FAMILY CARE
OF THE ELDERLY

OTHER RECENT VOLUMES IN THE
SAGE FOCUS EDITIONS

8. **Controversy (Third Edition)**
   Dorothy Nelkin
41. **Black Families (Second Edition)**
   Harriette Pipes McAdoo
64. **Family Relationships in Later Life
   (Second Edition)**
   Timothy H. Brubaker
89. **Popular Music and Communication
   (Second Edition)**
   James Lull
119. **The Home Care Experience**
   Jaber F. Gubrium and Andrea Sankar
120. **Black Aged**
   Zev Harel, Edward A. McKinney, and
   Michael Williams
121. **Mass Communication and Public Health**
   Charles Atkin and Lawrence Wallack
122. **Changes in the State**
   Edward S. Greenberg and Thomas F. Mayer
123. **Participatory Action Research**
   William Foote Whyte
124. **Experiencing Fieldwork**
   William B. Shaffir and Robert A. Stebbins
125. **Gender, Family, and Economy**
   Rae Lesser Blumberg
126. **Enterprise Zones**
   Roy E. Green
127. **Polling and Presidential Election
   Coverage**
   Paul J. Lavrakas and Jack K. Holley
128. **Sharing Social Science Data**
   Joan E. Sieber
129. **Family Preservation Services**
   Kathleen Wells and David E. Biegel
130. **Media Coverage of Terrorism**
   A. Odasuo Alali and Kenoye Kelvin Eke
131. **Saving Children at Risk**
   Travis Thompson and Susan C. Hupp
132. **Text in Context**
   Graham Watson and Robert M. Seiler
133. **Social Research on Children
   and Adolescents**
   Barbara Stanley and Joan E. Sieber
134. **The Politics of Life in Schools**
   Joseph Blase

135. **Applied Impression Management**
   Robert A. Giacalone and Paul Rosenfeld
136. **The Sense of Justice**
   Roger D. Masters and Margaret Gruter
137. **Families and Retirement**
   Maximiliane Szinovacz, David J. Ekerdt,
   and Barbara H. Vinick
138. **Gender, Families and Elder Care**
   Jeffrey W. Dwyer and Raymond T. Coward
139. **Investigating Subjectivity**
   Carolyn Ellis and Michael G. Flaherty
140. **Preventing Adolescent Pregnancy**
   Brent C. Miller, Josefina J. Card,
   Roberta L. Paikoff, and James L. Peterson.
141. **Hidden Conflict in Organizations**
   Deborah M. Kolb and Jean M. Bartunek
142. **Hispanics in the Workplace**
   Stephen B. Knouse, Paul Rosenfeld, and
   Amy Culbertson
143. **Psychotherapy Process Research**
   Shaké G. Toukmanian and
   David L. Rennie
144. **Educating Homeless Children
   and Adolescents**
   James H. Stronge
145. **Family Care of the Elderly**
   Jordan I. Kosberg
146. **Growth Management**
   Jay M. Stein
147. **Substance Abuse and Gang Violence**
   Richard C. Cervantes
148. **Third World Cities**
   John D. Kasarda and Allan M. Parnell
149. **Independent Consulting for Evaluators**
   Alan Vaux, Margaret S. Stockdale, and
   Michael J. Schwerin
150. **Advancing Family Perservation Practice**
   E. Susan Morton and R. Kevin Grigsby
151. **A Future for Religion?**
   William H. Swatos, Jr.
152. **Researching Sensitive Topics**
   Claire M. Renzetti and Raymond M. Lee

FAMILY CARE OF THE ELDERLY

Social and Cultural Changes

Jordan I. Kosberg
editor

SAGE PUBLICATIONS
International Educational and Professional Publisher
Newbury Park   London   New Delhi

This book is dedicated to my parents
Hilde and S. J. Kosberg
for being caring and vibrant role models

For information address:

SAGE Publications, Inc.
2455 Teller Road
Newbury Park, California 91320

SAGE Publications Ltd.
6 Bonhill Street
London EC2A 4PU
United Kingdom

SAGE Publications India Pvt. Ltd.
M-32 Market
Greater Kailash I
New Delhi 110 048 India

Printed in the United States of America

Library of Congress Cataloging-in-Publication Data

Main entry under title:
Family care of the elderly: social and cultural changes / Jordan
  I. Kosberg, editor.
        p. cm. —(Sage focus editions; 145)
    Includes bibliographical references and index.
    ISBN 0-8039-4279-6. — ISBN 0-8039-4280-X (pbk.)
    1. Aged—Home care—Cross-cultural studies.
HV1451.F35   1992
362.6—dc20   92-25037

92 93 94 95 10 9 8 7 6 5 4 3 2 1

Sage Production Editor: Diane S. Foster

Contents

Preface   vii

1. An International Perspective on Family Care of the Elderly:
   An Introductory Overview   1
   JORDAN I. KOSBERG

PART I: Young Countries   15

2. Family Care of the Elderly in Ghana   17
   CHARLES K. BROWN

3. Family Care of the Elderly in Mexico   31
   RAQUEL BIALIK

4. Family Care of the Elderly in Thailand   47
   MALINEE WONGSITH

PART II: Youthful Countries   65

5. Family Care of the Elderly in China:
   Changes and Problems   67
   ZHU CHUANYI and XU QIN

6. Family Care of the Elderly in Costa Rica   82
   FIDELINA BRICEÑO CAMPOS,
   FLORA SABORÍO HERNÁNDEZ, and
   FERNANDO MORALES MARTÍNEZ

7. Family Care of the Elderly in Egypt 95
   ABDEL MONEIM ASHOUR

PART III: Adult Countries 107
8. Family Care of the Elderly in Argentina:
   A Context of Crisis 109
   ROBERTO KAPLAN and NÉLIDA REDONDO
9. Family Care of the Elderly in Hong Kong 123
   NELSON W. S. CHOW
10. Family Care of the Elderly in Israel 139
    GILA NOAM and JACK HABIB

PART IV: Mature Countries 157
11. Family Care of the Elderly in Australia 159
    JOHN McCALLUM and ANNA L. HOWE
12. Family Care of the Elderly in Greece 179
    PETER STATHOPOULOS and ANNA AMERA
13. Family Care of the Elderly in Japan 196
    DAISAKU MAEDA and YOUMEI NAKATANI
14. Family Care of the Elderly in the United States:
    An Issue of Gender Differences? 210
    TIMOTHY H. BRUBAKER and ELLIE BRUBAKER

PART V: Aged Countries 233
15. Family Care of the Elderly in Austria 235
    JOSEF HÖRL
16. Family Care of the Elderly in Great Britain 252
    CHRIS PHILLIPSON
17. Family Care of the Elderly in Sweden 271
    LARS ANDERSSON

18. Conclusion:
    Family Care of the Elderly—Unique and
    Common Features 286
    JORDAN I. KOSBERG
    Index 300
    About the Editor 311
    About the Contributors 312

Preface

The world is changing at an increasingly rapid pace. In addition to the dramatic geopolitical changes, other forces less dramatic, less obvious, but no less tumultuous—forces of social, demographic, and cultural change —have permeated countries of the world. Traditional institutions are being challenged and are changing. One of the major institutions in any society, some would say *the* major institution—the family, is undergoing change; the structure, function, and composition of the family is being challenged as a result of many different dynamics in each country.

One of the traditional roles for the family has been that of caring for its elderly members. Unquestioned by traditional cultural norms and mores, supported by religious beliefs, necessitated by economic imperatives, and enforced by both informal sanctions and formal policies, family care of the elderly had been the major and, indeed, often the only, mechanism for the care of older persons who were economically, socially, psychologically, and physically dependent.

As a social worker, sociologist, and gerontologist, I was aware of these global changes. Familiar with international literature in gerontology, I was also fortunate enough to visit many countries in the world and to attend international conferences. Initially, through the sponsorship of the International Exchange Center on Gerontology at the University of South Florida (and, in particular, as a result of the encouragement of Dr. Harold

L. Sheppard, its former director), I attended three conferences that focused upon formal and informal care of the elderly and mainly included representatives from the United States and the Far East. I traveled three times to Malta at the invitation of the United Nation's International Institute on Aging (INIA) to lecture on social gerontology to representatives from developing nations. I am most grateful to INIA Director Dr. Alfred Grech for this opportunity to meet with, and learn from, those from many foreign countries.

In addition to visiting (and lecturing) in many countries, I have taught at Nankai University in Tianjin, China, and, during the spring semester of 1992, I was a Visiting Professor in the Department of Social Work and Social Administration at the University of Hong Kong. After visiting Hong Kong on many occasions, I was impressed with its agencies, programs, and facilities for the elderly. Social problems, however, also reflect strains on traditional methods by which the elderly have been cared for in Hong Kong (and, earlier, in China).

Back in 1986, during a conference in Taiwan, I had been asked to review a manuscript that reported on a recently-completed study. The title of the work, "Elder Abuse in Hong Kong," had surprised me and had called my attention to the social changes occurring in that country, which affected the ability of the family to care for elderly relatives. In retrospect it was this monograph, authored by a Hong Kong social worker and carried out under the supervision of leading Hong Kong gerontologists, that led to this book on family care of the elderly around the world.

The search for an organizing principle for such a book, with chapters representing different countries of the world, was an interesting challenge. Seeking a method by which to divide countries of the world into different categories, I chose to consider the proportion of the population who were 65 years of age and older as the organizing framework. Somewhat modifying a scheme of the Population Reference Bureau, in Washington, DC, for dividing countries of the world through use of chronological age (and using the Bureau's 1990 data), I arrived at the following categories:

Young Countries—with 4% or less of the population being 65 years of age and older.

Youthful Countries—with between 5% and 7% of the population being 65 years of age and older.

Adult Countries—with between 8% and 10% of the population being 65 years of age and older.

Mature Countries—with between 11% and 14% of the population being 65 years of age and older.

Aged Countries—with 15% or more of the population being 65 years of age and older.

My next task was to select (for inclusion in the book) three countries in the world to represent each of the five types of age concentrations of elderly. At the suggestion of the publisher, the United States was added as the 16th country. The method of selection was rather arbitrary. Effort was made to include representation from all parts (continents) of the world. After establishing a list of all countries that fell within each of the five categories of elderly concentrations, I first identified those countries from which I personally knew experts representing the social and/or health sciences and then asked friends and colleagues about appropriate individuals they knew. I set the policy that authors would live and work in their countries and thus excluded from consideration (a) those individuals who were no longer living in their native countries and (b) Americans (and others) who were experts on foreign countries.

Based upon the list of those individuals I personally knew, and those who were recommended to me, I chose individuals from 15 different countries (and from the United States) to contact with an invitation to write a chapter for this book. As testimony to their commitment to gerontology in their countries (and possibly to my convincing letter of invitation), all 16 individuals agreed to take on the responsibility of authoring, or coauthoring with a countryman a, chapter on family care of the elderly in their country.

It is necessary to point out that the countries chosen to be included are not, in any way, meant to be representative of all countries that fall within the age grouping of persons who are 65 years of age and older. In addition, it should be pointed out that this book did not begin with an a priori assumption that the proportion of elderly persons was correlated to any particular variables in countries.

Each author was asked to address, as best as possible, the following areas in his or her chapter:

1. *Traditional Characteristics of the Country*—demographic overview, traditional values, role of family care of the elderly, basic economic system, and attitudes toward the elderly.

2. *Societal Changes Occurring Over Time*—demographic changes, economic and education changes, Westernization and industrialization; changes in im-

migration, emigration, and mobility; urbanization, important current events, changes in birth and death rates; changes in the rate of divorce, remarriage, intermarriage, arranged marriages; changes in the role and importance of the elderly and in family care of the elderly.

3. *Consequences of Societal Changes*—strengthened role of the family; positive role of the elderly in the family; findings of family stress and burden; family members who are unavailable, ill-suited, and ill-prepared to provide care; and the existence of abuse and maltreatment of the elderly by family members.

4. *Responses to the Changes in the Country*—programs and services to support family caregiving; alternatives to family care; public policies for social, economic, and family welfare; perceived responsibility for the care of the elderly by government, private sector, organized religion, voluntary sector, family, and individual.

5. *Future Predictions*—for the care of the elderly by the family and by formal service systems in the country.

I would like to thank the authors for their willingness to write and for their cooperation in meeting deadlines for chapter drafts in a timely fashion. English was not the primary language for the majority of authors (and not often used by several). Many of the authors were apologetic about their command of the English language (authors had been requested to submit chapter manuscripts in English). Such apologies were unnecessary. On some occasions, however, I had to translate into more understandable language the information they had provided to me. Should my translation of an author's terms or meanings be incorrect, I apologize for such misinterpretations.

I would also like to thank the authors for their critical assessment of family care of the elderly in their countries. There may be a tendency to minimize problems occurring in one's country when describing situations at home to others from elsewhere in the world, but the authors of this volume did not steer away from identifying problems and pressures facing their countries, and their candor should be appreciated by all those who read their words. Indeed, inasmuch as one of the purposes of this book is to share experiences between countries, the factual description of social change on the care of the elderly and the interpretation of consequences is vital to this book's intent.

This book could not have been published without the encouragement and support of Christine Smedley, Associate Editor of Sage Publications. Thanks, also, to Diane S. Foster, Sage Senior Production Editor. I also want to acknowledge the useful suggestions of the reviewers of my initial prospectus.

The communication with, and coordination of, authors from many countries in the world necessitated much time, effort, and support. This project was undertaken while I was a Professor in the Department of Gerontology at the University of South Florida. I would like to acknowledge the assistance of faculty and staff from the Department, my Graduate Assistants, and the staff from the International Exchange Center on Gerontology.

Finally, I would like to acknowledge the support and encouragement of Dr. Juanita L. Garcia—my colleague, friend, and wife. Much of the cultural awareness I have developed (for use in communicating with individuals from diverse societies in the world) has come from her insights, experiences, and guidance. She has tolerated my somewhat compulsive nature in working on this book with understanding (and not without some degree of humor).

Jordan I. Kosberg

1

An International Perspective on Family Care of the Elderly

An Introductory Overview

JORDAN I. KOSBERG

This introductory chapter on family care of the elderly in different countries of the world will provide a brief overview of general issues that pertain to such care. In addition, the social changes that can affect countries will be discussed as will the possible consequences of these changes on family caregiving to the elderly. The chapter will provide a discussion of the relationships between the stage of development of a country and the impact on the elderly and the care of the elderly by informal and formal support systems. Finally, the objectives of the book will be presented.

The Aging of the World

The countries in the world are aging. The United Nations (1988) has estimated an increase in those 65 years of age and older in the world from 6% of the total population in 1985 to 9.7% of the population by the year 2025. According to U.N. statistics (1988), the proportion of elderly in more-developed nations will increase from 11.5% in 1985 to 18.9% in 2025; the proportion of elderly in less-developed nations will increase from 4.2% in 1985 to 8.0% in 2025.

In 1988 the International Institute on Aging (INIA) indicated that, as of 1985, 56.5% of the world's elderly lived in less-developed nations. This figure for less-developed nations was projected to reach 61.5% by the turn of the century and 71.9% by the year 2025. As an indication of the growth of the elderly population, INIA (1988) estimated that—between 1985 and 2025—the elderly will increase by 77% in developed countries and by 207% in developing nations.

The United Nations (1988) presented a breakdown of projections of those 65 years of age and older by regions of the world for 1985 and 2025. In Africa there will be an increase from 3.1% to 4.1%; in Latin America, from 4.5% to 8.5%; in North America, from 11.8% to 19.7%; in Asia, from 4.7% to 9.6%; in Europe, from 12.7% to 20.1%; in Oceania, from 8.5% to 13.4%; and in the former U.S.S.R., from 9.6% to 14.8%.

According to Myers (1990), "The major demographic forces that change the size of a population and its age composition are levels of fertility and mortality" (p. 28). Specifically, the increase in the number and proportion of the elderly in any nation and, collectively, in the world, results from a decrease in both births and deaths. This is brought about by many possible factors, including improved medical technology, mass education, the use of birth control, emigration, and others. These changes, in turn, are seen to result from urbanization and industrialization and the changing roles for women. (While this chapter will not discuss these topics, they will be addressed relative to individual countries within the chapters that follow.)

Coupled with demographic changes are economic, social, and cultural changes in countries around the world (INIA, 1988). The consequences of these changes can be prodigious and affect all major institutions in a country. Certainly to be affected is the major caregiving institution in any society: the family.

Family Care: A Tradition

Care of the elderly by members of the informal support system is characteristic of all countries in the world (Chappel, 1990). Such a mechanism includes family, friends, neighbors, and members of a collectivity (such as a village, tribe, or clan). Generally speaking, such care is provided voluntarily without remuneration. Care by family members (whether blood relatives or those by marriage) predominates among the alternatives within the informal support system.

There are potentially many explanations for family care of the elderly. Certainly the influence of historical tradition is important. If the responsibility of caring for the elderly in a society had always been with the family, then it had become expected by the elderly (and provided without question by the family). In such a traditional context family care was provided by social or cultural custom. In cases where such care was not willingly provided, informal sanctions against the (irresponsible) family members became as important as formal sanctions (such as fines or incarceration).

In addition to cultural imperatives for family care, and supportive of it, were religious teachings. Most religions of the world, if not all, support the notion of family responsibility for the family elders (as well as other dependent members of the family). For example, Oriental religions and Confucian influences emphasize the norm of filial piety. Judeo-Christian religions implore its adherents to honor one's father and mother.

Female members of the family have been the major caregivers of elderly persons. Such has been found to be true not only in the United States (Brody, 1981), but also for most of the countries in the world (Gibson, 1984). Part of this explanation is due to the tradition of females as caregivers (i.e., wives, daughters, daughter-in-laws, sisters, grandmothers). In the past women remained within the home, thus making them available to provide care to elderly relatives (while the men usually worked in jobs outside the home).

Women have generally performed a nurturing role (in raising children and caring for the ill members of the family) as a result of the deliberate socialization for gender-specific roles. Furthermore, inasmuch as women had been younger than their husbands, there had always been a good probability that a wife (in her later years) would be responsible for the care of her (older) impaired husband. As will be discussed in many of the chapters of this book, such reliance on females is being challenged by changes in many countries in the world.

Only with increased inability to maintain independent community living would an older person become dependent on the family and come to reside within the home of a family member. This is characteristic of most countries in the world (Gibson, 1984; Kosberg, 1985). Two of the greatest fears that an older person can have is that of an accident (and being unable to call for help) and institutionalization.

Relationships between the elderly and their family members have varied from culture to culture. In most societies, however, intergenerational relationships have been the basic social fabric of a culture and the elderly have been well integrated within the family (Tout, 1989). While some would maintain that such a notion of intrafamily relationships is characteristic of preindustrial societies (Cowgill, 1986), others have suggested that reciprocal relationships between the elderly and their families exist in both extended and nuclear family structures (Harris & Cole, 1980; Chappell, 1990).

Family Caregiving: Causes and Consequences

Although separate dwellings may be maintained by some elderly, family members often must provide assistance for many of the activities of daily living, including meals, medication, transportation, housekeeping, and personal grooming tasks. Gibson (1984), in a comprehensive article on international family support patterns for the elderly, found that a similar desire for independence by the elderly exists worldwide. Only with increased impairments and decreased ability to provide for one's self does the family play a major role in care provision.

Ideally, families should willingly, and voluntarily, take on caregiving responsibilities for their elderly relatives. Yet the motivations may be inappropriate. Garrett (1979-1980) has questioned the extent to which genuine desire and affection are the bases for kinship obligation for the care of elderly relatives. Miller (1981) has discussed middle-aged children as the "sandwich generation"—individuals who have responsibility for both their elderly parents and their dependent children at a time when they are worrying about their own future.

Brody (1985) sees guilt as a major motivation to provide that care, stating: "Guilt may be a reason that people assert that they and their own families behave responsibly in caring for their old, but that most people do not do so as was the case in the good old days" (p. 26). And some family members have taken on caregiving responsibilities because of benefits to be received from the elderly relative (i.e., property, rent, possessions) or to be received in the future (i.e., inheritance, land, a home). Such motivations do not necessarily lead to good care.

Research findings around the world have documented caregiver burden resulting from meeting the needs of elderly relatives (Gibson, 1984; Kosberg, 1985). These burdens on family members are influenced by the level and nature of impairments, the existence and involvement of family support given to the major family care provider, and the degree to which the older person is a "provocateur" (Kosberg, 1988b).

As a country's population ages, the likelihood increases that adult children, themselves, will be elderly. An elderly husband and wife may both be impaired and unable to be effective caregivers. Some relatives are inappropriate, unmotivated, and ill-suited to provide care for an impaired and frail elderly relative. Some family systems are already overwhelmed by other problems (i.e., alcoholism, unemployment, overcrowding), and the additional responsibility for the care of an elderly relative may result in a breakdown of the family system (Kosberg, 1988a).

While only the negative aspects of family caregiving have been presented thus far, possibly due to researchers who have concentrated on the adversities from caregiving, it should be pointed out that research has found positive consequences as well. For example, Colerick and George (1986) found caregivers to have positive feelings of accomplishment and self-satisfaction; Hooyman, Gonyea, and Montgomery (1985) found increased life satisfaction; Brubaker (1985) has discussed improvements in family and spousal relationships; and Lewis and Meredith (1988) reported on the reaffirmation of the feminine identity resulting from the provision of care to an elderly relative.

Nevertheless, excessive and unrelenting caregiving demands can result in social, physical, psychological, economic, and psychosomatic adversities to family members. The result may be an inability to provide effective care to meet the needs of the older person.

The ultimate adversity is elder abuse and maltreatment. A growing body of literature (Kosberg, 1983, 1988b) indicates the existence of elder abuse and maltreatment resulting from acts of omission and commission by others (mainly family members). The problem of abuse and maltreatment exists in many countries and is not limited to only industrialized nations of the world (Kosberg & Garcia, 1991).

Finally, the more relatives an older person has does not necessarily equate with a more effective informal support system. There may be conflicts between family members. For example, some members of an extended family may be upset with other relatives who are perceived to be shirking responsibilities for the care of an elderly relative. Fiore, Becker, and Coppel (1983) have written about the family system as a potential source of stress to family members, and when family members are stressed, they may take out their anger and frustration on the source of the problem: the older relative.

Family Care and Economic Prosperity

Intergenerational relationships between members of the family might well be a function of the general economic prosperity of a society (or of a family). This is to suggest the possibility that a pooling of economic resources by members of the family may be the motivation for intergenerational interdependence. Further, the need for a family division of labor may permit younger adults to secure employment outside the home, while the elderly remain in the family dwelling to care for young children, maintain the home, and cook for the employed family members.

Worach-Kardas (1983) has pointed out that family responsibility for elderly, as opposed to public (that is, governmental) responsibility, is often a function of economic conditions in the country. "The state's responsibility for meeting citizens' needs looks different in times of prosperity than in times of crisis." (p. 594). While true, it is also a fact that when hard economic times befall a nation, so too are its citizens affected. Shifting responsibility from government to families in hard economic times would, no doubt, add burdens to those already burdened.

Governments generally have always encouraged family care of the elderly. When faced with low economic growth, extensive unemployment, competition for public expenditures, and increasing monetary demands, relief of the responsibility for elderly members of society through family care is, indeed, welcomed. Whether the form of government is a full-fledged welfare state or one based upon individualism and more limited government responsibility, the problem of competing demands for limited resources always exists.

The problems for a government might be exacerbated, should the number and proportion of the elderly be increasing. As will be discussed in the chapters in this book, such growth in the elderly is taking place in every country. Thus the public expenditures may be seen to be increasing in the areas of social and health services for the elderly. An increased emphasis may be placed upon the family to care for their elderly relatives.

Another motivating factor is when governments encourage or, perhaps, require family support of the elderly. Such policies that seek to mandate (however subtly) family responsibility have moral and religious origins. Elizabethan Poor Law (established in Great Britain and influential in early United States policies) emphasized the principle of primary family responsibility. The goal, states Garrett (1979-1980), was "to protect the public from the burden of supporting persons who had family able to provide assistance" (p. 781).

Although Gibson (1983) has indicated that "a number of developing nations and some industrialized nations indeed mandate such responsibilities" (p. 12), specific mandates for requiring family support are currently seldom seen in countries in the world. As Gibson (1984) states: "Most . . . industrialized nations have abolished legal requirements obligating filial financial responsibility for elderly parents, or are in the process of doing so" (p. 78).

Yet some vestiges can be seen when families are required to bear economic costs for care or when they must provide instrumental assistance (e.g., transportation) to use available public (or private) services for their elderly relatives. While there are some countries that do mandate family responsibility for the elderly, such requirements are virtually impossible to enforce because few older persons are willing to report their nonsupporting adult children (Gibson, 1984).

Inaction by state and national government to meet the needs of the elderly through the enactment of public policy for the elderly and their families may result in consequences for the families similar to those that would mandate family responsibility. When there are no alternatives provided by a government, families are often left without alternatives to relieve them of such responsibilities. Thus they are forced to provide care. This is especially problematic when a family care provider has no other relative, or anyone else, who can assist in meeting the needs of the older relative (or in providing periodic respite from the ongoing caregiving demands).

Although public resources may well be needed for those elderly without families or for those whose families are unavailable to provide care, governments do worry about providing incentives for families to shirk their caregiving responsibilities. In providing alternatives to family care, families may be relieved of the responsibility that should be undertaken on behalf of their elderly relatives. As Greengross (1981) writes about British policy:

> Many official pronouncements . . . suggest that any extension in the provision of formal services would undermine family responsibility further and encourage relatives to rely on the state, shirking their duty and abandoning their elderly parents to institutional care. (p. 21)

The creation of public housing estates (that is, apartment buildings) for the elderly in one country in the Far East, plus the introduction of additional forms of social settings, has resulted in alternatives for family care and a waiting period of more than 6 years (Hong Kong Council on Social Services, 1987).

Gibson (1984) has discussed disincentives to family care for the elderly and gives examples of countries where older persons lose their welfare services or benefits when living with family members. While some countries may fail to provide financial assistance for the in-home care of an elderly relative, public support may exist for institutional care. On occasion, when there may be only one informal caregiver (for example, the elderly spouse), an impaired elderly person is ineligible to receive home-delivered health, social, or personal care services. Home health care, it may be reasoned, is designed to supplement, but not replace, the informal support system of an elderly person. Thus it may be determined that the spouse cannot provide the care needed by an elderly person (inasmuch as the home health care services are provided only a few hours each week). Institutionalization may be the only recourse for the spouse.

In times of economic austerity a nation may rethink its priorities, and this may lead to new policy initiatives or to competition between different groups (INIA, 1989). For example, in the United States the intergenerational conflict has been initiated by the conservative Americans for Generational Equity, which has advanced the view that the United States cannot continue to provide public resources to the elderly at the expense of its children and youth. Faced with a stagnant economy and mounting discontent with its cradle-to-grave welfare system, a socialist country may face the prospects of cutting taxes and social and health benefits (including those to the elderly and families who care for them).

In those countries with rapidly mounting health care costs that far exceed the public's ability to afford unlimited care for all, the possibility is being discussed—the reality is being implemented—for the creation of eligibility criteria for the use of expensive and limited health care resources, operations, and procedures. And chronological age is a most common criterion to be used for such decisions.

The Impact of Modernization

The countries represented in this book not only vary greatly in the proportion of elderly citizens, but also in many other characteristics. One important dimension that differentiates the countries is in the stage of modernization (alternatively, often referred to as a stage of development, industrialization, or Westernization). "Third world" countries have been defined to be in preliminary or early stages of modernization, but are not industrially advanced (Barrow, 1986). The United Nations has referred to countries as Less Developed Countries (LDCs) and More Developed Countries (MDC) (United Nations, 1980).

In a relative sense, countries in the world range from less modernized nations to those that are fully modernized. The definition of modernization given by Cowgill (1986) follows:

> Modernization is the transformation of a total society from a relatively rural way of life based on animate power, limited technology, relatively undifferentiated institutions, parochial and traditional outlook and values, toward a predominantly urban way of life based on inanimate sources of power, highly developed scientific technology, highly differentiated institutions matched by segmented individual roles, and a cosmopolitan outlook which emphasizes efficiency and progress. (pp. 185-186)

Although this book uses a chronological definition of old age, by the categorization of countries into one of five concentrations of those 65 years of age and older, such a definition is but one method by which to determine the size of the elderly population. As Cowgill (1986) states: "Old age is defined in terms of chronological age chiefly in modern societies" (p. 7). While most of this book's authors define old age in the passage of years, it is important to note alternative definitions.

Age can be defined in functional terms (Clark & Anderson, 1967). One is considered old when no longer able to perform tasks previously undertaken. According to Barrow (1986), "A person may be old when the body loses vigor to the extent that it lacks either the strength or mobility required to do adult work" (p. 394). Old age can also be defined in formal terms often dependent upon taking on new roles or losing old ones. For example, in some societies a person is considered old upon becoming a grandparent for the first time or on retiring from employment.

Much has been written about the inverse relationship between the state of modernization of nations in the world and the status of the elderly. This hypothesized relationship was initially articulated by Cowgill and Holmes (1972) in *Aging and Modernization* and expanded upon by Cowgill (1986) in *Aging Around the World*. The notion is that as countries become more modernized, the importance of the elderly in society is reduced. According to this view, the less-developed countries have greater roles for older persons and see them more positively; more-developed nations—those that are technologically advanced, with a mobile population, experiencing rapid social change—will accord the elderly lower status. An assumed corollary is the inverse relationship between developed nations and prevalence of family care to the elderly.

At variance with such a view of the linear relationship between stage of industrialization (or modernization) and the status of the elderly is the work of Palmore and Manton (1974). In their article, "Modernization and Status of the Aged: International Correlations," indicators of modernization (e.g., labor force in agriculture, literacy, youths in school) and the status of the aged were analyzed from 31 countries. The authors concluded that while the status of the elderly does decline in the early stages of modernization, after the period of modernization has occurred, the status of the elderly stabilizes and then rises. The explanations for this rise are a result of factors "such as the growth of new institutions to replace the farm and the family in maintaining the status of the aged such as retirement benefits, more adult education and job retraining, policies against age discrimination in employment, etc." (p. 210).

Other research challenges the Modernization Theory (Cowgill, 1986; Keith, 1990). Any discussion of the impact of modernization—and its relationship to the role and status of the elderly—must include an acknowledgment of the contribution of the economic condition of a nation at a particular point in time. Industrialized nations (e.g., the United States, Sweden) may undergo recessions and depressions; thus making it difficult to meet the needs of their citizens. Conversely, less industrialized nations (e.g., Saudi Arabia, Oman) may experience times of prosperity and be able to act charitably to their citizens.

Purpose of This Book

This book attempts to neither confirm nor reject the merits of the Modernization Theory nor any grand notion of causes for the decline, maintenance, or increase in the status of the elderly or in family care to the elderly in countries of the world. Such an inquiry necessitates an empirically-derived study (which is beyond the objectives of this book).

Indeed, family care of the elderly does not seem to take on an especially significant role in the work on modernization, although Cowgill and Holmes (1972) did observe: "With modernization the responsibility for the provision of economic security for dependent aged tends to be shifted from the family to the state" (p. 190). One might wonder whether this "shift" also refers to noneconomic areas as well, such as the public provision of housing, transportation, nutrition, health care, and other areas.

This book was conceived to provide an analysis of the past and present role of family caregiving, the impact of social change on such care, and to project what is likely to occur in the future. It does not emanate out of an explicit (nor implicit) desire to confirm or reject any theory or to engage in empirical comparative analyses. The goals are more modest, but perhaps no less important. Changes are occurring in countries of the world regardless of the stage of development. Inasmuch as family care of the elderly has been the traditional and major mechanism by which the needs of the nation's most dependent elderly have been met, this book asks how family care is "holding up" in the face of these changes.

The answers to such a question, as seen to exist by the authors who represent 16 different countries in the world, have prodigious ramifications for general knowledge development, but also have more applied consequences. Information may provide suggestions for meeting the needs of the elderly who are less likely to be cared for by their families in the future.

Each chapter will, to an extent, alert readers to the variations in family caregiving within each country. Greater differences may be within the types of countries (by age concentrations) than between them. Similarly, greater variations in family caregiving patterns may be within a particular country than between countries with similar proportions of elderly persons.

Accordingly, it is necessary to discern the contributions of different characteristics of the members of a society on the nature of family care given to elderly relatives. Demographic factors include gender, race, religion, martial status, level of education, urban or rural location, and subculture (among others). And while national prosperity was suggested to influence a country's desire and ability to provide assistance to those in need, individual and family prosperity (or, rather, socioeconomic status) should be assessed so as to determine its contribution to family caregiving.

In addition to individual or group variables, readers are requested to assess the public responses to the changes occurring in the countries discussed in this book. Such information might provide others with both insights and ideas as to what possible alternatives to family care of the elderly may be initiated in their own countries.

Certainly there is an interrelationship between the role of the formal support system and the informal support system (mainly the family).

Although the formal support system is not the major focus of this book, readers should be interested in any discussion of pension systems (private and public), employment (ageism and opportunities), physical and mental health care systems, institutional care, personal social services, educational opportunities, housing, and supportive services. (For an in-depth description of community services for the elderly in 35 countries in the world, see Kosberg, in press.) Along with a determination of the existence of formal policies creating resources that supplement and, when needed, replace family care of the elderly, readers are urged to get a sense of the equity in these formal resources; the ability to reach and serve all in the country without random (unplanned) or systematic (purposeful) exclusion of any group of needy elderly persons.

The world is "shrinking," and we are moving toward a "world community" resulting from both a world economy and a world ecology. No country is immune to the impact of other countries, however close or far away. In this "world community," the exchange of ideas, technologies, and people is essential. While the study of international gerontology attempts to identify the differences that exist among countries in the world, so, too, does it look for universals (or commonalities) (Kosberg, Sohn, & Sheppard, 1991). From common experiences can follow suggestions for government actions. It is hoped that this book will be read by those from many countries in the world who will see implications for public action from the experiences of represented countries both at similar stages of development and at more developed stages.

In identifying countries at a comparable level of development or those that otherwise share similar characteristics and problems, readers will engage in "cross-national borrowing" of ideas and solutions regarding the interaction between families and governments.

For others, the chapters that discuss the experiences in countries that are more modernized (with larger proportions of elderly persons) will provide clues for national planning and policy development for a likely future scenario. As Cowgill (1986) states:

> Those people (whose countries are now beginning to experience modernization and development) will have learned from our experience both what to avoid and which adaptations will serve them well. Some of their value systems, such as filial piety and familism, may help them avoid the extreme devaluations of the aged experienced by the pioneer societies in the field of aging. (p. 200)

Countries in the world are changing, and the family is a major institution undergoing change. As the family changes, so too does its ability to continue to meet traditional roles and responsibilities—especially as related to the elderly members of the family.

The following chapters, then, address the experiences of social change on the elderly, on family care for the elderly, and on the governmental response (if any) to changes in the major, traditional mechanism for meeting the needs of the elderly in the nations of the world. As Cowgill (1986) suggests: "Demographic aging is producing new pressures and new needs, and so our cultures are in the process of changing and adapting to these new needs" (p. 4). What follows are the processes and adaptations in family care (in 16 countries) relative to such aging.

References

Barrow, G. M. (1986). *Aging, the individual, and society,* (3rd ed.). New York: West.

Brody, E. M. (1981). "Women in the middle" and family help to older people. *The Gerontologist, 21*(5), 471-480.

Brody, E. M. (1985). Parent care as a normative family stress. *The Gerontologist, 25*(1), 19-29.

Brubaker, T. H. (1985). *Later life families.* Beverly Hills, CA: Sage.

Chappel, N. L. (1990). Aging and social care. In R. H. Binstock & L. K. George (Eds.), *Aging and the social sciences* (3rd ed.) (pp. 438-454). New York: Academic Press.

Clark, M., & Anderson, B. (1967). *Culture and aging.* Springfield, IL: Charles C Thomas.

Colerick, E. J., & George, L. K. (1986). Predictors of institutionalization among caregivers of patients with Alzheimer's diseases. *Journal of the American Geriatrics Society, 34,* 493-498.

Cowgill, D. (1986). *Aging around the world.* Belmont, CA: Wadsworth.

Cowgill, D., & Holmes, L. (1972). *Aging and modernization.* New York: Appleton-Century-Crofts.

Fiore, J., Becker, J., & Coppel, D. B. (1983). Social network interactions: A buffer or a stress? *American Journal of Community Psychology, 11,* 423-439.

Garrett, W. W. (1979-1980). Filial responsibility laws. *Journal of Family Law, 18,* 793-818.

Gibson, M. J. (1983). *Family support of the elderly mentally ill: An international overview.* Paper presented at the World Congress for Mental Health, Washington, DC.

Gibson, M. J. (1984). Family support patterns, policies, and programs. In C. Nusberg (Ed.), *Innovative aging programs abroad: Implications for the United States* (pp. 159-195). Westport, CT: Greenwood.

Greengross, S. (1981). Caring for the carers. In F. Glendenning (Ed.), *Care in the community: Recent research and current projects* (pp. 18-30). Stoke-on-Trent, England: Beth Johnson Foundation.

Harris, D., & Cole, W. (1980). *Sociology of aging.* Boston: Houghton Mifflin.

Hooyman, N., Gonyea, J. G., & Montgomery, R. J. V. (1985). The impact of in-home service termination on family caregivers. *The Gerontologist, 25,* 141-145.

International Institute on Aging (INIA). (1989, February). *Preliminary findings of survey on training needs in developing countries.* Report presented at the Expert Group Meeting on Short-Term Training in Social Gerontology, Valletta, Malta.

Keith, J. (1990). Age in social and cultural context: Anthropological perspectives. In R. H. Binstock & L. K. George (Eds.), *Handbook of aging and the social sciences* (3rd ed.) (pp. 91-111). New York: Academic Press.

Kosberg, J. I. (Ed.). (1983). *Abuse and maltreatment of the elderly: Causes and interventions.* Littleton, MA: John Wright-PSG.

Kosberg, J. I. (1985). *Policies encouraging and requiring family care of the aged: A critical assessment.* Paper presented at the XIIth International Congress of Gerontology, New York.

Kosberg, J. I. (1988a). *Family care of the aged in the United States: Policy issues from an international perspective.* Tampa, FL: International Exchange Center on Gerontology, University of South Florida.

Kosberg, J. I. (1988b). Preventing elderly abuse: Identification of high risk factors prior to placement decisions. *The Gerontologist, 28*(1), 43-50.

Kosberg, J. I. (in press). *International handbook on community services for the elderly.* Westport, CT: Greenwood.

Kosberg, J. I., & Garcia, J. L. (1991). Social changes affecting family care of the elderly. *Journal of the International Institute on Aging, 1*(2), 2-5.

Kosberg, J. I., Sohn, K., & Sheppard, H. L. (1991). International imperatives for gerontological education. *Educational Gerontology, 17*(5), 477-486.

Lewis, J., & Meredith, B. (1988). Daughters caring for mothers. *Aging and Society, 8,* 1-21.

Miller, D. A. (1981). The "sandwich" generation: Adult children of the aging. *Social Work, 26*(5), 419-423.

Myers, G. C. (1990). Demography of Aging. In R. H. Binstock & L. K. George (Eds.), *Handbook of aging and the social sciences* (3rd ed.) (pp. 19-44). New York: Academic Press.

Palmore, E., & Manton, K. (1974). Modernization and status of the aged: International correlations. *Journal of Gerontology, 29,* 205-210.

Services for the Elderly Division, Hong Kong Council of Social Services. (1987). *A background paper on services for the elderly in Hong Kong.* Unpublished paper.

Tout, K. (1989). *Aging in developing countries.* New York: Oxford University Press.

United Nations. (1980). Selected demographic indicators by country, 1950-2000: Demographic estimates and projections as assessed in 1978. (Ser. R 138). In G. M. Barrow (Ed.), *Aging, the individual, and society* (3rd ed.) (pp. 407-408). New York: West.

United Nations. (1988). Economic and social implications of population aging. (ST/ESA/SER.R/85). New York: Author.

Worach-Kardas, H. (1983). The Polish family tradition. *The Gerontologist, 23*(6), 593-596.

PART I

Young Countries[1]

Young countries are defined as those in which the population aged 65 and older represents 4% or less of the total population. In this book such countries are represented by Ghana, Mexico, and Thailand.

Ghana, located in Western Africa, had a mid-1990 population of 15 million people. By the year 2020 the population is projected to more than double to 33.9 million people. In 1990 it was estimated that 45% of the population in Ghana was under 15 years of age and that 3% of the population was 65 years of age and older. It was also estimated that almost one third of the citizens (32%) lived in urban areas. Charles K. Brown, Ph.D., Director of the Centre for Development Studies at the University of Cape Coast in Cape Coast, is the author of the chapter on Ghana.

Mexico, located in North America, had a population of 88.6 million people in mid-1990. The population is projected to dramatically increase to 142.1 million people by the year 2020. While 42% of the Mexican population was under 15 years of age (and the largest population of young represented in this book), in 1990, 4% of the population was 65 years of age or older. About two thirds of the citizens of Mexico (66%) live in urban areas. The author of the chapter on Mexico is Raquel Bialik, head of the Department of Extension and Academic Exchange, Faculty of Medicine, the Universidad Nacional Autonoma de Mexico, in Mexico City.

Thailand, located in Southeast Asia, had 55.7 million people in mid-1990. By the year 2020 the population is estimated to increase to 78.1 million people. It was estimated that, in 1990, 35% of the population was under 15 years of age, and 4% of the population was 65 years of age or older. With an urban population of only 18%, Thailand is the most rural country represented in this book. The author of the chapter on Thailand is Malinee Wongsith, Associate Professor, Institute of Population Studies at Chulalongkorn University in Bangkok.

Note

1. All information used to describe these three countries comes from *1990: World Population Data Sheet of the Population Reference Bureau, Inc.* Washington, DC, 1990. Mid-1990 population estimates are based upon census or official national data or upon U.N., U.S. Bureau of the Census, or World Bank projections. Year 2020 projections come from the same sources.

2

Family Care of the Elderly in Ghana

CHARLES K. BROWN

Introduction

In most societies the family occupies a central position in strategies advocated for dealing with aging. Its capacity to care for its older members, however, seems to depend on three variables: (a) its social and economic situation, (b) whether it comes under the ambit of a social security system or not, and (c) its actual nature or structure as a social unit. The available evidence suggests that families are under severe pressure in most of the developing world: where widespread poverty constrains their social and economic situation, where the coverage of social security is very limited, and where the structure of the family unit is undergoing far-reaching changes.

In recent times several commentators have pointed to the breakdown of the extended family in which the elderly always remained part of a stable community unit ordered by blood ties. They have pointed to the social and economic changes taking place in many developing and traditional societies that have resulted in the gradual erosion and substantial breakdown of the traditional familial support for the elderly. For example, modernization had created institutions that have assumed the functions, tasks, and duties previously fulfilled by the children, and rural/urban migration has resulted in the residential segregation of generations, enabling young people to live in the built environment of the urban sector with its prioritizing of nuclear accommodations. Likewise, the introduction of industrial occupations has made it inconducive for younger persons to care for elderly relatives, and modern education fosters individualism, straining the old community ties of interdependence. It is also asserted that the search for profit, competition, and salaried activity works against the old systems of community and mutual caring, while modern mass media tends to erode the best values of traditional culture and care systems. Finally, women, the traditional caregivers, are increasingly joining the labor force.

The disintegration of the family, the recognition of its social role, and the abandonment of old persons are the inescapable results of the model of industrial civilization prevalent in the developed countries. The extended family structure in these countries has given way to the nuclear or conjugal family, thus affecting the pattern of traditional family care of the elderly.

The purpose of this chapter is to give an overview of the issues that pertain to family care of the elderly in Ghana. Specifically, the chapter discusses traditional characteristics, values, attitudes, and family caring practices in Ghana; the demographic, economic, and cultural changes that have occurred over time; the consequences of the changes as related to the roles, responsibilities, and abilities of families to care for the elderly; the responses that have been made to these changes in the form of social policy, programs, and services; and the future prospects regarding family care of the elderly in Ghana.

Demographic Overview of the Population

Aging Trends

The most outstanding feature of the age structure of Ghana's population is its youthfulness. The proportion of persons less than 15 years old was 44.6% in 1960, and this figure will increase to 46.0% by the year 2000. In contrast, the proportion of persons aged 60 and over was 4.2% in 1960, increasing to 4.5% by the year 2000 (see Table 2.1).

The low proportion of the elderly in the Ghanaian population should not obscure the increase in absolute numbers of the elderly who constitute an important economic and demographic group. The population aged 60 and over in Ghana is estimated to rise by a factor of 8.5, from 286,000 in 1960 to 2,425,000 in 2025, or an increase larger than that projected (5.6%) for the total population. The aging of the population, however, will not get underway until well after 2025. Continued high rates of fertility,

Table 2.1 Estimated and Projected Percentage of Total Population in Major Functional Age Groups (0-14, 15-59, 60 and over) Ghana, 1960, 1980, 2000, 2020, 2025

Age Group	1960	1980	*(In percentages)* 2000	2020	2025
0-14	44.6	46.3	46.0	34.0	30.3·
15-59	51.2	49.2	49.5	60.3	63.2
60+	4.2	4.5	4.5	5.7	6.4

SOURCE: United Nations (1982)

coupled with slowly declining mortality rates, has in fact resulted in a high gross reproduction rate and an improved survival of its large cohorts. Only after the year 2020, when fertility rates are projected to fall quite rapidly, will the conditions be given for the aging of the population.

A slight increase in the number of the persons aged 60 and over in the total population was recorded from 4.2% in 1960 to 4.5% in 1980 and in 2000. By 2020 this proportion is expected to rise to 5.7% and by 2025 to 6.4%. Long-term projections suggest that it will take until about 2075 for fertility declines ultimately to bring the weight of the 60-plus age groups to a situation comparable to what is currently to be found in many developed countries (United Nations, 1985). The estimated and projected population aged 60 and over, by sex and age group, for the period 1960-2025 indicates that the total number of the elderly will increase from 286,000 persons in 1960 to 992,000 by 2000. By the year 2025 the number will more than double to 2,425,000 elderly persons. Indeed, between 1960 and 2025, the older population is projected to increase by a factor of 8.5.

The policy implications of the rapid numerical growth in the elderly population in Ghana during the period 1980-2025 become clearer if one compares the growth in the elderly population to that in the population as a whole. While the total population will increase by 229.5% between 1980 and 2025, the elderly component will increase by 365.5% as the cohorts of children who will become the elderly population over the next 40 years will be successively larger. This will result from the high fertility rates of recent decades, coupled with increased life expectancy, especially among the young.

With regard to the sex ratio, it is worthy of note that within the elderly population, the females have consistently outnumbered the males since the 1960s and will continue to do so even after 2025.

The total dependency ratio (defined as the ratio of persons aged 0-14 and 60-plus to the population of working aged people 15-59) was estimated to be fairly stable during the period 1960-2000. By 2020 (and up to 2025 and possibly beyond), however, the total dependency ratio for the country is expected to decline substantially (66 in 2020, and 58 in 2025). The decline in the total dependency ratio after 2000 may be explained by the decrease in the child age dependency ratio (brought about by the decline in the fertility rate) and the fairly constant aged dependency ratio during the period 2000-2025.

The above account should not be misconstrued to mean that Ghana does not yet have a problem of the aging of her population. On the contrary, this should be seen as the right time to evolve a comprehensive program that should provide health and social service infrastructures for the population aged 60 and over in Ghana.

Traditional Beliefs About Old Age and Aging

This section will examine some of the traditional beliefs about old age and aging that exist in the Ghanaian society. This is especially relevant, as these beliefs have served as the main basis for the continuing sustenance and maintenance of elderly persons.

In both traditional and modern Ghanaian society, old age is regarded as a blessing, and old people are regarded as sacred. This is because there is the belief that an old person is nearer the state of the ancestors than the young. Closely related to this belief is the idea that an old person has experienced all the vicissitudes of life and, thus, is adequately equipped for the life thereafter. The older person's long life is, indeed, required as the proof of one's righteousness (Sarpong, 1982-1983).

Old age is also considered to be dignified and, therefore, deserving of honor, respect, and sympathy. It is believed that the respect that the young owe the aged compels the former to tenderly look after the latter. In the Ghanaian society, to neglect one's aged father or mother is to commit an unpardonable act of ingratitude. Parents look forward to the day when they will receive the reciprocal treatment of love and affection from their children. In fact, a child cannot neglect this duty without losing considerable face. As the Akans put it: "When someone has looked after you for you to grow your teeth, you should also look after the person to lose his/her teeth."

Old age in Ghana also commands obedience. To fail or refuse to do what an old person tells or orders one to do is to leave oneself open to trouble. The child who persistently refuses to obey his elders is not expected to get on well in life and is doomed to a life of total failure. Because it is believed that the words of an old person are prophetic and can be maledictory, young people do not dismiss the admonitions of the old with impunity. This gives the aging an authority that is not enforced by brute physical force but, rather, it is enforced in the moral obedience that should be forthcoming from young people.

Ghanaians are also encouraged to be with the elderly as much as possible, especially because wisdom is attributed to old age. The number of years lived is supposed to be commensurate with a person's store of wisdom. Old people, renowned for their wisdom, are consulted on every issue.

Old age is also associated with knowledge. An old person is the repository of the mores, folkways, and traditions of society. The elderly must teach the young how to comport themselves in public ceremonies, funerals, festivals, and the like. Likewise, they hold pragmatic local knowledge, particularly of herbs, medicinal drugs, and plants, and they know where certain valuable items may be hidden and how some things are made. Often the care and loving that are lavished on the old serve as an inducement to get them to reveal some secrets of life to those near (Sarpong, 1982-1983).

The Ghanaian also holds the elderly in fear or awe. The curse of an old person is much dreaded, believed to carry with it the mark of indelible calamity. Many stories are told in which the ridicule or contempt of the old by the young is severely punished by the ancestors.

The elderly are to be treated with love and affection, rather than contempt, revulsion, or avoidance. The good elderly are, in turn, looked upon as affectionate and loving to children and grandchildren, generous in giving. They must not be too demanding, however, and must be grateful when something is done for them. In the same vein, the young must have love and respect for their elders. In effect, the relationship that should exist between the elderly and the young should be that of mutual love, mutual dependence, and mutual advice. The good elderly person is the one who gives good advice, and a good young person is the one who takes the advice of the good elderly person (Sarpong, 1982-1983).

In summary, it may be said that the care of the aging has been borne most willingly in traditional Ghanaian society by the family and the general community because of the invaluable contribution that the aging can make toward the affairs of the community. Indeed, the folkways, mores, values, and artforms (such as dances and games) all remind the people of Ghana of the wisdom, knowledge, experience, and authority of the aged and, therefore, of their obligations toward them. There is little wonder that the members of the extended family in traditional society do all they can to help the old person until he or she departs in dignity (Brown, 1984).

Aging and Social Change

Changes in the Role of the Elderly

Various factors have affected the traditional roles formerly performed by the elderly. These include formal education, industrialization, migration, Christianity and Islam, and technology. With its inculcation of new values, an inquiring mind, and the projection of new models of social relations, formal education has brought into conflict the traditional roles and authority of the elderly. Teachers and other contemporary social leaders, rather than the elderly, are now the counselors from whom the young seek advice (Brown, 1984). Industrialization and job opportunities tend to make the youth more independent and make them ignore, and sometimes even challenge, the authority of the elderly.

The attraction of the youth to the urban centers from rural areas generates a melting pot of cultures, and the new migrants turn to their peers for advice instead of the elderly or their parents. Also, with the migration of the youth to the urban areas, the elderly are deprived of the care they would have had from the youth (under traditional practices).

The advent of Christianity and Islam have weakened the influence of the elderly in traditional structures and practices. For example, traditional herbal practices, in which the aged played an important role, are now frowned upon by some Christians and Muslims because of the traditional rituals. The aged are, therefore, losing their authority as custodians of traditional healing practices among some sections of the population. Finally, the decline of traditional technology, in which the youth served their apprenticeship under the aged, has resulted in the loss of their authority.

Changes in Family Care of the Elderly

In the traditional extended family system, the various divisions of labor on the farm (by sex and by age) often allowed an interchange of roles as the young grew into adults and as adults grew into old age. It was this interdependence that formed the strength of the family support system. The system undertook the many caring responsibilities for the elderly and, in a large measure, old people remained the responsibility of individual families, who provided comfort and support in times of anxiety, loneliness, and helplessness.

With increasing social change, this interdependence—which had formed the strength of the family support system—has been eroded by the separation of the generations through migration, death of key family members, and lack of surviving siblings of elderly persons. Indeed, one could say with some justification that the onus of responsibility for the care of the elderly has shifted from the extended family system toward the nuclear family (with an especially important role being played by spouse and children). In this regard the special role performed by one's children is seen to be very crucial. Brown (1984) has shown the important filial obligation that siblings have toward their parents in the form of providing food (or money for food), running of errands, attending to the daily needs of their parents, occasionally paying for medical bills and house rent, supplying clothing, and providing emotional satisfaction and encouragement.

On the other hand, Apt (1981) has indicated that while most Ghanaians are still willing to take responsibility for their aged parents, young people frequently complain of their own financial inability to care as much as they would wish for aged relatives. She points out that the overall effect of modernization is pressure on the nuclear family, and younger wage earners in particular, to provide for themselves and with little available for aged parents who may be at a distance and inaccessible to receive personal care. Although Apt (1981) hoped for a continued system of family care, the indicators suggested to her that, in comparison with the present generation of people over 60, newer generations of the elderly will be unlikely to have help and security from children. The problem, as she points out, is that not only will people have fewer children, but that because of migration, the children will simply be less available to support their aged parents and, frequently, less able to contribute material assistance.

Consequences of Societal Changes

The Old and Family Relationships

In spite of the profound changes in the institution of the family in Ghana, the family has retained many caring responsibilities for its older members and, in a large measure, old people have remained the responsibility of individual families.

In a survey, Brown (1984) found that there was generally a warm and cordial relationship between the elderly and their children and relations. Once a month, at least 61.7% of the elderly were visited by their children who did not stay with them, while 31.2% were visited by other relations during the same period. Similarly, the reciprocal visits by the elderly to their children and other relations were fairly regular. At least once in every three months, 60.8% paid visits to their children who did not stay with them, while 51.1% indicated that, during the same period, they paid visits to other relations not staying with them. On the whole, Brown (1984) found that the contacts with their children were thought to be very adequate (28.4%), adequate (31.8%), and satisfactory (23.9%). Similarly, contacts with other family members were thought to be very adequate (5.7%), adequate (35.2%), and satisfactory (42%).

Thus the relationship of the older persons with their children, and other family members, in the Ghanaian society appears to be satisfying and rewarding. One may therefore ask: "What accounts for the maintenance of intergenerational ties in spite of the several factors that operate to disrupt them?" Perhaps the main reason is the cultural imperative to "honor thy father and mother," which is inculcated from the earliest years and reinforced continually in the socialization process through societal norms.

Social Change and Family Care of the Elderly

Brown (1984) has shown that the onus of responsibility for the care of the aged in Ghana has shifted from the extended family to the nuclear family, with an important role being played by spouses and children.

The results of a sample survey of the elderly, conducted in the Greater Accra Region of the country, showed that the main sources for the upkeep of the elderly were the elderly themselves (34.5%), their children (33.7%), and their pension, gratuities, and savings (13.4%). Indeed, the support from other relatives was minimal (7.7%), thus supporting the view that there has been a substantial breakdown of the traditional extended familial support system for the elderly. When asked specifically whether they received any support either in-kind or in-cash from their extended family relations, however, almost one-third (31.8%) replied in the affirmative. It will, however, be interesting to find out the extent to which this finding is valid for all parts of the country; especially in rural areas, where the extended family is generally regarded as the first line of defense for its members.

Community Participation and Social Networks of the Elderly

The available evidence indicates that the elderly continue to play an important role in their communities. This is seen not only in their involvement in the operations of the existing representative institutions of the community, but also in their efforts toward the improvement of their working and living conditions.

Brown (1984) operationalized participation in the existing local institutions into four areas of activity: (a) participation in the election of the local chief, (b) participation in the election of the members of the Village Development Committee (VDC), (c) voting in the last general and presidential elections, and (d) membership in voluntary organizations. The results of his study generally support the assertion that the elderly play a fairly active role in the operations of the existing local representative institutions. For example, 47.2% of the sample took part in the election of their chief; 61.4% were instrumental in the election of the members of the VDC; 80.1% voted in the general and presidential elections held in June 1979; and 40.3% belonged to some voluntary organizations that dealt with local development administration (43.7%), matters of local welfare (19.7%), economic development (11.3%), and religious and charitable programs (11.3%). In their involvement with voluntary associations, 62% played an active role by regularly attending meetings and taking an active part in the deliberations. Not surprisingly, 63.4% held various executive positions in these voluntary organizations.

In addition to participating actively in the existing representative institutions in their local communities, Brown (1984) found that the elderly were also very much involved in various efforts toward improvements in the living conditions of their communities. For example, 63.1% took part in communal labor, in spite of their mean age of 68.4 years, and 54% had voluntarily contributed various items and sums of money toward the improvement of their communities. To reemphasize the importance of participation in local affairs, 95.5% were of the view that every inhabitant should take part in communal labor or "voluntary" work, while 90.9% also expressed the opinion that the elderly should play an active role in the affairs of the community. Various reasons were given to explain why the elderly should play an active role in community affairs, of which the most important were the following: to give advice, counsel, and guidance in public affairs (63.5%); to share the experience, wisdom, and knowledge of old people with other members of the community (12.2%); to educate young people in the tradition and customs of the community (12.2%); and to give moral support and encouragement to those at the helm of affairs (8.3%).

The role being played by the elderly appear to be greatly appreciated by other members of the Ghanaian society. Brown (1984) found that 90.9% of his sample were of the view that the local people regarded them as useful members of the community. Again, 93.2% were of the impression that they were needed by people around them and that they were, therefore, greatly encouraged to give of their best for the development of the community.

To conclude, Ghanaian society provides opportunities for older people to participate in some aspects of community life, and the elderly, in turn, play an important role in the development of their communities. There are, however, several obstacles in the development process. Aside from physical and health problems, there might be conditions, processes, and provisions in the social system that affect their efficient performance. These include such things as provisions in the labor market, social insurance, and pension scheme; changing roles; cultural lag; changes in technology; and differences in the value systems of the society. Given the rapid increase in the absolute numbers of the aging, it is necessary to address these problems so as to benefit from their knowledge, skills, and potential. The important question to ask is: "How do we enable the aging to overcome these obstacles and, in the process, improve their participation in the development of their communities?"

In the first place, the aging could be encouraged, and retained, to contribute more effectively to various developmental activities through the processes of community development and organization, cooperative development, local development administration, and through effective programs of adult education, functional literacy, and agricultural development activities, and by making use of appropriate technology. Furthermore, policies and programs aimed at promoting the participation of the elderly must be closely linked with those activities designed to improve their situation as members of an extremely vulnerable group.

Support Systems for the Elderly

Government Policies for the Welfare of the Elderly

It appears that both the colonial British Administration and the post-independence regimes have implicitly relied on the ability of the family network to cope with the problem of individual aging. Indeed, no concrete policies have evolved that anticipate the problems of population aging in Ghana. The result is that in Ghana, at the moment, no laws or a comprehensive national policy focus specifically on the needs and welfare of the aged, although the general laws on retirement and pension affect the aged. Indeed, a National Commission on the Aged was not established until 1982 to advise the government on all matters related to the welfare of the aged.

While one would argue that there are no specific policies for the welfare of the aged, some government departments that deal with social welfare, community and rural development, public health, and adult education, cater, in some ways, to the needs of the elderly. For example, the problems of the needy, including the aged in the urban areas, come under the schedule of the Department of Social Welfare, whereas the Department of Community Development caters to the elderly in the rural areas. Similarly, the social security and pension schemes make some provisions for the elderly. Under the Social Security Act 1965, (Act 279) and the Social Security Decree, 1972 (N.R.C.D. 127), all workers (whether in the public or private sector) should be covered by the Social Security Fund. Workers are required to contribute 5% of their earnings toward the fund, while their employers contribute 12.5%, thus making a total of 17.5% of the worker's wage. Under the pension scheme the worker has the following retirement benefits: a superannuation or old-age benefit, an invalidity benefit, and a survivor's benefit.

With these benefits, the retired worker is supposed to take care of himself and his family for the rest of his life. Because these benefits are not constantly adjusted to take care of inflation and changes in the cost of living, however, they do not provide the elderly with an adequate level of protection sufficient to maintain their financial independence. This is, indeed, a far cry from the lofty and laudable ideals the initiators of the Social Security Bill had in mind when it was introduced in February 1965 —"to ensure carefree, comfortable, and happy old age, instead of living like parasites on the all too meager income of some relations" (Republic of Ghana, 1965).

Furthermore, the present retirement schemes are inadequate in that they cover only the small minority of the elderly who have been fortunate to pass through a period of paid employment in the public and private sectors. The schemes do not cover self-employed persons, agricultural workers, peasants, and farmers, all of whom are more numerous than wage earners. Thus for this category of workers, there is no insurance against old age except in the traditional family system.

The Family Support System

As has been pointed out, the onus of responsibility for the care of the elderly has shifted significantly from the extended family system toward the nuclear family, with an important role being played by spouses and children. Despite tremendous difficulties in looking after their own needs; spouses and children have, in a large measure, assumed the responsibility for caring for the elderly.

One feature of the family support system that continues unabated, however, is that of providing a fitting burial for the dead, especially when death occurs in old age. Subject to local ethnic and tribal variations, and the impact of religious doctrine and affiliation, this last obligation is the main benefit of being survived by one's children and relatives (Brown, 1990).

A major weakness of family support in Ghana is that it is not formal; its effectiveness depends on the demographic and life-cycle evolution of the family unit and its members. In this connection the introduction of formal programs that assist the family, especially its younger members, in providing support for elderly relatives will enhance the quality of life of the elderly.

Support From Voluntary Associations

Voluntary associations have been more alert than government in recognizing the needs of the elderly and coming to their aid. Church organizations (such as Hope Society and St. Vincent de Paul of the Catholic Church of Ghana), as well as other voluntary organizations (such as Boy Scouts, Red Cross, Help-Age International, and Ghana National Association of Teachers) have all provided voluntary social services and material help for the elderly.

The elderly, themselves, have formed some associations aimed at ensuring the general welfare of the elderly and their appropriate and satisfying roles in society. These elderly people's associations, which include the Union of Retired Persons, The Veterans Association of Ghana, and The Senior Citizens Club, can be seen as a measure of the pervading sense of failure on the part of both the government and the family to cope with the various problems and needs of the elderly in Ghana.

Future Projections Regarding Family Care of the Elderly

It is now apparent that the traditional social structures of Ghana are no longer able to adequately care for and support the elderly. There is also a trend of further breakdown owing to degenerating economic and social circumstances.

The state-based social security systems in Ghana are not developed enough to absorb the increasing demand for services and facilities for the elderly. Indeed, the family and the local community still constitute the primary sources of care for the elderly. The aging trend, however, suggests that unless family and community traditions of mutual aid can be strengthened, a vast service infrastructure will be required to replace and expand previous informal care. Given the scarcity of economic resources and the competing demands from the large population of youth, it will be extremely difficult to develop a social security system that provides full coverage to the population. A possible solution to the problem is to find a proper balance between the family and government assistance. This is to suggest a system that will help the family continue to be responsive to the affective needs of elderly relatives and, yet, to provide outside care when critically required. Such a family-oriented policy should include provision of community and home-based care for the elderly in the spheres of health, housing, and social welfare; the availability of professional assistance, financial aid, and counseling services to families caring for disabled or chronically ill aging relatives; the institution of respite care to provide periodic relief to families caring for chronically ill or disabled elderly; and the introduction of concrete measures in support of the family, such as income tax incentives, allowances, and housing subsidies.

Indeed, a combination of service and financial policies will be required to strengthen the capacities of the family to respond to the needs of its aging members and to permit the continued integration of the aging in family life.

Undeniably, informal care in the home plays a major role in maintaining the elderly in the community. As has been pointed out, in the future, the number of relatives available to provide care is likely to diminish because of declining family size and the increasing proportion of women in paid employment. Possibilities for encouraging the development of new types of informal care networks need to be explored and informal care needs to be backed up by a wide array of medical and social services. When all has been said and done, however, the ultimate aim is to enable the elderly to remain with their families (and in their familiar environment) for as long as possible, so as to promote their independence and to give them the right to choose their own life-styles and destinies.

References

Apt, M. A. (1981). *Aging in Ghana* [Mimeo]. Legon: University of Ghana.

Brown, C. K. (1984). *Improving the social protection of the aging population in Ghana.* [Issuer Technical Publication Series.] Legon: University of Ghana.

Brown, C. K. (1990). *Aging and old age in Ghana.* Tampa, FL: International Exchange Center on Gerontology, University of South Florida.

Republic of Ghana. (1965). *The Hansard,* Vol. 38, p. 1083.

Sarpong, P. K. (1982-1983, December-January). Aging and tradition. In *Aging and social change. Proceedings of the 34th Annual New Year School* (pp. 13-20). Legon: Institute of Adult Education, University of Ghana.

United Nations. Department of International Economic and Social Affairs (1982). *World population prospects: Estimates and projections as assessed in 1982.* (No. 83 XIII.5). New York: Author.

United Nations. Department of International Economic and Social Affairs (1985). *The world aging situation: Strategies and policies.* (No. E85.IV.5). New York: Author.

3

Family Care of the Elderly in Mexico

RAQUEL BIALIK

Introduction

Mexico, with 80 million inhabitants (and increasing each year by 2 million), is an old and heterogeneous country with blended characteristics from the indigenous Indian and the Spanish colonial past, creating a *mestizo* culture.

We can very well speak of distinct Mexican environments. In rural areas the native Indians still maintain their traditional Indian dialect and native indigenous values, modes of life, and culture. They have poorly developed agriculture, mainly for self-consumption and with little for barter. The mestizo rural population is well integrated into the national economy and its institutions.

On the other hand, urban areas are becoming characteristic of present-day Mexico—a country becoming more and more urban. In the 1940s Mexico's population was 80% rural, and by the 1970s, 45% of the population lived in urban areas. In the 1980s more than 50% and in the 1990s 60% of Mexico's population resided in urban areas (CEED, 1981).

Mexico City, the capital (a megalopolis), is the most populated city in the world, with 20 million inhabitants and a growth projection to 30 million dwellers by the year 2000. By then the country of Mexico is expected to reach a population of 105 million people. In addition to Mexico City, there are a few other large cities, including Guadalajara, Monterrey, and Puebla.

The overall picture of Mexico shows a highly centralized economy with very few developed areas that attract large quantities of the labor force from scattered rural communities. These individuals often settle in shantytowns in the suburbs.

The political system, until very recently, has been a one-party, authoritarian, and presidential system. Since the profound economic recession of the 1980s, the dominating party has lost much of its great influence, and the country has begun to experience a pluralistic party system. Change, democratization, and more public participation are anticipated for the 1990s.

Demographic Overview of the Population

The study of the population growth and changes in Mexico results from the consequences of fertility, mortality, and migration. Mexico follows the general tendency found in most Latin American countries. Following the Spanish conquest, there had been a tremendous decline in the native population (due to war, famine, epidemics, labor conditions—especially in the mines). Crisis periods alternated with relative stable periods, permitting the equilibrium and growth of the Mexican population. At the end of the colonial period, in the early nineteenth century, there were 6 million inhabitants in all of Mexico (with high-fertility and high-mortality rates). The first population census with "modern characteristics" (undertaken in 1895) registered 12.6 million Mexicans (Jiménez Ornelas & Minujín, 1984). Life expectancy was then 30 years.

After the 1910 Armed Revolution, when one million people were lost, the annual population growth rose to 1.7%, corresponding to the first stage of demographic transition. At the end of the 1930s a reduction in mortality and the maintenance of very high levels of fertility raised the population growth to one of the highest peaks in the demographic history of mankind (Alba, 1989).

From 1970 to 1974 the annual growth rate was 3.38%, representing the second stage in the demographic transition. After 1974 fertility began its descent, mainly because of modern birth control techniques and programs (especially the use of the I.U.D. in urban areas). The third stage had a 2% annual growth rate and will end when fertility reaches a low and stable level together with a low mortality (Urquidi & Morelos, 1982). A fourth stage will be reached when population growth will approximate zero (Benítez Zenteno, 1984).

Table 3.1 Population by Age Groups (thousands and percentages)

Year	Total	0-14	%	15-64	%	65+	%
1950	27,375	11,805	43	14,649	53	921	3.4
1960	37,073	16,912	45	18,907	51	1,254	3.4
1970	51,176	23,878	46	25,507	49	1,791	3.5
1980	69,393	31,013	44	35,913	51	2,467	3.6
1990	89,012	34,821	39	50,875	57	3,316	3.7
2000	109,180	37,243	34	67,331	61	4,606	4.2
2010	128,241	37,704	29	84,096	65	6,441	5.0
2020	145,956	37,988	26	98,398	67	9,570	6.5
2025	154,084	38,231	24	104,005	67	11,848	7.7

SOURCE: United Nations (1988)

Other reasons for fertility reduction are more intense: women's participation in the industrial labor force, older ages at marriage, higher educational levels, urbanization, and family changes. Fertility rates are different
according to geographical areas and to socioeconomic groups.

From 1975 to the present, a 40% reduction in the population growth rate
has brought consequences to the age-structure of the population and has
transformed the aging structure. The birthrate has been diminished to 30
births per 1,000. Youngsters (15 years of age or younger) represented 39%
of the population in 1990 and are expected to become less than 30% in
the year 2010 (see Table 3.1). While the population 65 years and older
already shows a tendency of a greater relative weight, it will represent 4.2%
in the year 2000 and reach 7.7% of the total population in the year 2025,
thus doubling its numbers in the next 30 years.

Mexico has 30 deaths per 1,000 and is expected, in the next 30 years,
to reach a medium annual growth rate of 1.09%, with a general fertility
rate of 2.3 children per couple. There will be 17.7 births per 1,000 and 6.4
deaths per 1,000; implying a life expectancy of 73.2 years. In terms of life
expectancy rates, in the 1930s it was 36.3 years, while in the 1970s it had
risen to 62 years. Life expectancy differs by gender (as shown in Table 3.2).

Life expectancy also differs greatly among regions in the country (with
a 12-year differential). For both sexes, and most particularly among the
younger population, deaths due to infectious and parasitic diseases have
been rapidly declining (because of vaccination), even though they are still
present (as will be discussed). Between the ages of 45 and 65 years, male
mortality is almost double that of female mortality. Between 15 and 45
years, especially among men, violent deaths are the highest causes of

Table 3.2 Life Expectancy at Birth

Year	Male	Female
1930	35.30	37.55
1940	43.34	46.48
1950	50.48	53.96
1960	57.20	60.10
1970	60.05	63.31
1980	62.83	67.11
2000	68.40	72.00

SOURCE: Bronfman, M. (1988)

death. The fall in infant mortality has been much more pronounced in urban settings, and there is still much inequality in death rates, depending on the different social sectors of society.

The main characteristic of the Mexican mortality rate, from 1940 to the present, is its considerable drop. This does not mean, however, that there has also been a substantial improvement in the living standards of the great majority of Mexico's population.

Although health has improved through the years, Mexico still presents a dichotomized profile. On the one hand, it has the characteristics of underdeveloped countries: 40% of its infant population has some degree of malnutrition (2% of which is severe); epidemics in the last 20 years (measles, malaria, equine, encephalitis, typhoid fever, dengue—melindre) have resulted from an unhealthy environment and a lack of services (such as drinking water, drainage, and very poor health education). On the other hand, Mexico is resembling other developed countries with chronic-degenerative diseases, accidents, and neoplasia among the first causes of death of its aging population. Table 3.3 shows causes of mortality among adults.

A total of just $64 per capita is spent yearly for health, representing 2% to 5% of the National Gross Product, with 85% going to treatment and only 15% going for prevention. Since the beginning of the 1980s there has been a reduction in health expenditures in Mexico (IMSS, 1985).

Economic System and Its Effects

It was not until 1911 that the economic grounds were set for the development of "Modern Mexico" with its articulation to the capitalistic world economy. From being a typical agricultural society, with a 2% an-

Table 3.3 Main Causes of General Mortality (1982)

Cause	No. of Deaths	Rate × 100,000	%
Accidents	52,839	72.4	12.8
Heart Disease	50,072	68.6	12.1
Gastrointestinal Infections	35,271	48.3	8.6
Respiratory Infections	30,838	42.2	7.5
Malignant Tumors	29,476	40.4	7.1
Perinatal Infections	25,480	34.9	6.2
Diabetes Mel.	16,775	23.0	4.1
Hepatic Cirrh.	16,001	21.9	3.9
Cerebrovascular Disease	15,898	21.8	3.9
Homicide	13,323	18.2	3.2
Other causes	126,372	173.1	30.6

SOURCE: National Institute of Statistics, Geography and Information. Ministry of Programming and Income (1982/1988)

nual growth and a contribution of more than 28% to the national product, Mexico started developing its manufacturing sector, which absorbed much of the primary labor force. Industry and urban centers grew.

During the period of 1930 to 1950, agriculture absorbed 40% of the occupations; while in the period 1950 to 1970, industrial activities increased to 38.5% and services to 54.4%. This indicates a very strong tendency toward tertiarization, which, as is well known, implies high levels of sub-occupation. This expansion of the tertiary sector explains the growth of women's participation in paid jobs that have been incorporated into extradomestic and nonagricultural activities. In Latin America 35% of all females are in the labor force (Garcia, 1988).

The modern Mexican economy can be divided into different periods: (a) growth with inflation and devaluation (1940-1958), (b) growth with price stability (1958-1970), (c) economic crisis and recession (1970-1990), and (d) recuperation (1990s). In the 1970s Mexico's economy underwent a period of stagnation with a sharp decrease in private investments (especially in industry). Important oil fields were discovered in two southeastern states, but this did not solve the overall crisis, and Mexico entered the 1980s in a deep economic recession.

Work opportunities in the rural areas have been greatly reduced and massive migration has taken place to three or four developing urban centers in Mexico, which, in turn, has forced emigration toward the border of the United States.

Salaries had dropped as much as 50% in the late 1980s, and Mexico's economy started a slow growth (especially with the policy that opened commerce, based upon Free Commerce Agreement [FCA]). Until now, Mexico's economy has had a growing technological dependency.

Another alternate solution to overcome the economic crisis was decentralization. Many companies are growing and providing occupations in new centers. Small plants and companies and family workshops received subcontracts to manufacture parts of specific products (mainly in automobile and garment industries).

Even though in the last few years there has been a tendency to lower demographic growth, the national economy still suffers a crisis that has prevented an improvement in the living conditions for the majority of Mexicans. The age group 14 to 64 years, in which the economic activity rests, will increase considerably at the close of the century; it will consist of 66.5 million people. This figure represents a big challenge for the creation of new jobs that will meet this population growth (estimated at 3% annually) and stop the expulsion of thousands of workers.

The Mexican economy is essentially a market economy in which the amount and quality of the goods and services consumed depend basically on income (COPLAMAR, 1989). In addition, very serious disparities still persist that cut across social stratification and regional differences (almost as wide as in the beginning of the twentieth century). While 10% of the poorest families obtain 1% of the income, 5% of the richest families receive 25% of the income. The former spend their incomes on essential goods and have negative savings (expenses being higher than income), while the latter spend their incomes on products and services beyond (some, far beyond) those needed for mere survival.

If income distribution remains unaltered, Mexico will need to increase its economic development to 9% during the next two decades, and only in this way will it be able to satisfy the basic needs of its lower strata. A typical household will need an average income of two to three times the minimum wage in order to provide for the needs of its members.

Recession coincides with public political unrest. The population is demanding democratization and participation, and the middle class, which has the highest level of education, includes those who are organizing themselves in order to obtain political power.

Employment

The general trend has been the disproportionate rise in nonagricultural activities, especially in the services and in bureaucratic activities. Unemployment in the labor force is now more than 10%, and underemployment stands at more than 40%.

More than one million new jobs per year are needed in order to cope with the population and its needs. Real income loss represents 50% in the last 5 years. This, in part, explains emigration, abandoning agricultural activities, and pauperization in the urban cities (especially in metropolitan areas).

Migration

The very rapid population growth has encouraged massive movements with internal rural-urban migration creating larger and larger urban centers with many regional differences and inequalities. Impoverished peasants, often young people looking for jobs, move to the cities where they seek work in the industrial sector and, more and more, in tertiary service activities. About 42% of the migrants move before marriage.

Women who migrate from rural areas to urban areas tend to have lower levels of education. Most are illiterate, and many do not even speak fluent Spanish (and keep their native culture). Many members of this labor force go into domestic services (as maids) or become peddlers. The north has attracted young women to work in the textile and electronics industries (*maquiladoras*) (Arizpe, 1978).

Men who migrate to the United States become seasonal workers, mostly in the agricultural sector. Men who migrate within the country often find marginal occupations in the construction (building) industry, earning minimal wages. Seventy percent of these migrants have rural backgrounds, and they absorb the norms and modes of life found in urban areas.

Mexico City was the main recipient of mass migration for decades. From 1980 to 1990 this trend diminished because it is becoming less attractive to dwell in this city due to administrative limitations, land-use regulations, and increased land value. Other causes are the fear of another earthquake (such as the 1985 quake), and better educational, living, and working opportunities elsewhere in the country (Brambila, 1985).

There is a high incidence of co-residence among migrant families. In this way, families of the same origin and background (town, state) form urban networks that represent one of the most important resources for different needs (i.e., in time of illness or emergency). Thus traditional behavior patterns coexist with the new urban life-styles.

Migration occurs basically for economic reasons. The problem is that at present the Mexican economy cannot create as many new jobs as are needed in the urban setting, thus causing marginality and misery. In the period 1950 to 1975, one million Mexicans were supposed to have migrated to the United States to look for jobs. Immigration to Mexico is very limited. It stems mainly from Central America and the United States, and very few come from Europe and Asia. Immigration accounts for less than 0.5% of the total population.

Education

Less than 40% of the household heads residing in Mexico City have finished their elementary education. The middle class has the highest educational level of attainment.

Since 1982, with the severe economic crisis, there has been a tremendous drop in the growth rate of all educational levels. Of the total population 6 years of age and older, 56% has had some elementary schooling. Only 63% of first graders pass to the next grade. One of the adverse implications, for Mexico, is a delay in the educational progress of many students, which, in turn, results in a delay in the sequence by which they fill social roles in society.

Desertion from school is especially dramatic in the rural areas, where youngsters are needed for agricultural work (which is considered more important than school) (Padua, 1990). In the large cities children from marginal families beg, wash car windows, and become vendors, among other things, to bring home a few pesos to the family.

Thirty-nine percent of the elderly population is illiterate. The percentage of illiteracy is higher among elderly women (49%).

Education is directly correlated to occupation. Of the total economically-active population, 27% has had no formal instruction and 30% has had only 3 years of elementary school. This level is much lower in agricultural areas, especially among the indigenous peasants. Thus job qualification standards (most particularly in modern technical activities) are necessarily low, and the possibility of obtaining higher levels of vocational education is very limited for the majority of the population. This, in part, explains the low salaries and the unequal distribution of income. Educational opportunities are highly concentrated and depend upon social class and geographical location. For example, the states of Chiapas and Guerrero still have the highest rates of illiteracy and lowest rates of educational attainment.

Industrialization and Urbanization

Mexico began its industrial development and economic transformation since the 1940s. During the next 4 decades Mexico followed an industrialization policy based on the substitution of imported manufactured goods for its own goods manufactured in urban areas.

Industrialization has constituted the main strategy for Mexican development. Rural to urban migration takes place mainly to four metropolitan areas: Mexico City, Guadalajara, Monterrey, and Puebla. These areas are expected, in the near future, to absorb 75% of all the population (together with other developing urban regions). These few areas are highly urbanized, densely populated, and an obstacle for widespread regional development (and the historical pattern of concentration and dispersion is still present).

More than 120,000 marginal, somewhat isolated, and very dispersed small rural communities in Mexico have fewer than 2,500 inhabitants, accounting for 30% of the population. Sixty percent of the households have one to two rooms, with 5.8 people living in an average household. In addition, 30% of the households have no running water, and 40% have unpaved floors (Padilla, 1989).

The Role of the Family in the Care of the Aged

Since pre-Hispanic times, family links have been very strong. In addition to the relationship among grandparents, parents, and children, former clans and tribal associations have now become community and neighborhood bonds. These special relationships convey the institution called *compadrazgo,* which brings together the *compadres* (buddies) and *padrinos* (godparents) with the *ahijados* (godchildren) into a closer relationship than may be found in the actual family.

Yet the family has always been the basic social, economic, and legal institution in Mexico, with rights, responsibilities, and expected cooperation among all its members. Monogamy and patrilineality are the norm, and the extended family has always played an important role in all family affairs. This has been most evident among the rural population, which, until only a decade or two ago, comprised the vast majority of the Mexican people.

With the industrialization process, accompanied by rural to urban migration, the structure of the family has become more and more nuclear and more disrupted. Divorce is uncommon (approximately 25,000 divorces occur yearly); marital separation takes place without legal action and is much more prevalent than is divorce.

It is a socially-recognized responsibility of the family to take care of all its members, including its elderly, sick, and poor. This includes all members of the extended family. The old have always participated in family life (with decision-making power and social status), but their place in the family has become weakened by the "new modes of life" in contemporary society. Their economic participation, too, has diminished. Retirement plans, very limited in scope, are insufficient for the independent living of the elderly, so more and more of them are becoming dependent upon their children (mainly their sons) or on some sort of institutional help. Only 5% of the elderly in Mexico live alone.

The Mexican family is very strong. Through family channels, most of the socialization of cultural values are transmitted to individuals. Although the father is still the main provider (altered in younger urban families), the mother is the central figure of family cohesion. The age of marriage is lower for women without a formal education or with only a few years of elementary school, with the average age of marriage for women 17.3 years in rural areas and 18.7 years in larger cities.

Politically, socially, and psychologically, family members are prepared to assume the responsibility to take care of their elderly relatives, but priorities have changed. First, young adults solve their necessities and those of their children and only after that are the needs of the old considered. Although the elderly do receive care, it may not be sufficient.

Another problem exists when the old remain alone due to family migration, death, abandonment, or poor communications. Some of these individuals will be institutionalized; others will remain on their own. At present no more than 10% of the population 65 years old and over is incorporated into social security systems, and the family continues to be the nucleus where the needs of the elderly are met.

In the 1980s, 60% of elderly men and 17% of elderly women were employed. There is a tendency, however, to reduce their participation in remunerated activities. This reduction in paid income will increase to 44% in the year 2000 and to 25% in 2025 for elderly men and to 10% in 2000 and only 4% in 2025 for women over 65 years of age. This means that the

Mexican elderly (especially the women) will depend for their support on their families, and will do so more and more.

As was discussed, illiteracy among the elderly is more than 40% higher among women, reaching 87% among elderly indigenous women. This has had negative effects on their working opportunities and explains why these groups have found their main economic activities in agriculture and domestic services.

From a research project undertaken by Bialik, 1989, of 1,000 elderly women in Mexico (both urban and rural), one third had no personal income and 12% had incomes of less than $5 a month. It was found that 36% were sustained by their children (34% of whom lived with family), 26% by the spouse, 8% by government agencies, 5% by other family members, and 18% were self-supported. Only 10% of the sample had paid employment outside the home.

Although the research covered many aspects, the focus was on the perception of the elderly toward their own families. The main reason for the happiness of the elderly in old age was their family; thus their family was the major source of satisfaction. In addition, feeling useful was stressed as a good method by which not to feel old and this, again, has to do with the role played by the elderly in their domestic and family environment. The role of parent and grandparent still made the elderly participate and feel important.

Expectations of the elderly toward family members differed by sex and by generation. From their daughters, love and caring were expected. From their sons, they expected economic help and sustenance. From the grandchildren, the elderly expected affection and respect. These expectations were less realized in urban settings. It was in urban areas where different social networks were being established to meet the needs of the elderly, especially by neighbors and through church affiliations (Bialik, 1989).

After the 1980s, when the economic crisis had profoundly affected the lives of the majority of the Mexicans, adverse changes had been felt within the family. There were lowered rates of consumption in every sphere of society (educational, recreational, nutritional). The disruption of many families was caused by forced migration (within the country and abroad) of the younger and stronger members of the family, as they sought better working conditions to make a better life for themselves.

This crisis is less acute in the 1990s, but the family structure has suffered a profound change. It has become more urban and nuclear, and reorganizing into an incomplete extended urban family (where the young married couples have to stay for long periods of time with their parents, due to lack of housing, unemployment, etc.).

Families in metropolitan areas often live in crowded and/or dangerous areas. The elderly, obviously, are having a difficult time and are becoming more of a burden to the urban family than they had ever been to the family in rural areas (González Casanova & Aguilar Camín, 1990). Because Mexican traditional values praise love and care within the family, it is uncommon to find maltreatment toward the elderly. Rather, "oblivion," or second-class treatment, is what can, on occasion, be found in urban society (in particular).

From the study of elderly women in Mexico (Bialik, 1989), it was found that the institutionalized elderly comprised the least cared for group and their level of functioning was the worst. Those who lived in public old-age homes were the ones who scored the lowest in biopsychological and social functioning. Although fed, given medical care, and provided with recreational activities, they were still unhappy, lonesome, and felt "locked up." Most of these institutionalized elderly were urban women without family or with family members who did not want any contact whatsoever with these elderly relatives.

The "Council of the Elderly," which had been created to make decisions affecting the elderly, no longer exists and is more "wishful thinking" by some pro-elderly agencies than it is fact. Mexican old people are tolerated. This is the general attitude. A 1984 study in Mexico found that old men were better liked by the general public than were old women. A later study, however, (Bialik, 1988) found that old women perceived themselves as still being useful and felt that their main source of pleasure in life came from their families; only 4% felt lonely and mistreated. Social attitudes are becoming more accepting, and in 1979 the government enacted policies to give care and assistance to the elderly of Mexico.

Programs and Services to Support Family Caregiving

In Mexico governmental policies toward elderly care have emphasized family responsibility to keep the elderly in their homes and own milieu, thus maintaining their links in their communities. The Declaration of the Rights of the Old emphasizes that families have the responsibility to care for their elderly in the midst of the family. This Declaration has led to the creation of government programs for families with limited resources. The main means has been through the National System of Integral Development of the Family (DIF), which implements such services as free medical care, laundry, recreation, and meals.

The Mexican Institute of Social Security has protected 32 million people, mainly workers, and the ISSSTE, an agency that protects state employees, covers 6 million persons. About 16% of those on social security are retired and are granted retirement benefits, but the rest are without any old-age insurance.

Another institution that gives protection to the elderly is the National Institute for the Aged (INSEN). Created by presidential appointment in 1979, INSEN gives integral assistance to the aging population (60 years and over), particularly the ones who lack social security and have no access to sanitary services. Its programs include economic assistance through the issuance of identification cards, which permit discounts of goods and services from 50% to 100% savings (in transportation, medical services, drug supplies, and basic need articles). It also provides centers to help with self-sufficiency (through paid employment and training workshops). In addition, the agency has a legal protection office and sponsors old-age homes and recreational clubs. INSEN also sponsors educational campaigns, geriatric and gerontological education, and preparation for retirement. Finally, to meet many other needs, the agency is responsible for occupational therapy workshops, day residences, and recreation and vocational activities.

At present, after more than 10 years of its existence, INSEN has one million affiliated members and 3,000 service providers. The month of August has been declared "the month of the old." Campaigns for information and specific actions are undertaken and spread throughout the country. One event that has been very successful is the annual ball, "Una Cana al Aire" (which means, in Mexican slang, to misbehave). This event, which began in Mexico City, is now celebrated in many other cities. These efforts have led to changes in the general perception of the public toward the elderly and have opened new channels of communication and understanding. Ultimately a better acceptance of the elderly in community life has developed.

The DIF, which was already mentioned, has similar programs for the elderly, and so there are several institutions working for the elderly and retired populations. Also, some private institutions, mainly religious groups, give assistance to the old.

Religion is a primary institution, especially Catholicism (although Protestants are increasing in their numbers in rural areas), and it plays a very important role among the Mexicans, especially the elderly. From the author's research (Bialik, 1989), 93% still practice their religion frequently, from which they obtain peace and hope, and they have high expectations from their priests to accompany them and give them moral support in old age.

Since 1977 two geriatric societies in Mexico organize training courses, congresses, and scientific meetings and publish and distribute gerontological information. The teachings of geriatrics and gerontology have developed only lately. The Instituto Politécnico Nacional has begun a specialty in the School of Homeopathy and, very recently, has developed a master's degree in geriatrics. The National University has a 3-year master's degree program in geriatrics for medical students. A private university, Universidad Iberoamericana, has academic links with the "University of the Third Age" and gives academic credits to elderly students who register in special courses dealing with gerontology.

Conclusions

Working with national statistics can be truly misleading, especially if one is working at local levels. As was discussed, Mexico is a mosaic of traditional versus modern modes of life. Implementation of actions—to be realistic and functional—should best be based upon research results and given viable solutions. Mexico, like so many other countries, suffers from a lack of continuity between policymakers and researchers. Programs are often implemented without the benefit of solid scientific data.

Old age in Mexico is here to stay; numerically, it is becoming increasingly significant. If, in 1990, the elderly represented 3.7% of the total Mexican population, in 30 years (by 2020) the proportion of elderly is projected to double.

The economic participation of the elderly has increasingly been reduced and, because social security systems are insufficient and meager, it is clear that there will be an increase in the helplessness and distress of the old. Retirement policies in Mexico, also, are very limited in scope and will have to be better planned and implemented.

In the coming decades, two of every three elderly persons will be women, and these women are the most dependent upon family care. The family is the institution for which solutions must be sought so that effective care may be provided to their elderly relatives. Mexicans' cultural background is well molded for such a responsibility. It is, then, a matter of good and timely planning that will permit Mexicans to effectively cope with this heterogeneous group: the elderly.

References

Alba, F. (1989). *La población de México. Evolución y dilemas* [Mexico's population. Evolution and dilemmas]. Mexico City: El Colegio de México.

Arizpe, L. (1978). *Migración, etnicismo y cambio económico. Un estudio sobre migrantes campesinos a la ciudad de México)* [Migration, ethnicity and economic change. A study on migrant peasants to Mexico City]. Mexico City: El Colegio de México, Centro de Estudios Sociológicos.

Benítez Zenteno, R. (1984). Población, desarrollo y políticas de población en México. [Population, development and population policies in Mexico]. In R. Benítez Zenteno (Ed.), *Los factores del cambio demográfico en México* [Factors in Mexican demographic change] (pp. 11-18). Mexico City: Siglo XXI, S.A. de C.V.

Bialik, R. (1989). *Migración y formación familiar en México* [Migration and family formation in Mexico]. Mexico City: El Colegio de México.

Brambila, C. (1985). *Migración y formación familiar en México* [Migration and family formation in Mexico]. Mexico City: El Colegio de México.

Bronfman, M. (1988). *La Mortalidad en México.* Mexico City: El Colegio de México.

Centro de Estudios Económicos y Demográficos (CEED) (1981). *Dinámica de la población en México* [Mexican population dynamics]. Mexico City: El Colegio de México.

Coordinación General del Plan Nacional de Zonas Deprimidas y Grupos Marginados (COPLAMAR). (1989). *Macroeconomía de las necesidades esenciales en México. Situación actual y perspectivas al año 2000* [Macroeconomics of the essential needs in Mexico. Present situation and perspectives to the year 2000]. Mexico City: COPLAMAR and Siglo XXI.

García, B. (1988). *Desarrollo económico y absorción de fuerza de trabajo en México 1950-1980* [Economic development and labor force absorption in Mexico 1950-1980]. Mexico City: El Colegio de México.

González Casanova, P., & Aguilar Camín, H. (1990). *México ante la crisis* [Mexico facing the crisis]. Mexico City: Siglo XXI.

Instituto Mexicano del Seguro Social (IMSS) (1985). *Salud, necesidades esenciales en México* [Health, essential needs in Mexico]. Mexico City: Coplamar and Siglo XXI.

Jiménez Ornelas, R., & Minujín, A. (1984). *Los factores del cambio demográfico en México* [Demographic change factors in Mexico]. Mexico City: Siglo XXI.

National Institute of Statistics, Geography and Information. Ministry of Programming and Income. (1982/1988). In E. Gonzalez Carbajal (Ed.), *Health Diagnosis in Mexico* (p. 30). n.p.: Editorial Trillas.

Padilla, A. (1989). *México: Desarrollo con pobreza* [Mexico: Development with poverty]. Mexico City: Siglo XXI.

Padua, J. (1990). "Los desafíos al sistema escolar formal" [The challenges to the formal school system]. In El Colegio de México (Ed.), *México en el umbral del milenio*

[Mexico on the verge of the millennium] (pp. 307-344). Mexico City: Centro de Estudios Sociológicos, El Colegio de México.

United Nations. (1988). *World Demographic Estimates and Projections, 1950-2025* (ST/ESA/SER:R/79). New York: Author.

Urquidi, V.,& Morelos, J. B. (1982). *Tendencias y políticas de población* [Population trends and policies]. Mexico City: El Colegio de México.

4

Family Care of the Elderly in Thailand

MALINEE WONGSITH

Introduction

In Thailand, where socioeconomic development in the past decade has been accompanied by an effective family planning program, the impact of rapid social and economic change can be observed on the family structure and functions. As Thailand moves from an agricultural society to a more urbanized and industrialized one, the family structure shifts from an extended unit to a nuclear one. Even though the family is a universally fundamental unit of society, its meaning in the society is changing drastically (Carter & McGoldrick, 1988). Adults, a major part of whose life spans were devoted to child rearing, are now spending less than half of the time formerly needed for such activities. Due to a low birth rate, family size is decreasing, with effects on the changing role of women. Social exposure offers better status for women; but, at the same time, the divorce and remarriage rates are increasing. Such changes, characteristic of modern development, are resulting in a change in family structure and traditions.

Not only has the structure of the family been changed but also the familial roles, although the family generally continues to serve as a source of support and the majority of the Thai elderly live with family members or have access to family members for assistance. There is a shift, however, in the frequency and quality of support. With increasing modernization

AUTHOR'S NOTE: Special thanks are due to Dr. Carl M. Frisen for his valuable comments.

and education, the size of the nuclear family has declined and the extended family has been dispersed. The traditional ties of family and face-to-face support of the young for the old have diminished. Many elderly are totally abandoned and are not able to adapt to a new environment.

The Setting

Thailand is a tropical country in the Indo-Chinese peninsula of Southeast Asia with an estimated 1990 population of about 56 million. It covers 198,500 square miles, much of which consists of flat alluvial plains and river valleys devoted primarily to rice farming. To the south, the country becomes a narrow extension of the Malay Peninsula. The Kingdom is generally considered as comprising four main regions.

The north, with 19% of the nation's population, includes both sparsely settled mountainous areas and densely settled river valleys. The northeast, with 35% of the population living mainly on a semiarid plateau with relatively infertile soil, is the least developed of the regions. The central region, including the Bangkok metropolitan area, contains 33% of the national population. Its fertile alluvial plains, combined with the presence of Bangkok as the center of governmental and economic activity, make it the most developed and most densely settled region. The south, comprising peninsular Thailand, has 13% of the population, including 80% of the country's Muslims. The south is devoted largely to rubber, coconut, and fruit cultivation; and tin mining is an important activity.

The 1980 midyear population of Thailand was estimated at 46.7 million people by the United Nations. The final results of the 1990 census are not yet available, but the United Nations medium projection for mid-1990 is 55.7 million. Table 4.1 provides a picture of demographic changes in Thailand since 1970. The number of the elderly 65 years of age and over has increased from 1.1 million in 1970 to 1.6 million in 1980 and an estimated 2.2 million in 1990. In terms of percentage, this is an increase from 3.0% in 1970 to 3.5% in 1980 to 3.9% in 1990. The proportion of elderly who were female was estimated at 56% in 1990. The old-age support ratio rose from 5.9 in 1970 to 6.2 in 1990. Projected trends of change in the size and proportion of the elderly population are discussed later.

Traditional Values in Thai Society

The religion of the vast majority of Thai is Buddhism, from which much of the dominant value system is derived. For example, the idea of "merit"

Table 4.1 Population Size, Age and Structure, Based on United Nations Estimates, 1960-1990. (medium variant)

	1960	1970	1980	1990
Population (000)				
Total	26,392	35,745	46,718	55,702
60+	1,188	1,715	2,528	3,453
65+	725	1,077	1,650	2,175
70+	421	4,616	968	1,282
75+	210	313	484	671
% of total population				
60+	4.5	4.8	5.4	6.1
65+	2.7	3.0	3.5	3.9
70+	1.6	1.7	2.1	2.3
75+	0.8	0.9	1.0	1.2
% of population female				
60+	53.6	39.5	54.7	54.6
65+	54.9	56.1	56.1	55.9
70+	55.8	58.4	58.5	57.8
75+	56.7	60.4	58.5	59.9
Population 65+ (000)				
Male	327	473	725	961
Female	398	604	927	1,216
% of population 65+ years				
Male	1.2	1.3	1.6	1.7
Female	1.5	1.6	2.0	2.1
Support ratio	5.2	5.9	6.2	6.2

NOTE: Support ratio = pop 65+/pop 15-64
SOURCE: United Nations (1991)

and "demerit" is adhered to widely. The Thai also have a strong sense of child-parent obligation, or filial piety, that imposes heavy obligations upon children concerning their behavior and responsibility toward their parents (Cowgill, 1986). Children are believed to owe their parents absolute obedience and support in their old age and to owe them appropriate funerals to make merit for them.

Seniority is widely revered, and the aged are highly regarded. Thai also have a sense of superordination and subordination, with the head of the family exercising power over other members. Finally, the Thai system is conceptually centered on women, who perform the overall functions in family, although they are not more powerful or influential than men (Potters, 1977).

Basic Economic System

For centuries the economy of Thailand has been predominantly agricultural, based on rice as the staple food. Since 1955 there has been a rapid and substantial growth of other crops, and industry is now growing rapidly in performance.

During the past 2½ decades there have been significant changes in the Thai economic structure. Due to the intervention of the government, which was becoming increasingly aware of the need to shift the structure of the economy and to reduce the dependence upon agriculture and a few primary products, rapid industrial expansion has taken place in the production of consumer goods. The changing product share of the agricultural sector was reduced from about 40% in 1961 to only about 17% in 1985 (Kiranandana, Wongboonsin, & Kiranandana, 1989). Thailand has also done well in the services sector with tourist attractions. Huge investments have given rise to fast industrialization with increases in manufactured exports by an average 40% per annum during 1987-1989 (*Bangkok Post,* 1990). This structural transformation from agriculture to a modern economic sector has many social and economic implications. The rural agricultural sector could not be developed at the same speed as the urban industrial sector and, as rural-urban differences became wider, they gave rise to more rural-to-urban migration, creating many problems.

Role of the Family

Age is still a basic determinant of status in Thailand (Cowgill, 1972). The elderly are treated to positions of honor both in public gatherings and in the home. All Thai are trained to show respect for elders. The Thai child is taught the gesture and ritual appropriate to persons of different ages.

More than any other institution, the family has provided the central focus of social life for older people in Thailand. In the past the predominant family structure was the extended family, where more than two immediate generations live together. In the extended family, the elderly could always carry out useful activities (such as caring for young children, cooking meals, and housekeeping), while active family members were out working. The elders' experience and suggestions were required and highly valued.

Thus it is the family that normally takes full responsibility for its aged members. Within the family responsibility is usually shared among members according to their age and abilities. Studies have shown that children are major sources of support to their parents, particularly when parents are too old to work or care for themselves (Chayovan, Knodel, & Siriboon,

1990; Kamnuansilpa, 1980; Xuto, 1982). This support takes both economic and social forms and is viewed as repayment to parents for having borne, cared for, and raised the child (Knodel, Chamratrithirong, & Debavalya, 1987).

The concept of parent repayment is quite strong. Parents expect, and are entitled to, support from their adult children as repayment or obligations, which encompass both economic and noneconomic dimensions. For example, during illness, the aged parents need physical care and psychological comfort as well as financial help in purchasing medicine or paying for medical services. Even after parents die, children are expected to pay respect to the deceased parents. With a deeply entrenched sense and practice of repayment involving the provision of support to the aged, old-age support from family members, especially children, persists in current society, but the form of support appears to be shifting.

It should be borne in mind that though the elderly are highly respected in Thai society, age alone is no guarantee of respect. To maintain respect the elders should behave in a manner befitting them (Kaufman, 1960).

Societal Change Over Time

Demographic Change

Dramatic changes have been occurring with respect to vital rates. The total population increased from 8 million in 1911 (first census taken) to 11.5 million in 1929 and 17.4 million in 1947. The average annual growth rate during this period was generally not very large because of the high level of mortality.

The gain to a total population count of 27 million in 1960 resulted from a rapid decline in death rates due to modern medical treatment and sanitation practices. Mortality among Thai was declining continuously, while birth rates remained high. As a result, the population growth rate at that time increased to 3.2%.

The decline in fertility of the Thai population began in the early 1960s. The total fertility rate, which indicates the average number of births a woman could expect to have as implied by current age-specific birth rates, fell from 6.3 in 1964-1965 to 2.2 per woman in 1985-1986 (Chayovan, Wongsith, & Saengtienchai, 1988). Major factors in the rapid decline in fertility were the approval by the Thai cabinet, in 1970, of an official policy to reduce the population growth, and the Thai readiness to accept family planning. The National Family Planning Program (NFPP), formally established under the auspices of the Ministry of Public Health, was fully operational by 1972, leading to the decline in fertility and a lower population growth rate (Bennett, Frisen, Kamnuansilpa, & McWilliam, 1990).

Socioeconomic Change

Demographic change in Thailand has resulted from declining trends in fertility and mortality with increases in longevity and in mobility of the population among the regions as well as from rural to urban areas (Kiranandana et al., 1989). These demographic dynamics affect socioeconomic processes and interact with them.

With the low growth rate, the number of dependent young is declining, while the numbers of working age and elderly populations are increasing, especially in the rural areas where 80% of Thai reside. With limited land availability and current advances in technology, the increase in the rural working age population exceeds the labor absorption capacity of the agricultural sector. Labor surplus has moved to urban areas, especially Bangkok, leading to urban industrial unemployment. Although agriculture is a very important sector in the Thai economy, the industrial sector has begun to play a more important role.

In brief, Thailand's economy has been undergoing dramatic change from an agricultural economy based on a narrow range of support commodities, for example, rice, rubber, teak, and so on, to a strong industrial base. Industrialization and the unavailability of additional land for agriculture continue to be the driving force for rural-urban migration.

The mobility patterns of the population have a significant impact on the elderly. Adult children cannot remain with elderly parents, and the form of support they provide for the elderly has shifted. Although migrants send remittances, they tend to be sent most frequently by husbands or wives, by the older generation to the younger generation, and, least frequently, by younger to older. This has considerable negative significance for older people left behind and who hope for financial support from the out-migrants (Tout, 1989). Those who remain behind in the rural areas (mainly women, children, and elderly) often lack adequate means for subsistence.

As the society moved from agricultural to a more urbanized and industrialized society, the pattern of education has also changed. Vocational and technical education enrollments have increased to conform to the country's development needs and the government policy of promoting vocational and technical education. Enrollment in secondary and higher education has also increased. Generally, the educational quality has been upgraded as has educational opportunity. There is no sex discrimination in the educational system in Thailand.

Economic growth and technological advancement, which affect educational patterns, affect the elderly. The elderly may find their knowledge and long experience not suitable for various new technologies. The transmitted knowledge that once was useful to the new generation tends to become obsolete in a modernizing society.

"Modernization" usually carries with it the implication of change for the culture and movement of the society away from traditional practices that it previously accepted (Korson, 1978). For instance, in Thailand traditional familial values toward marriage seem to have been changing as society modernizes and other conditions change. Social and economic changes have resulted in a greater frequency of conflict within the family which, in turn, can lead to divorce. There are no precise figures on divorce and separation rates in Thailand, because many marriages (as well as divorces) are not registered on the government rolls, and many separations seem to follow an on-again-off-again pattern (Phillips, 1965). It does appear, though, that the legitimate divorce rate in Thailand is increasing and the highest rate is found in Bangkok (NESDB, 1989).

Consequences of Societal Change

In order to understand the effect of changing social, demographic, and economic conditions on family roles, it is essential to understand the Thai family structure. It varies with the sequence of family life. The large majority of newlyweds start their married life as part of the parental household (Smith, 1973). There is no set rule as to parental choice, so it is impossible to say whether Thai marriage is patrilocal or matrilocal (Cowgill, 1986). Most of the newlyweds stay temporarily with the parents until the first child is born or until they become economically well off, when they then set up a separate household. If one of the newlyweds is the youngest child, the new family tends to stay indefinitely with the parents. This pattern of rotation of residence produces various structures of households. Early in marriage couples live in stem families.[1] Later most of them move out and live as nuclear families until the first child is married, when they may again become a stem family, remaining a stem family until the parents die.

Although, traditionally, the aged are obligated to care for the young and the young are obligated to help the elders as best as they can (Potters, 1977), changes introduced by social and economic development are

Table 4.2 Percentage of Households by Household Structure and Age of Household Heads, 1980, Thailand

Household Structure	Under 60	60+	65+	70+
Unrelated individual	3.7	7.5	9.0	10.8
Nuclear family	76.1	40.0	36.2	33.9
Extended family*	20.3	52.5	54.8	55.3

*Including vertical (stem), horizontal (joint), and vertical and horizontal.
SOURCE: National Statistical Office (1980)

transforming the way of living. The household structure has largely changed from an extended to a nuclear family type, which is less suitable in accommodating the elderly. Table 4.2 provides information on living arrangements for household heads who are under age 60 years and those 60 and older. The data reveal that the proportion of nuclear families with household heads aged under 60 years was 76%, while 55% of the household heads aged 65 years and over lived in extended families. Increased urbanization will result in a trend toward more nuclear families in the future. The decline in fertility means that there will be fewer children for elderly parents to live with and fewer children to assume the social, economic, and emotional responsibility of caring for the old.

Other continuing changes in Thai society are altering the form of support the young provide for the elderly. Farming is no longer the most attractive way of earning a living because there is a shortage of land and income is unpredictable. With more job opportunities in the big city, many of the young move to Bangkok and become unskilled laborers. Some return to the village during harvest season, while others work only in the city. Under these circumstances, a shortage of field laborers leads to low productivity in the rural areas. Many elderly are left behind to care for small children.

Traditionally Thai elderly lived with, or within, the same village as their children, allowing frequent contact. Children could help support and comfort parents in old age. The children provided labor in farm activity and assistance during illness, primarily in the form of physical care and psychological comfort and also through financial help in purchasing medicine and paying for medical services. The responsibility of the children to the aged parents included the provision of food and clothes, social visits, help around the house, and help with cooking.

As migration has increased, many adult children no longer remain with or nearby the elderly; thus the contact and even the forms of support have shifted. Frequency of contact is decreasing and those who have migrated send remittances home for those who remain behind in the village. Monetary remittances from wage labor or nonagricultural jobs outside the village are replacing help in activities requiring labor. Increasingly, outmigrants fail to remit financial support to the elderly. The elderly are faced with the monetization of daily life and may have difficulty earning cash incomes of their own. They may have to fight for subsistence and adopt informal types of agriculture or commerce, with less benefit potential, in order to meet their needs. Data from the study of the Socio-Economic Consequences of the Aging of the Population in Thailand (SECAPT) also confirm that the percentage of the rural elderly currently working is higher than urban elderly, and a higher percentage report that income is insufficient (Chayovan et al., 1988).

All surveys show that the elderly are likely to report more illness than the population at-large and the duration of illness is longer among the elderly. With physical health problems, the elderly need health care and almost one half of the aged respondents to SECAPT expressed the need for some type of health care; more rural than urban elderly feeling this need.

The consequences of societal change are not only physical but also can be psychological (in terms of depression, loneliness, and the degree of satisfaction with life). Deteriorating physical condition, physical disability, death of a spouse, children leaving home, and lack of adequate sources of income are causes of depression and loneliness (Weeks, 1984). Recent studies have pointed out that Thai elderly are faced with the problems of adjustment to changing society and loneliness (Kumnuansilpa, 1980; Xuto, 1982). Data from SECAPT revealed that a higher percentage of the elderly not living with their children feel loneliness. This is the result of the departure of the children from the family home, leaving aged parents with no one readily available to take care of them.

A few elderly Thai are childless, and a few are estranged from their children. Even though the data on extent of childlessness are not available, SECAPT data show that about 4% of the Thai elderly live alone (with a higher proportion in rural than urban areas). Attention should be given to the elderly living alone, especially the poverty-stricken elderly in rural areas.

Responses to Change in the Country

Most studies conclude that the concept of children giving support to the elderly is still practiced and accepted in Thailand. For example, SECAPT data showed that almost half of the elderly depend upon children, or spouses of children, as the main source of income. It was found, however, that two major problems of the Thai elderly are inadequate income and health problems. Traditionally the extended family has taken care of these matters.

With social and economic changes, the extended family is less frequently maintained, the household has decreased in size, and the nuclear family has become standard in the society. Therefore it is a common practice to develop specialized programs for housing and care of infirm older people. In the case of Thailand, various programs provide for the elderly, though the number receiving assistance is small. Although the family network still continues to be the main source of provision for the elderly, many old-age assistance programs have been introduced. They vary considerably in the area covered and the scope of services provided.

Old-Age Pension Plans

The existing old-age pension plans can be classified into three groups: government, state enterprise, and private enterprise employees (Kiranandana et al., 1989).

Government Employees

Government employees receive benefits in the form of a lifetime pension or a lump-sum payment upon retirement. The compulsory age of retirement is 60 years, but early retirement can be taken after age 50 or 25 years in service. Those who have government jobs continuously for 10 years or longer are eligible to receive a lump sum of money. Those who work for 25 years or longer can choose either a lump sum or monthly payments. The amount of the lump-sum benefit is calculated by multiplying the final monthly salary by the number of years in service. For those qualified for a pension, the monthly benefit is equal to 2% of the final monthly salary times the number of years in service.

State Enterprise Employees

The state enterprises contribute fixed percentages of the monthly total salary paid to the pension fund, and benefits are paid to the employees upon retirement in a lump-sum payment. The retirement age and early retirement are allowed in the same manner as for other government employees.

Private Enterprise Employees

Most of the pension plans for private enterprise employees are operated in the form of provident funds with contributions from both employers and employees. Under the Royal decree on provident funds, issued in September 1983, and effective on January 1, 1984, each employee contributes not less than 3% of the wage or salary earned, while each employer's contribution should not exceed 15% of the wage or paid salary. Benefits are paid to employees according to the terms specified in each employer's provident fund. Only large private enterprises provide old age or retirement benefits to their employees, however.

Various Types of Assistance for the Elderly

Thailand is in the early stage of establishing a social security program. The Fifth National Economic and Social Development Plan (1982-1986) called for noninstitutional care for the elderly, encouraged private-sector participation, and emphasized the role of the family in taking care of the elderly. A variety of services provided by government and nongovernment sectors are briefly described.

Government Services

Most of the welfare programs for the aged are under the responsibility of the Departments of Public Welfare and Social Services, Ministry of Interior, and some supportive programs are carried out by the Department of Medical Services, Ministry of Public Health and the Department of Nonformal Education, Ministry of Education.

Institutions for the Aged. Bangkae Home for the Aged was the first home, established in 1953 under the responsibility of the Department of Social Services, Ministry of Interior, with the main purpose of rendering residential care to needy persons who meet the following requirements: over 60 years of age for females and over 65 years for males, homeless, have no relatives with whom to live, or are not able to live happily with their own families. The number of homes has increased to 12. Three categories of programs are offered: free of charge, hostel, and private home. Services provided to the residents include lodging and food, clothing, personal living effects, religious rites, medical services, physical exercise and therapeutic activities (for physical rehabilitation), recreational activities, traditional festival activities, social work services, and traditional funeral services. Hobbies and vocational therapeutic activities such as embroidery or handicraft are arranged.

Elderly Social Services Centers. In addition to residential care for needy elderly persons, the Department of Public Welfare established the first elderly social services center in August 1979 in the compound of Bangkae Home for the Aged. Eight centers provide services to both males and females over 60 years of age who live in nearby areas and to the heads of households who have problems in caring for elderly persons. Services provided in these centers include therapeutic and rehabilitative care, recreation, day care, family assistance, and counseling services. Also included are opportunities for social and community participation for the residents of the homes for the aged. Parallel to the services centers, home visits are made in the surrounding communities so as to give advice and primary medical treatment to elderly persons. The Elderly Social Services Centers have aided in promoting health conditions for the elderly, in general, through prevention and rehabilitation. The government plan for the future is to establish more social services centers for the aging population in various provincial areas. The activities of these centers should enable the elderly to remain with, and in the care of, their families, thus reducing the need for additional homes for the aged.

Social Center for the Aged. In order to expand the coverage of services for the aged, the Department of Social Services has set up a social center for the aged in Bangkok. This center focuses its services on educating the aged and providing social activities for them. The center also serves as a temporary home for the aged in cases of urgent need.

Nonformal Education Program. Education plays a very important role in keeping elderly persons alert and aware of the outside world and helps them to continue to be physically and mentally active. With this in mind, nonformal education projects have been initiated, including the formation of vocational interest groups, education through mass media, village reading centers, audiovisual education, and so on, through the Department of Nonformal Education, Ministry of Education. Nonformal education is used not only to keep people abreast of currents events, but also to promote understanding of, and preparation for, old age.

Health Care. In view of the problems facing the aged due to deterioration of health, the government included a program for prevention and cure of illness and provision of therapy for the aged as a part of the Fourth Five Year Plan (1977-1981). Because the demand for health care services increases with the growing number of aged, in 1979 the Ministry of Public

Health set up the Advisory Committee for Planning Health Care Programs for Aging. Several programs on health care for the elderly are augmented in general hospitals throughout the country. Up to now many hospitals have operated geriatric clinics, and the others are encouraged to render special care for the elderly. Moreover, the Ministry of Public Health has integrated preventive and curative services for the aged into the primary health care program.

In 1980 a Special Geriatric Health Service Program was initiated. Its main activities include training of personnel in health care for the elderly and widening public knowledge in this field through the mass media. One year later a National Committee on Coordination of Health Care for the Elderly was formed as a planning and coordinating body. In recognition of the emerging problems of an increasing elderly population and the importance of proper planning for the future, the government set up The National Committee on the Elderly of Thailand in 1982.

Nongovernment Services

Active participation of the private sector is an important element in the achievement of overall welfare goals. In the field of aging, as in other welfare and development fields, the private sector has played an active role through clubs, foundations, and associations. Many offer services for the aged through various kinds of activities. Unfortunately there are no complete records of the organizations involved. These private organizations are operated on a voluntary basis in the form of foundations or clubs.

Foundations for the Aged. Various foundations offer care for elderly persons. The most widely known, the Wai Wattana Nivas Foundation, provides housing and services for homeless males over 60 years old. Presently about 500 elderly persons are under the responsibility of this foundation, most of them Chinese and almost half in poor health. The welfare services of this foundation include housing and food, physical and mental rehabilitation, vocational therapy, and so on. Other foundations providing similar services are the Taranu-kraw Foundation and St. Louis Foundation. Many activities focus on humanitarian and developmental aspects of the aging. Some private hospitals in Bangkok and the provinces provide free health care for the poverty-stricken aged.

Senior Citizen Clubs. One hundred eight senior citizen clubs have been established in 72 provinces within Thailand. Each club has its own activities, primarily concerned with health, religious, and recreational services. There are also associations formed by elderly persons who are all retired from the same organization or the same profession (such as the Retired Interior Officials Association, Retired Militarian Association, etc.). These associations carry out activities similar to Senior Citizen Clubs. In addition to these organizations, welfare services are found in the field of private business. Some private firms have retirement and pension policies, others do not, and the range and coverage of services vary from one organization to another. The personnel of state enterprises, and large-scale private firms, are entitled to receive welfare services, while those elderly who were self-employed or worked with small-scale establishments usually have to rely on their families.

Public Policies

The overall assistance programs for the elderly confirm that the Thai have become aware of the aging problem, but the tendency is to fall back on the traditional system, which emphasizes the role of the family. To ensure that the family will care for the increasing numbers of the elderly, the government seeks to reinforce the individual family to care for the aging parents and to curb the mass migration which is splitting up family units.

In order to cope with the care for the aged, The Subcommittee on Research and Long-Term Planning drafted a National Long-Term Plan for the Elderly (1986-2001) (DMSMPH, 1985), identifying problems in the following areas: health, education, income, employment warranty, and cultural and social welfare.

Generally both government and the private sector have long been active in the assistance given to the elderly population. The long-term plan, however, proposes a policy of encouraging more participation of the private sector and expanding social welfare services, especially noninstitutionalized care. Practically, the feasibility of such a policy and the pace at which it can be implemented are not known at this stage. Further research should be conducted to assess the outcome of the announced policy.

What can be said at this point is that the current role of the Thai Government is to confirm that the traditional role of providing support and care for the elderly should be continued. The family is still seen as the fundamental unit in the support of the elderly. Children are the main source of support in terms of financial, physical, and psychological matters.

The Projected Pattern of Care for the Elderly and Its Implications

Because the results of the 1990 census are not yet available, future growth can be assessed based on the medium variant of the NESDB projections published in 1988. These show that the population 65 years of age and over is expected to grow from 2.1 million in 1990 to 4.2 million in 2010, a 20-year gain of 2.1 million or 100%. During this time the total population growth is projected at 26%. Compared with most developed countries, the proportion of those 65 years old and over in 2010, estimated at 6%, does not represent a drastic increase from 4% in 1990. The problem is that Thailand, having reduced its high fertility to replacement levels in less than 30 years, has altered the family structure and size so that providing home care for the elderly poses more serious problems. At the same time, current government policy continues to emphasize and rely primarily upon the traditional pattern of support.

It may be useful to look briefly at three burdens that will fall upon the children in providing care for their parents. They are the provision of financial support, housing, and health care. With increasing urbanization and industrialization, the income gap between the rural and urban residents is widening. The average annual household income in 1988 ranged from $3,740 (U.S. dollars) in Bangkok to $1,421 (U.S. dollars) in the northeast, a predominantly agricultural area. Thus with less than adequate income from farming, migration of northeastern residents to Bangkok and other urban areas has resulted in many villages being populated largely by children and elderly. Urban residence, however, is no assurance of adequate income, as evidenced by the more than 200 slums that exist in Bangkok.

The rapid growth of nuclear families, especially in urban areas, also poses a problem of providing for the additional housing needs of parents no longer able to maintain the old family home. Again, the problem is most acute for unskilled migrants in the large urban centers. Perhaps the most serious problem is providing adequate health care to those who are ill or incapacitated. The incidence of illness increases significantly with age, while the number of children available to provide financial and personal care has declined. This can become a very serious problem when physical or mental illness requires the provision of long-term care. Currently neither government nor private facilities are in a position to meet adequately the needs of the elderly who are chronically ill.

In summary, Thailand is aware of problems associated with the aging of the population, but government policy tends to emphasize the traditional system of care within the family. Not enough attention is being paid to the extent to which changes in family size and structure are affecting family function and making the traditional care system for the elderly increasingly difficult to maintain.

Note

1. The stem family is a family in which only one married child stays in the parental home and inherits the homestead. The other children move elsewhere upon marriage.

References

Bangkok Post. Economic Review. (1990, December). Year-End Bangkok (p.11). [Special issue].

Bennett, T., Frisen, C., Kamnuansilpa, P., & McWilliam, J. (1990). *How Thailand's family planning program reached replacement level fertility: Lessons learned.* [Population Technical Assistance Project]. (Occasional Paper No. 4). Washington, DC: USAID.

Carter, B., & McGoldrick, M. (1988). *The changing family life cycle: a framework for family therapy* (2nd ed.). London: Gardner Place.

Chayovan, N., Knodel, J., & Siriboon, S. (1990, September). *Comparative study of the elderly in Asia.* (Research Reports, No. 90-92). Ann Arbor, MI: Population Studies Center, University of Michigan.

Chayovan, N., Wongsith, M., & Saengtienchai, C. (1988). *Socio-economic consequences of the aging of the population of Thailand.* Bangkok: Institute of Population Studies, Chulalongkorn University.

Cowgill, D. O. (1972). The role and status of the aged in Thailand. In D. O. Cowgill & L. D. Holmes, (Eds.), *Aging and modernization* (pp. 91-102). New York: Appleton-Century-Crofts.

Cowgill, D. O. (1986). *Aging around the world.* Belmont, CA: Wadsworth.

Department of Medical Services, Ministry of Public Health (DMSMPH). (1985). *Long-term plan for the elderly in Thailand.* Bangkok: Author.

Kamnuansilpa, P. *Modernization, self-image, and some problems concerning the aged* (in Thai). Bangkok: National Institute of Development Administration.

Kaufman, H. K. (1960). *Bangkhuad: A community study in Thailand.* New York: J. J. Augustin.

Kingshill, K. (1976). *Ku Daeng: The red tomb, a village study in northern Thailand 1954-1974* (3rd ed.). Bangkok: Suriyaban.

Kiranandana, T., Wongboonsin, K., & Kiranandana, S. (1989). Population, aspect of development in Thailand: Health/nutrition, education and old age security. In Population Division, ESCAP (Ed.), *Frameworks for population and development integration* (Vol. 2, pp. 295-344). (Asian Population Studies Series No. 93). Bangkok: ESCAP.

Knodel, J., Chamratrithirong, A., & Debavalya, N. (1987). *Thailand's reproductive revolution*. Madison: University of Wisconsin Press.

Korson, J. Henry. (1978). Modernization and social change—the family in Pakistan. In M. S. Das & P. D. Bardis (Eds.), *The family in Asia* (pp. 169-207). New Delhi: Vikas.

Kumnuansilpa, P. (1980). *Modern, self-image , and some problems concerning the aged* [in Thai]. Dangkok: National Institute of Development Administration.

National Economic and Social Development Board (NESDB). (1988). *Population projections for Thailand, 1980-2015* (2nd ed.). Bangkok: Author.

National Economic and Social Development Board (NESDB). (1989). *Social indicators in 10 years and social indicators: 1987*. Bangkok: Author.

National Statistical Office. (1980). *Economic and social indicators*. Bangkok: Office of the Prime Minister.

Phillips, H. P. (1965). *Thai peasant personality*. Berkeley and Los Angeles: University of California Press.

Potters, S. H. (1977). *Family life in a northern Thai village*. Berkeley and Los Angeles: University of California Press.

Smith, H. E. (1973). The Thai family: Nuclear or extended. *Journal of Marriage and the Family, 35*(1), 136-141.

Tout, K. (1989). *Aging in developing countries*. New York: Oxford University Press.

United Nations. (1991). *The sex and age distribution of population* (revised ed.). New York: Author.

Weeks, J. R. (1984). *Aging: Concepts and social issues*. Belmont, CA: Wadsworth.

Xuto, N. (1982). *Thai old people* (in Thai). Bangkok: Social Research Institute, Chulalongkorn University.

PART II

Youthful Countries[1]

Youthful countries are defined as those whose population aged 65 and older represent between 5% and 7% of the total population. Such countries are represented, in this book, by China (The People's Republic of China), Costa Rica, and Egypt.

China is estimated to have had a population of 1,336 million people in mid-1990. Despite efforts to control population growth, it is estimated that the population will increase to 1,735 million by the year 2020. While about a quarter of the Chinese population (26%) was under 15 years of age, in 1990, 6% was 65 years of age and older. It was estimated that 29% of the population lived in urban areas of the country. The authors of the chapter on China are Zhu Chuanyi, Research Fellow, and Xu Qin, Assistant Researcher, both from the Chinese Academy of Social Sciences, located in Beijing.

Costa Rica, located in Central America, is the least populated country represented in this book, with a population of 3 million people (estimated for mid-1990). The population is projected to increase to 5.3 million people by the year 2020. In 1990 it was found that 36% of the population was under 15 years of age and that 5% of the population was 65 years of age or older. It was also found that about 45% of the Costa Rican citizens lived in urban areas. The authors of the chapter on Costa Rica are Licenciada Fidelina Briceño Campos, Chief of Division, Department of Social Development, Licenciada Flora Saborío Hernández, Head of the Department of Social Development, and Fernando Morales Martínez, M.D., Consultant Geriatrician, National Hospital of Geriatrics, all from the Costa Rican Social Security Bureau, located in San José.

Egypt had a population estimated, for mid-1990, at 54.7 million. This figure is projected to almost double to a population of 101.9 million by the year 2020. In 1990 it was found that 41% of the population was under 15 years of age (the second-largest proportion of young represented in this book) and 5% of the population was 65 years of age and older. It was found that 45% of the population in Egypt lived in urban areas. The author of the chapter on Egypt is Abdel Moneim Ashour, M.D., Professor and Director, Geriatrics Unit, Faculty of Medicine, Ain Shams University in Cairo.

Note

1. All information used to describe these three countries comes from *1990: World Population Data Sheet of the Population Reference Bureau, Inc.* Washington, DC, 1990. Mid-1990 population estimates are based upon census or official national data or upon U.N., U.S. Bureau of the Census, or World Bank projections. Year 2020 projections come from the same sources.

5

Family Care of the Elderly in China

Changes and Problems

ZHU CHUANYI

XU QIN

Background

Today, China has a population of 1.1 billion; the aged segment of which is approximately 100 million, constituting one fifth of the world's elderly population (which is slightly more than the sum of those for the United States and the former Soviet Union) (Xiao, 1990). It is estimated that the aged in China will increase by about 3% annually during the next 50 years, which far exceeds the 1% population growth rate of the nation. By the end of the century the aged in China will reach 130 million, more than 10% of the country's total, and place China in the ranks of the aged populations.

In China, family plays a prominent part in the twilight years of the elderly. In long years of history China survived mainly on an unitary agricultural economy, characterized by self-subsistence. Patriarchy and patriarchal systems predominated in the family; and the essential means of production—land—was in the hands of the family head. Ever since Confucious' time, 2,500 years ago, people were taught to honor, respect, and love the old. Mencious (372-289 B.C.) advocated "Love other's elders as you would love your own," which was regarded as the code of conduct of that time. In the "Book of Rites" it was clearly pointed out: "Widowers, widows, orphans and the handicapped will all be provided for." In the Qin Dynasty (221-206 B.C.), a stipulation was made in the law that "Loving fathers and dutiful sons are the props of a regime." During the reign of Emperor Xuan (73-47 B.C.) of the Han Dynasty, it was pointed out that "In guiding the people to observe filial piety, the nation will be in great order," and there was also a legislation that a son might be sentenced to death should he fail to fulfill his filial duty. "Tang Lu" (Tang Dynasty, A.D. 618-907) listed the lack of filial piety as the worst of the 10 unpardonable evil-doings.

The imperial edict in the reign of Hong Wu, of the Min Dynasty (1368-1644 A.D.), pointed out that "a civilian aged 70 and over is allowed to have one son specially to take care of him, who may be exempted from corvée." During the Qin Dynasty (1616-1911 A.D.), it was legally provided that "Those who do not support and wait upon the old well should be flogged 100 lashes," but families that abide by the rule were given preferential treatment to reduce or remit feudal land tax or *corvée*. Therefore, in the legislation of all the dynasties, filial piety, esteem, and respect for the old were laid down as the code of conduct and moral criterion. Family care has been built as a national tradition in the minds of the people, lasting for centuries.

In 1954 the Constitution, promulgated by New China, stipulated that "Citizens of the People's Republic of China have the right to material assistance from the State or society in times of old-age, sickness or disability" and the Marriage Law prescribed that "sons and daughters have the obligation to support their parents," and "prohibit members of a family to abuse or abandon one another." In the Law of Inheritance and the Criminal Law, one can find provisions on taking care of, and safeguarding, the rights of the elderly. Thanks to the historic tradition of promoting "filial piety" in society, the elderly in China enjoy more protection and respect than those in the West.

Today, in rural areas in particular, such a tradition is, in the main, handed down from generation to generation. The aged are still provided for mainly by the family. In case the family is unable to fulfill its duty, the community provides support according to custom. For many years society has attached great significance to kinsfolk and neighborhood relations (i.e., they frequently visit and help one another, and maintain ties). In recent years, as a commodity economy develops, the elderly are moving from traditional courtyards to multistoried buildings. So neighborhood relations are even more significant to the caretaking of the elderly. Now a new custom is being formed among neighbors to help the older persons.

The incapacitated childless widows and widowers without relatives in rural areas receive assistance from the community.

Unlike the West, where a "relay" model prevails whereby parents only have the responsibility to support their younger generations, the Chinese tradition (since ancient times) requires every couple to be held responsible for supporting both the older and the younger generations. As China is undergoing a period of great changes in its economic and social structure, however, the tradition of family care is being affected in different respects. Family care of the elderly, its coordination with social security, and the establishment of a new old-age pension scheme (under the present circumstances) have become major social issues of concern to the government and to the general public.

Changes in Chinese Society

Provision for the aged is one of the basic functions of a family. Despite the fact that family care remains the fundamental way of support, it is seriously challenged by economic and social structural changes.

Impact of Industrialization, Urbanization, and Modernization

Since the end of the 1970s, China's policy of reform and opening to the outside world has greatly boosted labor productivity, adjusting industrial mix in the course of change, raising the share of the secondary and tertiary industries in the national economy, and, as a result, many new cities and towns have developed and become industrial, commercial, and service centers. Township businesses emerged in large numbers in the villages. The interflow between urban and rural areas is increasingly expanding, and young farmers are rushing to the towns, many even to big cities. They manage industrial or commercial businesses or become employees, leaving women and the aged back at home in charge of agricultural production and domestic chores. Quite a number of young people have left their aged parents and gone to cities or towns for work, later getting married and settling down. Thus the function of caring for the aged by the family is being weakened.

Changes in Family Size and Structure

In the process of industrialization, urbanization, and modernization, families in China are undergoing steady and profound changes both in structure and size. The traditional united families and a portion of the trunk families are being replaced by core families. Particularly in recent years, the number of babies born to the family is on the decrease, and simultaneously the proportion of core families is on the rise. Therefore the size of the family is gradually getting smaller. The average sizes of a family in Beijing, Tianjin, and Shanghai in 1947 were 4.87, 5.11, and 5.11 persons, respectively. In 1987 the figures decreased to 3.71, 3.78, and 3.57. At the national level the figures decreased from 4.4 persons in 1982 to 4.3 in 1987. The greatest change has taken place in Heilongjiang Province, where the rate of 9.43 persons per family in 1947 dropped to 4.17 in 1987. Thus, in 40 years, family size has been reduced by more than half (Xiao, 1990).

Compared with the West, among the elderly population in China, the proportion of three generations living under one roof is great, while the proportion of the aged or aged couples living alone is still very small. In economically more developed urban and rural areas, however, families of the aged have shown signs of minimization and living alone. According to a survey conducted in 1987, the ratios of single-member and two-member families at the city, township, and county levels were 26.16%, 19.04% and 9.36%, respectively (Tian, 1989).

Socialization of livelihood, that is, shifting away of the production and consumption functions from a family and the pluralist development of culture, have prompted the family system in China to change. As the housing conditions improve and social security through old-age pension develops, the family is bound to change accordingly. The proportion of sons and daughters living apart from their elderly parents will rise further. Undoubtedly such a change will greatly weaken the traditional function of family care.

Changes in the Life-Style and Values

As a result of economic development, people's life-style and values are changing. As time moves on, the differences of the two generations in their life-style, way of thinking, ethics, interests, and hobbies are continuously growing, thus enhancing the disparities between the two generations in the family. Being economically independent, the sons and daughters no longer rely upon the aged nor do they want to live in the way as practiced by the elderly. Yet older persons may be financially dependent upon their children.

When their material needs are satisfied, however, the elderly may be attracted by the colorful cultural life and pursue a new life-style. Of course they would like to live apart from their children in a bid to be relieved from memories of the "wear and tear" of the past and to enjoy their twilight years in a relaxed way. The improvement of living conditions (e.g., when a member of an urban family acquires a new flat or a farmer constructs a new house) often constitutes an opportunity for two generations to live separately.

In addition, the development of the commodity economy leads to changing the way of provision for the aged in the rural areas. Traditionally, young people in the countryside supported the older people. Currently, in some coastal areas or suburbs of big cities (where commodity economy is more developed), the elderly have begun to be subsidized in monetary forms.

The social security program in China has been set up for a long time, mainly in urban areas. Nowadays suburbs of a number of large and medium-sized cities or economically more-developed villages have started pension schemes or cooperative old-age insurance programs for farmers. Thus in those places the traditional idea of family care is being altered. Many farmers, whether young, middle-aged, or old, place their hopes on a change of the system of traditional family care. Hereafter, inevitably, the sense of placing hopes on social security for their loneliness in their twilight years will spread far and wide.

Progressive Aging of the Elderly Population

A decline in the mortality rate is a direct consequence of economic growth. In the next 50 years, as the average life expectancy of China's population rises, so will that of the elderly population. A survey conducted in 1931 revealed that males and females aged 60 were expected to live another 14.19 years and 15.12 years, respectively. In 1981 the figures rose to 15.72 and 18.19 years (Xiao, 1990). This means that the aged people in China are living increasingly longer. Meanwhile the ratio of these venerable aged is also rising. In 1953 only 4.46% of the population aged 60 and over were in the 80 and over bracket. By 1987 it went up to 7.62% (Xiao, 1990). In 1986 Shanghai was the first city that joined the ranks of the aged, where the venerably old peaked at 25.18% (Xiao, 1990), meaning that one out of four elderly persons in Shanghai is of venerable age. At that age, many are physically weak, susceptible to illness, handicapped, bedfast, and in need of constant care in their daily life. Therefore there are more difficulties in providing services to them in the family than needed by younger persons. In Shanghai, for example, some of the married sons and daughters have to support not only their aged parents, but also grandparents, which is entirely beyond their means.

Forces Affecting Traditional Family Care

Besides great challenges for social security, resulting from the impact on family care of the elderly imposed by industrialization, urbanization, and modernization, there are, in China, some special political and social forces that affect the traditional function of family care. These forces need careful and targeted consideration in the establishment of a new old-age security system.

First and foremost, since the 1950s China has undergone tremendous political, economic, and social change, and the social status and role of the aged in society has varied in different periods.

In the early 1950s the "Labor Insurance Regulations" came into effect in cities, and employees of enterprises and government began to enjoy old-age benefits and free medical service. They became economically more independent, and their positions were correspondingly heightened. The land reform carried out in the countryside empowered the father-and-son generations to have a control over their means of production.

After the cooperative movement took place in the mid-1950s, land was collectivized and members of the family disowned their means of production. As a result of the historic tradition and the experience of the aged, which was rather important in underdeveloped agricultural production, the elderly received the respect of their descendants. By the end of each year, in times of bonus-sharing, usually it was the aged who went to the cooperative or commune-production brigade in the capacity of family head to receive the income for the whole family.

During the years 1966-1976, the period of the "Cultural Revolution," it was encouraged to "criticize all"—"suspect all." Young people were the radicals in the movement. Suddenly they turned out to be "masters of the country," and a "new authority" in the house. When fathers lost control over their means of production, they also were no longer the inherent authoritative heads of the family. The past situation, where the son submissively obeyed orders issued by the father, could hardly be perpetuated. The tradition of respecting the old, and family care for the elderly, was jeopardized to a certain extent.

In the 1980s, social life was restored to normal, and the people were called upon to bring back the fine traditions of Chinese society. The responsibility of supporting the aged parents by sons and daughters was re-affirmed in the Constitution. In this way the status of the aged in the family was again recognized. Thus, as a social stabilizer, the family resumed once again its function of supporting the aged.

At the present stage most of the families living with the elderly are enjoying a harmonious and happy life. It is estimated that 80% to 90% of the aged are respected and supported by their sons and daughters. So they are in good spirits, physically sound, and leading a happy life.

Nevertheless some elderly do face various problems in their old age. Local investigations, since 1987, have shown that there are about 1% to 4% of the families in which the younger generation does not respect the old, nor does it support them, and even go so far as to maltreat them. Though the percentage is not high, the phenomenon is not unusual. Especially in recent years, the incidence of maltreating the aged has taken place in various parts of the country.

Although family care of the aged is established in legislation and moral traditions, it all depends on the consciousness of sons and daughters to practice it. Subjectively speaking, some of the younger generations do not have a clear sense of law and, therefore, are unaware of their responsibility and obligation to support the old. The remaining traces of the "Cultural Revolution" can still be found in a small proportion of the young people, who do not show adequate esteem for the aged. In recent years, as China is carrying out a policy of opening up to the outside world, some people erroneously think that it is the responsibility of society to provide for their aged parents instead of their responsibility. And a fewer number of young people seek personal pleasure, regardless of the plight of their family or their parents. They do not respect, and are reluctant to support, the elderly, who they find unprofitable (without inheritance, housing, or being inca-pacitated, etc.). Objectively speaking, wide participation of women in the work force is changing their traditional role in taking care of the old. As government advocates equality between men and women in all fields, the employment rate for women—both in urban and rural areas—is very high. This is especially true for younger women. In their spare time it is hard for women to find time and energy to take care of the old. There are some grown-up sons and daughters in impoverished areas, in particular, whose families have a poor financial foundation. Because they are badly off themselves, they find it difficult to carry out their responsibility. In some families the aged are long-term patients (lying in bed or in need of con-stant care in their daily life), but their children are working outside, busy traveling on business, or otherwise incapable of providing family care. A

Chinese saying goes: "Once bedridden due to long-illness, no son is filial." In this case, when the older person becomes incapacitated and needs constant care, the person may be isolated and cut off from any help. Hence family care has its limitations.

Second, the policy of family planning in China is having a considerable impact on family care. The progressive growth of the population in the 1950s and 1960s has exerted great pressure on the socioeconomic development, which severely checked the improvement of people's living standards. China had no choice but to choose family planning to control its birth rate in a bid to achieve a good cycle of population growth and economic development. In more than 10 years of practice, family planning has made enormous achievements. It has, however, also brought about some new social problems, one of which concerns family care. By the end of the 1970s, when the government vigorously advocated one child for one family, single-child families (both in urban and rural areas) grew in multitudes. Since the early 1980s the percentage of one child per young mother has reached almost 100% in the urban areas of Beijing, Tianjin, and Shanghai. By the turn of the century, when these single sons and daughters grow up to marriage or child-bearing ages, their families are to face a situation of "four, two, one." That is to say, each couple will have to support one child and four aged-persons. Then family care will be confronted as a serious social problem. Of course most of the aged in the cities are entitled to old-age benefits and, because employment is common among women, it is actually not much of a problem for such families to support the aged financially, except in day-to-day care.

In the countryside, the establishment of a social security scheme takes a long time. Moreover, it is almost impossible for a single son or a single daughter to support four elderly persons. Furthermore, very seldom do parents of the couple live in the same village; but, on the contrary, they live quite a distance apart. Manual labor is often required in daily life; therefore the elderly rely more on their sons and daughters in rual areas than if they lived in the cities. In addition, transportation is inadequate in the rural areas, adding more difficulties in providing care and services for the aged. In big cities, around the year 2000, a wave of single-son and single-daughter families will exist; but physically, ideologically, or organizationally, China is not yet fully prepared for this. Relevant policies have to be formulated, and the implementation of programs and plans worked out as time is drawing near. At this moment China is carrying out a single-child policy, which is the only correct measure in the interests of the nation, but to the aged in the countryside, should they become physically weak, vulnerable to illness, or be childless, they are bound to be faced with problems. Yet, should initial social security (even in the nature of a subsidy) be started in rural areas, it would be possible for older persons to benefit from social development (i.e., they may support themselves with less reliance on the family). If this can occur, it will be conducive to implementing the one-child family policy even in rural areas.

Third, China is a developing country vast in territory. The provision for the elderly varies from urban to rural areas and from developed to underdeveloped areas. A national investigation of the elderly population in 1987 showed that 64% of the elderly's main source of income was retirement benefits, whereas in the villages only 5% were entitled to an old-age pension (Xiao, 1990). On the other hand, in cities, 17% of the main source of income for the elderly was derived from their sons and daughters (or other relatives); in villages the figure was 38%. Statistics showed that compared with cities, social security benefits for old-age are progressively lower in villages, although family care is better. In the rural areas family care is the principal part of old-age security, and social security is only supplementary. Recently, in 1,400 counties and towns all over the country, more than 10,000 villages have put into effect their old-age pension schemes in the nature of a varying amount of subsidies. More than 700,000 older farmers enjoy pension benefits, and 3 million and more destitute, incapacitated, older farmers (without any source of income) are supported by collective economic organizations (Wang, 1989). Therefore it can be reasoned that the number of the elderly receiving public assistance in various forms amounts to 23 million—approximately one fourth of the total aging population. Yet one third of the elderly still are outside social security benefits.

In addition to the disparities between the urban and rural areas, regional differences in old-age protection also exist in China. The suburbs of Beijing, Tianjin, Shanghai, and the more developed areas in Jiangsu and Guangdong (on the basis of their collective economies) have established their own cooperative old-age security schemes. In areas of economically less-developed or underdeveloped villages, the level of collective security for old age is rather low, some even go without it. For example, Shanghai pensioners constitute 72.9%, 78.6%, and 27.4% of the elderly, respectively, at the municipal, township, and county levels; whereas those for Hubei are 59.6%, 36.5%, and 4.2%, respectively (Yang & Xu, 1990). There are even differences within a single province. In the city of Harbin, in Heilongjiang Province, pensioners constitute 50.12% of the elderly, whereas in the city proper and townships of Zhaodong City, Heilongjiang Province, the figure is 40.61% (Yu, 1990; Wu Xiang, 1990).

In China, farmers in rural areas, the self-employed in cities and townships, and workers and employees in some small collective businesses, engage in various kinds of manual labor (or jobs) until the age of 70 or even 80. When they become incapacitated, most of them have to rely on their sons and daughters, or other family members. Under present circumstances, with the State and the collective economies inadequately prepared for universal old-age social security, family care—for a long period of time—will remain the principal means of old-age protection in China.

Public Efforts for Meeting Needs

In the last few years increasingly more people in China have come to realize that to resolve the problem of old-age protection, it will be necessary to explore various methods of integrating family care with social security. This must be done in the light of the actual conditions (and possibilities of socioeconomic development) at the present stage; proceeding from the realities found in different regions of the country. The following is an overview of how China is meeting, and can meet, the needs of the elderly.

Reasonable Sharing in Funding

In China the aging of the population came before the economy developed so insufficiency of resources is the main difficulty in providing old-age benefits. To work out a solution, ways must be sought to open up channels for financing an old-age foundation. At the moment the State is preparing for a reform of the social security system for which the basic idea is for finance-sharing among the State, the collective, and the individual. In cities and townships, except State-run enterprises or undertakings, a multitiered old-age social security scheme of different standards should be established in enterprises of collective, joint venture, and private ownerships. In the rural areas pilot projects should be worked out and later popularized stage-by-stage. Today some relatively developed rural areas are trying out various programs, such as old-age insurance or old-age allowances, mainly based on the collective economy (with a sharing by the individual and by the family and subsidized by the State).

From the history of the industrialized countries, one sees (as a rule) the universal phenomenon of eventually setting up a social security system in the rural areas, but for China the road is a long and arduous one, especially because of the severely imbalanced economic development in the rural areas. Social security systems in different forms, and with varying standards, will be in existence for some years to come.

"Five Guarantees" and Cooperative Medical Service

For many years widowers, widows, orphans, and other dependents, both in urban and rural areas, have been enjoying the "Five Guarantees" (i.e., food, clothing, shelter, medicine, and funerals are guaranteed, but at a minimum level). In cities they are supported by the State and in villages by collective economic institutions. At present, of the 3.37 million aged eligible for the "Five Guarantees," 91% are beneficiaries. By the end of 1988, 36,000 old-folks homes were set up in the countryside and more than 10,000 villages had "Five Guarantees" service centers, ensuring basic needs. Lately the grass-roots autonomous organizations use volunteers and the relatives from the neighborhood and are organized to serve those older persons who come under the "Five Guarantees" but live scattered throughout the community. Statistics in 1989 of all elderly revealed that those institutionalized in the old-folks homes amounted to 14.1%, those supported by the collective in-kind and in-cash (but living scattered) amounted to 73.5%, and those supported by the collective both in-kind and in-cash but living with their relatives or neighbors amounted to 12.65% ("China blazes," 1990).

The aged in China enjoy medical service of different forms. Functionaries of State organizations or government undertakings enjoy free medical care. Workers and employees of enterprises enjoy medical service according to their labor insurance. The elderly family members of workers and employees of State-run enterprises enjoy 50% free medical benefits. Most of the medical expenditures of the rural elderly are borne by themselves or their sons and daughters. In the 1980s, when the contract responsibility system came into force in rural areas, the cooperative medical service (which existed for a time) began to die out and farmers were again without the means to care for their serious illnesses. As the cooperative medical service is advantageous to the elderly, many parts of the country are actively setting up and developing various forms of cooperative medical insurance schemes. According to a survey conducted in 1985, among the rural residents, 81% paid their own medical bills; only 9.6% of rual residents were covered by the cooperative medical service. Another survey, conducted in 1988, found that 66% of rural elderly paid their own bills, 30% were covered by one form or another of collectively-funded medical service (such as the cooperative medical service, medical insurance, unified planning of medical service, etc.), and only 1.8% were covered by free medical service or the Labor Insurance Regulations (Gu, 1991).

Rules, Regulations, and Legislation for the Elderly

For the sake of protecting the legitimate rights of the aged, localities across the land are enthusiastically formulating legislation, trying to include respect for the old and providing care for the aged into the rules and regulations that should be adhered to by all Chinese. To date, laws and regulations to this effect have been made in 23 provinces, cities, and autonomous regions. As an example, it is clearly stipulated in the "Provisions on the Protection of Legitimate Rights of the Elderly of Tianjin" that "Grown-up sons and daughters are duty bound to ensure the living standards of their parents with a humble or no income not inferior to their own average." Furthermore, "Grown-up sons and daughters, whether living together with their parents or not, are duty bound to take care of their family needs," and "Grown-up sons and daughters are not allowed to seize the residence of their elders, or to compel the aged to move to other places."

Local governments at all levels, while expanding the old-folks homes, are carrying on with legislative activities on the "Five Guarantees," so that they will be given legal grounds and regulations. Presently, 19 provinces, municipalities, and autonomous regions have issued "Provisional Rules for Supporting the 'Five Guarantees' Households in Villages" and "Provisional Regulations on Rural Old-folks Homes," so as to ensure that services to those eligible will be properly settled.

With the implementation of the contract responsibility system in the rural areas, distribution of income has shifted from the hands of the production brigade to the family, and—as a result—disputes concerning family care arise. Dafeng County in Jiangsu Province took the initiative (in 1985) to start an "Agreement on Provision for the Aged," whereby sons and daughters would go to the village notary to get the agreement notarized, explicitly defining the responsibility of family members, including the methods and the amounts to implement family care. Signing of the Agreement renders the legal provision, "Sons and daughters have the obligation to support their parents," a powerful and effective means of public supervision over the provision of family care in the rural areas. In villages of many provinces, the signing of the "Agreement on Provision for the Aged" in varying forms has become popular. Hence such agreements become new ways of consolidating family care with Chinese characteristics.

Community Services

Community services in China are not well-developed, compared with the West. In practice, however, attention has been paid to new forms suitable to the Chinese situation. In cities and towns community services mainly rely upon the neighborhood committees and in villages, mainly on county, township and village communities. The conditions and resources available to the community are being supplemented, in carrying out social services, through self-help or mutual-help. To meet the basic needs in life with one's own resources is an important aspect of China's social security system. Guaranteed services, convenient services, and community facilities are the three main forms of services.

"Guaranteed services" are most common, and take a household as a unit, for which all volunteers are mobilized. The volunteers include members of the neighborhood committees, retirees, students, employees, military men, housewives, and so on. Services are rendered to widowers or widows, retirees, the handicapped, mental patients, and poor residents in way of "Single-Item Service, Two-Way Mutual Help Service," and "Coordinated Comprehensive Service." In 1986 there were 36,000 Guaranteed Service Groups organized for 66,000 destitute aged. By the end of 1988 the figures grew to 54,000, working for 88,000 aged (which registered increases of 50% and 33%, respectively) (Zhu, 1990). Today, various kinds of Guaranteed Services are advancing toward a broader scope, wider coverage, and more varieties. Experience proves that this is a way to social security, best suited to Chinese traditions and conditions, with less investment and better results.

Different Forms of Old-Age Security for Rural Areas

China has a vast territory, and tremendous differences exist in culture, population, and natural conditions. Therefore each locality is seeking its own way to social security, proceeding from its economic, ethnic, and local conditions and in the light of actual needs.

For example, in Changchun City, Jilin Province, old-age security combines the following five features:

1. Paying the elderly a certain amount of old-age benefit in better-off villages and townships.
2. Setting up Provident Funds for old-age. Farmers deposit an amount of money as their financial conditions permit, and draw from it when they grow old.
3. Allocating specific plots of land, forest, or pastureland for economic gains to be used to subsidize the elderly in need.
4. Setting up "Daughters' Funds." Transforming the allowances earmarked for couples practicing family planning into "Daughters' Funds," and—together with the contributions from the families—depositing funds in the bank for use in old-age.
5. Levying an old-age "tax." The collective levies an old-age "tax" on each household, for every unit of land contracted, to support the elderly.

The scheme in Fanggan Village of Laiwu City, Shangdong Province, is to set up an old-age fund with collective labor. The essence of their old-age security is based on the principle of labor accumulation. That is, before they grow old, farmers contribute in terms of labor days and take measures to publicize the results of the more effective efforts.

Conclusions

While promoting social security for old-age, the government should pay attention to family care, by taking various measures to prevent the breakdown of this tradition, and by injecting new opportunities. First, the government should provide those adult children having financial difficulties from caregiving with additional "family assistance." Second, the policies formulated concerning old-age provision should all favor consolidating and strengthening family care (e.g., in household registration, housing construction, and distribution considerations). Services for the aged should be added to the community service programs (e.g., organizing homemakers). At the request of the residents, and according to the conditions available, temporary apartments for the elderly are being set up to solve the caregiving troubles of their children. Finally, the government, community, and enterprise should join hands in creating an appropriate living environment for the elderly. In a community it is necessary to build necessary stores, hospitals, activity centers, and to have adequate transportation facilities—so that all of the aged may be satisfied in the vicinity within which they dwell.

As a developing country, China is closely following the changes that are taking place and problems brought about in family care. While earnestly learning from the experiences of, and drawing lessons from, other countries, China is establishing an old-age security system congruent with Chinese characteristics and with present and future Chinese realities in mind.

References

China blazes a trail for five guarantees program. (1990, January 5). *Society News*, p. 2

Gu, X. (1991, April). Study on medical service schemes in rural China. *Journal on Gerontology, 4*, 21.

Tian, X. (Ed.). (1989). *Data on sampling survey on elderly population age 60 and over 1987*. Beijing: Population Department, State Statistical Bureau.

Wang, K. (1989, September 15). Various ways of old-age security in rural China. *Social Security News*, p. 2.

Wu, X. (1990, January). New tendency of rural old-age security, Guangdong. *Social Work Research, 1*, 60.

Xiao, Z. (Ed.). (1990). *Collection of statistical data on elderly population*. Beijing: Hua Liang.

Yang, Z., & Xu, Y. (Eds.). (1990). Strategic research on aging problems in Shanghai. In *Life style of the elderly in villages and cities*. Shanghai: Shanghai Municipal Aging Committee and Shanghai Society for Gerontology.

Yu, N. (1990). Characteristics of old-age social security in Heilongjiang province. *Field of Sociology, 6*, 11.

Zhu, C. (1990). *Guaranteed services—community services with Chinese characteristics*. Unpublished manuscript.

6

Family Care of the Elderly in Costa Rica

FIDELINA BRICEÑO CAMPOS
FLORA SABORÍO HERNÁNDEZ
FERNANDO MORALES MARTÍNEZ

Introduction

This chapter initially provides demographic-political facts and other data that will serve as a reference to social policies and to cultural changes observed in the Costa Rican family.

In addition, this chapter will present some hypotheses that may explain the possible rebound of social policies in the changes in family behavior along with some measures to assist, maintain, and fortify family ties.

Finally, data based on actual programs in operation and studies of the Third Age within Costa Rica will be presented.

Political Issues

Costa Rica, due to its historical background, has developed differently from its neighboring countries. It has a greater land distribution, an important social legislation, and a more effective electoral regime, which allows it to maintain a representative democracy. Indeed, Costa Rica has been governed by a Democratic political system for a century and void of any army since 1948. Primary and secondary education is mandatory, and tuition is free. Women have full political rights, and governing officials are not allowed to be reelected. The official religion of Costa Rica is Roman Catholicism.

The country's critical economic situation, which surged in the latter part of the 1970s and has escalated in recent years, has had a great impact on the development of the country's social policies. The State is responsible for the formulation, administration, and implementation of social policies and is responsive to popular demands.

The Costa Rican government is coordinated by the legislative, executive, and judicial branches, and its Public Administration for Planning is organized by the following sectors according to activity:

Social Sectors:
  Health
  Education and Human Resources
  Labor and Social Security
  Housing and Urban Development
  Cultural and Recreational

Economic Sectors:
  Agriculture and Animal Husbandry
  Industry and Commerce
  Energy, Mining and Natural Resources
  Transportation
  Finances, Public Credit
  Foreign Trade
  National System of Science and Technology

Each sector is represented by a group of ministries and institutions that coordinate activities within the same field of action so as to achieve proposed objectives.

The Health Sector Institutions are organized and function using regional and sector criteria. Thus they emphasize local specialization and decentralized distribution. The Health Ministry oversees health promotion and mass media dissemination of knowledge and reports. The Costa Rican Social Security Bureau (Caja Costarricense de Seguro Social) is nationwide and is responsible for health, recovery, rehabilitation, and pension schemes. The bureau supports and assists the Health Ministry in prevention and promotion of health activities. The National Insurance Institute (I.N.S. Instituto Nacional de Seguros) is in charge of the care, rehabilitation, and indemnification of persons covered by insurance involving professional risks and the obligatory insurance for motor vehicles.

The Costa Rican Institute for Water Supply and Sewage is in charge of water management and sewage services.

The health policy in the 1970s originated with the implementation of a universal coverage by means of basic strategies. The primary focus was on the universalization of Social Security and the nationwide extension of coverage of services.

In the latter years the task was to strengthen the capacity of units of the local level and the articulation among them and to Local Systems of Health (SILOS). These systems were conceptualized as a group of resourceful interrelations, sectorials, and extra-sectorials responsible for the health of a population in a geographic area defined by its epidemiological characteristics, demographics, socioculture, and economic and admini-strative policies. The actions are directed primarily to define the mechanics and instruments for the programming of the SILOS. In addition, efforts are made to develop the managerial capability to make possible decentralization to the local level of human resources, technologies, financial accountants, and supplies. The formulation of information systems capable of supporting measures of the Local Systems of Health and the establishment of mechanisms to incorporate the participation of the community in the process at local and regional levels were also goals of such efforts.

Costa Rica and the Elderly

Costa Rica has an area of 51,900 square kilometers and a population of 3 million people. It is located in Central America, bounded in the north by Nicaragua and the south by Panama.

The infant mortality rate in 1950 was 94 per 1,000 and 19 per 1,000 in 1990. The global rate of fertility (fecundity) in 1950 was 6.7 and 3.3 in 1990.

In 1991, 6.4% of the population was 60 years of age and older, and the proportion is projected to increase to 7.4% by the year 2000. In Costa Rica 45% of the population lives in urban areas and 55% lives in rural areas. The mortality rate for the 65 and older age group was 62.2 per 1,000 in 1970, declining to 48.9 per 1,000 in 1987 and to 48.5 per 1,000 in 1988.

To indicate the life expectancy of the group of 60 and older by gender, statistics (frames) are included in Table 6.1.

The conclusion to be reached is that life expectancy in Costa Rica has greatly increased over the past decades and is projected to continue to in-

Table 6.1 Life Expectancy From Birth in Costa Rica

	1950-1955	*1970-1975*	*1990-1995*	*2000-2005*	*2010-2015*	*2020-2025*
Both Sexes	57.26	68.08	75.19	75.90	76.27	76.48
Male	56.04	66.05	72.89	73.52	73.85	74.00
Female	58.55	70.22	77.60	78.39	78.82	79.09

SOURCE: CELADE/ACDI (1990)

crease into the twenty-first century. Thus more people will survive into old age. To these figures are added the absolute number (and the projection) of those 60 years of age and over. Currently there are 192,917 residents over 60 years, with projections of 275,900 by the year 2000 and 616,253 by 2020. The implication of such projections is that the older population in Costa Rica is increasing at a rapid and dramatic rate.

The study, "Three Methodological Approaches for the Study of the Social Condition of the Elderly: The Costa Rican Case," utilized the latest census data (from the year 1984) and established a sociodemographic profile for the concentration of elderly persons (their spatial distribution) and their sociodemographic and economic characteristics.

Among the results, the following are believed to be especially important in providing a view of the elderly in Costa Rica. Approximately 75% of the elderly were concentrated in the central region and the metropolitan area (San José) of the country. The majority (64%) of the elderly were married, 80% were illiterate, and 26% were found to be active in their social lives. Of those still working, 53% were working in the primary sector (agriculture) and 31% were working in the services sector. The elderly proportion who lived alone was less than 10% (and, therefore, it can be concluded that the majority of the elderly were still a part of a family system).

The most common source of income for those 60 to 65 years of age consisted of pensions for men (in 45% of the cases) and financial assistance received from grown children for women. After age 65 pensions were the most important source for both men and women. The most widespread pensions were those from the "Regimen No Contributivo" (Noncontributive Regime), which focused upon persons of low income. Those who indicated having received some form of pension included half of all elderly women and a little more than a third of all elderly men. These pensions mainly benefitted persons from the rural areas as well as those of advanced ages.

In reference to housing, 18% of the elderly lived in houses occupied by two persons, more than half live in moderate-sized homes for three to six persons; and 21% were part of very large family households.

It had been found that 56% of the elderly live in their own homes. The remainder lived in the homes of their relatives (or other persons). With reference to health, 99% of the elderly made use of services given by the Costa Rican Social Security Bureau. According to data from the 1987 study "Egresos Hospitalarios y consultas al médico de las personas de 60 años y más" (Caja Costarricense de Seguro Social, 1990), the elderly go to the doctor and to the hospital more often due to the fact that they represent 6.1% of the population and make up 12.6% of the doctor's appointments and 12.6% of the hospitalizations. These data have been the same since 1985, when they were first reviewed. Nevertheless, the average stay in the hospital for the group 60 to 64 years of age was observed to be 14.5 days in 1985 and 13.1 days in 1987.

The major causes of dysfunction in the elderly are heart disease, malignant tumors, and cerebrovascular diseases. This age group has the highest rate of physician visits per individual, and the primary causes are related to hypertension, arteriosclerosis, and diabetes mellitus. Presently the five most frequent causes of hospitalization for the Costa Rican elderly (affecting 35% of the hospitalizations) are chronic obstructive pulmonary diseases, ischemic heart diseases, malignant tumors, diabetes mellitus, and visual problems. In 1980 malignant tumors constituted the primary cause of hospitalization of the elderly. Such problems, however, have decreased to the third most common cause for hospitalization of the elderly.

Sociocultural Changes

The fact that the elderly have been considered an important group to be protected by the state and community is certainly encouraging. The sociocultural changes in Costa Rica may well produce several consequences that affect the care of the elderly. These factors will have to be reviewed in order to balance necessary policy changes without harming basic cul- tural values and principles.

In Costa Rica there exist some policies in matters of protection of the Third Age (as reference is often made to elderly persons). These policies may produce significant changes in the family role and have a direct effect on the rate of the institutionalization of the elderly. One such change is likely to be the care of the elderly within the family structure, which is the main alternative to the construction of nursing homes.

There are elderly persons who cannot rely on their family or the family does not have the resources or facilities to care for their elderly relatives within their homes. These older persons are not, necessarily, in the majority. That there are homes for the elderly in Costa Rica, however, has provided a place to institutionalize them and relieve the family of the responsibility of caring for their elderly relatives.

Massive housing programs have also influenced the changes in family roles. The reduced physical space in such housing impedes the presence of elderly relatives, displacing them even against the wishes of relatives.

The elderly displaced due to space limitations in housing programs increase occupancy statistics within homes for the aged and also lead to increases in the number of "elderly wandering in the streets." The book *The Costa Ricans* (Hiltunen, de Biesanz, Zubris, & de Biesanz, 1979) includes illustrations of this phenomena with the following examples:

> The director of one of the elderly homes in Costa Rica subsidized by taxes and private donations says that the majority of the residents of these homes continue to be those who need special care due to mental disturbances or serious physical impairments, but the proportion of elderly placed there by their working daughters or by adult sons who are not willing to take care of them is increasing.

A retired teacher complains:

> Thirty years ago it was considered an honor to care for elderly parents. Many daughters did not marry because their parents needed help. If a teacher asked for a leave of absence in order to take care of her sick parent, she would be granted permission and many times the director himself would preside over her class. This has changed.

> A study made by the Instituto Mixto de Ayuda (Social Institute of Mixed Social Services) showed that 71% of the people over 64 years of age who now live with their relatives prefer to live in homes for the elderly.

Such changes, produced in the level of cultural and family values, are due not only to the policies of the state (regarding nursing homes), but also to the lack of space in the family houses. In addition, there are other factors of a social nature, such as the socioeconomic situation of Costa Rica, which has worsened during the last 20 years.

The information cited above is described in a study titled "Education of Poverty in Costa Rica," which was presented at the 50th Congress of

Social Security in Costa Rica in 1991 by the Deputy Director of the Institute for Mixed Social Aid and Welfare. It was pointed out that from 1980 onward, the situation in Costa Rica can be described as one with deteriorating living conditions. As a result the crisis has generated an increase in the incidence of poverty; thus leading to a 10-year decline in the indicators of living conditions.

It is established in the same study that the existing relationships between unemployment, underemployment, and poverty are being increased in the rural areas of Costa Rica. During this period of crisis, the poverty rate rose from 98,000 poor families in 1977 to 173,000 in 1983. This implies an increase in the incidence of poverty from 24% to 34% of all the families in the country.

In 1986, just as in 1977, the poverty rate showed a total of 134,000 families living in poverty. This means that 25% of the total number of families are poor and, from the previous data, 14% are living under extreme poverty, and 11% are living under basic poverty levels.

According to a study carried out by CEPAL (Consejo Económico para América Latina) in 1988, 14.9% of the families were living in extreme poverty, while the percentage of families that could not satisfy the basic needs rose to 24.5%. This study allows us to point out that there is a relationship between poverty and unemployment. From the 25% of poor families there were 40% unemployed and 32% underemployed. Women headed 36% of poor families, and 75% of the families living in extreme poverty were in rural areas of the country.

The above information should be considered when referring to changes in the values and family attitudes. Thus the following question needs to be answered: What can a woman do when she is a head of the family and needs to support her children, and in addition she has an elderly person under her responsibility?

The answer seems to be obvious, and it is important to join efforts in the search of the best solutions for the different age groups of the population in an equal and consistent manner.

Such solutions are under study. Analysis and planning of programs that strengthen family ties are also under way. A current example of support is the integral approach of the elderly strengthening family ties, with models such as the day hospital, day care centers, and domiciliary visits. In 1991 the government began a new housing program for independent elderly. The policy behind the program states: "In any new housing project, a special area for this purpose must be considered."

The fundamentals of these models help strengthen family ties and acknowledge the realities confronted by some families who care for the elderly during their workdays. Moreover, they contribute to prevent negligence in the treatment of the elderly. There exists a segment of the population, however, which due to diverse circumstances, either does not rely on the members of a family or has physical conditions that require special care in nursing homes.

If the programs that address the Costa Rican family's needs are strengthened, this will lead to a more positive and humane method by which to help the elderly enjoy the company of their family. This is especially the case if these programs include assistance with the basic essentials, such as housing and nutrition.

Elder abuse has been found to be a problem. In a recent study carried out by the National Geriatrics Hospital, Dr. Raul Blanco Cervantes pointed out the elevated percentage of abused elderly which appeared to be related to the total dependent condition of the elderly. This was found for 22.8% of more than 500 elderly patients studied during the years 1987 to 1989. Of a sample of 51 total abandoned elderly studied during the years 1990-1991, 35% were in severely deteriorated condition—physically and/or mentally. The risk factors, and indicators of abuse detected, are limitations to independence and autonomy because they threaten the security and well-being of the elderly. At present, Congress is in the process of formulating a new law to legally protect those elderly persons who are vulnerable to being abused.

Social Programs and Policies for the Elderly

While reviewing the programs in force and their role in the Costa Rican society, one encounters the problems of the entire population, which bear a great analogy of those of the elderly, in particular. The social policy developed within a sectorial organization has contributed to the delineation of particular fields in each sector. It has also helped to specify the direction of each of the programs that try to maintain a connection with several channels of coordination. The sectors in the social area are responsible for proposing and executing the social policy.

The State's ability to administer social policy has been restricted due to problems originated by the State's financial and administrative inefficiency. Along with this situation, the State has tended to reform its measures with restrictive policies on public expenses in accordance with international financial agreements. The State's restructured policies are likely to affect welfare and social aid institutions that have been abolished according to priorities that emphasize efforts directly related to the Productive Sector.

In actuality, an administration is being planned that will be character- ized by the decentralization of services and the readaptation of the admini- strative apparatus. The result of such efforts should be an increase in managerial capacity and restructuring of available services. The restruc- tured formulas in force are as follows: (a) the reduction of vacant markets, (b) the regulation of contracts and new markets, (c) the commissioning of diverse institutional services, (d) the regulation and restriction of the financial mechanisms of public expenses, and (e) the supervision and evaluation of available resources.

During recent years a plan to rebuild the Social State has been designed. The State's intervention in providing social services has played an impor- tant role in the development achieved by Costa Rica. Social programs are addressed to groups considered at high risk. Such groups include those with physical impairments, women, young children, and the elderly.

The policies in the fields of health, education, and culture do not con- form to specific demands. Instead their effects have been generalized and manifested in improvements in specific areas. Other programs of services, such as water management and sewage, and telephone and electricity, have directly influenced the way of life of the population.

Within other policies, other issues are emphasized, such as the distri- bution of lands, the settlement of the rural areas, social credit, rural health, food supply, and rural housing. Some policies are directed to the urban population. These efforts can incorporate the productive sector or society, as illustrated by efforts to eradicate slums, various housing programs, and the creation of child care centers, among others.

In regards to the elderly, the programs directed to this population have been coordinated between institutions and intersectorials. The Consejo Nacional de la Tercera Edad (National Council for the Elderly) and its Tech- nical Secretary Council were founded as a viable alternative to approve and develop policies and strategies in this field and to contribute to the improvement of the quality of life for the aged in Costa Rica. This Council was created in 1984, according to an executive decree, as an answer to the National Development Plan. In January 1990, reauthorization was made for an advisory organization to coordinate the executive power (in keeping with the definition and execution of the National Integral Policy for the Third Age).

The Minister of Health, or Vice-Minister, is the manager over the following institutions:

- Health Ministry
- Labor Ministry and Social Security
- Public Education Ministry
- Culture, Youth, and Sports Ministry
- National Planning and Economic Politic Ministry
- Institute for Mixed Social Aid
- Costa Rican Case for Social Security
- Social Protection Council
- Private Sector Representative

The president of this Council is the Minister of Health.

The Technical Secretary Council has the function of advising and assessing those organizations related to the Third Age (in the execution of national policies in this field). This organization is comprised of public officials of a high technical level, the institutions that form the Council, and a representative of the following organizations:

- National Crusade for Protection of the Elderly
- Costa Rican Gerontological Association
- Geriatric Physicians Society
- Centers of Higher Education (The University of Costa Rica)

This group of institutions from the public sector, as well as from the private sector, is responsible for planning efforts to care for the needs of the elderly of Costa Rica within their families and communities.

The National Development Plan for the period 1990-1994 emphasizes the reincorporation of the elderly into activities that would maintain them as productive and useful members of society as well as create opportunities for them in recreation, education, and the general society.

The existing plans have been operating in an isolated manner. This situation has been studied by experts of the Third Age and, as a result, other activities have been considered, which are indispensable for an integral focus upon the elderly population. Thus the "Strategic Institutional Plan for the Elderly" (Plan Institucional Estratégico de la Tercera Edad) has been effected, and the organizational structure began in 1991.

With this plan in operation, the elderly will obtain proper and quality care. On the other hand, with the creation of postgraduate studies in

Geriatrics (a four-year program), individuals will be trained to specialize in meeting the needs of the elderly beginning in 1992.

At present the National System for Elderly Care is being worked out by the National Council for the Elderly and its Technical Secretary. It is believed that the care of the Costa Rican elderly will be improved. In turn, there will be a reduction in the rates of hospitalization and institutionalization in homes for the aged. Thus, as a consequence of the actions directed by the State, the role of the elderly will be strengthened with regards to the family, integral care, and community participation.

To illustrate these efforts, some data—reflecting the results of the application of policies and programs—can be found in the different services and programs developed by this group of national institutions. These efforts seek to complement each other so as to provide efficient and global services that are orientated toward the well-being of the elderly. They promote the access of the elderly to health services, housing, education, recreation, and other services. All these resources are granted through comprehensive medical services, nursing home care, and socioemotional aid. Efforts are especially targeted to those living in extreme poverty.

Conclusion

After reviewing the information presented in this chapter, we can conclude that the situation of the elderly in Costa Rica should be analyzed within the context of family realities. The family is being affected by aspects such as changes in the cultural values, situations of poverty, as well as by the social policies designed to protect the elderly (which have not fulfilled their objectives).

The Costa Rican state has set the groundwork toward the achievement of the integral development of the Costa Rican, through the impulse of a socioeconomic process that enables an ample participation of all the groups, in the creation of a new society where solidarity, social justice, and common welfare prevail.

The actual goal is to create the correct combination of private and public sectors working hand-in-hand in the promotion of the economic growth and in the execution of a social policy that is oriented mainly toward overcoming poverty. Yet this must be done without overlooking other goals that the country has identified, particularly those related to the fields of health and medicine.

A strategy has been designed that embraces three general levels of action:

1. aspects related to welfare and social assistance,
2. activities oriented toward the development of strengthening social organizations for the production and generation of stable and well-paid employment, and
3. integral strengthening of the family and the improvement of the participation of women in economic, social, and political activities.

This integral vision of development contemplates the full and active participation of the different sectors of the population in the achievement of economic growth with special emphasis on the incorporation of minority groups (one group of which is the elderly).

Work is being done in Costa Rica toward the identification of new alternatives in the social services granted by the state. Such efforts are necessary in order to propose programs and projects that will make more rational use of the resources. This should permit social services to better expand its coverage and to better improve the general quality of services being offered to the Costa Rican citizen.

The above efforts should be accompanied by serious and profound institutional reform that would enable the public institutions to adapt themselves in a suitable way to the new needs and demands of the social groups. This is especially important for those groups of Costa Ricans who are in poverty.

References

AISSCAP. (1978). *Los programas de protección a los ancianos en las instituciones.* Seminario sobre la Población en 3ra. Edad XXII. Reunión del Consejo Superior de AISSCAP. San José, Costa Rica.

Caja Costarricense de Seguro Social. (1990, Agosto). *Egresos hospitalarios y consultas al médico de las personas de 60 años y más, 1987.* San José, Costa Rica: Dirección Técnica de Servicios de Salud.

CELADE/ACDI. (1990). *Tres enfoques metolológicos para el estudio de la condición social de los ancianos.* San José, Costa Rica: C.C.S.S.

Hiltunen, M., de Biesanz, M., Zubris, K., de Biesanz, R. (1979, Diciembre). *Los Costarricenses* (Iera edición). San José, Costa Rica: Editorial Universidad Estatal a Distancia.

Jiménez-Rodríguez, S. (1991). *El abuso del anciano.* San José, Costa Rica: Hospital Nacional de Geriatría Dr. Raúl Blanco Cervantes.

Morales Martínez, F. (1987). Long term care services in Costa Rica. *Danish Medical Bulletin, (Special Supplement 5)*, 38-40.

Morales Martínez, F. (1991). *Cambios demográficos en Costa Rica y Latinoamérica.* San José, Costa Rica: Hospital Nacional de Geriatría Dr. Raúl Blanco Cervantes.

Raabe Cercones, C. (1990, Junio). *El nivel de vida de los ancianos Costarricenses.* San José, Costa Rica: Secreteria Ténnica de la Tercera Edad, Ministerio de Salud.

Secretaria Nacional de la Ténnica Edad. (1989). Primer simposio nacional sobre programas educativos y de capacitación, relacionados con la 3era: Edad. *Memoria.* San José, Costa Rica.

Universidad de Costa Rica, Colegio de Trabajadores Sociales de Costa Rica, ALAETSS, CELATS. (1990, Junio). *Contexto socioeconómico y politico de Costa Rica* (Capítulo II). San José, Costa Rica: Author.

Universidad de Costa Rica, Colegio de Trabajadores Sociales de Costa Rica, ALAETSS, CELATS. (1990). *Las políticas sociales en Costa Rica* (Capítulo II)I. San José, Costa Rica: Author.

7

Family Care of the Elderly in Egypt

ABDEL MONEIM ASHOUR

Methodological Background

Most of the figures used in this chapter come from several sources of information: the *Statistical Yearbook of the Central Agency for Public Mobilization and Statistics* (CAPMAS), census reports, and the "General Report on Egypt" of the Social Indicators Study.

The first reference, published in June of 1990 (by CAPMAS), is the last of a series first published in 1961. The report includes selected statistics on the social, demographic, and economic status of Egypt derived from many governmental agencies. The series gives trends of changes over the last 30 years. Additional demographic data on Egypt come from population census reports. Started in 1882, 11 of the census surveys have already been conducted, the last one in 1986, with about 10-year intervals between each. The Egyptian census is done by the de facto method, which, of course, has its methodological limitations. The reliability and validity of census data and areas covered vary among the years and have improved over time. There is particular confidence in census surveys that have been conducted since 1927.

The 1986 census was based on population samples. A large survey, comprising 80% of the household families and individuals in public housing, covered information of a general nature on the identity and demographics of persons and homes. A smaller sample, comprising 20% of the families, concerned itself with more detailed information on such specific issues of social mobility, fertility, immigration, and housing conditions.

Whenever necessary, the information collected by sampling was manipulated by the proper statistical methodology.

The second major source of information for this chapter comes from the "General Report for Egypt of Social Indicators for Development Study" (Saleh, Abdelkader, & Khalifa, in press). By social indicators, reference is specifically made to a movement that considers not only inputs (such as programs or interventions), but also outputs (such as welfare indices). These indicators form the basis of a social report of the country, which is issued periodically, and also help policymakers in planning and evaluation.

The Social Indicator movement was the basis for some form of social national report in more than 15 developed countries, starting in the late 1970s. The movement reached Egypt in 1979. Initially, Social Indicators surveyed Egyptian families but has been recently extended to other Arab families. This study was sponsored by the Arab Regional Center of UNESCO and the Egyptian Academy for Scientific Research and Technology. The authors of the first general report on this study (Saleh et al., in press) have given their permission to use findings in this chapter.

A final source of information for this chapter is from research findings and insights of a multitude of authors who are experts on Egyptians and Egypt (e.g., Abdalla & Kamham, 1986; Azzer & Affifi, 1990; Hamdan, 1984; Hopkins, 1987; Palmer, Leila, & Yassin, 1986).

Profile of Egyptians

According to the census in 1986, Egyptians numbered 48.2 million. United Nations global estimates and projections of the population from 1988 made revisions and estimated that there were 54.05 million Egyptians in 1990. Currently the Egyptians comprise 1% of the world's population and 10% of Africa's population. Rural-to-urban population ratio is 55.4:44.6, according to the census.

Male-to-female population ratio is 51.3:48.7, with an index of 105.2, according to the social indicators survey. A highly comparable figure of 104.7 comes from the census; pointing to the high cross-validity between the two systems of data collection.

Figures on the population over 65 years old come from the social indicators survey. Those 65 to 69 years of age represented 1.8% of total Egyptians. Those 70 to 74 represented 1.2%, those 75 to 79 represented 0.6%; those 80 to 84 represented 0.3%; and those 85 and over represented 0.4%.

There were very little differences between the proportion of men and women.

From the 1986 census it was found that 2.4% of the population was 60 to 64 years of age; 1.1% was 70 to 74; and 1% was 70 and over. That is to say that 3.8% of the population is 65 and older, and 6.2% is 60 and older.

Again, there is little sex difference between all the age groups over 60 years. While the national ratio for male:female is 1:1; the ratio is .9:1 for those 60 to 64, 1.16:1 for those 65 to 70, and back to 1:1 for those 70 and over.

As for the rural to urban distribution of the elderly, compared to the national ratio of 56.1:43.9, it is found that the ratio is 55:45 for those 60 to 64 years of age and 59:41 for those 65 and older. It is clear that there is a trend of rural overrepresentation, beginning at age 65.

To complete the description of the Egyptian population, census figures indicate that half the population is under 20 years of age; 14.8% is below five; 13.1% is 5 to 9 years old; 11.6% is 10 to 14; and 10.4% is 15 to 20.

In 1988 it was found that the marital status of Egyptians over 18 years of age was as follows: 31% of males and 20% of females had never married; 65% of males and 64% of females were married; 22% of males and 12.7% of females were widowed; and .5% of males and 13% of females were divorced. These national figures of marital status do not differ greatly between rural and urban populations.

According to 1986 census figures, the total number of those 20 years and older was 26.6 million (13 million males and 13.6 million females). There were 1.8 million Egyptians 65 and over who constituted 6.6% of those 20 years and older.

In Egypt it was found that there are 1.6 million Christians and 25 million Moslems. The male:female ratio is around 1:1 for both religious subgroups. The census found that 12.5% of the 65 and older population of Egyptians are widowers, three times higher than the national average for the 20 and older population (which is 4%). Those 65 and older form 3.5% of all widowers. The national ratio for male:female widowers is 1:6. For the 65 and over group the ratio is 1:2 for Moslems and 1:4 for Christians.

It has been found that .7% of those 65 and older are divorced, much less than the national Egyptian average of divorce for the 20 and over population (of 4%). The 65 and over divorces form 5% of all divorced. The national ratio for male:female divorce is 1:3. For those 65 and older, it is 1:1.6 for Moslems and 1:0.6 for Christians. Sixty-eight percent of Egyptians 65 and over are married, which is more than twice the national average of married for those 20 and older (which is 30%).

Those 65 and older form 12% of married persons 20 and older. The national ratio of married males to females is 1:0.5. For the 65 and older group, the ratio is 1:1 for both Moslems and Christians. To reach 65 years of age in Egypt is to double the chances of being married. More than two thirds of the Egyptians 65 and older are married.

The census found that 0.8% of Egyptians 65 and older never married. This is, of course, much less than the national average of 27% for those 20 and older who never married. The 65 and older age group form 0.2% of never married Egyptians who are 20 years of age and older. The national ratio for males:females who never married is 1.5:1. For those 65 and over, it is 1.2:1 for Moslems and 1:1 for Christians.

Profile of the Country

Housing

Because Egypt is a large oasis in a larger desert, the populated land is only about 39,000 square kilometers and the population density, in 1990, was around 1,450 persons per square kilometer (one of the highest in the world). Egypt is the most densely populated agricultural country in the world. In Cairo the 1988 population density was 28,259 persons per square kilometer. In that year Metropolitan Cairo had 8.76 million inhabitants.

From the social indicators survey, information was obtained on the suitability of Egyptian houses. In urban Egypt 81% of the dwellings had pipeline water, but 14% had no water supply at all. In rural areas 30% had pipeline supplies, and 50% had no water supplies at all. Public taps were available for 57% of rural homes and for 53% of urban homes that had no water supply to their households.

Electricity was available to 97% of urban households and to 84% of rural ones. Sewers were available to 78% of urban households and to only 12% of rural ones. Water closets were completely lacking in 8% of urban households and in 37% of rural ones. Bathrooms were lacking in 37% of urban and 80% of rural households.

Refrigerators, washing machines, cooking ovens, and water heaters are grossly lacking, especially in rural households. By marked contrast, 66% of urban households have color television sets, which is true for 47% of rural households.

Inhabitants of urban households expressed satisfaction with their dwellings in 65% of the cases and satisfaction with surroundings in 72% of the cases. In rural areas the corresponding levels of satisfaction were 82% and 89%, respectively.

As to ownership of dwelling buildings, 78% belonged to the private sector in urban areas and 92.7% in rural areas. The state owned only 3.8% of the buildings in urban areas. In urban areas the inhabitant was the owner in 45.6% of the cases and was a renter in 54.4% of the cases. In rural areas inhabitants owned 97.9% of the units and only 2.1% had to pay rent.

For all households, on the average, in both rural and urban areas, there was a 30-minute walk to schools (of all grades), health services, and sports grounds. From the 1986 census, figures are quoted to depict the state of crowding in dwellings. The 48.2 million Egyptians formed 9.7 million families who were accommodated by 7.7 million buildings with 11.3 million housing units. The number of people residing in public buildings was about 210,000.

Education

Education is not only an index of quality of life but also an index of development. As found by the social indicators survey, 40% of all Egyptians have never gone to school. This pertains to 29.5% of the males and 51.7% of the females. This trend is regressive, as 28% of those 5 to 14 years of age never attended school, as compared to 65% of those 40 and older.

By the same token, illiteracy figures are high: 27% of urban husbands and 49% of rural ones are illiterate, as are 54% and 75% of urban and rural wives, respectively. Illiteracy is coming under some control (3.7% and 11% rates for young men in urban and rural areas, respectively, and 10% and 43% for young urban and rural women). The middle-aged form a high illiterate base and a very low percent of high school graduates. This trend is shared by the 65 and older population. Females living in rural areas form the broad base of illiteracy. Absolute numbers of illiterates are increasing, now numbering 20 million. And, as will be discussed, education is highly linked to fertility.

Only one third of Egyptian youth are in school, and only 20% of them obtain the secondary school certificate. Technical education after high school remains low. Adult education is presently only in a nominal form, and is taken advantage of by only around 10% in urban areas and less than 5% of those in rural areas. Such education amounts to mainly vocational training and lasts for just a few months.

For the Egyptian elderly the following levels of education have been found: of the half million persons 75 years of age and older, 75% are illiterate (with a male-to-female ratio of 1:2.5); of the half million persons 70 to 75, 80% are illiterate (with a ratio of 1:1.5); of the 8.82 million who are 65 to 70, 70% are illiterate (with a ratio of 1:1); and of the 1.1 million who are 60 to 65, 75% are illiterate (with a ratio of 1:1.5).

Finally, the national average for illiteracy, in the same census, is 50% for all Egyptians 10 years of age and older. Of the 34 million Egyptians who were at least 10 years old in 1986, some 1.1 million had a bachelor's degree from a university. The male-to-female ratio for these college graduates was 3:1. For those 65 years of age and older, only .3% (or 22,000) had a college degree. The male-to-female ratio was 30:1.

Employment

Labor in Egypt is the most important source of income. According to the 1986 census, Egyptians over 15 years of age numbered 29 million, of whom 14.7 million were males and 14.2 were females. Those employed numbered 12.8 million, of whom 11.2 million were males and 1.4 were females. Of those employed, 1.5 million were in sales or services; 4.1 million were in agriculture; 2.75 million were unskilled laborers; and 1.2 million were in other forms of employment.

The share of the senior citizens in the labor force is depicted in the following figures. For all of Egypt, of the 1.8 million persons 65 and older, 240,000 are working within the labor force. Of these, 70,000 are wage workers (who amount to less than .1% of the total work force) and 147,000 are self-employed (and amount to .5% of all self-employed Egyptians). There are 27,344 employers who are 65 years of age and older and who amount to 5.5% of all the employers in Egypt.

In urban Egypt 75,000 persons over 65 are within the labor force (and amount to .1% of that force). In rural Egypt 173,000 persons over 65 are in the labor force (and amount to .24% of that force). Most elderly working in rural areas are self-employed and in urban areas most are wage workers. Of all those who are not able to work or who do not want to work, the elderly account for 67% in urban areas and 45% in rural areas.

Some indicators have found that work satisfaction is related to the type of work and profession. Those with the lowest satisfaction were wives and young, never married females in rural areas. The main causes for dissatisfaction include tedious work (41%), low pay (21%), and lack of job security (21%). It has been found that 22% of the work force, who are

15 years of age and older, have tried to travel abroad to find work. This would be a reflection of the level of dissatisfaction with one's present job. Very few of those studied (12% of the urban sample and 9% of the rural sample) believed that their work revenues can cover their needs (and permit them to save part of their earnings).

It was also found that there is early entry and late exit from the labor force, especially in rural areas, and for both males and females. For example, 37% started working at the age of 12 or younger. It can be assumed that with greater economic gains in the country, the number of those working in agriculture will be reduced in favor of work in other areas. Twice as many men work in agriculture as do women.

Egyptians are hard workers; 56% work 5 to 6 days a week, 18% work less than 5 days a week, and 26% work all 7 days a week. It has also been found that 45% work an average of 7 to 10 hours a day, 27% work 6 hours or less a day, and 28% work 10 hours or more a day.

It has been found that 44% of the labor force is employed in the private sector, 28% in government, 15% in a family business, and 12% in the public sector. Employment in family business and private sectors has been on the increase since the mid-1970s, with a decreasing role for government. Unfortunately the current labor market in Egypt does not provide enough satisfactory work opportunities for the people. There are pressures for the expansion by the private sector and in family businesses. A trend also exists in the number emigrating to find opportunities for employment in other countries.

Health and Health Services

Life expectancy at birth in urban Egypt rose from 57.6 years in 1981 to 61.4 years in 1985; and in rural Egypt it rose from 51.3 years to 55.1 years during the same period. This increase is mainly a result of the drop in mortality. Most deaths between the ages of 5 and 15 occur in rural areas. Families with at least one member needing continuous care amount to 34% of all families in urban areas and 23% of all families in rural areas.

The main disabilities are heart conditions, nervous disorders, polio, and kidney problems. The major obstacle to family care for chronic illness lies in financial difficulties. This is especially true for more than half (67%) of all rural caregivers. Occupational health care problems have occurred in rural employment. While medicine is generally available, the cost of medication is a major problem for many persons.

Egyptian people do not rely on the public health services because of poor standards of care. Instead they seek private physicians and, yet, cannot afford such care (in 72% of the cases), and this is especially true for widowers.

To give the proper credit to the government, there are free medical services available to Egyptians. In 1989 there were 102,000 hospital beds (generally governmental). The hospitals were mainly for patients needing treatment for endemic diseases, chest diseases, psychiatric problems, and for those seeking maternity and infant care. Unfortunately no figures exist of the number (or type) of geriatric services or the use of general health care services by the elderly.

Finally, Egyptian families generally believe that science can lead to healing. Yet there still exist those who hold nonscientific health beliefs, and who utilize nonscientific health services and practices.

Social Changes

Of the 47.7 million Egyptians, 20.8 million reside in urban areas; 17 million were born in the urban sites within which they still dwell. Internal movement to urban areas of the country includes about 13% of the population. One third of the elderly living in urban areas had relocated from rural areas; only 9% of rural elderly had relocated from urban areas.

In general, 23% of the Cairo residents were born elsewhere in the country (46% for those 65 and older); 31% of the Ismailia residents were born elsewhere (57% for the elderly); 23% of those living near the Red Sea (a recently developed urban area) were born elsewhere (56% for the elderly). Such movement, it was learned from social indicator surveys, involved mainly younger males going from rural to urban areas. Thus there has been fairly substantial internal mobility within Egypt.

Emigration from Egypt is currently found for 2.12% (or one million) of the total Egyptian population, and 2.8% of the males were working outside the country. Most are, in fact, males (8:1) who leave behind their wives. They usually come from rural areas and, when they return to Egypt, move to urban areas.

Recent trends in marriage and divorce have produced many changes in Egyptian society. The social indicator surveys have found that there is a sharp difference between urban and rural areas. Females tend to marry earlier than do males; the average age of marriage is 27 for males and 21 for females.

It was learned that 2.7% of urban males and 2.4% of rural males had more than one wife. The number of living children was inversely related to the level of education in both urban and rural areas. There are positive attitudes toward the need for family planning, for smaller families, and for male children.

Knowledge regarding birth control was up to 95.9% and was related to level of education. It was not one's religion, but, rather, the desire to have (or not have) more children that motivated individuals to engage in birth control practices. Between 57% to 80% of family members contemplated using family planning. Thus, if these attitudes are true, Egypt can contemplate an easing of its population explosion in the near future.

Social and Family Support of the Elderly

Religion and religious institutions enjoy authority and respect in Egypt. Many services at the grass roots level are offered through the assistance of organized religion. In a study of the elderly (Azzer & Affifi, 1990), it was found that 90% believed that religion was a source of great strength and comfort to them. For many retired persons, religious practice is a compensatory activity; the five daily prayers provide a needed daily routine. Fellow worshipers form a network for socialization. For the majority of old people in Egypt, religion provides a purpose for their daily lives that would, otherwise, be more idle and less meaningful.

Religion also defines the relationship between generations within the Egyptian family. The Koran includes various principles on support of both emotional and financial obligation between the aged and (especially) their male offspring.

In one survey of a sample of elderly who were in need (Azzer & Affifi, 1990), it was found that financial support was mainly received from children (45% of the cases), from friends or neighbors (3.4% of the cases), from brothers or sisters (1.4% of the cases), and from public assistance (.4% of the cases). When help was needed with daily tasks, it was generally in housekeeping and preparing meals (for about 60% of the subjects). The most helpful, in meeting these needs, were sons (41%) and daughters (32%). It was found that 12% of the elderly subjects had their needs unmet, and this has important implications for needed policies in the country.

It was found that sons, daughters, and wives ranked the highest in meeting the need for emotional support of the elderly. Elderly who admitted that they felt lonely often, or on occasion, included 42% of the males and 59% of the females. Findings also indicated that 50% of the females and 56% of the males believed that they did not receive the respect they deserved; thus they felt a lack of emotional satisfaction. More than half of the subjects were visited by their children on a daily basis.

In case of emergency, 66% of the elderly felt that they could count on someone to support them in crisis; most felt they could rely on their sons. The highest percentage of all kinds of support was usually provided by the eldest offspring. Yet it was found that both financial and emotional needs of a significant proportion of the elderly who were in low- or very low-income categories did not have their needs met. Generally this was because the offspring, themselves, were in similar income categories and could not afford to provide (or were psychologically unable to give) the care needed by their elderly parents.

The elderly were found to provide care for others: 50% of the sample indicated that they provided help with daily tasks, 67% indicated that they provided emotional support to others, and 46% indicated that they provided financial help. These forms of help were given by the elderly to their sons, daughters, and neighbors; and 53% of the elderly indicated that they had provided emergency help within the past year.

The type of support provided most often by the elderly was less than that received. The major types of assistance included gifts, care of sick relatives, and care of grandchildren.

Formal Support for the Elderly

The Egyptian constitution recognizes and encourages both formal and informal support. Formal support includes a modern social security program that provides social and health insurance services, as well as disability, unemployment, and old-age assistance (Act No. 79, 1985). There is, however, the need for improvements in the formal system in the areas of coverage and eligibility qualifications, among other areas.

The following information suggests how much the welfare system is in need of serious modifications and improvement. It has been found that 39% of the elderly, although entitled to a pension, still mainly rely on the support of their children. Also, 52% of the elderly are not entitled to a pension and must rely on the support of their children. The average monthly sum received per person from pensions is Lire Egyptiene (L.E.) 54 (with a minimum of L.E. 35).

Another government program is called universal social security (Act No. 112, 1980). This is a program that can be used by many (especially the elderly) who are not covered by the previously-mentioned pension program. In 1987 there were about one million beneficiaries. The average monthly benefit was a mere L.E. 8.5.

In addition to the inadequacies in the coverage of these formal financial programs, there are also programs that provide social welfare services (and can include home delivery, transportation assistance, recreation, etc.). All these program may be underutilized. Although the programs do provide benefits for some of the Egyptian elderly, as well as the destitute, they are not utilized by all who are eligible because many eligible persons are unaware of the existence of the programs. Furthermore, bureaucratic inefficiency also can result in the underutilization of formal programs available for the elderly.

A health insurance services program (Act 75, 1964) covered 6% of the population in 1988. This program does not extend to all pensioners. For a yearly contribution of L.E. 7, an individual received an average expenditure for treatment (in 1985) of L.E. 60. Thus there was (and is) a heavy burden placed upon the program's financial resources, and more funds are needed to extend the coverage of the program and improve the quality of care given under this program.

In addition to these formal services, in Egypt there are some 49 homes for the elderly across the nation that provide care for about 1,950 individuals. There are also about 50 old-age clubs in the country.

The amount of government and voluntary social support is depicted in the following figures. The number of insured employees, in 1989, was 13.5 million, and the value of their participation amounted to 3 billion Egyptian pounds. Pensions and compensations for insured employees amounted to 2.2 million Egyptian pounds. The trend is for better coverage.

A network has existed, since 1989, for some 10,000 nongovernmental societies, which cover various areas of need for the citizens of Egypt. The major fields of coverage include cultural, educational, and religious services. These are followed by services focusing on social aid, family care, and maternal and child care. In addition, some 90 societies provide care for the aged; however, only 58 of these societies focus specifically on the elderly.

There is a trend for combining social development with social aid. While there is vast experience with, and facilities for, child day care, it is hoped that the Egyptian elderly will benefit in the future from an extensive network of day care resources.

Conclusion

In conclusion, the family is the main social institution in Egypt that provides support for the elderly, despite social change and socioeconomic pressures. Children are the most likely family members to provide care; and it is especially true that sons, or the eldest child (male or female), is most likely to have the greatest responsibility.

Neighbors provide support to the elderly in emergencies and may offer care and support in case of need.

On the other hand, elderly reciprocate services to their family members, and this gives them satisfaction and consolidates their importance and position in the family.

Income-generation programs, day centers, domiciliary care, and substitute pension schemes are badly required in Egypt to supplement what the family is able to provide to their elderly relatives.

Support of the Egyptian family is also badly needed—educationally, materially, and morally. The situation is Egypt is serious, but it is far from hopeless.

References

Azzer, A., & Affifi, E. (1990). *Social support system for the aged in Egypt, National Center for Social and Criminological Research and United Nations University.* Cairo: NCSCR Press.

Census 1986. (1990). *Report on the general characteristics of population and housing conditions* (Vol. 1). Cairo: CAPMAS.

Hamdan, G. (1984). *The personality of Egypt.* (In Arabic). Cairo: The World of Books.

Hopkins, N. S. (1987). *Agrarian transformation in Egypt.* Cairo: The American University Press.

Palmer, A., Leila, A., & Yassin, E. (1986). *The Egyptian bureaucracy.* (Arabic text). Cairo: The American University Press.

Saleh, N., Abdelkader, M., & Khalifa, A. (in press). *Social indicators for development, general report on Egypt.* (Arabic text). Cairo: Arab Regional Centre for Research and Documentation in Social Sciences.

Statistical yearbook of the central agency for public mobilization and statistics (CAPMAS) (1990). Cairo: Author.

PART III

Adult Countries[1]

Adult countries are defined as those whose population aged 65 and older represent between 8% and 10% of the total population. Such countries are represented, in this book, by Argentina, Hong Kong, and Israel.

Argentina, located in temperate South America, had a mid-1990 population estimated at 32.3 million people. The population is projected to increase to 43.5 million persons by the year 2020. In 1990 the population under 15 years of age represented about one quarter of the total population (34%) and the population 65 years of age and older represented 9% of the total population. It was found that 85% of the Argentine population lived in urban areas of the country. The authors of the chapter on Argentina are Roberto Kaplan, M.D., and Nélida Redondo, M.S.S., both from Hospital Italiano in Buenos Aires.

Hong Kong, located in East Asia, is estimated to have had a population of 5.8 million in mid-1990 and will increase to 6.9 million people by the year 2020. In 1990 it was found that 22% of the population were under 15 years of age and 8% were 65 years of age and older. It was estimated that 93% of the population lived in urban areas (making Hong Kong the most urban country represented in this book). The author of the chapter on Hong Kong is Nelson W. S. Chow, Ph.D., Professor and Head of the Department of Social Work and Social Administration at the University of Hong Kong.

Israel, located in the Middle East (also identified as West Asia), is estimated to have had a population of 4.6 million in mid-1990. By the year 2020 the population is estimated to increase to 7 million people. In 1990 Israel was found to have a population with almost one third (32%) under the age of 15 years, and those 65 years of age and older represented 9%

of all Israelis. Almost 90% of the population lived in urban areas. The authors of the chapter on Israel are Gila Noam, M.A., Senior Researcher, the JDC-Brookdale Institute of Gerontology and Adult Human Development; and Jack Habib, Ph.D., Director, Joint Distribution Committee-Israel, and Professor of the Department of Economics and Baerwald School of Social Work at Hebrew University; both authors are located in Jerusalem.

Note

1. All information used to describe these three countries comes from *1990: World Population Data Sheet of the Population Reference Bureau, Inc.,* Washington, DC, 1990. Mid-1990 population estimates are based upon census or official national data or upon U.N., U.S. Bureau of the Census, or World Bank projections. Year 2020 projections come from the same sources.

8

Family Care of the Elderly in Argentina

A Context of Crisis

ROBERTO KAPLAN
NÉLIDA REDONDO

Introduction

It is estimated that 70% of the one billion people over 60 inhabiting our planet in the near future will be living in the developing world. Latin America is no exception. A sharp increase of elderly population is expected here; from 6.4% in 1980 to 10.8% in 2025. Argentina faces a similar prospect: a "leap" is expected from 13% in 1987 to 16% in 2025 (Rubinstein, Epstein, & Kaplan, 1990).

The vastness of the territory, the relatively low density of population, and an impressive immigratory movement at the turn of the century have shaped a country—from the sociodemographic viewpoint—with singular characteristics. Another element that contributes to sharpening such multiple peculiarities is the country's high degree of urbanization.

Argentina, in the southern cone of the American Continent, has a surface of approximately 3 million square kilometers and a population of 33 million inhabitants. Just as a comparison, India, with almost the same territory, has 20 times the Argentine population.

AUTHORS' NOTE: We wish to thank Mercedes Quaglia for her invaluable help in the translation of this chapter into English.

The country (as well as the two neighbors, Chile and Uruguay) has other features that make it different from the rest of the subcontinent: it is among those countries having a population over 65 that is above 8% of the total amount ("adult" country) with a net predominance of Caucasians unlike the other countries in the continent that have an indigenous or African predominance.

This ethnic-racial feature should also be considered "late," because it does not stem from the origins of the conquest by Spaniards or Portuguese. It was only at the end of the nineteenth century that the "white" immigration started. Up to then, even if the flow of Iberians to America had been constant, it was relatively small in number. By 1810, in accordance with estimations of the time, there were only 3,276,000 whites in the entire region of Spanish America (Rouquie, 1990).

The incorporation of the new territories into the world market, as well as the expansion of the new cultures, created a great demand for labor. This coincided with the growing possibilities for Europeans to sail overseas, moving away from overpopulated Europe.

Regulations disrupting immigration into the United States made millions of impoverished Europeans look for hope in the South. They set out for the temperate areas in the south of Brazil, where the cultivation of coffee offered growing possibilities. Yet, as slavery disappeared, uninhabited lands required new settings for agrarian production (especially in Argentina and Uruguay).

Thus between 1867 and 1930 Argentina received 6,330,000 immigrants, 3,385,000 (more than half of all) of whom decided to stay in the country. According to the first census, in 1869, the "Argentine desert" had 1.7 million inhabitants. The influence of the early foreigners, in shaping Argentina, determined one of the most acute changes in the New World. Thus the population duplicated in Argentina every 20 years until 1914, when foreigners amounted to 30% of the population. The flow only stopped in 1930, and resumed in 1945. By the end of World War II, immigration occurred with a much lower intensity.

Another outstanding feature of the demographic framework is, undoubtedly, the degree of urbanization. Latin America, as a whole, has an urbanization rate very close to that of developed Europe: 68%. This is twice the Asian rate and three times that of Africa. Argentina, Chile, and Uruguay are among the 15 most urbanized countries in the world, regardless of the criterion used (i.e., either agglomerated of over 20,000 or more than 100,000 inhabitants). Almost one fourth of the Latin American population, lives in cities.

A paradox makes itself evident: in a country with a strongly developed agrarian economy such as Argentina, more than 80% of the population lives in the cities. Within the metropolitan area of Buenos Aires, moreover, is concentrated one third of the total population of Argentina (Kaplan, 1987). This area also encompasses 45% of the industrial activities, 55% of the workers, and 45% of the national electric power used in the country.

Aging of the Population

Argentina is an example of those countries considered to be "late" (since 1950) in the occurrence of elderly populations (Myers, 1982). Even though such countries (e.g., Argentina and Japan) are now following different directions, they all have significant increase rates.

In Argentina the National Census of 1970 showed a new phenomenon: the nation had aged. The inhabitants over 65 now amounted to 7% of the entire population. That was the culmination of a process that had started a hundred years before, a period when fertility and mortality evolved—with peculiarities—in accordance with demographic transition patterns. In Argentina, mortality did not decrease before or at a higher pace than fertility and, on the other hand, the combination of the different decrease rates modified the size of the gap between mortality and fertility (vegetative growth). This was never either very large or very small, however. The vegetative growth rate has never been below 13% or above 20%, showing a declining tendency in the long term, through an oscillating pattern in the short term (see Pantelides, 1983). Meanwhile the massive European immigration had an impact on both the total and the vegetative growth of the population at the turn of the century.

The causes for this demographic transition and for the large immigration waves from overseas are associated with the enormous social and cultural transformation of Argentina between 1860 and 1914. Just as in many other countries in the nineteenth century, Argentina consolidated its national unification between 1860 and 1880 and the country entered the world market as a large exporter of foodstuff—agrarian and livestock products.

Some remarkable social, political, and economic transformations were to have an effect on demographic factors. Economic growth allowed a series of improvements in environmental hygiene, public transport, dietary intake, the opening of hospitals and schools of medicine, and the control of epidemics and infectious diseases. All this was to lead to a fast reduction of mortality. It should be noted that the situation in Argentina differed, in this sense, from that of other Latin American countries where reduced mortality occurred later on (from the 1940s), through health campaigns to eradicate infectious and parasitic diseases (Chesnais, 1988; Recchini de Lattes & Lattes, 1975; Somoza, 1973).

The prominent process of urbanization in Argentina, reinforced by the settling of large immigratory waves from overseas, was to have an influence on the decrease of fertility. In fact, immigrants contributed to an important expansion of the urban middle classes, and the latter were to be protagonists of a reduction in the number of children. Surveys of fertility in Argentina would confirm that the most significant decrease in birth rate took place within some subgroups of the population: the most urban ones, the foreigners, and those with a higher literacy level (Rothman, 1973).

The analysis of demographic forces indicates that the aging of the Argentine population was not regionally uniform. Buenos Aires and the Center-Littoral region were the areas where the above-mentioned demographic transition patterns took place (at higher levels than those of the country as a whole). Buenos Aires, in particular, showed (in 1980) the lowest birth rate in the country and had achieved such a decrease of mortality that life expectancy at birth was 72.2 years (INDEC, 1988). Buenos Aires and Center-Littoral were certainly the most aged regions in the country.

Other areas, even if they had not had such an evolution in birth rates and mortality, have undergone a population aging due to the emigration of young natives. Other areas have started the transition later on. Hence aging is still in its early phase. The northern and southern regions have the youngest populations in the country. The former has high mortality and fertility rates, and the latter has high fertility and positive net migration.

Likewise, the aging of the Argentine population varies on the basis of social strata. Unfortunately no data are available to describe and quantify the change of demographic factors in different social strata. It is only known that the decrease in birth rates, all through the century, took place among the urban, foreign, and literate population. On the other hand, there are no data regarding the evolution of mortality in the different social strata, but it is assumed that the upper and middle strata, in urban areas, have a relative advantage in their access to highly developed health services, environmental comfort, and adequate nutritional patterns, as well as other factors that lower the levels of mortality. Therefore it can be concluded that the urban middle strata includes the ones that have undergone the most acute process of aging. In the lower strata, because both fertility and mortality levels are high, the population remains younger.

Social Trends of the Aged in 1980

The last decades of the twentieth century do not evidence, in Argentina, such a promising reality as that of the end of the nineteenth century. In Argentina, as well as in other Latin American countries, from the 1980s on, there is evidence of an acute process of economic involution. The GNP has been decreasing over the years, as a consequence of coexisting factors of a persistent fiscal deficit and an unaffordable foreign debt (within a context of sustained recession). This macrostructural situation has affected, and is still affecting, the standard of living of the nation's elderly. Obviously this group has become one of the most vulnerable sectors of the Argentine population.

In 1980 the National Census in Argentina indicated that the population over 60 amounted to nearly 3.3 million people (11.8% of the total amount), while the population over 65 had reached 8.2%. Compared with the 1970 Census, the Argentine population had increased its aged population, but at a slower pace than in previous decades. Also, in 1980, it was found that 86.1% of the elderly population lived in urban areas (Argentina, 1982).

The percentage of elderly people covered by the Social Security System might be considered high in Argentina, even though no data are available from the authorities. By Social Security System is meant the general program for individuals, both working and retired. It covers the whole range of workers' life contingencies: health, incapacity, aging, and so on. The 1980 National Census of Population found that 79.2% of the men over 75 declared themselves retired or pensioned. The female population over 75 were found to have a much lower level of coverage: 47.7%. A significant segment, however, gets some coverage from the Social Security System (i.e., spouses of beneficiaries get financial assistance and health delivery services).

At present the elderly population in Argentina is facing a severe economic crisis due to the acute breakdown of the whole Social Security System. The system had grown fast in the 1950s, providing large coverage, mainly for workers from the formal sector of the economy. During the last 20 years, and in accordance with the aging population, the Social Security System added further programs for the elderly population besides the regular pension (such as family allowances, health care, and housing programs) (Golbert, 1989).

The National Fund for Retirement had undergone its first great crisis by the end of the 1960s, mainly, as a result of having matured too early and due to the unwise administration of funds within an inflationary context (Isuani, Feldman, & Golbert, 1986). By National Fund for Retirement is meant a subprogram of the Social Security System, in fact the earliest one, in charge of paying pensions and is mainly financed with contributions by active workers.

In the 1980s, failing to accomplish the aims of universality, equality, and solidarity, the Social Security System became acutely unbalanced, a tendency that has been increasing to the present. The most serious consequence is the decrease in pensions; the loss of purchasing power of pensions has exceeded—by far—that of the salary of active workers. The most important loss (in absolute and relative terms) in the purchasing power of pensions took place between June and July of 1989, when the Argentine economy went through hyperinflation (Golbert, 1989).

At the beginning of the 1990s the elderly ranked as one of the poorest sectors of Argentine society. Based upon information provided by a large research program, "Survey on Poverty in Argentina" (and its chapter "Poverty in the Buenos Aires Conurbation") (INDEC, 1989), it was found, in 1988, that 25% of the population over 60 in Greater Buenos Aires were in a category referred to (in this survey) as "pauperized." This category includes, according to INDEC (1989),

> families that at certain moments had been able to improve their relative situation and had had an acceptable standard of living who, due to a permanent reduction in their pocket salary, are now living in the same conditions—regarding consumption—as the structurally poor.

These data warn about the negative impact that the crisis of the Social Security System might have had on the standard of living of a significant sector of the elderly population in Argentina. This is easy to understand when taking into account the fact that pensions are the main source of income for the elderly of Argentina. In fact the data supplied by an epidemiological research study carried out in five Argentine cities (PAHO, 1989), reprocessed by another survey (Pantelides, 1988), disclose the high percentage of elderly people who declare that the main source of their income is their pension.

Indeed, the percent of those who receive a regular income from sources other than pension, or from employment, is low. States Pantelides (1988):

> Many of the people surveyed may combine several sources of income. As the answers are not excluding, the real situation of the interviewed with regards to this variable is impossible to ascertain. (p. 119)

Regarding income from investments, little is known about the elderly's savings during their economically-active life. Thus figures are quite low.

The prosperity that the Argentine economic structure allowed during the 1940s and the 1950s can be seen in the significant percent of elderly people who are the owners of their own dwellings: more than 65% of those living in the five selected cities (Pantelides, 1988). Likewise, a case study carried out in an "urban poverty pocket" of Buenos Aires shows that the purchase or building of their own dwelling was a feasible possibility even for those in the lowest socio-occupational strata (Redondo, 1990). "Urban poverty pocket" refers to an area in the city where a high percentage— 50% or more—of the population live in homes where basic needs are not met. On the other hand, savings were negatively affected by the Argentine inflationary process. Most of the elderly people who participated in the survey pointed out that their savings had devaluated and drained before they reached old age (Redondo, 1990). Thus the data available are enough to explain why the percentage of elderly people who declare they get revenues from investments is low, despite the fact that they were adults at a time when society offered good economic conditions.

The percentage of elderly people who indicate that they receive money from their children is low, as well. The question arises then if Argentina, within the present context of an economic crisis, the family is involved in the care of their elders? An attempt to answer this question, even though the information available is exiguous, is approached in the following section.

Family and Elderly Population

In 1980 Argentina was following the general tendency of urban and aged societies in the structure of their households. This was also true for the distribution of the population in a wide range of living arrangements from the unipersonal household to a three-, or more, generation family.

The elderly population, in turn, seemed to have independent dwelling patterns. Redondo (1990) reported that, in 1980, 49.7% of the elderly lived in two "typical" social situations: 38.9% in a nuclear family and 10.8% in unipersonal households (See Table 8.1).

Table 8.1 also shows that sex and age are strong predictors of variations in the distribution within these categories for both sexes. With increasing age, the percentage of residents in nuclear families decreases, while those in unipersonal households increase. On the other hand, the percentage of elderly men living in nuclear family households is higher than those for

Table 8.1 Percentage Distribution by Sex and Age of the Population Over 60 Living in Households According to Family Types

| | | | | *Total in the Country—1980* | | | | | |
| | *Total Population* | | | *Men* | | | *Women* | | |
Type of family	Total	60-64	65+	Total	60-64	65+	Total	60-64	65+
N	3,248	1005	2243	1438	475	964	809	530	1279
Total	100.0	100.0	100.0	100.0	100.0	100.0	100.0	100.0	100.0
Unipersonal	10.8	8.3	11.9	8.8	7.3	9.5	12.4	9.2	13.3
Multipersonal									
Nuclear family	38.9	46.9	35.4	49.1	52.3	47.6	30.7	42.1	26.0
Nonnuclear fam.	38.4	35.9	39.4	34.8	34.1	35.2	41.3	37.6	42.7
Multipersonal									
Nonfamily	11.9	8.9	13.3	7.3	6.3	7.7	15.6	11.1	17.5

NOTE: N = expressed in thousands
SOURCE: Redondo (1990)

women. In contrast, the percentage of women living in unipersonal households is higher than that for men. This is due to the different life expectancy between men and women. In addition, the current generation of elderly married at a time when men married much younger women.

A third modality of residence, frequently found for the elderly in Argentina, is the multipersonal nonfamily household. This refers to those situations when an elderly person shares the household with other nonnuclear relatives. This includes relatives who are not spouses or children (e.g., brothers or sisters, grandchildren, or nonrelatives). The percentage of elderly people living in this type of household is slightly higher than that of the unipersonal home. The distribution by age and sex is similar in both; the percentage is higher among women and increases in the group of the eldest. This distribution shows that the sharing of the home with nonrelatives may be an alternative arrangement to the unipersonal home and offers economic and emotional advantages. Such arrangements alleviate the housing shortage, diminish livelihood expense, and make mutual care and help easier.

Finally, it must be pointed out that in Argentina, in 1980, the percentage of elderly people living with extended families was still significant. In this type of household, men's distribution shows no variations by age, while women's increase in the group of the eldest. Thus this type of family represents yet another option when facing widowhood and the loss of autonomy or independence.

The family structure of the elderly shows a certain relationship with demographic aging for different regions in Argentina. In the most aged areas there were larger percentages of unipersonal households (mainly among the elderly female population) and lower percentages of extended families. This is seen in Table 8.2.

Likewise, the ratio of potential dependence of the population living in the different types of households indicates that among the population over 60 there is the tendency to live in unigenerational homes (Redondo, 1990).

In short, the information seems to confirm the fact that in Argentina the evolution is similar to that of other "aged" countries: The elderly choose to remain in their own households, independent of their adult children. With increasing age and growing risks of widowhood and loss of autonomy, however, the elderly find their adult children's households a valid alternative in the Argentine society.

Naturally, in order to live in an independent household, some conditions should be fulfilled. This includes having a dwelling of their own or whose rent they can afford, enough income to cover their basic needs, and good health. In an empirical survey carried out in the Metropolitan Area of Buenos Aires (Pantelides, 1988), it was found that a housing shortage is an unsurmountable problem for elderly people who would like to live in their own households, and one of the main causes for admittance in "homes for the elderly poor" (see Kaplan, 1987). As earlier discussed, however, the percent of the aged who do not own a dwelling is low in Argentina. Indeed one of the main problems is the generalized descending social affluence in society, with the hardest impact on the elderly population whose pensions have fallen close to the poverty line. This may turn into a threat to the quality of life for a high percent of the elderly living in independent households.

Nevertheless the tendency to live in independent dwellings does not mean that the elderly are deprived of family support. Care is particularly likely from adult children, even when they do not live with their elderly parents.

For example, in information obtained from a survey (PAHO, 1989), Pantelides (1988) has found that, in general, the elderly declared they did receive help for their daily living activities as well as in cases of illness. For daily living activities the help comes mostly from their spouse, second, from a daughter, then from other relatives, and last from a son.

In cases of illness those who live alone very frequently declared that they received help from a daughter, in the first place, and, second, from other relatives. It must be taken into account that those who live alone are

Table 8.2 Percentage Distribution of the Population Over 60 Living in Households According to the Type of Family—1980—Areas Ordered by Population Aging

Type of Household	Buenos Aires City	Buenos Aires Province	Santa Fe Province	Cordoba Province	Entre Rios	Greater Buenos Aires	Mendoza Province
Total	100.0	100.0	100.0	100.0	100.0	100.0	100.0
Unipersonal	13.8	12.4	11.3	10.3	10.2	9.9	6.7
Multipersonal nuclear family	41.0	42.5	41.9	39.5	38.4	41.8	37.0
Multipersonal nonnuclear family	29.5	33.0	35.8	38.3	39.5	39.0	46.4
Multipersonal nonfamily	15.7	12.2	11.1	11.8	11.8	9.3	9.8
Population aging. % of 65+/Total population	14.9	9.6	9.5	8.3	8.2	7.4	6.4

SOURCE: Redondo (1990)

mainly widows whose immediate family are their children. For those who share their dwelling with others, the care seems to come from their spouse or from a daughter, in this order.

It was found that most of the elderly in Argentine cities declared that they did not receive money, housing, or food from their relatives, but that they did receive company and care. Most of the elderly indicated that their relatives did not provide them with money, clothes, or food, but that they offered company and care instead. This was found for between 52% and 72% of the elderly (depending on the city) (Pantelides, 1988). Unfortunately the surveys did not specify age or generation of relatives.

Thus, at least from the elderly's viewpoint, family bonds priorize company and care rather than the exchange of goods. The data available from the above-mentioned survey in an "urban poverty pocket" coincided in this sense. According to Redondo (1990),

> for most of the interviewed, children do not represent a permanent economic support. Thirty percent of the elderly people living in that area do not have children. Those who have children do not ask for their help because either they believe that they cannot afford it or simply in order to keep an image of independence. (p. 266)

Notwithstanding, the survey pointed out that the elderly felt very satisfied with their bonds with adult children and other relatives, and they relied on their company and care in case of illness or other contingencies.

Information available through qualitative research in popular urban sectors (CEPEV, 1989, 1990) agree in showing that, from the elderly's viewpoint, there are two aspects of crucial importance. On the one hand, is the wish to keep their housing and economic independence from their adult children as well as from other relatives; on the other hand, is the wish not to add conflicts to younger families because the elderly notice— correctly—that the impoverishment of the whole society has put an enormous burden on younger generations.

In Argentina the traditional role of gender stresses the role of daughters in supporting the daily living activities of their elders. This is especially true in cases of illness, regardless of the impact of social changes in society.

As in other societies, the Argentine woman has continuously been increasing her participation in the labor market. In the middle strata of the population most of the increases in female labor have been associated with higher educational levels (particularly with the growing number of university women graduates). In turn, within lower social classes, the crisis within the industrial sector of society (in the last decade) has brought about men's unemployment or underemployment. This has encouraged women to work in the services area, mainly in domestic work. Thus keeping the traditional patterns of gender in the care of the elderly implies an extra burden for women. This situation will tend to sharpen with the expected increase of population aging and the growing proportion of very old people.

Conclusions

The last hundred years have held a sad parable for Argentina. By the end of the nineteenth century the sustained socioeconomic growth brought about a demographic evolution that resulted, almost a hundred years later, in an aged population. Far from a promising future, however, a huge economic crisis has shaken Argentine society in the last decades of the twentieth century, and it is seriously affecting the standards of living of its elderly population.

In Argentina—as an urbanized and aged society—the people show evidence of preferring unigenerational housings, giving priority to their housing and economical independence from their adult children. This does not imply a weakening of the bonds between the elderly and their families; but, rather, all the data suggest a high quality of reciprocal relationship of duty and care. Indeed, faced with increasing age and the subsequent loss of autonomy, the extended family is still a valid alternative.

The impoverishment of Argentina in the recent years has, however, affected the standards of living in large urban population sectors, putting strong pressure on the family and weakening their capability of looking after their elderly members. The possibility of their providing economic help has diminished, and there is a greater demand for a larger extra-home labor share from women. And, yet, it has been women who have been the caregivers for the dependent members of the population: the children, the ill, and the frail elderly.

In order to alleviate the negative effects of the present crisis, a series of changes are required that should necessarily include the promotion of modifications in the traditional patterns of gender roles, encouraging sons to take a more active participation in the care of their elders. At the same time the utmost efficiency of social policies should be demanded so as to achieve a rational distribution of the scarce resources, giving priority to the highest risk sectors of the elderly population: the very old, the very frail, the poorest, and those who are alone.

Finally, efforts should take into account the fact that the complexity of the problems faced by the aged will only be solved by the joint action of all the social elements of Argentina's society: the family, the state, and the elderly themselves.

References

Argentina. (1982). *Censo nacional de poblacion y vivienda 1980—serie d, poblacion total del pais, Buenos Aires* [1980 national census of population and housing—total population].

Centro de Promocion y Estudios de la Vejez (CEPEV). (1989). *Investigacion participativa con ancianos residents en un bolson de pobreza urbana: El barrio de La Boca* [Participatory research with elderly people living in an urban poverty pocket: the Boca district]. [Mimeo]. Informe investigacion IAF.

Centro de Promocion y Estudios de la Vejez (CEPEV). (1990). *Investigacion participativa con ancianos residentes en un bolson de pobreza urbano: Villa Jardin* [Participatory research with elderly people living in an urban poverty pocket: Villa Jardin, Greater Buenos Aires]. Informe Investigacion IAF.

Chesnais, J. C. (1988). *La revancha del tercer mundo* [The Third World's Revenge]. Buenos Aires: Editorial Planeta.

Golbert, L. (1989). *Envejecer en Argentina: Bienestar y privaciones* [Aging in Argentina: Wellbeing and hardships]. [Mimeo]. Informe de investigacion, Buenos Aires.

Instituto Nacional de Estadisticas y Censos (INDEC). (1988). *Tabla de mortalidad—1980-1981. Total y por jurisdicciones* [Table of mortality, total and by areas]. (Cuadernos INDEC). Buenos Aires: INDEC.

Instituto Nacional de Estadisticas y Censos (INDEC). (1989). *La pobreza en el conurbano Bonaerense* [Poverty in the Buenos Aires conurbation]. (Estudios INDEC No. 13). Buenos Aires: INDEC.

Isuani, E, Feldman, J., & Golbert, L. (1986). *Maduración y crisis del Sistema Previsional Argentino* [Ripening and crisis of the Argentine Pensions Fund System]. In Boletin Informativo Techint (ISSN: 0497-0292) No. 240, pp. 57-92. Buenos Aires: Techint Enterprises.

Kaplan, R. (1987). Care for the elderly: Could teaching nursing homes be of value in Argentina? *Danish Medical Bulletin, Gerontology special supplement.* (Series No. 5), pp. 28-31.

Myers, G. (1982). The aging of populations. In R. H. Binstock (Ed.), *International perspectives on aging: Population and policy challenges,* pp. 1-39. (Policy Development Studies No. 7). New York: UNFPA.

Pan American Health Organization (PAHO). (1989). *A profile of the elderly in Argentina.* (Technical Paper No. 26.) Washington, DC: Author.

Pantelides, E. A. (1983). *La transicion demografica argentina: Un modelo no ortodoxo* [The Argentine demographic transition: A nonorthodox model]. In *Desarrollo Economico—Revista de Ciencias Sociales, 22*(88), pp. 511-534.

Pantelides, E. (1988). *Servicios sociales para la tercera edad en el gran Buenos Aires* [Social services for the aged in greater Buenos Aires]. (Mimeo). (Informe Investigacion IDRC). Buenos Aires: IDRC.

Recchini de Lattes, Z., & Lattes, A. (1975). *La poblacion Argentina* [The Argentine population]. (INDEC, Serie de Investigations Demograficas). Buenos Aires: INDEC [National Institute of Statistics and Census].

Redondo, N. (1990). *Causas y consecuencias socioeconomicas del envejecimiento poblacional argentino* [Socioeconomic causes and consequences of Argentine population aging]. [Mimeo]. (Informe de Investigacion CONICET). Buenos Aires: CONICET.

Rothman, A. M. (1973). La fecundidad en la Argentina entre 1869 and 1970 [Fertility in Argentina between 1869 and 1970]. In *Temas de poblicion de la Argentina. Aspectos Demograficos*, pp. 41-62 [Population issues in Argentina. Demographic aspects]. (Serie E, No. 13). Buenos Aires: CELADE [Center of Demography for Latin America].

Rubinstein, A., Epstein, E., & Kaplan, R. (1990). Envejecimiento poblacional en al mundo; Analysis de la situacion argentina. Inpacto en el sistema de salud [World population aging: An analysis of the Argentine situation. Impact of the health system]. *Revista Hospital Italiano, X*(2), pp. 61-77.

Somoza, J. L. (1973). La mortalidad en la Argentina entre 1869 y 1969 [Mortality in Argentina between 1869 and 1969)]. In *Temas de poblacion de la Argentina, aspectos demografios*, pp. 21-40 [Issues on Argentine population. Demographic aspects]. (Series E, No. 13). Buenos Aires: CELADE.

United Nations. (1956). *The aging of populations and its economic and social implications.* New York: U.N. Department of Economic and Social Affairs.

9

Family Care of the Elderly in Hong Kong

NELSON W. S. CHOW

Introduction

Among different societies in the world, Hong Kong is probably the best place for a study of the changing role of the family in supporting the elderly. On the one hand, more than 98% of the population in Hong Kong is Chinese by race and known for a tradition of respecting the old (Chow, 1987). On the other, economic development in the last 40 years has made Hong Kong one of the most developed and affluent cities in East and Southeast Asia (Chen, 1979). With such economic success, it is only natural for one to expect Hong Kong to encounter similar problems as other industrial societies such as the aging of its population, the weakening of its family system, and the loosening of some of its traditional values. In other words, as a result of the economic changes, the Chinese families in Hong Kong may no longer be capable of taking care of their elderly members as in the past, and there would be a greater pressure on the state to provide the necessary support and care (Chow, 1983). To what extent would the above assumptions be correct? As Hong Kong grows in affluence and becomes more urbanized, would families there necessarily give less attention to their elderly members? Could the traditional value of respecting the old resist the onslaught of the modern forces of industrialization and urbanization? If Hong Kong is following in the footsteps of other industrial societies in requiring a greater input from the state in providing care for the elderly, should the same public social services system be adopted? Are there other alternatives for Hong Kong that would suit its situation better?

This chapter on family support of the elderly in Hong Kong is written to answer the above questions. The discussion will begin with a description of the situation of the elderly in Hong Kong. The traditional values surrounding the Chinese family system and the way in which the elderly should be cared for are then examined. The societal changes that have occurred as a result of the industrialization process and their impact on family support of the elderly will follow. The discussion will be concluded with an evaluation of the efforts made by both the people and the government of Hong Kong in providing care for the elderly.

Family Support and Filial Piety

Just as in other industrial societies, the population of Hong Kong is aging rapidly. Twenty years ago, in 1971, more than half of the population in Hong Kong was under 21 years old, while those aged 60 and above accounted for just 7.4% (Chow, 1990). In 1981 the proportion of the population aged 60 and above increased to 10.3% and further increased to 12.8% in 1991. As Hong Kong has, by early 1991, a total population of more than 5.7 million, the number of the elderly came close to around 730,000. This figure may not seem excessive compared to similar ones of the Western industrial societies, but it should be noted that people who are growing old in Hong Kong are often migrants, having moved to Hong Kong in the late 1940s and early 1950s. They are, therefore, the first generation who have experienced aging in a modern industrial society (Chow, 1988a). In other words, the environment and, thus, the value orientation within which they now grow old is very different from the one with which they were acquainted when they were young. This has resulted in a discrepancy between the kind of care they may expect from their families and what they are actually receiving from them. Studies on family care of the elderly conducted in Hong Kong clearly indicate that while the elderly generally expect their families and, in particular, their children to take care of them, the latter have often been found to be either unwilling or unable to do so (Law, 1982). Therefore the expectation of the elderly toward family care does not always mesh with the reality.

Despite the changing situation, evidence indicates that filial piety still remains as one of the most fundamental values of the Chinese in Hong Kong. A survey in 1985 reported that 87.6% of the respondents either agreed or strongly agreed, according to Lau and Kuan (1988), that "the first thing to do in order to build a good society was to have everyone practicing filial piety" (p. 59). And filial piety can only be influential when it is linked up with the significant position occupied by the Chinese family system (Fei, 1985). Latourette (1964) described the traditional Chinese family system as one that "had a leading part in economic life, in social control, in moral education, and in government" (p. 565). The importance of the traditional family system, therefore, did not come only from the many roles it undertook on behalf of the wider society (Baker, 1979). Furthermore, five cardinal relationships were identified in traditional China as existing between kings and subjects, fathers and sons, husbands and wives, among brothers, and, last, between friends. It is important to note that three of the above five applied to family members with the most fundamental relationship being that between parents and children. In the old Chinese classics, particularly in the teachings of Confucius, children were admonished not only to support their old parents but also to show them respect (Freedman, 1979). Filial piety was, thus, important not only in ensuring that the elderly were properly taken care of by their families but also as a means to regulate the behavior between family members or even those within the wider society. As Yang (1959) wrote:

> While the functioning of filial piety was limited to relationships between parents and children, their veneration of age was traditionally a means of inspiring respect and obedience by the young toward all the other senior members of the family and society as a whole. (p. 51)

Based on the notion of filial piety, a network of relationships was established in traditional China with distinct entitlements and obligations. It is difficult to ascertain the extent to which these entitlements and obligations are still true of the Chinese in Hong Kong, but up to the 1960s the Hong Kong Government (1965) still believed that a public policy on the elderly was not necessary and argued:

> It is of the greatest importance that social welfare services should not be organized in such a way as to make it easier for social disruptive influences to gain a hold over the community, or to accelerate the breakdown of the natural or traditional sense of responsibility—for example by encouraging the natural family unit to shed on to social welfare agencies, public or private, its moral responsibility to care for the aged or infirm. (p. 5)

This belief of the Hong Kong Government had to be modified in later years when the Working Party, set up in 1972, reported that the need of the elderly for public social services could no longer be ignored and that the family system could not totally be relied upon to provide the necessary care and support for the elderly members (Working Party on the Future Needs of the Elderly, 1973). Notwithstanding the acceptance of a public policy on the elderly, however, the Hong Kong Government has never failed to stress the important role of the family in taking care of its elderly members. The most recent policy paper on social welfare (Hong Kong Government, 1991) states that

> social networks are part of Chinese culture and tradition and have always existed in Hong Kong. They are most clearly demonstrated in the role of the family as the primary providers of care and welfare. (p. 18)

The government further stated that "The family unit is a vital component of society. . . . The family is a source of support and strength in the care of the infirm and the elderly" (p. 19). Thus it is clear that while the traditional notion of filial piety is gradually diminishing in its importance, as is family support of the elderly, the Hong Kong Government is only prepared to adopt a policy that, rather than taking over the responsibility of the family, aims mainly at supplementing what the family fails to provide. The question remains, of course, to what extent is this kind of policy successful in providing care for the elderly?

The Diminishing Family Role and Care in the Community

Apart from the fading notion of filial piety, another challenge to family support of the elderly came from the drastic changes the family system itself has undergone in Hong Kong (Lee, 1991). The Chinese family has often given the image that it must be an extended one in which, says Latourette (1964), "parents enjoyed a serene old age, honored by all, with their descendants about them, and tenderly cared for as declining years brought physical weakness" (p. 572). In reality, except for the wealthy ones, the traditional Chinese family has never been large, and the image is certainly not true in present-day Hong Kong (Lee, 1991). Since the early 1980s the average size of the Hong Kong family has been found to be less than four persons, and the figure for 1991 was 3.4. Furthermore, the results of the 1986 bi-census showed that out of 596,456 elderly persons,

65,559 (11.0%) were living alone, 250,931 (42.1%) were living with their unmarried children, and only 162,483 (27.2%) were living in what is generally described as extended families, with the rest in other types of accommodations (Central Committee on Services for the Elderly, 1988). Evidence indicates that more and more elderly persons in Hong Kong must face the reality of leading an independent life without the immediate availability of support from their family members. This change in the pattern of family support is attributable to the following phenomena.

First, as previously mentioned, the majority of the elderly in Hong Kong have migrated to live here after World War II, and some of them have never succeeded in getting married and building a family (Ikels, 1983). As a result, and it is probably true of most of those who now live alone, they simply have to do without the support of a family. Another reason to account for the increasing number of the elderly living alone is that in the last few years a substantial number of families, about 20,000 a year, have emigrated, very often leaving behind their elderly parents (Chu & Lo, 1989). Last, even if the elderly have children in Hong Kong, the development of new towns, which now accommodate about 40% of the total population, has often attracted the young married couples, while their elderly parents remain in the old districts. A recent report on housing for the elderly found that in some of the old public housing estates, the percentage of aged residents may be as high as 1 in 4, whereas in the new towns, the percentage may be less than 1 in 20 (Working Party on Housing for the Elderly, 1989). In other words both internal and external migration have the same effect of reducing the amount of family support of which the elderly can avail themselves.

The above changing phenomena have not gone unnoticed. It has been mentioned that in 1972 the Working Party had been established to look into the needs of the elderly and to make appropriate recommendations for the government to follow. The Working Party reported a year later. Admitting the diminishing role of the family in providing care for the elderly, the Working Party suggested an approach that later became the direction for further development of services for the elderly in Hong Kong. In brief, the approach proposed was to concentrate on "care in the community" as the guiding principle. This meant, said the Working Party on the Future Needs of the Elderly (1973), that

> services should be aimed primarily at enabling the elderly to remain as long as possible as members of the community at large, either living by themselves or with members of their family, rather than at providing the elderly with care

in residential institutions outside the community to which they are accustomed. (p. 15)

The services referred to included community nursing, home help, day care, laundry and canteen services, social and recreational activities, hostel accommodation, and sheltered employment. Respite care has been added recently. Members of the Working Party (1973) further believed that this approach "makes the best sense from the point of view of the elderly themselves, their families, and the community at large" (p. 15).

In theory the care in the community approach has its attractions as it is in line with the Chinese tradition, which stresses the importance of the elderly's remaining as members of the community and being accepted by their own families. Few objections can be raised, at least conceptually, against the "care in the community" approach but, as Little (1979) had pointed out, "While lip-service is given to the value of community living for the elderly, home-delivered services to supplement family care are in most countries seriously deficient" (p. 10). This is also true of the situation in Hong Kong. The shortage of services has now become a permanent phenomenon despite the repeated demonstration by surveys on social service needs of the elderly that the supply is lagging far behind the demand (Hong Kong University, 1982). By the end of March 1991, the demand for 30 multiservice centers for the elderly has only been met by a provision of 17, with a shortfall of 13; the demand for 30 day care centers by a provision of 9; and the demand for 247 social centers by a provision of 155 (Social Welfare Department, 1991b, Chapter 6).

Other than a lack of support services to enable the elderly to remain as members of the community, the adoption of the care in the community approach has also resulted in an underdevelopment of residential services for the elderly. Thus by early 1991, despite a demand for 8,150 places in government-subsidized care and attention homes, only 3,232 were provided, with a shortfall of 4,919 (Social Welfare Department, 1991b, Chapter 6). The severe shortage of government-subsidized places has created a market for unregulated (and often substandard) private homes, which, though with a short history since 1982, now provide accommodation for more than 10,000 infirm elderly (Kwan, 1988). In brief, the care in the community approach has yet to become a reality in Hong Kong.

While the supply of community support services is unable to catch up with the demand, other shortcomings of the care in the community approach are also exposed. First, when the Working Party (1973) put up its recommendation for the adoption of this approach, members admitted that they "looked for solutions which . . . would cost less, would make the least demand on scarce manpower resources and that could be implemented reasonably quickly" (p. 44). Although the adoption of the approach may cost less to the government, however, it is obvious that families that have elderly members to take care of are bearing the expenses either directly or indirectly. A study of the elderly awaiting admission into care and attention homes revealed that the main reason for application into these homes is that most families could no longer afford to have someone staying at home to look after the elderly. Even when they managed to do so, it often implies a sharp reduction in family income as someone would not be able to go out to work (Chow, 1988b). From the angle of family finance, the care in the community approach is definitely an extremely expensive one.

Recent studies have also found that the Working Party, in making its recommendation, has failed to examine in sufficient detail the dynamics and relations among the family, the community and the elderly themselves. In his study on the dynamics of family care for the elderly, Young (1990) found that the life satisfaction of the elderly was not determined by the support that they received either from their own families or the community. He refuted, therefore, the proposition of the Working Party that, when some care was provided either by their families or the community at large, the elderly would be content in a familiar environment. Indeed, in proposing the care in the community approach, the Working Party has never made clear the role of family care in relation to other community support services and the part that the family should play in the care of the elderly. What has been assumed is that the Chinese family in Hong Kong should continue to perform its function as caregiver for the elderly and that as long as the elderly were living in the community, and best with their families, they should be happy. What kind of community, however, are the elderly in Hong Kong living in? What type of care can they expect from their families and neighbors?

The Changing Community and Family Care

When the Working Party (1973) adopted the care in the community approach as the guiding principle for the future development of services for the elderly, it referred to the community either as the environment that the elderly knew or as sources from which the elderly could possibly obtain care and attention (p. 15). Thus the community possesses a geographical dimension and, at the same time, implies a set of social relationships within which help is available. This insistence on the role of the community has not changed over the years, as the recent policy paper on social welfare (Social Welfare Department, 1991a) stated that while social welfare services should be made available to all, "such an objective cannot be achieved without the support of an input from the community through the establishment of networks of informal care and support provided by families, friends and neighbors" (p. 18). Even if one can accept the contributions of the "community," however, one has still to ask: Does this network of informal care and support exist naturally or does it have to be created? What are the sets of social relationships that exist to provide the elderly with the necessary care and support? What is the relationship between this network of informal support and the system of formal care? What is the role of family care in all these formal and informal networks?

In a report of the Barclay Committee published in the United Kingdom in 1982 (Barclay Report, 1982), *community* was defined as "a network or networks of informal relationships between people connected with each other by kinship, common interests, geographical proximity, friendship, occupation, or the giving and receiving of services or various combinations of these" (p. 199). As far as Hong Kong is concerned, the networks of relationships established between the elderly and other people as a result of kinship, geographical proximity and a giving and/or receiving of services will be most applicable. It has been mentioned that the unextended nuclear family in Hong Kong has long been the norm rather than the exception, and that due to various reasons, about 1 in 4 of the elderly are either living alone, with another person, or in collective households (Central Committee on Services for the Elderly, 1988).

For those who are living with their children, as the average household has fewer than four persons, the number of family members who are able and willing to help must be very small. In a study on the size of the informal support network, defined as those persons who were ready to offer help, Ngan (1990) found that 13.6% of the elderly respondents had not even one person to offer help while 58.5% had one to three persons. And those ready to help were mostly family members or their immediate kin. In another study on the health situation of the elderly, Lee and Chi (1990) found that fewer than two persons were ready to offer help to each elderly respondent, when sick or injured, and these (again) were mostly family members and close relatives. Hence, although kinship relationships still form an essential element of the community from which the elderly can receive care and support, it is rapidly dwindling in size and is often restricted to one to two immediate family members.

If the community of kinship relationships is diminishing in its importance, is there any possibility for it to provide compensation by the relationships established among neighbors, especially as families in Hong Kong are progressively split because of internal migration? Nearly all data available on the degree of neighborliness in Hong Kong, measured in terms of the frequency of contacts between neighbors, indicate that the situation is less than desirable (Chan, 1990). In a study on the life-style of the elderly in Hong Kong, respondents answered that when they needed help in their daily life, they would first turn to their children (48%), followed by their spouses (24%), and only 11% mentioned their friends and neighbors (Chow & Kwan, 1986). More recent studies by Ngan (1990) and Young (1990) also obtained similar results.

This situation is, in fact, not particular to Hong Kong. A 1960 national survey of social networks in adult life in the United States (Antonucci & Akiyama, 1987) also reported that "82% of the support networks consisted of family members, only 18% consisted of friends" (p. 523). Thus one can conclude that while neighbors might, in the future, become a more important source of help for the elderly in Hong Kong, there is little likelihood that they can replace family members. Ideologically, as discussed above, the obligations on neighbors to help are not as strong as that on the family.

There is, of course, another possibility from the formal care network, comprising the services provided either by the government or the nongovernment organizations, to replace the informal care of the family. But as mentioned earlier, the provision of services for the elderly is lagging so far behind the demand that only those elderly who, for one reason or another, are deprived of other sources of help can have an access to them. The availability of family support, in fact, often presents itself as an obstacle rather than an asset for an elderly person in seeking help from outside of the family.

To summarize, the "community" that exists in Hong Kong as a source of help to the elderly is mainly the family to which the elderly belong. Neighbors and service networks—at best—only play a supplementary role for a small number of those who either have no family of their own or are fortunate enough to obtain help from their neighbors or social welfare agencies. While the family in Hong Kong still provides a community for the majority of the elderly, the rapidly decreasing percentage of the elderly living with their grown-up children implies that the community, which formulates the basis of the care in the community approach, is weakening in strength. Furthermore, currently it is very rare to find an aunt or other close relatives, who are usually very good helpers, to become a member of the household. The increasing number of married women employed outside of the family is another phenomenon that has, and will continue to, weaken the caring function of the family. Indeed it is often the simple unavailability of caregivers within the family, rather than their unwillingness to provide care, that has posed the most serious threat to the family as a caring institution. A survey of residents of private nursing homes for the elderly (Kwan, 1988) found that the absence of care-givers at home was the major reason for admission. Thus it can be con-cluded that although the family remains as the most important community within which the elderly can obtain care and support, the extent of help available is both limited and diminishing in scope. On the other hand, there is no sign at the present moment that neighbors and service net-works are emerging as viable alternatives to provide care for the elderly.

Factors Influencing Family Care of the Elderly

As the family continues to be the most important source of help to the elderly, and will continue to do so in many years to come, it would be worthwhile to further examine the exact nature of care it provides as well as the factors influencing the performance of its caring role. Before such an examination it should be mentioned that a compulsory public retire-ment pension scheme is still absent in Hong Kong. It is, therefore, not uncommon for the elderly to turn to their grown-up children for financial support; and for those who have no children to support them, their last resort would be to apply for public assistance. At present, about 10% of the elderly in Hong Kong are receiving public assistance at around $150 (U.S. dollars) a month (Social Welfare Department, 1991a). The other form of cash payment is the old age allowance at around $50 (U.S. dollars) a month, which is available to all Hong Kong residents upon reaching the age of 65. As only a small portion of the elderly are receiving retirement pensions, many families in Hong Kong must continue to take the respon-sibility of looking after the financial needs of their elderly members, and the task is admittedly not an easy one.

Besides financial support, the other forms of care more frequently offered by the family, as found in the study on the life-style of the elderly previously mentioned, included escorting the elderly to go out, washing, shopping, cleaning, and cooking. Even in areas where the elderly most needed help, support was provided to less than a third of the respondents, those who were usually the more senior ones of 70 years and above (Chow & Kwan, 1986, p. 51). Lee and Chi (1990) also found that about half of their respondents did not need any kind of assistance in their daily living; for those who needed help, the extent was confined to one or two items. The majority of the elderly living in the community do not, in fact, require a great deal of care from their families. Rather than putting an immense burden on their family members, the study on the life-style of the elderly found that many of the elderly were more often doing a lot in providing support for their families than the other way around. Regarding the elderly respondents who were living with their grown-up children, the study reported that 76% of them helped in looking after the home when other family members went out; 68% helped in doing various household chores; and 39% helped in taking care of their grandchildren (Chow & Kwan, 1986, p. 52). Furthermore, the study also found that those who provided help in housekeeping and looking after their grandchildren usually maintained a better relationship with other family members.

This confirms the observation once made by Walker (1987) that "we know from research, for example, that the provision of family care is based on reciprocity, exchange, and other interdependence rather than individualistic values" (p. 378). In her study on the relationship between social support and health status of the elderly in Hong Kong, Ho (1989) also concluded that "just the sense of belonging maintained by the frequent contact and interaction with the network members, and the perception that support would be needed, have important beneficial effects on health" (p. 10).

Hence despite all the rhetoric about filial piety in a Chinese society, it does not seem that this age-old tradition has been particularly influential in fostering a harmonious relationship between the elderly and their children, and thus the likelihood that the former will receive support from the latter. It is, admittedly, difficult to definitely verify or refute the relevance of traditional concepts such as respecting the old; but as far as the provision of family care to the elderly is concerned, evidence indicates that certain factors, such as the extent of assistance that the elderly themselves can offer to other family members, are as important, if not more so, as the simple rhetoric of filial piety. In other words, the establishment of a harmonious and reciprocal relationship between the elderly and their family members may be more important than simply exhorting the young to respect the old.

The Complementary Roles of Formal and Informal Care

Accepting that family care is limited in scope and there is little chance for neighbors to become a viable alternative "caring community," what is left to be examined is the extent to which formal care can complement family care. In adopting the care in the community approach as the guiding principle for the future development of services for the elderly, the Hong Kong Government (1979) committed that it would provide

> a range of community services and improved cash benefits that will encourage families to look after their elderly members, or which will enable old people on their own to live independently, and in dignity, in the community for as long as possible. (p. 14)

As discussed above, the promise of the Hong Kong Government to provide the elderly with the necessary community support services has not materialized. As a result, many of the elderly living in the community are unable to lead an independent life, not to mention a dignified one. The inadequate provision of community support services has also produced two unintended effects when the care in the community approach was first proposed.

First, as services are not available to all who need them, they are offered to those perceived to be in the greatest need, who often happen to be the frail elderly people without a family. Even among recipients of public assistance, the proportion of lonely elderly is much higher than those living with their families, about 9:1 (Social Welfare Department, 1991a). This situation is not special to Hong Kong; a national study (Stone, Cafferata, & Sangl, 1987) of caregiving for the frail elderly in the United States reported that "Less than 10% [of caregivers] reported the use of paid services, and those who did rely on formal care were assisting the most severely impaired elders" (p. 625). Although the care in the community approach in Hong Kong also includes the lonely elderly, particularly the frail ones (as its target of assistance), the overconcentration of both cash assistance and community support services on this group implies that most families with elderly members can scarcely obtain any outside help. Hence with the community support services concentrated on the lonely elderly and more families increasingly finding themselves unable to look after their elderly members, it is not surprising that the care in the community approach in Hong Kong has been ridiculed as "care by the family," or even "the elderly people caring for themselves."

Second, as families caring for elderly members often fail to obtain outside support, some inevitably take the task in a negative manner and this has often made the elderly feel unwanted. Chi and Lee (1989) found that elderly people who were satisfied with their lives were those who were financially independent, healthy, and active. Those requiring support and care from their families were less satisfied. It is difficult to conclude that families actually make their elderly members feel unhappy, but they would certainly find the task much lighter if they could obtain outside help.

There is no doubt that the care in the community approach adopted in Hong Kong has only partially achieved its objectives. The failure is mainly caused by the inadequate provision of community support services that leaves, as a result, most of the families caring for elderly members without the necessary support. In other words, community support services have yet to play a complementary role to family support as they were intended to do. The two systems of community support services and family care are, therefore, not forming a complete "caring community" for the elderly. While both are needed, they seem to be serving two different groups of elderly people: one with families and the other without, and only on rare occasions would there be interaction between the two types of support.

Integration of Formal and Informal Care

The above examination of the care in the community approach adopted in Hong Kong indicates that despite the fact that the family system still formulates the main source of help, there is an increasing demand for formal community support services. So far the two systems are serving two different target groups of elderly persons, and they have yet to truly integrate with each other. Indeed it is questionable whether formal and informal support should be identified as two separate systems. Walker (1987) suggested that the rigid division between the formal and informal sectors should be overcome and it is better to think more in terms of "social support networks," which "may comprise both formal and informal helps, professional and nonprofessional personnel" (p. 381). Bulmer (1987) also suggested that, in addition to the family, different types of networks should be built up to provide social support for the elderly: personal, volunteer, mutual aid, neighborhood, and community empowerment.

So far as Hong Kong is concerned, it will be a long time before the formal and informal sectors can be fully integrated to enable the elderly to live in the community in dignity. For the majority of them the family continues to be their most reliable source of help. Despite the family's diminishing functions, it is important to ensure that family members are not overburdened in their task of caring for the old and, hence, forced to give it up by institutionalizing the elderly. There are already signs that many families are doing exactly this as seen by the increasing number of private nursing homes. More adequate provision of formal support services, which are presently mainly taken up by the lonely elderly without families, would probably help to relieve the burden on the family caregivers; but the help available from friends and neighbors should be further explored. A study (Chow, 1988c) conducted in the Tuen Mun new town in Hong Kong found that as residents there are farther away from their relatives, they tend to turn more to their neighbors for help and assistance and a higher degree of neighborliness has resulted. Attempts have also been made to organize mutual-aid groups among the elderly themselves.

Conclusion

What can be ascertained is that with the changes in values and the structure of the family system, the elderly in Hong Kong can no longer take it for granted, as in the past, that family care will be available to support them. The most recent policy paper on social welfare (Hong Kong Government, 1991) also admits that though "In Hong Kong . . . it is accepted as a family responsibility to look after older members as far as possible . . . these values are subject to challenges and pressures as society develops (p. 30). Thus the provision of care outside of the family is no longer optional, but, rather, must be recognized as playing an equally important role in enabling the elderly to live in the community in dignity.

References

Antonucci, T. C., & Akiyama, H. (1987). Social networks in adult life and a preliminary examination of the convoy model. *Journal of Gerontology, 42*(5), 519-527.

Baker, H. D. R. (1979). *Chinese family and kinship.* London: Macmillan.

Barclay Report. (1982). *Social workers: Their role and tasks.* London: Bedford Square.

Bulmer, M. (1987). *The social basis of community care.* London: Allen and Unwin.

Central Committee on Services for the Elderly. (1988). *Report of the central committee on services for the elderly.* Hong Kong: Hong Kong Government Printer.

Chan, C. L. W. (1990). Community care in Hong Kong: Questions to the answered. In Community Development Resource Book Editorial Committee (Eds.), *Community development resource book 1989-1990* (pp. 25-32). Hong Kong: Hong Kong Council of Social Service.

Chen, E. K. Y. (1979). *Hyber-growth in Asian economies.* London: Macmillan.

Chow, N. W. S. (1983). The Chinese family and support of the elderly in Hong Kong. *The Gerontologist, 23*(6), 584-588.

Chow, N. W. S. (1987). Western and Chinese ideas of social welfare. *International Social Work, 30,* 31-41.

Chow, N. W. S. (1988a). *Caregiving in developing East and Southeast Asian countries.* Tampa, Florida: International Exchange Center on Gerontology, The University of South Florida.

Chow, N. W. S. (1988b). *Caregiving for the elderly awaiting admission into care and attention homes.* Hong Kong: Department of Social Work and Social Administration, University of Hong Kong.

Chow, N. W. S. (1988c). The quality of life of Tuen Mun inhabitants. *The Asian Journal of Public Administration, 10*(2), 194-206.

Chow, N. W. S. (1990). Aging in Hong Kong. In B. K. P. Leung (Ed.), *Social issues in Hong Kong* (pp. 164-178). Hong Kong: Oxford University Press.

Chow, N. W. S., & Kwan, A. Y. H. (1986). *A study of the changing life of the elderly in low-income families in Hong Kong.* Hong Kong: Writers' and Publishers' Cooperative.

Chu, I. P. L., & Lo, K. Y. (1989). An exploratory study on adjustment of the elderly separated from family members who had emigrated to overseas countries. *Hong Kong Journal of Gerontology, 3*(2), 34-36.

Fei, X. T. (1985). The caring of the old in families undergoing structural changes. In C. Chien (Ed.), *Proceedings of the conference on modernization and Chinese culture* (pp. 3-12). Hong Kong: The Chinese University of Hong Kong.

Freedman, M. (1979). *The study of Chinese society.* (Essays selected by E. W. Skinner.) Stanford: Stanford University Press.

Ho, S. C. (1989). Social support parameters and health status among the Hong Kong elderly. *Hong Kong Journal of Gerontology, 3*(2), 4-12.

Hong Kong Government. (1965). *The aims and policy for social welfare in Hong Kong.* Hong Kong: Hong Kong Government Printer.

Hong Kong Government. (1979). *Social welfare into the 1980s.* Hong Kong: Hong Kong Government Printer.

Hong Kong Government. (1991). *Social welfare into the 1990s and beyond.* Hong Kong: Hong Kong Government Printer.

Hong Kong University, Department of Social Work. (1982). *A study of the welfare needs of the elderly in Hong Kong: The needs of the elderly living in the community.* Hong Kong: Author.

Ikels, C. (1983). *Aging and adaptation: Chinese in Hong Kong and the United States.* Hamden, CT: Archon.

Kwan, A. Y. H. (1988). *Residential life of the elderly in private elderly homes in Hong Kong.* Hong Kong: Writers' and Publishers' Cooperative.

Latourette, K. S. (1964). *The Chinese, their history and culture.* New York: Macmillan.

Lau, S. K., & Kuan, H. S. (1988). *The ethos of the Hong Kong Chinese.* Hong Kong: The Chinese University Press.

Law, C. K. (1982). *Attitudes toward the elderly.* Hong Kong: Department of Social Work, The University of Hong Kong.

Lee, J. J., & Chi, I. (1990). Determinants on life satisfaction among the Chinese elderly in Hong Kong. *Hong Kong Journal of Gerontology, 4*(1), 29-39.

Lee, R. P. L. (1991). The past and the future of the family and kinship system in Hong Kong. In C. Chen (ed.), *Proceedings of the conference on the Chinese family system and its changes* (pp. 129-144). Hong Kong: The Chinese University of Hong Kong.

Little, V. C. (1979). Open care of the aging: Alternative approaches. *Aging, 301*(2), 10-23.

Ngan, R. M. H. (1990). The availability of informal support networks to the Chinese elderly in Hong Kong and its implications for practice. *Hong Kong Journal of Gerontology, 4*(2), 19-27.

Social Welfare Department. (1991a). *Study of public assistance recipients 1989.* Hong Kong: Social Welfare Department.

Social Welfare Department. (1991b) *The five-year plan for social welfare development in Hong Kong: Review 1991.* Hong Kong: Hong Kong Government Printer.

Stone, R., Cafferata, G. L., & Sangl, J. (1987). Caregivers of the frail elderly: A national profile. *The Gerontologist, 27*(5), 616-626.

Walker, A. (1987). Enlarging the caring capacity of the community: informal support networks and the welfare state. *International Journal of Health Services, 17*(3), 369-386.

Working party on housing for the elderly. (1989). *Report of the working party on housing for the elderly.* Hong Kong: Hong Kong Government Printer.

Working party on the future needs of the elderly. (1973). *Services for the elderly.* Hong Kong: Hong Kong Government Printer.

Yang, C. K. (1959). *The Chinese family in the communist revolution.* Cambridge: Harvard University Press.

Young, S. (1990). *The dynamics of family care for the elderly in Hong Kong.* Unpublished doctoral thesis. Hong Kong: University of Hong Kong.

10

Family Care of the Elderly in Israel

GILA NOAM
JACK HABIB

Demographic Overview and Demographic Changes

Israel's population comprises a wide variety of cultural groups differing in their norms and traditions, educational levels, and demographic structures. The heterogeneity of Israel's population is the result of the immigration of more than 2 million Jews to Israel since the founding of the State in 1948—a phenomenon that almost tripled the original Jewish population. The relatively high proportion of elderly in the various waves of immigration (i.e., about 8% of all immigrants since 1948 were at least 60 years of age upon arrival in Israel, and 18% to 20% were between the ages of 45 to 64) has been a significant factor in the remarkable rate of the aging of Israel's population.

Three major population groups are generally distinguished in Israeli society—Jews of Eastern descent (i.e., of Asian-African origins), Jews of Western descent (i.e., of European-American origins), and the non-Jewish population, which comprises 18% of the total population, primarily Moslems, Christians, and Druze.

Mortality and infant mortality rates in Israel are quite low (10 per 1,000 and 6.6 per 1,000, respectively). Life expectancy at birth is 73.8 years for Jewish men and 77.0 for Jewish women, and 72.5 and 75.5 for non-Jewish men and women, respectively. The proportion of Israeli-born among the Jewish population is on the rise, and includes about two thirds of the population. Among the elderly, however, the vast majority (96%) are still foreign born, and among the foreign-born elderly about three quarters are of European and Western origins and a quarter are from Asian and African countries. These proportions are expected to change, such that by the year 2000 the proportion of elderly of Western and European origins will decline to about 50%, and the proportion of those of Asian-African origins and Israeli born will increase to 38% and 10%, respectively (Be'er & Factor, 1990a).

The rate of growth of the elderly population (age 65 and over) has been very dramatic. The absolute number of Jewish elderly has increased ten-fold since 1948, and the percentage of elderly in the Jewish population has increased almost three-fold (from 3.8% in 1948 to about 10% in 1989). The difference in the age structure of the Jewish and non-Jewish populations is striking—only 3.4% of the non-Jewish population is over the age of 65 as compared with about 10% among Jews.

Sociodemographic Characteristics of the Elderly

The elderly are characterized by a generally low level of education. Some 14% of men and 25% of women aged 65 and over have had no formal schooling, in sharp contrast with the rapid rise in the educational level of the younger generations. This creates a clear "generation gap" with regard to education. Educational diversity is quite high among the elderly, however, and a significant percentage of the Jewish elderly (about 13%) have had postsecondary schooling. Geocultural origin is highly correlated with educational level. Only 6% of the elderly of Western origin received no education as compared to half of those of Asian-African origin and almost 70% of non-Jewish elderly (see Table 10.1).

Over time, a clear trend toward rising educational attainments among the Jewish elderly can be noted. For example, in 1961, 30% of the elderly Jewish population had had no formal schooling, but by 1983 this was the case for only 17%. The trend is particularly notable among elderly women, for whom the percentage with no schooling declined from 40% to 22% over this time period (Noam & Sikron, 1990). While it can be anticipated that the proportion of elderly with no formal schooling will continue to decline, there is no evidence that the gap between the educational level of the elderly and nonelderly populations is declining as well. Within the Jewish population the intergenerational gaps in education are particularly notable among those of Asian and African origin. The percentage of elderly with no formal schooling is more than double that of the nonelderly in these groups.

Table 10.1 Selected Indicators of the Aged Population of Israel

	Total Population	Total Jews	Ethnic Origin Eastern Jews	Western Jews[1]	Total Non-Jews
Total population aged 65+[2] (thousands)	361.3	337.8	85.3	252.3	23.5
% aged 65+[2] of total population	8.9	10.1	5.6	18.5	3.4
% aged 75+[2] of total aged	35.4	35.1	33.1	35.8	39.1
% women of total[2]	53.1	53.3	52.9	53.5	50.3
% of married[2]					
Total	60.0	60.2	57.6	61.1	56.2
Men	81.1	80.9	82.6	80.4	83.4
Women	41.3	42.0	35.3	44.3	30.8
% with no formal education[2]					
Total	20.3	16.9	50.1	5.7	69.4
Men	14.5	11.4	33.7	3.9	57.5
Women	25.3	21.6	66.6	7.0	81.4
Living arrangements[3] (percentages)					
Men alone	6.4	6.5	5.8	6.8	4.3
Women alone	21.7	21.9	22.3	21.9	17.9
Couple	50.7	52.7	35.5	58.5	21.8
Couple with others	9.8	8.1	18.5	4.6	34.9
Other	11.8	10.7	17.9	8.0	21.2
Total	100	100	100	100	100
Elderly living in long-term care institutions	4.1	4.4	3.2	4.8	0.3

NOTE: 1. The vast majority of Israeli-born Jews are of European origin (according to father's country of birth) therefore they are included in the Europe-America category.
2. SOURCE: The Aged in Israel: A Selection of Census Data. (1983). (Census of population and housing publication no. 11). Jerusalem, 1986.
3. SOURCE: Based on survey by the Central Bureau of Statistics of a probability sample (n = 4, 189) of the Israeli population aged 60 and over, 1985.

The educational level of non-Jewish elderly is particularly low, and no indication of dramatic change can be discerned. Between 1961 and 1983 the percentage of those with no formal schooling remained stable—about 77%. A very large gap exists between the educational level of the elderly and the nonelderly among the non-Jews. In 1983 the median of years of schooling for the nonelderly was about 9 years of schooling, as compared to one year among the elderly. This gap reflects the increasing exposure of the younger non-Jewish population to the educational opportunity system and to compulsory education, while the elderly cannot avail themselves of these opportunities.

Some 60% of the elderly are married, with the percentage of married men being almost double that of women—81% and 41%, respectively. The percentage of elderly living alone is quite small—28% among Jews and 22% among non-Jews, and the majority of elderly reside with their spouses —62% of Jewish and 57% of non-Jewish elderly. There are clear differences between the two groups, however, with regard to household composition. Among the Jewish elderly not living alone, most (52%) reside in single-generation households, while among the non-Jews this is the case for only 22%. Clear differences with regard to household composition may also be noted between elderly men and women. The percentage of women living alone (35%) is more than two and a half times greater than of men (13.6%). These differences have clear implications for gender differences in the availability of social support.

The economic status of the elderly is quite heterogeneous. On the average, the relative income position of the elderly compares very favorably with most Western countries, but the percentage with low incomes close to the poverty line is very high. Slightly over a third of the elderly receive supplementary grants from the National Insurance Institute, which are granted to those for whom the old-age pension allowance constitutes the major source of income.

The percentage of work-related pensions received by males is twice that of females (46.8% and 21%, respectively), and more men have income from current employment. The percentage receiving work-related pensions is higher among younger cohorts of the elderly population, reflecting relatively recent developments in the pension system and the increase in the accumulation of rights to work-related pensions. Nevertheless it will take some time before more significant numbers of elderly will be eligible for such pensions.

In comparison with other countries, labor force participation among the elderly in Israel is high, and the trend towards early retirement is much less evident. Among the young-old (ages 65 to 74), about 40% of the men are employed, and even among those 75 and over, 17% continue to be employed. Employment among elderly women is much rarer (11% of women over the age of 65), reflecting the fact that for the present generation of elderly women employment outside the home at a younger age was not common.

Despite the fact that labor force participation among the elderly in Israel is relatively high, there are indications that it is decreasing, particularly among men. In 1966, 43% of elderly Jewish men were in the labor force, as compared with 23% in 1989. Rising unemployment and the need to absorb large numbers of immigrants in jobs may render employment of elderly Israelis problematic. A slight increase in the labor force participation of women over age 60 can be discerned. For both men and women there is a positive relationship between European origin, level of education, and participation in the labor force.

Traditional Values

Among the most central components of the Israeli social ethic is the commitment to the "in-gathering of exiles" and the absorption of immigrants, perceived as being at the very heart of Israel's role as the center for Jews the world over and as the place of refuge for Jews in distress.

The "Law of Return" stipulates that virtually no element of selectivity should characterize the immigration policy. Indeed, over the State's 43-year history, hundreds of thousands of immigrants have been absorbed from a very broad range of countries, and linguistic and cultural backgrounds, with virtually no selectivity being put into effect despite the tremendous difficulties involved in absorbing such numbers of new immigrants.

Another central social value is the settlement of Jews throughout the country, including relatively underdeveloped and outlying areas. Over the years the policy of scattering the population throughout the country was implemented primarily by settling new immigrants in the outlying areas. A certain level of tension arose between the simultaneous attempts to realize both the goal of integration of immigrants into the mainstream of Israeli society and the dispersal of the population.

The Economic System

Israel is a highly industrialized country, with only about 5% of the population employed in agriculture. Several unique types of cooperative settlements characterize the agricultural sector, including the *kibbutz* and the *moshav*. Among the non-Jewish population, family plots of varying size still constitute a source of supplementary employment and income.

Israel is a modern welfare state, but for many years the government's involvement in the economy was greater than that of most governments of such states. It is characterized by a very strong commitment to full employment, linked to the commitment to absorption of immigrants (Ben-Porat, 1989).

In recent years privatization of services has increased dramatically, partly because of the difficulties faced by the public sector in coping with social challenges in meeting the demand for services. For example, between 1987 and 1989 the number of private-sector beds in long-term care institutions grew at a rate double that of the growth in the number of beds in the institutional system as a whole (17% versus 9%), and over these 2 years the private sector contributed almost two thirds of the increase in the number of beds (Be'er & Factor, 1990b). Another dramatic example of the recent expansion of private services is the entry of the private sector into the provision of home care services in the wake of the Community Long-Term Care Insurance Law (see below).

The Role of the Elderly in the Community and in the Family

Activity in the labor force is one channel of social participation in which, as noted above, a considerable proportion of the elderly population is involved. In addition, there is a growing interest in the potential contribution of the older population to voluntary activities, in light of the need to provide the elderly with opportunities to continue to make a meaningful contribution to society. There is also the need to attract new population groups to voluntary activities, as more and more women—the traditional manpower reservoir for such activities—become less available for volunteer activities, in light of their growing participation in the labor force.

National data (Steigman, 1988) indicate that 10% of those 60 and older are involved in some form of voluntary activity, whether through formal organizations or privately. Efforts are now concentrated at expanding the involvement of those segments of the elderly population that have been less active in voluntary activities up to now—that is, those with lower education and class status and of Asian-African origins.

In general, the nonwork activities of the elderly tend to vary by geo-cultural origin. Those of Asian-African origin are generally more involved in family-related activities, while those of Western origin are more extensively involved in relations with their peers. National survey data

(Steigman, 1988) indicate that about a fifth of the elderly are members of clubs, and participation in adult educational programs is on the increase.

Generally, the basic respect for the elderly, which has always been an integral part of the Israeli value system, continues to be expressed on various levels. Beyond the various customs reflected in individual daily behavior (such as getting up to give the elderly a seat on the bus), the fact that services for the elderly are among the few areas with regard to which public budgets have been expanded, without engendering any public debate or evidence of intergenerational conflict, seems to be indicative of continued adherence to this value.

Despite this, evidence exists of negative attitudes of professional service providers toward the elderly, including the reluctance of health professionals to specialize in geriatrics (Bergman, 1970), to have elderly or chronically ill patients on their case load (Shuval, Javetz, & Shai, 1988), and reluctance of social work students to specialize in social work geared to the needs of the elderly (Katan & Aviram, 1986). Furthermore, a study on the knowledge and attitudes of teenagers concerning the elderly (Eaglstein & Weinsberg, 1985) revealed considerable ignorance about the elderly and several negative stereotypes. The issue of abuse of the elderly has recently come to the fore, and in 1989 the Ministry of Police issued a report summarizing the recommendations of a committee that had examined the subject (Ministry of Police, 1989). The report did not present data on the scope of the problem but recommended the establishment of a telephone hot line, the expansion of social services in hospitals to deal with cases of abuse, and the dissemination of information to the elderly on their rights.

The Elderly and Their Families

In Israel, as in most societies, it has been clearly established that the informal support system plays a major role in the care of the elderly (Habib, Factor, Naon, & Brodsky, 1986; Krulik, Hirschfeld, & Sharon, 1984; Morginstin & Werner, 1986). At the same time there is a widespread belief that the role of the family is changing or, at least, will change in the future. It is argued that norms of care for the elderly differ among Israel's various cultural groups and, yet, that these will converge as the strength of family ties weaken within the more traditional population groups.

Family care of the elderly may be examined on various levels. First, the potential for family support and care may be estimated on the basis of the availability of a spouse, children and siblings and of the elderly individual's living arrangements and proximity to children. Proximity to family members, and living arrangements, serve to facilitate family ties and, at the same time, may also reflect their strength.

Second, analyses of frequency and patterns of interaction between the elderly and their families may be conducted. Finally, the actual flow of various forms of emotional and instrumental support between the elderly and members of their families may be viewed as a direct indicator of family care.

Elderly men enjoy greater access, at least potentially, to informal support than do elderly women. While 81% of elderly males are married, only about half that number—41%—of elderly females are married. Among males, there are no significant differences in marital status among ethnic groups, but among females, the differences are clear. A higher percentage of women of Western origin (44%) are married as compared with those of Eastern origin (35%) and non-Jewish women (31%). To a great extent, these differences stem from differences in the husband-wife age gap among the various groups, and are expected to narrow with increasing modernization of marital patterns.

All subgroups in the population are characterized by a very high percentage of elderly with living children—88% for Jewish and 95% for non-Jewish elderly. The gap among various origin groups is more pronounced when examined in terms of average number of children. While for Jews of Eastern origin and for non-Jews the average number of children is 5 and 5.5, respectively, for Western Jews it is less than half—2.2.

A somewhat larger gap exists between Jews of Western and Eastern origin with regard to the presence of siblings—78% of elderly Eastern Jews have at least one living sibling as compared with 63% of Western Jews and 73% of non-Jews. The most notable difference among population subgroups exists with regard to the presence of friends and neighbors. For example, while only 44% of Eastern-origin elderly reported having friends, parallel percentages for those of Western origin and for the non-Jews were 75% and 86%, respectively.

The presence of family members at close distance to the elderly person facilitates ties between them and renders support more readily available. Considerable differences exist among the various ethnic groups with regard to proximity of the nearest child, reflecting the differences among them in the average number of children. While about 10% of Western Jewish elderly have a child living in the same household, about a third of the Eastern Jewish elderly and half the non-Jewish elderly reside with at least one child. Similar differences prevail among ethnic groups with regard to percentages having a child residing in the same neighborhood. A study on the kinship networks of the elderly in Israel (Noam, 1989) obtained information on the actual distances between the elderly's place of residence and that of their nearest child. The average distance was only about 5 kilometers.

Data from a study on the living conditions and family-life of rural Arab elderly in Israel (Weihl, Azaiza, King, & Goldsher, 1986) indicated that the vast majority (almost 80%) of Arab elderly who do not reside with a child, but have a child residing in the same village as the parents, often in adjacent homes. As a result, they often make use of facilities or services available in their children's homes.

Against this background of generally close residential proximity between the elderly and their families, actual patterns of interaction may be examined. Contacts with children are virtually universal, and of those having children, only 4% to 8% do not see a child at least once a month. The frequency of meetings is much higher among non-Jews; 81% see their children once every 2 days, as opposed to 44% of all the elderly; but there is only a relatively small difference between Jews from Eastern and Western backgrounds in the frequency of interaction between the elderly and their families. Contacts with siblings, friends, and neighbors are more frequent among the elderly of Western origin and, thus, seem to substitute for their fewer contacts with children. On the other hand, the greater availability of all network members among non-Jews is paralleled by higher rates of contact with all network components. In addition to visiting, telephone contact is prevalent, with 62% of the total elderly population speaking with their children on the phone, almost all at least once a week.

A recent study focused on the qualitative dimensions of the elderly mother/daughter relationship (Noam, 1991). Factor analysis was used to obtain a picture of the perceptions of the relationship by both mothers and daughters. Both perceived intimacy, the possibility of relying on the other for help and advice, respect for the other's autonomy, values, and the like as being relevant dimensions of the relationship. The first factor—relying on the daughter for help—explained 20% of the variance in quality for mothers, while for daughters the first factor was intimacy, explaining 24% of the variance in quality. Positive and significant correlations were found for mothers between the degree of mother's disability and scores on the ability to rely on the daughter and intimacy. For daughters, four dimensions of quality were found to be significantly and negatively correlated with mother's disability. That is, the more disabled the mother, the more negative is the relationship perceived with regard to evaluation of the mother as a person, tension in the relationship, the desire to be like the mother, and the evaluation of the mother's help to the daughter.

The Role of the Family
in Provision of Care to the Elderly

The role of the family in provision of instrumental assistance to those elderly needing personal care (in bathing, dressing, eating, or transferring in and out of bed) and homemaking (cooking, cleaning, laundry, and shopping) is a function of both the extent of need for such assistance and the availability of such assistance from various sources.

The percentage of elderly in need of support in performing the activities of daily living (ADL) varies significantly among the different ethnic groups. Among the non-Jews it is more than double the overall average (21.6%), while only 6.3% among those of Western origin and 12% among those of Eastern origin are in need of help. There seems to be a cultural, or normative, factor underlying these differences, perhaps associated with the differential significance attached to maintenance of independence in these various groups.

As expected, the percentage of elderly persons dependent in ADL increases with age from about 4% at ages 65 to 69 to 11% at ages 75 to 79, and to almost a third among those aged 85 and over. At all ages, the rate of ADL dependency is higher among women, especially in the 75 and over age group. Some 12% of elderly women, as opposed to 8% of elderly men, are dependent in personal care, and 20% of women as compared with 11% of men are dependent in mobility.

Compared to Jews, non-Jews receive help in ADL from children and siblings far more frequently, but less frequently receive help in ADL from spouses. When controlling for need, the extent of support is relatively similar across the ethnic groups, although several differences remain. Another fact of interest is that among Jews, help is most often received by someone living with the elderly, while among non-Jews, nonresiding relatives are also very important sources of assistance. It is only among Jews that neighbors or public support play any significant role, with public support much higher among those of Western origin but still reaching only 13% of the dependent elderly.

Defining dependency in homemaking tasks is somewhat problematic. It is difficult to distinguish between those who are incapable of performing homemaking activities for physical reasons and those who may not do so, or be reluctant to do so, for cultural reasons. Furthermore, dependency may be defined in terms of the individual elderly person or the household unit. Data presented here relate to dependency in accordance with the self-assessment of the individual's inability to perform homemaking tasks for whatever reason and irrespective of whether there is someone else in the household, such as a spouse, capable of performing these tasks.

Dependency in ADL, as thus defined, is very widespread. A very high proportion (58% of the elderly) cannot perform at least one of the four household tasks. The dependent percentage ranges from 52% among those of Western origin to as high as 86% among non-Jews. Women are less dependent in cleaning (35% of women versus 54% of men) and in cooking (14% of women versus 61% of men), but more in shopping, and the pattern of dependency seems to be influenced by traditional sex roles (Habib & Sundstrom, 1990).

For all ethnic groups spouses are more dominant in the provision of help. Indeed the spouse seems to be the most frequent source of help as compared with other family members. This is most pronounced among those of Western origin. The pattern, with respect to other sources of help, is similar to that noted with regard to ADL. Privately-purchased help has become an important source of help, however, particularly among those of Western origin (25%). Among those who are independent, help from the spouse is also very widespread (as is to be expected). Help from family is most prevalent among non-Jews and Jews of Eastern origin, whereas purchased help once again is much more common amongst Jews of Western origin.

Care of the disabled elderly in the context of the kibbutz (Israel's cooperative settlements) has recently been examined (Bergman, King, & Bentur, 1988). In principle the kibbutz assumes collective responsibility for all the needs of its members. It is, therefore, of particular interest to examine the extent of family caring in such a context in which, presumably, the family could be "exempt" from caregiving responsibilities. It is clear, however, that here, too, the family continues to play a very important role: 19% of the elderly receive help and care from family members only (8% from their spouse only). Sixty percent of the elderly receive care from both informal and formal sources of support, and 21% only from formal support sources. The percentage of kibbutz elderly cared for exclusively by family members is naturally higher among married elderly and those who have other family members on the kibbutz. In addition to supplementing the family's role, the kibbutz also recognizes the needs of families to provide care and encourages the provision of such care (on occasion, by recognizing it in lieu of fulfillment of other work obligations). For instance, 35% of all family members providing assistance with heavy housework and 46% of those providing assistance with dressing received work credit for their caregiving.

Weihl, Azaiza, King, & Goldsher (1986) found a massive volume of support provided by children to parents in the rural Arab sector. They concluded that, modernization notwithstanding, family ties remain very strong both in terms of quantity of contacts and the extent of mutual assistance. Indeed Weihl et al. note that the levels of intergenerational assistance found among the Arab population exceed those found in studies of Jewish elderly.

As has been often emphasized, the elderly are also a source of assistance to their children. The most frequent type of assistance provided by the elderly within the family is help with care of grandchildren, which involves about one third of the elderly and over half the non-Jewish elderly. Advice-giving, as another form of assistance provided by the elderly has also been studied and found to be extensive among both Jews and non-Jews (Shuval, Fleishman, & Shmueli, 1985; Weihl et al., 1986).

The Impact of Caregiving on Family Members and the Response of Public Policy

Several studies in Israel have examined the burden of care on informal caregivers, generally focusing on the primary caregiver. A study of caregivers of elderly who receive public home care services found that a sense of burden, in a range of areas, was widespread (Brodsky, Habib, Factor, Naon, & Dolev, 1986). Almost two thirds reported physical strain, emotional stress, and time restrictions. Economic burden was reported by 25%, and about 40% complained of having to perform unpleasant tasks. With the exception of time restrictions, spouses generally tended to report heavier burdens.

These findings are consistent with studies from other countries (Brody 1985; Doty 1986). They cannot, however, provide us with any overall sense of the severity of the problem for the caregivers themselves.

Several studies in Israel have translated the concept of family burden into overall summary measures. Brodsky et al. (1986) found that 55% of informal caregivers of homecare service recipients reported that the overall burden is too heavy, 28% that they cannot continue to help to the same extent, and 8% that they cannot continue at all. On all these measures, spouses reported greater burden than did children.

In a recent study on elderly mothers and their daughters (Noam, 1991), daughters were asked to assess their ability to care for their mothers in specific circumstances, referring both to the mother's degree of disability (such as incontinence or confusion) and the inconvenience the caregiving might cause for the daughter (infringing on her time, her work, etc.). Among daughters of independent and disabled mothers alike, percentages of daughters who responded that they would be able to care for their mothers were quite high, although fewer daughters of disabled mothers favorably assessed their capacity to care. For example, while 70% of working daughters of independent mothers expressed their belief that if caregiving made it necessary for them to temporarily leave their jobs they could continue to provide care; neverless, the percentage is lower among daughters of disabled mothers—about 42%. In general, however, daughters expressed a high degree of willingness and commitment for providing care; even in cases of severe disability, on the one hand, and in cases of severe disturbance to the daughter's routine or daily life, on the other.

Programs and Services to Support Family Caregiving

The particularly strong commitment by Israeli families to maintaining the elderly at home is one of the main factors explaining the low rate of institutionalization in Israel. Caregiving families are aided by community services such as personal and housekeeping services, home-delivered meals, professional nursing, and medical home care integrated into the basic primary health service system, and a growing network of day care centers, among others.

In Israel there is no program of compulsory health insurance covering the entire population. Most of the medical care received by the elderly (and the general population as well) is provided by National Sick Funds, which are organized on an insurance basis and include a broad range of health services. Virtually all (about 94%) of the elderly have health service coverage for ambulatory and hospital care.

Nevertheless, existing services seem inadequate relative to growing needs. There is a broad consensus in Israel that community services for the elderly and their families must be expanded to better meet the needs of the elderly and ease the burden on the family. This was among the major factors leading to the adoption of a Community Long-Term Care Insurance Law as an expansion of social services for the aged under social insurance.

In April 1986 the Israeli Parliament completed the enactment of this innovative law, which was fully implemented in April 1988, when it became possible to apply to the National Insurance Institute for community services. The law's primary goal is to provide such benefits on the basis of social insurance principles: Personal entitlement and clearly defined eligibility criteria. It represents an important shift from budgeted to entitlement service programs for the elderly and from largely selective, income-tested benefits to largely universal benefits.

The target population served by the new law are those elderly who are severely functionally disabled in ADL or those who require constant supervision. The basic entitlement is for in-kind services.

One significant by-product of the law was the immediate and rapid increase in service providers, especially in the private sector. Approximately half of the eligible elderly are receiving care via private service agencies, whereas these were almost nonexistent prior to the enactment of the law.

Despite the expanded entitlements, there remains a strong emphasis on the role of the family. The new law was intended to complement, rather than replace, the existing system of service provision or family care and responsibilities, as the benefit covers only a small part of total needs. Moreover, in Israel the family is held financially responsible for financing many of the services received by the elderly—the most notable of which is institutional care. In contrast to trends in other countries, there is a tendency to strengthen the enforcement of these provisions and, at the same time, there is also a great sensitivity to the need to support family caregivers in a variety of ways. Besides the Community Long-Term Care Insurance Law, there has been a considerable expansion of various forms of respite care, with a particular emphasis on day care facilities for the disabled. Today the network of such facilities covers almost the entire country. Furthermore, many handbooks, manuals, and educational materials designed to inform the elderly and assist the family in caregiving have been recently published. Most notable among them is a guide for families who care for the cognitively-impaired elderly (Cohen, 1987). The National Insurance Institute (NII) in cooperation with ESHEL (The Association for the Planning and Development of Services for the Aged in Israel) has developed a program for training family members of impaired elderly at home (Morginstin & Werner, 1986) and a series of films and videos have been produced and made available to professionals around the country (Csillag, Werner, & Kraniel, 1986).

Despite a number of recent initiatives, self-help groups and group work with families are not widespread, whereas individual counseling of families and the elderly is much more common. Counseling is carried out by Kupat Holim (the National Sick Fund) nurses in the context of a network of local primary care clinics and by specialized geriatric social workers within the network of local social welfare bureaus. A new system of co-ordinated care and case management for the elderly is currently being put into effect. The system is based on teams of nurses from the Kupat Holim clinic and geriatric social workers with responsibility for the same geographic area. These teams are responsible for undertaking comprehensive assessment and provision of care and for establishing communication with all other professionals and service providers (Brodsky et al., 1986). The creation of these teams is geared to enhancing the capacity of local service providers to address the needs of both the elderly and their families in the context of a comprehensive and coordinated effort and, thus, to arrive at an optimal balance of formal and informal support.

Future Trends and Their Implications for Family Care of the Elderly

Israel is in the midst of a new period of mass immigration. Prior to this it was expected that by the year 2000 the elderly population was expected to number about 462,000. This represents an increase of 17% in comparison with 1988. Among those age 80 and over, the increase in numbers is expected to be particularly dramatic in this period (37%). The number of dependent elderly persons has increased and is expected to continue to increase even more in the next decade along with the dramatic rise in the number of "old-old"—age 75 and over. Furthermore, the rise in the percentage of women and the expected changes in the ethnic composition of the elderly will also contribute to an increase in disability rates. While it is not yet clear what the full implications of the recent wave of mass immigration will be, it is estimated that 100,000 elderly will be added to Israel's population within the next 5 years, and this will surely have major ramifications in areas such as housing, income maintenance, health and welfare services, and so on (Brodsky & Bergman, in press).

The elderly population of the future is expected to differ considerably from the current population of elderly in several of its basic characteristics.

More and more of the Israeli elderly will be Israeli-born and well-integrated into Israeli cultural norms, better educated, and more knowledgeable as to their entitlements. This may contribute to intensified utilization of services. At the same time, as families shrink in size and as more and more of the traditional caregivers—that is, women—become active in the labor force, the question of the family's capacity to continue to provide care becomes a very real one. This, in turn, raises the question of whether the low rates of institutionalization, which have characterized Israel up to now, can continue to be maintained. Clearly more and more attention and resources will have to be devoted to the development of community services for the elderly and for their families.

On the other hand, as the number of employees covered by work-related pensions grows, retirement conditions will improve, and thus the dependence of the elderly on external sources of support—including their families—may be reduced considerably.

We can only speculate what the implications of the growing "Westernization" of Israeli society will be for the commitment by families to caregiving. Up to now such a commitment has been a dominant feature of intergenerational relationships in Israel.

References

Be'er, S., & Factor, H. (1990a). Demographic development of the elderly in Israel in the years 1988-2000 (Hebrew). *Gerontologia, Spring-Summer, 47-48.*

Be'er, S., & Factor, H. (1990b). *Long-term care institutions and sheltered housing: The situation in 1989 and changes over time.* Jerusalem: JDC-Brookdale Institute.

Ben-Porat, Y. (1989). *The Israeli economy: Growing pains.* (Hebrew). Tel Aviv: Falk Institute.

Bergman, S. (1970). The willingness of nurses to work in geriatrics: A survey of nursing school graduates: 1969 (Hebrew). Tel Aviv: n.p.

Bergman, S., King, Y., & Bentur, N. (1988). *The system of services and care for impaired elderly in kibbutz society: Summary of results for year one.* Jerusalem: JDC-Brookdale Institute.

Brodsky, J., & Bergman, S. (in press). Israel. In E. Palmore (Ed.), *International handbook of social gerontology: Contemporary developments and research* (2nd ed., pp. 208-233). Westport, CT: Greenwood Press.

Brodsky, J., Habib, J., Factor, H., Naon, D., & Dolev, T. (1986). *Patterns and burden of caregiving among spouses, children and others.* Jerusalem: JDC-Brookdale Institute.

Brody, E. (1985). Parent care as a normative family stress. *The Gerontologist, 25,* 19-29.

Central Bureau of Statistics. (1988). *1985 survey of israel elderly age 60 and over* (Unpublished).

Cohen, H. (1987). *Guide to families caring for the mentally frail.* Jerusalem: Joint Israel and JDC-Brookdale Institute.

Csillag, D., Werner, P., & Kraniel, E. (1986). *Training family members caring for the housebound elderly.* [VII Special Series. Series of Video Films]. Jerusalem: National Insurance Institute.

Doty, P. (1986). Family care of the elderly: Is it declining? Can public policy promote it? *Milbank Memorial Fund Quarterly, Spring,* 34-75.

Eaglstein, S., & Weinsberg, E. (1985). *Knowledge and attitudes of teenagers concerning the elderly.* Jerusalem: JDC-Brookdale Institute.

Habib, J., Factor, H., Naon, D., & Brodsky, J. (1986). *Family care and family burden in a survey of disabled elderly.* Jerusalem: JDC-Brookdale Institute.

Habib, J., & Sundstrom, G. (1990). *Understanding differences in the patterns of support for elderly men and women: A comparison between Sweden and Israel.* Paper presented at Annual Symposium of EBSSRS (IAG), Dubrovnik, Yugoslavia.

Katan, J., & Aviram, U. (1986). *Professional integration of social work graduates in Israel: A follow-up study.* Tel Aviv: Tel Aviv University.

Krulik, T., Hirschfeld, M., & Sharon, R. (1984). *Family care for the severely handicapped children and aged in Israel.* Tel Aviv: Sackler School of Medicine, Department of Nursing.

Ministry of Police. (1989). *Survey and recommendations for actions to minimize crime vis-à-vis the elderly.* Jerusalem: Author.

Morginstin, B., & Werner, P. (1986). *Long-term care needs and provision of services for the elderly: Summary of selected data.* [Survey No. 51]. Jerusalem: National Insurance Institute.

Noam, G. (1989). *Kinship networks of the elderly.* Jerusalem: JDC-Brookdale Institute.

Noam, G. (1991). *The quality of elderly mother—adult daughter relationships and implications for caregiving.* Jerusalem: JDC-Brookdale Institute.

Noam, G., & Sikron, M. (1990). *Sociodemographic trends among the elderly population in Israel: 1961-1983: Analysis of census data.* Jerusalem: JDC-Brookdale Institute.

Shuval, J., Fleishman, R., & Shmueli, A. (1985). *Patterns of exchange between the elderly and their children.* Jerusalem: JDC-Brookdale Institute.

Shuval, J., Javetz, R., and Shai, D. (1988). *Physicians' perceptions and approaches.* Jerusalem: JDC-Brookdale Institute.

Steigman, N. (1988). *Promoting voluntarism by the elderly.* Jerusalem: JDC-Brookdale Institute.

Weihl, H., Azaiza, F., King, Y., & Goldsher, E. (1986). *Living conditions and family life of the rural Arab elderly in Israel.* Jerusalem: JDC-Brookdale Institute.

PART IV

Mature Countries[1]

Mature countries are defined as those whose populations aged 65 and older represent between 11% and 14% of the total population. Such countries are represented in this book by Australia, Greece, Japan, and the United States.

Australia had a population estimated to be 17.1 million persons in mid-1990. By the year 2020 the population is projected to increase to 22.9 million people. About 22% of all Australians were estimated, in 1990, to be under 15 years of age and 11% to be 65 years of age and older. It was determined that 86% of the Australian population lives in urban areas of the country. The authors of the chapter on Australia are John McCallum, Ph.D., from the National Centre for Epidemiology and Population Health at The Australian National University, and Anna Howe, Ph.D., Head of the Office for the Aged, Australian Commonwealth Department of Health, Housing and Community Services, both located in Canberra.

Greece is estimated to have had a population of 10.1 million persons in mid-1990. The population is projected to decrease to 9.9 million persons by the year 2020. In 1990 it was found that 20% of the Greek population was under 15 years of age, and that 13% were 65 years of age and older. About 58% of the population in Greece lives in urban areas of the country. The authors of the chapter on Greece are Peter Stathopoulos, Ph.D., Professor, and Anna Amera, MSW, both from the School of Planning, Technological Institute of Athens, in Athens.

Japan had a mid-1990 population estimated at 123.6 million people. The population is projected to slightly increase to 124.2 million people by the year 2020. In 1990 it was found that one fifth (20%) of the Japanese population was under 15 years of age and that 11% were 65 years of age

157

and older. More than three quarters (77%) of the Japanese population live in urban areas of the country. The authors of the chapter on Japan are Daisaku Maeda, MSSA, Professor at the Social Work Research Institute of the Japan College of Social Work, and Youmei Nakatani, MSW, Researcher, from the Department of Social Welfare and Social Research of the Tokyo Metropolitan Institute of Gerontology, both located in Tokyo.

The *United States* is estimated to have had a mid-1990 population of 251.4 million persons. By the year 2020 the population is projected to increase to 294.4 million persons. In 1990, 22% of the American population was estimated to be under 15 years of age and 12% of the population was estimated to be 65 years of age and older. Almost three fourths (74%) of the population in the United States lives in urban areas of the country. The authors of the chapter on the United States are Timothy H. Brubaker, Ph.D., Associate Professor, Family and Child Studies Center, School of Education and Allied Professions, and Ellie Brubaker, Ph.D., Associate Professor, Department of Sociology and Anthropology, both from Miami University, Oxford, Ohio.

Note

1. All information used to describe these four countries comes from *1990: World Population Data Sheet of the Population Reference Bureau, Inc.,* Washington, DC, 1990. Mid-1990 estimates are based upon census or official national data or upon U.N., U.S. Bureau of the Census, or World Bank projections. Year 2020 projections come from the same sources.

11

Family Care of the Elderly in Australia

JOHN McCALLUM
ANNA L. HOWE

Traditional Characteristics of the Country

Demographic Overview of the Population

Three features of Australia's population have a key bearing on family care for the aged. First, Australia is a relatively young population compared to other developed countries. The 1986 Census showed 10.6% of the population was aged 65 years and older. There are now historically low birth and death rates, resulting in low total population increases. By June 30, 1990, the population had increased by 253,100 or 1.5%. This figure was lower than the post-World War II average but higher than most developed nations (e.g., the United States, Canada, and New Zealand). Natural increase (births minus deaths) has remained positive since 1947, but the rate has declined during the last 3 decades.

Second, Australia is an immigrant society. Net migration (immigration minus emigration) has accounted for about 40% of Australia's postwar population growth. Some 5 million people have settled permanently in Australia since 1947. The 1986 Census showed that 22% of the population indicated it was born overseas and another 42% had at least one parent born overseas (National Population Council, 1991). The impact of immigration on the aging of the population and some special features of care of the ethnic aged are a major theme of this chapter.

Third, in contrast to the above features of an advanced Western nation, the care practices of the indigenous people of Australia, the Aboriginals and Torres Strait Islanders, are those of a traditional gerontocracy. Their poor survival rates to old age are similar to developing countries, with the exception that the diseases of affluence (such as cardiovascular diseases) are more prevalent than in poor countries of the world. With a total population of approximately 300,000 in a population of around 17 million, they are, numerically, a minority group.

Social and Political Values

The Australian egalitarian tradition first defined by Sir Keith Hancock is of a particular type, emphasizing "equal" treatment rather than just returns from different contributions. For example, Australia had flat-rate and means-tested, rather than earnings-related, benefits for retirement from 1908. Another expression can be found in the industrial award of the Harvester judgment in 1907 that fixed a living, minimum wage for low-paid, low-skill workers and a parallel policy that protected the industries that employed them behind a high tariff wall.

The current Commonwealth Government has placed emphasis on four principal elements of social justice: equity—fairness in the distribution of resources; equality—equal, effective, and comprehensive civil, legal, and industrial rights for all; access—fair and equal access to services; and participation—the opportunity to participate fully in personal development, community life, and decision-making (Prime Minister, 1989, p. 3). Specific guidelines for management of Commonwealth programs accompanied this statement of objectives (Department of Finance and Department of Prime Minister and Cabinet, 1989).

Public recognition of multiculturalism is a relatively recent development within this notion of social justice, fostered by the growing strength of ethnic community organizations in mainstream politics. Since the 1970s there has been an explicit adoption of multiculturalism by the federal government.

The current Commonwealth social justice strategy underlies all the aged-care programs. One of the roles of the new Geriatric Assessment program established in 1987 is: "to facilitate access of the elderly to appropriate residential services upon request or referral." Similarly, the Home and Community Care program (HACC), established in 1985, embodies a goal of "equal access" regardless of location, culture and language, physical access, and without discrimination on the grounds of ability to pay, gender, race, marital status, religion, sexual preference, or type of disability. The Australian tradition of government intervention to achieve social justice has been reinterpreted in the new programs developed in an aging society.

Role of the Family in Care of Aged

The family has been the exclusive basis of care for the elderly throughout most of Australia's history. Apart from provision of the age pension, government entry to welfare and social services for aged care dates only from the early 1950s. While the scale of public provision has grown substantially during the last 4 decades, the relationship between family care and public support is one of supplementation, not substitution.

Spouses and children are the primary providers of care for the Australian elderly; spouses, because of their proximity and moral obligations, provide the most care to the Australian elderly. A profile of carers is provided by the findings of a recent survey of aging and disability conducted by the Australian Bureau of Statistics (ABS, 1988), which included questions on both family care and use of formal services. The carers part of the survey focused on the severely handicapped, defined as those who required supervision or assistance from another person in one of three key areas of daily living. Carers were defined as persons living in the same household as the severely handicapped person, and who were the main providers of care.

Just over half of the total severely handicapped population aged 60 years and older (54%) were found to have a coresident carer. Spouses account for 90% of carers for those aged between 60 and 69 years, but this drops to 72% over age 70 years. Men were the majority of coresident carers among the elderly, mainly because older women were more likely to be widowed and living alone. The higher proportion of nonspouse carers at older ages indicates the changes in household composition and family structure consequent upon widowhood and the need for care.

Daughters become more important as carers after age 75, making up a third of all coresident carers for this age group. Daughters are also likely to be the majority of noncoresident carers. Even after the disabled person reaches age 75 years, sons still account for fewer than 10% of all carers. The advanced ages of those being cared for by daughters suggest that, in many cases, the daughters themselves will be well into middle age when caregiving responsibilities make major demands on their time.

People older than 75 years of age, predominantly women, were the least likely to have a carer and least likely to be living with immediately family and relatives, as well as most likely to be living alone. Severely handicapped men were more likely to have a carer (74%) than women (58%). This difference is accentuated with increasing age. In the 75 years and older group, 67% of men had carers compared to only 39% of severely handicapped women.

Societal Changes Occurring Over Time

Demographic Changes

The Australian population is aging due to effects of changes in birth, death, and immigration rates. The proportion of the population aged 65 years and older remained almost constant at around 8% from the first postwar census, in 1947, to the 1971 census. Since then, it has risen to just over 10% in 1986, when more than 1.6 million Australians were aged 65 years and older. The proportion of aged is projected to reach 12% by 1996 and 14% by 2011. In 1991, 11% of the Australian population was aged 65 years and older. It is expected to take 45 years for the proportion aged 65 years and older to increase from 10% (as it was in 1986) to 20% of the population, which is expected in 2031 (McCallum, 1990).

Life expectancy at birth in Australia has risen continuously during the twentieth century (with the exception of the period during the 1960s, when death from cardiovascular disease increased particularly for men). Between 1905 and 1989, life expectancy at birth increased by 18 years for men and 21 years for women. Life expectancy from age 65 years, by contrast, increased only marginally in the first 6 decades of the century— 0.9 years for men and 2.5 years for women. During the last 2 decades this has increased at a greater rate, 2.5 years for men and 3.0 years for women (McCallum, 1990). In 1988 life expectancy at age 65 years was 14.8 years for men and 18.7 years for women.

The cohorts of the extended baby boom, born 1950 to 1970, were boosted by the arrival of relatively high rates of immigrants post-World War II. These factors have two outcomes for aging of the population. First, dependency ratios in Australia remain stable until well after the turn of the century as the baby boom cohorts move through the work force. Second, as immigrants begin to reach older ages in large numbers toward the end of the century and in the following decades, the cultural diversity of the aged population changes markedly. The ethnic component of the Australian aging population is bringing new perspectives to issues in family care of the elderly in Australia.

Economic and Educational Changes

The aged population has become increasingly better educated during this century. Universal primary education was established in all states by the turn of the century as declining birth rates and improved survival of children saw more effort being put into the education of each child. The minimum leaving age also rose steadily in the early years of the century. These developments meant that the majority of the current cohort aged 80 years and older attended school until at least age 14. The extension of secondary and tertiary education is apparent in the higher proportion of the 60 to 64 years cohort who remained at school to later ages. Interestingly, these patterns are very similar for men and women, except that women lagged in participation in tertiary education.

Continuing education is common throughout working life, but not extending very much into retraining for older workers. Older workers themselves appear willing to accept offers of retirement packages rather than pushing for retraining that would equip them to remain in the work force. One factor contributing to this pattern appears to be an expression of the "fair go" ethos on the part of older workers, who feel they should make way for younger people joining the work force.

Longer life expectancy at older ages has been accompanied by shorter periods at work. At the end of the World War II more than half a man's remaining years of life after age 60 years were spent in paid work; by the end of the 1980s less than a third was spent this way. The declines in labor force participation of older Australian men in the 1970s were as strong as those in any country in the world (BLMR, 1983). Projections from the Department of Employment Education and Training show that the pace of these declines has slowed for men over age 60 years but that younger men 55-59 years are expected to reduce their participation rate from 70% in 1996 to 66% in 2001.

The implications of these changes have raised public interest and government concern. The Commonwealth Government House of Representatives Standing Committee on Community Affairs conducted an inquiry, "Is Retirement Working?" in 1988-1989 (House of Representatives Standing Committee on Community Affairs, 1990), and a senate committee is currently examining the implications of the extension of life expectancy.

Increased Westernization/Industrialization

Australia's early immigrants brought with them the patterns of family support for the elderly found in nineteenth-century Britain (Quadagno, 1982) with developed expectations of community and public sector help in this task. Australia has always been a highly industrialized nation, but recent trends in female work force participation have affected these patterns of family care for the elderly.

Childbearing in Australia in postwar years has been concentrated in the early 20s and most families are completed by the time a woman is 25. During the years of raising children until they are teenagers, few women are likely to have parents in their 70s or 80s needing care. The parents of this generation are in their 50s and 60s and still active and independent. It is, rather, this older generation of women who may have very elderly and frail parents, and by the time this generation reaches their mid-70s, their daughters will be in their 50s.

Women have been through a major restructuring of their middle years with declining numbers of children born to them and increasing participation in education and paid work. They are increasingly less likely to work at ages 10 to 19 years because they are participating in education, but they are more likely to work after age 20 years. In 1986 women aged 20-29 years (born 1957-1966) spent 70% of their time between ages 20-24 years in full-time work compared with 50% for women aged 50 to 59 years (born 1927-1936). Two-income families rose from 41.5% to 44% between the 1981 and 1986 censuses.

Women's participation in the workforce, always less than that for men, has been increasing at adult ages, up to age 55 years, where there have been minor declines in participation until the last two years. Older women have relatively stable, low participation rates, but this stability in aggregate masks an increase in the part-time participation rates for older women.

Changes in Immigration, Emigration, and Mobility in the Country

Immigration has not only contributed to the growing size of the aged population, but is also making it increasingly diverse. Four broad phases of immigration can be identified. Before World War II most migrants were British with relatively few from non-English speaking countries. In the postwar years the first immigration waves were composed largely of refugees and displaced persons from Northern and Central Europe for whom

English was not a first language. Many of these individuals were without family, and while many established families in Australia, some groups (e.g., Poles) are still characterized by high proportions of single men.

Later immigration waves were drawn to Australia under programs designed to bolster the work force and contribute to population growth. The countries of origin shifted first to Southern Europe, with major immigration from Greece, Italy, and Yugoslavia, and subsequently to the Middle East, with growing numbers coming from Lebanon, Egypt, and Turkey. Originally a male-dominated immigration, many of these postwar immigrants sent back to their home countries for brides and other family members including older parents. The extent to which older family members are currently involved in family reunification is indicated by 3.5% of settlers arriving in Australia in 1989-1990 being aged 65 years and older compared to more than 10% of the population of that age. In 1989-1990 the median age of the population was 32.2 years compared to the median age of settler arrivals of 26.8 years (Bureau of Immigration Research, 1991).

As successive waves of immigrants reach old age, the aged population has come to show increasing cultural diversity. While refugee and work force-related immigration continue, a growing share of immigration has been taken up by family reunification, including reunification of elderly parents. The ethnic aged are defined officially in Australia as those born in non-English-speaking (NESB) countries. At the 1986 census, just over one quarter of the population aged 65 years and older were born overseas, divided evenly between migrants from English-speaking and non-English-speaking countries. The latter ethnic component of the aged population is set to grow far more rapidly than either of the Australian-born or the English-speaking born components. By the year 2000, 1 in 4 older Australians will be from a non-English-speaking birthplace.

Australians also change their place of residence frequently, creating considerable internal migration. In the 1986 census, 43% of the people who had been living in Australia at the time of the 1981 census were at a different place of residence. Some 87% of moves were within the same state. Only 12% of movers each year cross state boundaries, which is partly offset by outflows. Net gains were achieved between 1981 and 1986 by the states of Western Australia and Queensland due to cheaper housing, warmer climates, and economic inducements.

Changes in Urbanization

Australia is one of the most highly urbanized nations in the world. The population is concentrated in the east, southeast, and southwest coastal zones. In 1986 this was 3.3% of the total land area, supporting 81% of the population. The proportion of Australians living in cities increased consistently during the century up to 1976 (when 86% lived in cities with more than 1,000 inhabitants). As a consequence of extensive urbanization, significant problems in support for dependent elderly occur in rural and remote areas. These areas are normally defined in terms of the low population density of the Statistical Local Areas and are diverse regional centers (population 4,000 to 25,000), rural towns, retirement developments, company towns, Aboriginal and Islander communities, and dispersed families working in the outback or remote areas. Some 15% of older Australians 70 years and older live in rural or remote areas.

Natural disasters such as floods, bush fires, and cyclones are regular occurrences in remote areas of Australia. The needs of frail elderly people are dealt with along with those of other dependent persons. They may be evacuated early to alternative accommodation or receive disaster relief like persons of any age in their area.

Family Dynamics

While marriage and childbearing became more prevalent during this century, patterns of family formation have become less stable. Currently Australian women are marrying later and delaying birth of children. There have been significant increases in single-parent families and couples with children. Consequently, among older women different patterns are seen. Those born before 1916 have rates of "not being married by age 40 to 44 years" above 10%, compared to a rate of 5% of those born in 1926 (i.e., aged 65 in 1991). Similarly the number of surviving children for a woman of 60 years of age increased from 1.7 for those born before 1916 to 2.2 for those born in 1926. About 80% of women born in 1896 had at least one surviving child at age 60 compared to 90% of those born in 1926. These patterns do not indicate any concern about current availability of family supports.

The impact of divorce on family structure has become more significant. Until the early 1980s there was a marked increase in divorce rates associated with the introduction of "no fault" divorce in the early 1970s. In the 1950s and 1960s about 9% to 12% of marriages ended in divorce. This increased to 40.6% in 1982 but it has since stabilized at around 35% to 38%. The divorce rates among persons aged 65 and older were around 5% in 1986 compared to around 3% in 1966. One impact of divorce for the elderly is on access to grandchildren among those whose sons and daughters divorce. The major difference in marital status between men and women is in levels of widowhood, which, in 1986, were 14.5% for men and 48.5% for women aged 65 years and older.

Attitudes Toward, and Importance of, the Elderly

Popular perceptions of the elderly as a social group have changed in postwar years. There has been a widening differentiation between the well aged (or active retired) and the frail aged. Trends of earlier retirement and improved income among the young-old have created a new life-style that most Australians can expect to enjoy for a good 10 years from their early 60s to early 70s. The emergence of popular magazines, travel, and a "grey" market testify to the reality of this group. Many older people themselves project this self image.

At the same time it must be recognized that not all enter retirement willingly or with a positive outlook. A study of retired auto workers identified a group of "reluctant retirees" who had been forced to retire early due to ill health and whose plans for retirement had been preempted (McCallum, 1986).

Opinion surveys of the Australian population consistently show tolerance of the aged and support for public benevolence toward them. On the negative side this expresses a type of "compassionate ageism" by assuming the dependency of people simply because of chronological age. In opinion surveys throughout the period following World War II up to the 1990s, at least two thirds of the Australian public supported the abolition of means tests on the age pension. More Australians, about 40%, are opposed to compulsory retirement than Britons, Austrians, and Italians (McCallum, 1990).

With the emergence of "grey parties" in state elections during the 1980s and age issues in federal politics, there has been a changing perception of the importance of the aged. The "grey parties" appear now to have declined in influence after an initial burst of support due to frustration with pension policy changes. The political "quietism" of Australians coupled with a system of compulsory voting lowers the gains from such political activity. A system of universal health insurance further removes a major uncertainty of old age. One example of new opportunities for the elderly is the push for antidiscrimination legislation in states. This has been blocked in some states, appeared with multiple exclusions in the state of South Australia, and covers only compulsory retirement in New South Wales. While no dramatic changes in work participation are expected from this, a new respect for the rights of the older person is embodied in the legislation. Users' rights are more generally appearing in most areas of Commonwealth policy for the elderly, and new Consumer Forums are being sponsored by the Commonwealth Office for the Aged.

Consequences of Societal Changes

Stability of Family Care of the Elderly

Family care has been and is the mainstay of support for the elderly in Australia. Interest in family support in the early 1980s prompted major surveys and a number of smaller-scale studies. Some of the common key findings demonstrate the extent and variety of family support. Around four out of five tasks performed for older people living at home were provided by informal supports, predominantly spouses and family. Three-generation households were uncommon even early in this century, and two-generation conjugal households were the norm in similar proportions to the present day (Rowland, 1984). The two-generation families operate as modified-extended families in supporting the elderly and providing intimacy at a distance.

In a 1981 survey of people 60 years and older, 64% agreed that "when older people can no longer manage on their own, most want to stay at home with outside help." The next most popular answer was "to move to a home for the aged," that is, an alternative form of accommodation (17%), while taking up residence with children and moving to a nursing home (each 8%) were the most unpopular choices (Kendig & Rowland, 1983). Preferences, however, do not necessarily express the most appropriate form of care for persons when they actually have some health or support crisis, and opinions may change in that situation.

There has been only a minor reduction in the supply of sons and daughters available through the demographic transition. Rowland (1991) calculated ratios of women aged 50 to 64 years, the main years of responsibility for an aged parent, to the number of persons aged 80 years and older. The ratio is projected to fall from 3:5 in 1986 to 1:8 in 2031. The current ratio is already below 3 in countries such as Sweden and the United States. The potential for daughter involvement will decline in the 2020s, when the baby boom reaches 80 years and older. These ratios do not measure actual supply and demand for support; in particular, the provision of support by older spouses and the public sector. Further, only about 3% of the Australian elderly are without close relatives—spouse, children, and siblings. Thus the potential stock of family care providers for the current Australian elderly is relatively secure.

Continuation of the Elderly in Family/Community Life

The role of the elderly in the wider community is changing as retirement emerges as a more distinct and, generally positive, life-cycle stage. An older elite have money, conspicuous consumption, and political organization to shift community attitudes. Active older people, whether wealthy or not, are likely to provide more services to their families than they receive from them. As already noted, moreover, they are the major source of labor for support services provided in the home, namely as spouses of dependent elderly.

Old age, as well, can be a time of severely reduced "exchange" power due to loss of function, low income, and declining numbers of formal and informal ties. The evidence from surveys is that older people cope with adjustments and vulnerabilities of old age. Relatively few are depressed or demoralized after major changes such as retirement or widowhood (McCallum, 1986). Informal support is typically drawn from a core of 5 to 8 close bonds in addition to wider circles of acquaintants. It appears that expressive bonds can be negotiated even when personal resources are limited (Kendig, 1986). The voluntary, rather than obligatory, nature of these relationships is based upon emotional, rather than instrumental, rewards. New and old forces will ensure a positive role for the elderly in the community.

When it occurs, family breakdown appears to have a mixed effect on relationships between younger and older family members. While placing extra demands on younger women with children, divorce sometimes leads to reconstitution of three-generation families in which the older generation is able to accommodate younger members. This outcome has been found especially where older widows have "excess" housing space. Older members of families are also likely to provide child care services in such situations. These situations provide an example of intergenerational reciprocity. The household formations come about not necessarily because older family members require support or care, but rather because of the needs of the younger family members. These transfers may, however, lay the foundation for support at a later stage.

Contradictory demographic and labor market forces are at work in care of the elderly. Current elderly are the most likely of any generation in

Australia to have children available for support. On the other hand, married daughters in the current generation are the most likely to be working, compared to previous cohorts of daughters. Thus, while there is no shortage of supply of carers, the complications for those daughters who provide the care are increasing. The spouse carers are affected by different needs associated with their own advanced age rather than by multiple competing demands on their time and efforts. Whether women are being caught in the middle of responsibilities of caring for children and parents and between the traditional family responsibilities and the desire to fulfill their own potential in the labor force is open to question. However, most daughter carers will be aged 50 to 64 years and unlikely to have heavy responsibilities for care of children.

The issue of elder abuse is now emerging in Australia. An exploratory study of service provider experiences of abusive families in the city of Adelaide, South Australia, found initial resistance to discussion of the topic. Once this was overcome, some 120 cases were discussed of which physical abuse (25 cases) and economic abuse (34 cases) were the dominant types. Yet in this exploratory work prevalence could not be estimated (McCallum, Matiasz, & Graycar, 1989). The total numbers involved are estimated as less than one percent of the total caseload in the urban area (Kurrle, Sadler, & Cameron, 1991).

Ethnic Women Caregivers

Women in various ethnic groups provide a special case for the pressures of social change, not only between generations but also between traditional cultures and prevailing Australian mores. These pressures are most acute for the daughters of first-generation migrants of non-English-speaking background. The choices available to these women are complicated for them by the migration transition, which may be complex for them but not for their parents who still hold traditional values about support by daughters or daughters-in-law. Their parents can also have needs for support and information that derive from linguistic abilities and cultural background.

A focus group study of women from seven ethnic groups who provided extensive caregiving but did not work full-time outside the home probed issues of caregiving (McCallum & Gelfand, 1990). The parents' and the daughters' experience of living in Australia tended to vary with the time since migration to Australia and adherence to their cultural backgrounds. Ranked from longest to most recent arrivals, the groups were Jewish,

Italian, Greek, Croatian, Turkish, Arabic-speaking (Egyptian and Lebanese), and Vietnamese. The oldest age structures were in the Jewish community, predominantly from Eastern Europe, and the Italian born, at about 20% aged 60 years and older, compared to under 5%, for example, among the Vietnamese.

All the women expressed strong support for the extended family as the ideal way of caring for their parents. This view was held even more strongly by their husbands and by ethnic community leaders. At the same time the women recognized that this meant the lot of caregiving fell largely to them, and the expectation that women would care conflicted with a desire to work on the part of some. Although done ungrudgingly, the women derived less satisfaction than they might from caregiving because they felt neither their parents nor families were appreciative of their efforts. Thus while caregiving was an expected norm, it was not rewarded. The need for some social recognition of caring felt by these ethnic women is a view shared with their Australian-born counterparts.

The extent to which the caregivers were prepared to balance their cultural ideals of family care with an acceptance of the role of public support is seen in their unanimous agreement that public provision of support for the elderly in Australia surpassed arrangements in their home countries. The Italian women were most adamant in their view that Australia gave better support to carers and more respect to the elderly than occurred in Italy. Language still posed barriers to access for the some caregivers and even more so for their parents. Even though the women from the groups that had come to Australia some time ago had more adequate English than the more recently arrived groups, most had some difficulty in applying for benefits or services and in interacting satisfactorily with service providers.

When uncertain of service availability or unable to obtain detailed information, however, the women tended to fall back on family care. This response, in turn, precluded pursuing services. A further double bind developed: beliefs that services away from the home were not culturally appropriate persisted without being tested, and, with only limited use by the ethnic aged, services were not pushed to adapt to their needs.

Ethnic community organizations were significant as bridging mechanisms between the women caregivers and mainstream providers as much as in direct-service provision. These organizations were central to the development of ethnic-specific services; without them, it would not be possible to give effect to government programs in forms that were acceptable to the ethnic elderly and their caregivers. These services, in turn, inform the development of mainstream services.

Responses to Changes in Australian Society

While the provision of community care has been a feature of publicly-funded support for the aged since the early 1950s, the priority given to community care vis-à-vis residential care has fluctuated from time to time. The attention given to family care in relation to community services has been spasmodic and, until recently, the role of family care has been implicitly assumed in policy development. Explicit policy recognition of carers and the development of services to support their role has emerged since the early 1980s.

Growing policy interest at that time had lead to two major surveys, one conducted by the Department of Community Services in conjunction with the Australian Council on the Aging (1985) and the other undertaken in the Aging and the Family Project at the Australian National University (Kendig, Gibson, & Rowland, 1983). The findings of these surveys confirmed that the formal services then available contributed the minor share of support and that families, particularly elderly spouses and daughters, were the mainstay of care of the frail aged.

Home and Community Care Program

The clearest policy statement of the recognition of family roles in aged care in Australia has been made in the specific identification of carers as part of the target population of the Home and Community Care Program (HACC). The legislation under which the HACC Program has been implemented since 1985 designates the target population for the program as frail aged and younger disabled people and their carers. Within this broad client population, a number of groups with special needs are identified: the ethnic aged, those with dementia, older Aboriginals and Torres Strait Islanders, and older people in rural and remote areas.

The objective of HACC, as stated in the program guidelines, is threefold:

1. to provide a comprehensive and integrated range of home care services to the frail aged and younger people with disabilities and their carers;

2. to help these people to be more independent at home and in the community, thereby preventing their inappropriate admission to long-term residential care and enhancing their quality of life; and

3. to provide a greater range of services and more flexible service provision to ensure that services respond to the needs of users.

HACC covers 11 broad service types, and these can usefully be described in terms of the typology of services developed by Twigg, Atkin, and Perring (1990) with reference to assisting carers. A number of other elements of HACC service delivery, such as assessment and case management, can also be included. Several HACC services do not fit exclusively into one or the other category and are rather allocated on the basis of their main function. The five categories and the relevant HACC services are:

1. helping the carer manage: the Domiciliary Nursing Care Benefit, information and advisory services and counseling, including carer groups, education and training, and case management;

2. assisting the carer with practical tasks: home help, personal care, domiciliary nursing, transport, home maintenance and modifications;

3. providing relief from caring: respite services in the home or in day centers, complementing the provision of residential respite in nursing homes and hostels;

4. getting more from the system: assessment, information and advisory services, advocacy services, and user rights strategies; and

5. services provided to the dependent, which include all the direct care and support services listed above.

This mix of services combines some long-standing elements of community care with a number of recent innovations. Home nursing services have been subsidized by the federal and state governments since the early 1950s. The States Grants (Home Care) Act, the States Grants (Paramedical Services) Act, both passed in 1969, and the Delivered Meals Subsidy Act of 1970 indicate the kinds of services made available. The Home Care Act funded home help services and also supported Senior Citizens' Centers. Many of these centers grew out of social and recreation clubs and were not initially oriented to care services, although positions of welfare workers were also supported, sometimes in conjunction with Senior Citizens' Centers.

Respite Care

Respite care has expanded substantially under HACC. About one quarter of the Senior Citizens' Centers, now operating, offer programs for dementia care, and others cater for specific ethnic groups. HACC also funds in-home respite, with services using a mix of paid and volunteer staff and providing anything from a few hours respite a week to full substitute care for a week or more.

Residential respite care is also provided in nursing homes and hostels through special funding that provides an incentive to the provider to accept short-term admissions. In a number of cases residential care facilities have established respite units of 5-10 beds. Links have also been established with Geriatric Assessment Teams that provide booking services. The uptake of these services has grown steadily, and successive adjustments have been made in programs to overcome reported difficulties. In the course of the Aged Care Review, considerable interest was expressed in having day care centers provide short-term overnight respite; a few experimental services have attempted this type of operation, but there has as yet been no evaluation of their cost effectiveness or outcomes.

Innovative Services

A special Community Options component of HACC was fully funded by the Commonwealth from 1987-1988 to 1990-1991 to foster innovative approaches to service delivery, especially for individuals with complex care needs. Community Options Projects were developed along the lines of overseas case management approaches, notably those in Kent, England, and Wisconsin in the United States. The aim of the Community Options program was to develop more flexible responses to meeting the needs of individuals and to enable the "packaging" of services to meet complex care needs, bringing about change in the operation of standard services. From 1991 the funding for Community Options has been incorporated in the general HACC program.

Alternatives to Family Care

The absence of family support is a major factor in admission to residential care. Comparison of the sociodemographic profile of nursing home residents with the total population aged 75 years and older shows the attenuated family support of residents. On the basis of the 1986 Census and data on nursing home residents for 1990 (Department of Community

Services and Health, 1990), widowed women accounted for 48% of residents but only 28% of the total population; conversely, the proportions married (men and women) were 26% and 54%, respectively. Prior to admission, 20% of residents had lived with their spouse only, and 23% lived in other family groups (spouse and other family members, or other family members only). About 15% of the preadmission living arrangements involved children, suggesting that considerable adjustments in family composition are made in response to frailty. One third of residents had been living alone and 23% in nonprivate living arrangements.

A series of measures introduced during the last 5 years have brought about major changes not only in the provision of residential care, but also in the use of the services available. Thus while the number of nursing home beds grew by only some one percent over the 2 years to the end of 1990, the number of admissions per annum is estimated to have increased by 20%. This outcome is attributed to the introduction of preadmission assessment and to changes in the dependency profile of residents that has resulted in shorter stays. A central element in bringing about these changes has been the implementation of a funding system (based on five categories of resident dependency) that has created incentives to admit high-dependency residents.

These changes in access to residential care have significant implications for family care. The converse of the association between the lack of family care and admission to residential care is that remaining in the community is highly dependent on the availability of family care. In the past inadequate assessment and the limited provision of community care resulted in the early admission to residential care of relatively independent individuals who were without family care. At the same time families had to care for relatives to very high levels of dependency with very little assistance from services.

Provision of appropriate services to those without carers, including the expansion of hostel care, and to carers, together with assessment for admission to nursing home care, is bringing about a number of changes in patterns of care provision. Rather than shifting more care to family carers, the outcome is a redistribution of care for less-dependent individuals to hostels and to community services, including services assisting carers, and increased access to nursing home care for high-dependency individuals. In the Australian context, family care in the community and residential care are, thus, developing as complementary elements in an overall aged-care system rather than alternatives.

Policy Perspectives on the Future of Family Care

This chapter began with some general observations on social and political values in Australian society and, in concluding, it is appropriate to examine the values that are shaping current policy development on family care. An overemphasis on the negative aspects of caring can be most damaging. To characterize the person being cared for as a burden is demeaning and belittling. When seen only as a burden, the caring role becomes distasteful and something to be eschewed: only the unlucky will have to be cared for, and only the unlucky will have to take care of them.

The fallout from this negative view of caring is that care services are similarly characterized. Work in caring services is seen to provide few rewards; it is depressing; it is the last thing anyone would want to do. As the status of such work falls, it is not surprising that community services have difficulty in attracting and retaining staff. More generally, when caring is accorded little social value, public support for the provision of caring services wanes.

There is, however, an alternative value system inherent in caring, and one which should be fundamental to policies for aged care and be explicitly promoted in the provision of services. This value system recognizes the positive benefits of caring for individuals, both those who are cared for and their carers, and for society as a whole. Social recognition of the value of caring will not simply enhance the position of carers as making a worthwhile contribution to society, but will also mean that the public provision of service comes to be seen in the same way.

Such social recognition is not a matter of transferring the costs of care from the community to individuals, but, rather, reflects a realization of the complementarity between caring and care services. The view of carers, as co-clients, places carers in a positive relationship to services, recognizing them as deserving of support in their own right. Support for carers becomes an objective as well as meeting the needs of the person being cared for. It is this view of carers that has been adopted in such Australian programs as the HACC program, which identifies carers as a target group and mandates for the provision of services directly to carers as well as to the elderly.

A final comment on current policy perspectives on family roles needs to address the concern that policies supporting family care mean that government is discarding its responsibility and passing it back to family. Nevertheless, public support for community care, and specifically for carer assistance, is far greater than at any previous time in Australia. The view that more extensive support existed in the past and is now being withdrawn is illusory.

Likewise the interactions between community care and residential care are far more complex than a simple trade off. Rather than a one-for-one transfer from residential to community care, recent adjustments in the balance of care services in Australia have enhanced access to residential care for highly dependent individuals. Finally, current policy is based not only on the recognition of the extensive role of family care, but also on a view that government has a responsibility to support carers, and those they care for, so as to enable them to maintain their preferred ways of living. Support for carers is intended to give more options in making decisions about caring and assistance in realizing the choices made.

References

Australian Bureau of Statistics (ABS). (1988). *Carers of the handicapped at home.* (Cat No 4122.0). Canberra: Author.

Australian Bureau of Statistics. (various years). *Australian families and households.* (Cat No 2506.0). Canberra: Author.

Bureau of Immigration Research. (1991). *Australia's population trends and prospects 1990.* Canberra: Australian Government Publishing Service.

Bureau of Labour Market Research (BLMR). (1983). *Retired, unemployed or at risk.* Canberra: Australian Government Publishing Service.

Department of Community Services and Australian Council on the Ageing. (1985). *Older people at home.* Canberra: Australian Government Publishing Service.

Department of Community Services and Health. (1990). *Nursing homes for the aged: A statistical overview.* Canberra: Department of Community Services and Health.

Department of Finance and Department of Prime Minister and Cabinet. (1989). *Towards a fairer Australia. Social justice and program management: A guide.* Canberra: Australian Government Publishing Service.

House of Representatives Standing Committee on Community Affairs. (1990). *Is retirement working? A report on the community involvement of retired persons.* Canberra: Australian Government Publishing Service.

Kendig, H. L. (1986). *Ageing and families. A social networks perspective.* Sydney: Allen and Unwin.

Kendig, H. L., Gibson, D. L., & Rowland, D. T. (1983). *Health, welfare and family in later life.* Sydney: NSW Council on the Ageing.

Kendig, H. L., & Rowland, D. T. (1983). Family support of the Australian aged: A comparison with the United States. *The Gerontologist, 23,* 643-649.

Kurrle, S. E., Sadler, P. M., & Cameron, I. D. (1991). Elder abuse—An Australian case series. *The Medical Journal of Australia, 155,* 150-153.

McCallum, J. (1986). Retirement and widowhood transitions. In H. L. Kendig (Ed.), *Ageing and families. A social networks perspective* (pp. 129-148). Sydney: Allen and Unwin.

McCallum, J. (1990). Health: The quality of survival in older age. In Australian Institute of Health, *Australia's health 1990* (pp. 195-240). Canberra: Australian Government Publishing Service.

McCallum, J., & Gelfand, D. E. (1990). *Ethnic women in the middle.* Canberra: National Centre for Epidemiology and Population Health.

McCallum, J., Matiasz, S., & Graycar, A. (1989). *Abuse of the elderly at home: The range of the problem.* Adelaide: South Australia Government Printer.

National Population Council. (1991). *Population issues and Australia's future. Environment, economy and society.* Canberra: Australian Government Publishing Service.

Prime Minister. (1989). *Towards a fairer Australia: Social justice statement 1989-90.* Canberra: Australian Government Publishing Service.

Quadagno, J. (1982). *Aging in early industrial society: Work, family and social policy in nineteenth-century England.* New York: Academic Press.

Rowland, D. T. (1984). Old age and the demographic transition. *Population Studies, 38,* 73-87.

Rowland, D. T. (1991). *Ageing in Australia.* Sydney: Longman Cheshire.

Twigg, J., Atkin, K., & Perring, C. (1990). *Carers and services: A review of research.* London: Her Majesty's Stationary Office.

12

Family Care of the Elderly in Greece

PETER STATHOPOULOS
ANNA AMERA

General Characteristics of the Country

Geography

Greece is a small Mediterranean, Southern European country of approximately 130,000 square kilometers. Three quarters of its territory is considered mountainous. Of its 3,000 islands scattered in the Aegean and Ionian seas, only 150 are inhabited. The population of the country, according to the 1981 Census, was nearly 9.5 million. The rate of increase of the population, however, is only 0.4% per year. The elderly population is growing rapidly, and by the year 2000 it will reach a level of over 20%.

History

Greece is a relatively young state, about 170 years old, but a very ancient nation with a glorious civilizational past and a long and tortuous history. Located at the crossroads between East and West, Greece, throughout its history, has been visited or occupied by a variety of forces—Persians, Venetians, Genoese, Turks, the British, and Germans. In the twentieth century alone, Greece has withstood a number of wars, international and civil; its borders have been changed a number of times; and it has received and sent out several waves of refugees and migrants. For example, refugees from Asia Minor, mostly Greeks and Armenians, actually doubled the population of Greece around 1922. Hundreds of thousands of repatriates came from Egypt and from Western Europe in the 1960s and the 1980s. Presently Greece is receiving persons of Greek origin from Russia—from where a wave of some 500,000 is expected. Repatriation waves from Western Europe and from the overseas-migration-receiving countries (such as Canada, West Germany, and the United States) include a large proportion of elderly people coming to Greece following their retirement. Thus the percentage of elderly in Greece is increased and leads the Greek government to seek bilateral retirement-benefits agreements with many countries. So far treaties have been signed with only a few of them.

The above realities have changed Greece's population configuration repeatedly and have contributed to the formation of the Greek national character, which includes both the element of uncertainty in viewing the future and the conviction that—if a survival solution cannot be found within Greece—there is always the possibility of emigration, official or clandestine. Emigration always implies return, and permanent settlement always includes the fear of becoming a refugee.

Social Values

Uncertainty, due to the above realities, has molded certain national attitudes and values. The Greek is highly individualistic, but with a sense of self that encompasses the family, both from maternal and paternal sides, whether these people live under the same roof or are scattered in all continents. The family is the primary unit a Greek trusts and respects, feels responsible for, and is dependent upon. Loyalty is expected within the family, but inheritance difficulties may break up bonds. The Greek accepts the social control of the small community but does not accept such control within large, urban settings unless it is enforced. Traditional trust in the state and the government, due to Greece's history, is minimal.

The Greek person's approach to life is characterized more by resourcefulness and less by long-term planning or systematic methods. Urban living is more highly valued than rural living, as it promises more options, resources, and higher status. Urban life makes possible stable and dependable employment, improved living standards, diminished social control, and increased access to education and health facilities.

Investments are highly valued. Education is one of the most important. Other valued investments are real estate, gold and "strong" currencies, social insurance for health and retirement benefits, and—a late-comer—private life and health insurance (in the event that state-supervised schemes fail by the time one is old). The ultimate investment, however, is one's children: their education, their marriage, their property, their employment, and their status. Consequently, the bonds of reciprocal care are very strong in Greece and are seriously considered.

Socioeconomic Conditions

During the Second World War and the civil war, large numbers of people fled the rural areas and came to the large cities in Greece. This factor caused a large increase in the urban population. After the end of hostilities young people came to urban areas to seek employment at factories, in construction, and in public works. Since then the population in the rural areas has been declining. The rural population has declined from 57% in 1961 to 35% in 1981, according to the official census.

The process of industrialization began during the 1950s. Heavy industry consisted of steel, shipping, cement manufacturing and—more recently—textiles and plastics. Most manufacturing is located near the cities of Athens and Thessaloniki, as well as other large cities. Despite repeated efforts to attract foreign capital and technology, Greece has an average of zero rate economic growth during the 5 years leading to 1991. Currently its economy is in a serious crisis (Stathopoulos, 1991). Faced with a small private sector, the government has traditionally become the employer for a large segment of the work force. According to government reports, Greece has five times the number of civil servants that it needs, contributing to large budget deficits. Under the pressure of the European Community, the government is attempting to reduce the number of public employees and move toward the privatization of the public sector (with the resulting reduction in social services). Despite renewed efforts to attract foreign capital, it is strongly argued that Greece has entered a phase of deindustrialization (Papatheodossiou, 1990).

Government Structure

Greece has a centralized government structure. It is divided into 52 Prefectures (districts) on the basis of geographical, social, and economic criteria. The Prefector, who is appointed by the central government, coordinates the government's activities and oversees the operation of local authorities. In 1986 the government passed a law by which it has divided the country into 13 regions. Each region has a population between 200,000 to 700,000, except for the Attica and Thessalonica regions, which have 3,370,000 and 1,600,000 people, respectively. The establishment of the regions was a step toward the development of structures for more effective planning, delivery of services, and citizen involvement.

Health, education, and social services are mainly provided by the central government but are delivered on a decentralized basis, usually in the capital of each prefecture. More recently larger municipalities have also developed health and social services.

A serious problem in the delivery of services is the isolation of areas. Weather conditions during winter make most villages on the mountains and the islands inaccessible to health care and social service personnel. According to a government report (Ministry of Health, Welfare and Social Security, 1986), each social worker employed at the public welfare department of each prefecture has clients residing in eight communities (that also is true for the Athens area). For the mountainous, rural Peloponese region, the ratio is 1:236 communities. In terms of area covered, the ratio for Athens is one social worker to 56 square kilometers, while for the same Peloponese region it is 1:1,404 square kilometers. These data clearly indicate the magnitude of the problems in providing services to remote areas of the country.

Demography

Demographically, Greece is an aging country with a high tendency toward urbanization. Of its 9.5 million inhabitants, 40% live in Athens and Salonika and another 21% in other urban settings; 11% live in semi-urban communities of 2,000 to 9,999 inhabitants; and 28% live in some 5,000 communities of fewer than 2,000 inhabitants (National Committee for the World Congress on Ageing, 1983).

Greece has low birth and death rates as compared with other European countries, and life expectancy at birth is relatively high (i.e., 71 years for men and 74 years for women). These realities, plus the high emigration rates of the 1960 and 1970 decades, have contributed to the aging of the population. The aging of the population is expected to continue, but at a slower rate. According to the 1981 census, Greece has the seventh-oldest population among European Community countries, with 13% of its population over the age of 65. By the year 2,000 the segment of the population 60 years of age and older is expected to represent one fifth of the total. The percentage of women will be higher, as women outlive men. The percentage of widows will be even higher, as men tend to remarry. The fastest growing segment of the population is that of those aged 80-plus. In 1980 their numbers came to 74,500, but this number is expected to double by the end of the century. The very old (i.e., those over the age of 75) are found in both urban and rural areas; are mostly women, with finances lower than when their husbands were still alive and with increasing needs for services. Very few services exist in the rural areas, so there is a large migratory flow from the rural regions to the urban centers by elderly who come to the cities to find services and to be with their children. Those who come to the cities to be admitted into health facilities often return to their villages.

The percentage of the dependent elderly is no more than 7% (about 100,000 people), but those who are housebound—due to a variety of physical, mental or environmental reasons—represent one fourth of the elderly Greek population (i.e., about 400,000 people) (Heikkinen, Waters & Brzezinski, 1983). This picture becomes clearer, as to the severity of the problem, if one considers that (a) the dependency rate is high, coming to 55%, if the active population is taken as that between 24 and 60 years of age and (b) the young-old ratio is changing dramatically. While at the beginning of the century there were 11 old (over 65) to every 100 youths (under 15), today's ratio is 56 old to every 100 youths (Georgiadis & Amera, 1988). The dependency rate is lower than it was at the beginning of the century, but there is a significant difference: While 88% of the dependents had been children, now 61% are children, and the proportion of the elderly has increased more than threefold.

Low birth rates, in concordance with high life expectancy, bring the numbers of the elderly to increased levels. The 1961 census found 1,025,502 people over the age of 60. The 1981 census found that this group had increased by 600,000 and that their density was higher in the rural areas. The number of the very old present great interest because dependency is more likely.

Services for the Elderly

Formal services available for the care of the elderly in Greece have their base in the following sectors: (a) social security, social insurance, (b) state and local authority services, (c) the Church, (d) nongovernmental and other private nonprofit organizations, and (e) profit-making enterprises. These services will be summarized below.

Social Security, Social Insurance

All Greeks are covered by some social insurance scheme for health, retirement, and other benefits such as unemployment, child support, and widowhood, among others. Most of these schemes are contributory. In 1986 there were 330 different schemes, each with a different configuration of benefits, coverage, and amount contributed (Mossialos, 1990). Currently there are 32 organizations providing primary pensions and 63 providing supplementary pension benefits (Skoutelis, 1990). Although there are great differences in both benefits and contributions, and there are some pensioners who have 10 or 20 times the amount of the minimum pension, there is no Greek who is not somehow covered for all medical needs and for retirement benefits. Noninsured, indigent individuals over the age of 68 are covered through social welfare under the agricultural workers' scheme.

Due to the longevity of Greeks (and consequently the increased numbers of pensioners), the rapid rate of inflation, the small size of many retirement schemes, and the inefficiency of their administration, many schemes are practically bankrupt.

Under the threat of collapse of the whole social security system and the pressures from the European Community officials, the state is making another attempt to reorganize the system and reduce the number of the schemes to three or five. It remains to be seen if this effort will be successful, as many others failed in the past because of vested interests. Due to the above realities, the current neoconservative government encourages private insurance as a preferred alternative to the state-operated schemes. The urgency of the reform of the social security system is apparent when one considers the relevant statistics. O.E.C.D. estimates that, for the year 2000, the cost of pensions in Greece will represent 12.29% of the G.N.P. and 18.58% during 2050. For developed countries, on the average, the estimated costs for the corresponding years are projected as 12.24% and 20.15% (Ifantopoulos, 1988).

State and Local Authority Services

Traditionally, in the rural society with its characteristic extended patriarchal family structure, the elderly were cared for in the community. Only those who were destitute and totally incapacitated were placed in long-term residential institutions. The more recent trend in the government's policy is to recognize that the elderly should be taken care of as long as possible in the community, and that services should be provided not only to the destitute and seriously ill but to a broader segment of the elderly population as well. To achieve this aim and implement its policies, the state has developed a network of services described below.

KAPI

KAPI is the Greek acronym for Open Care Center for the Elderly or Community Day Center for the Elderly. The KAPI Centers offer medico-social services to the elderly of the community. Each center has a physician, a social worker, a visiting nurse, a physiotherapist, an occupational therapist, and one or more home assistants. Their goal is to contribute to the prevention of social, psychological, and physical problems; to encourage contact and cooperation with other age groups but also between the members of the center; to undertake research into the situation and problems of the elderly; to inform and educate and to enhance social participation; and to encourage self and group interest and activity.

Beyond the medical care (such as medical examination, electrocardiogram, examination for prostatic hypertrophy, PAP smear, chest X-rays, inoculations for influenza, etc.), the KAPI members are given advice and information regarding nutrition, prevention of accidents, counseling on social and psychological matters, and so on.

The program of social activities includes excursions, summer camp and vacations, dances, and other recreational and educational activities. Through occupational therapy, members receive self-care reeducation (for instance, after a stroke) or simply enjoy exercising hand and brain with arts and crafts. Members also organize their own interest groups—cooking, theater, choirs, gardening, computers, reading, and writing, and so on.

Almost all KAPI Centers have their own newspaper, published by the members. They also publish books of fairy tales and about old neighborhoods, traditions, recipes, proverbs, and so on, thus playing an active role in the maintenance of the Greek cultural heritage. Also, all KAPI Centers have mutual support and help groups that can prove of great importance when one is bedbound at home or in the hospital or when one is recently widowed.

There are 250 KAPI Centers in Greece, both in rural and urban areas. Most of them, however, are located in the greater Athens area. The KAPI Centers are operated by the local authorities and financed, to a large extent, by the central government. Thus the operation of the KAPI is subject to political pressures and often influenced by party nepotism toward its clientele by the mayors (Avramopoulou & Katsimbraki, 1990).

Thus, although KAPI centers have become an integral part of the social services system for the elderly in Greece, there is room for much improvement.

Housing

Every person over the age of 65 has the right to apply for a housing assistance and to be offered the lifelong use of a state-owned flat. The available flats are few, so people with difficulties have priority. This is a relatively new measure. Not very many years ago persons over the age of 65 had no right for shelter other than a bed in the Old Age Home. A recent measure that is of even greater importance is the rent-allowance. Homeless elderly who are not covered by any social insurance scheme are entitled to such an allowance. This is a measure that allows them choice and independence.

Social Hostels for Adults

Social hostels operate only in the Athens area. There are three of them and each one of them houses 50 people at a time (for periods up to 3 months). Social hostels operate for those adults who face temporary housing needs. They are open to adults over the age of 18, thus, avoiding age discrimination and age segregation. They may be used by dependent elderly whose children, or carers, need to be away for a period, or for adults who either have no place to stay or need (or wish) to be away from their home for a certain period. They are also very useful for people who come to the city from the rural areas in order to visit health facilities. The social services of the hostels are available to help with many problems.

Homes for Chronically Disabled Adults

Very few homes for the chronically disabled are in operation, and—where they exist—waiting lists are long. At this point, creating such units is of high priority, and 22 are being established in different parts of the country. The aim is to have one such home in each prefecture. Each unit is supposed to focus on physical, social, and occupational rehabilitation as well as on providing residential care. Disabled people who wish to, and can, remain in their own homes are provided with daily transport, which enables them to attend the rehabilitation programs.

All the measures mentioned above are state measures, some in full maturity and others developing. They have been recently conceived, in answer to real needs that are not yet fully and satisfactorily covered. Many of these measures are designed to relieve pressure placed on health facilities by persons who are over the age of 65. Mossialos (1990) reports that 4.2% of patients 65 years and older remain in hospitals for more than 41 days. The elderly, on the average, remain hospitalized for 16.6 days. In 1983 the average length of stay was 13 days for men and 12 days for women (Mossialos, 1990).

Each prefecture has a social welfare office. All state programs for the aged are implemented and/or mediated by that office. Thus there is a constant monitoring of the needs of the elderly, as well as other needs. All programs for the disabled are also implemented by that office. Home help services are beginning to be tested on the prefectural or the municipal levels. Two home nursing programs assist terminal cancer patients in the Athens and Piraeus areas; they are very effective, but they hardly cover the extent of needs. Additional state measures for the disabled, affecting the frail elderly, include financial assistance and tax rebates for the totally disabled.

The Church

The Eastern Orthodox Church of Greece has, historically, seen its role to comfort and care for the elderly who need its support. The church, through its dioceses and parishes, raises funds and provides mainly material assistance and services to elderly in institutions and, more recently, in the community. At the Archdiocese of Athens alone there are 2,500 volunteers who, on a regular basis, provide their services at the parish level. These volunteers are guided by parish priests and by (the few) social workers employed by the welfare department of the Archdiocese.

The Archdiocese of Athens consists of 141 parishes. There is an extensive network of self-help voluntary work provided to elderly persons. In each parish there is a welfare fund from donations and tray collections. The amount collected during 1987 was 365,000,000 drachmas (equivalent to about $2 million U.S. dollars), which is by no means insignificant. These funds are distributed to destitute persons in cash or for the purchase of medicine, eyeglasses, food, clothing, subsidy of rent, and so on. A large portion of these funds is used for the assistance of needy elderly persons.

The activities of the parishes include daily provision of meals, recreation, medical checkups, and ambulatory nursing care in 55 parishes. On a weekly basis, 11,215 meals are served, according to the Bulletin of the Archdiocese of Athens (1988). In addition to the provision of the above services, volunteers visit those elderly parishioners who, for whatever reason, are not able to leave their home. The volunteers do light housework, shopping, and food preparation for them.

The Archdiocese also runs 10 residential homes for elderly people and one nursing home for disabled bedbound elderly. The residential homes are for homeless elderly; they are small units and they serve from 5 to 40 persons on a long-term basis. The residents are self-caring, ambulatory, and capable of independent living. In most of these homes there is no paid staff except for the caretaker. Volunteers, under the guidance of the parish priests, take care of the needs of the residents. The extent, type, and quality of the provided services varies with the funds available, the availability of paid professional social work staff, and the leadership style and interest in the needs of the elderly by the parish priest.

Nongovernmental, Private Nonprofit Organizations

Nongovernmental organizations (NGOs) have played a very important role in the initiation and molding of services for the elderly in Greece. Outstanding among them are the Red Cross, the Volunteers' League, the Institution for Social Work, and the Center for the Care of the Family and the Child. These NGOs initiated new ideas in the care of the elderly people in cooperation with the Ministry of Health and Welfare, giving shape to services such as the KAPI, home help, tele-alarm, and many others that once researched, implemented, and proven useful and viable as solutions, were taken over by the state and local authorities. In Athens, at present, the Red Cross has one of the most extensive home help programs, and a significant training program for home helpers for the aged.

There are a number of other enterprises that take the form of private nonprofit organizations offering services to the elderly. These mostly include old age homes and private nonskilled nursing in hospitals and/or in homes.

Profit-Making Enterprises

The services offered by private enterprises suggest directions toward which community measures could expand, as they indicate demand and gaps in services. The proprietary sector offers (a) old age homes for both independent and dependent elderly and (b) private nurses for both hospitals and homes (hired by the patient or his family) for day or night shifts in acute or chronic cases.

There are many agencies providing this service, as Greece is in great need of trained and nontrained nurses. Many agencies work closely with hospitals, and it is possible to hire a private nurse through the office of the hospital head nurse. Many migrant women (from the Philippines, Sri Lanka, or Africa) find jobs through these agencies. Private agencies provide companions for the elderly who are frail or confused (Greek and foreign). Finally, private services are available for home help (cleaning, washing, feeding, shopping, etc.) and for transportation (taxi services).

Social Change and the Impact on the Family and the Care of the Elderly

All the services described above are developments of the post-World War II period and, more specifically, of the last 12-15 years. All estimates lead to the conclusion that, except for the social insurance and social security schemes and the health care system that cover all the elderly of Greece in more or less satisfactory ways, the rest of the services and measures reach only a segment of the aging population. It is said that only 1% of the Greek elderly are in institutions (Kanellopoulos, 1984), while there is evidence that about 7% of the Greek elderly are dependent and 25% are housebound (as has already been mentioned). The services developed in the last 15 years reach, at best, 10% of the aging population of the country—mostly through the KAPI Centers and, consequently, mostly the active old. The majority, thus, of the dependent elderly are taken care of within and by the family. This is the conclusion of sociological surveys and anthropological observations during the last 10 years.

The Greek Family and the Elderly

The Greek family is unavoidably influenced by the changes that are occurring. The last 40 years have seen Greece changing from a rural to an urban nation, from an agricultural economy to a service-oriented one attempting (unsuccessfully) to become industrial. Greece has changed from an isolated small nation to a member of the European Community, from a migrant-sending position to a migrant-receiving one, and from hunger in 1941 to a high enough standard of living that 35 years have been added to average life expectancy (placing Greece among the most advanced of the Western nations that have influenced its life-style and values). Yet the family remains the nucleus of Greek society. It is its focal point and most-supportive institution. This does not mean that the changes are not noteworthy. These changes are related to family size, focus (which is shifting from the extended to the nuclear), roles, responsibilities, and authority of its members (Teperoglou, 1990).

The size of the Greek family is becoming much smaller. The two-child family (a boy and a girl) remains the ideal—to the despair of demographers involved with national planning, who point to the defense and economic dangers resulting from the aging of the nation. Low fertility is not the only cause of family shrinking. During the first post-World War II years various members of the extended family, including grandparents, aunts, and uncles, lived under the same roof (Psychogios, 1987); however, the vast majority of contemporary Greek households embrace no more than the couple and its children. Internal migration, urban apartment living for most of the young, high rents, and limited mortgage possibilities for the purchase of one's own dwelling, and also the discovery of the meaning of "privacy" (a word that still does not exist in the Greek vocabulary) have contributed to significant shrinking of the size of the Greek family in terms of residence. Pensions and investments are encouraging elderly people to choose their privacy as well, and have their independence, which is something they prefer. Those who live under the same roof with their children feel they are not on their own turf (Tsaousis & Hatziyanni, 1990), even if the house originally belonged to them.

Despite its residential nuclearity, the Greek family is not isolated. Recent studies are concluding that, if nuclear in its appearance, the Greek family is extended—in essence and for all practical purposes. This is particularly true in relation to the grandparents. In fact, for at least one out of three families, the contact with the grandparents is daily (Moussourou, 1985). This contact is particularly strong when the family is young and the children are of preschool age, as the grandparents are usually involved with the everyday care of the children. The degree of this involvement is so high that it plays a determining role in the dynamics of the family, the interpersonal relationships of its members (Moussourou, 1985), and their perception of mutual dependence and responsibilities. Findings of several studies conclude that the Greek family is conjugal, but it functions within a broader network of relatives that support it in its day-to-day needs, influences its decisions, often assists it financially, and constitutes its primary social and recreational milieu (Teperoglou, 1990). The relatively high involvement of young children with their grandparents and, through them, with other family members (such as cousins as playmates and companions), allows the hypothesis that this network will continue to be important in their adulthood and will influence the upbringing of their own offsprings (Moussourou, 1985). It also molds the children's perception of the relationship between grandparents and grandchildren, leading youngsters to express the view that this relationship is one of the most important bonds for their own grandparents and to foresee that it will be of equal importance to them in the distant future (Amera, 1986).

One of the most significant changes of the postwar period is the entrance of women into the paid-work market. This change has affected roles, responsibilities, and authority between spouses, thus leading to greater equality (Teperoglou, 1990). Women's independence may have contributed to the greater number of divorces, whose impact is too soon to evaluate. In general, though, the employment of women is accepted because not only does it not disturb traditional processes, but it also helps the family to carry them through—even if it gives women a voice and independence (Lambiri-Dimaki, 1963). The education, migration, and employment of women substitute the "dowry" or give women the possibility to assist their father in amassing it. The wife's salary improves family finances, and a grandmother's pension often assists her children to educate their own offspring.

The participation of women with young children in the work force, or even their migration, is made possible by the willingness of grandparents to undertake the responsibility of the care of their grandchildren (Amera & Maratou-Alibrandi, 1988). These "debts" are usually honored when the grandparents become needy and/or dependent, as the general assumption still is (as is also the law) that children will take care of their parents in old age.

Although Greeks consider their children as the best security and investment, the traditional folk wisdom—stories, proverbs—have several statements of warning. One proverb, for instance, suggests: "Hold on to your money old man, for even if you have children you may also end up having troubles" (Amera, 1986). They also warn adults, however, that their own offspring will treat them the same way that they now treat their parents.

This sense of identification that the young have with the old, and the conviction that their fate will be the same as that of their parents, influences the behavior of those who are in the position of the carer. The majority of today's adults reject the idea of the impersonal institution for themselves and, consequently, reject it for those for whom they care. Caring for the old is, thus, a way of life corresponding to that of raising children; a responsibility families are reluctant to give up. The cost in time, energy, and money can be a gain in solidarity, meaning in life and peace of mind (Georgiadou & Amera, 1988).

The Care of the Elderly Relative

It has been ascertained that the family in Greece takes over many welfare roles. The care of the elderly, including the dependent elderly, is —to a large degree—the responsibility of the family in both urban and rural areas. This is particularly so in rural areas, however, where other services (provided by state, church, or private resources) are limited. Even so, a more careful examination of the issue is necessary, focusing more specifically (and with more method) on those individuals 75 and older who are more likely to have difficulties, disabilities, and dementias.

A study on the life-styles of older Athenians (Pitsiou, 1986) described family assistance patterns: there was a very high level of residential proximity with at least one of their children. There were daily contacts in 46% of the cases with children and 6% with siblings, and weekly contacts in 20% of the cases with children and 9% with siblings. The degree of contact seemed to decline somewhat as the parents got older, but tended to increase in the presence of illness or when the parents—especially the mother —changed residence and moved closer to the children. The elderly of the low-income group needed more assistance from their children than did those in the middle- and high-income groups.

The practice of caring for the elderly within the family is not without friction and conflict. Studies, such as the one by Spinellis and Pitsiou-Darrough (1990), on elder abuse and neglect, and the one by Amera (1990) on carers, point to several shortcomings and strains.

The phenomena of abandonments, neglect, abuse, or violence against the elderly, both in the community and the family, does exist (even though their frequency is very low and their actual numbers limited). The most common abuse within the family is verbal—indicating conflict and pressure; while in the community, burglaries and murders of elderly people occur with alarming increase. Some instances of abuse are due to ignorance. Cases of dehydration and poisoning due to medicine misuse appear with a certain regularity as do cases of bedridden elderly with bedsores that could have been prevented.

The departments of social services of most hospitals report a multiplicity of cases of abandoned elderly. The Athens General Hospital reported 225 cases for a 4-month period. Of these cases 40% were individuals who did not have any family, 35.5% were individuals whose family members did not want to care for them anymore, and 24.4% were persons from families facing serious hardships and not able to care for them.

Practically all hospitals have similar problems during the summer months and the holiday seasons: they become respite care institutions. This is because relatives abandon their elderly so the rest of the family can go on vacation. This practice is common among lower-class families—those who cannot afford to hire paid help to care for their frail, handicapped, or dependent elderly relative.

Particularly vulnerable are the elderly persons who have no family, live alone, or live with one other member of the family who is also old, ill, mentally ill, disoriented, or alcoholic. Their vulnerability relates not only to abuse, but also to the paucity of services. The impoverished are more likely to suffer from the absence of services, while the wealthy are more likely to suffer from exploitation and abuse.

Carers find very little support. Services are very few and private nurses and paid help are very costly. Long-term caring puts a strain on finances, careers, health, relationships, and mental well-being. The problems that carers mention are the problems of loss, fatigue, lack of sleep, lack of free time, interference with work and social life, inability to plan (as there is no way of knowing how long the situation will last), fear that when one situation will end another will appear (some carers have spent over 15 years in such a role), and the realization that by the time these responsibilities would end the carers—themselves—will be over the age of 60 and possibly will be needing care themselves. The question repeated by many carers is: "Our generation accepts this responsibility, as previous generations did, but when our time comes who will be in a position to care for us?"

Conclusions—Future Prospects

Greece, through concerted government and private efforts, has, in the postwar period, achieved an aging of its population attributed to a spectacularly improved standard of living and health care, to low fertility rates, and to high emigration levels. This achievement of adding more than 35 years to the average life expectancy has by now become a challenge. The challenge lies in the fact that the fastest growing segment of the population is that of 75-plus as well as the fact that the proportion of the elderly in the population is rising due to both longevity and the shrinking of the number of young people. Also shrinking is the size of the family, the institution that traditionally bears all welfare roles. Shrinking even more is the pool of carers, as women enter the work force in larger numbers. Carers are now older than they used to be in the past decades, often having aging needs of their own.

The state is now beginning to develop services for the elderly, but services for the dependent elderly are proving expensive and pension schemes are going bankrupt. Demands on health services are rising, as urban centers are getting larger and isolated island and mountain communities are getting smaller. Thus the creation and maintenance of a well-functioning network of state services is getting more difficult. The private sector is, as a consequence, getting very active; it also is very costly. And the probability of stress and strain on the family that cares for the dependent elderly is increasing.

Privatization is the wave of the future. An extra impetus to the private sector is given by Greece's geographical position and its touristical value as a place in the sun and a services-oriented economy. The "Florida phenomenon" is expected to bloom here, as well with elderly retirees from the northern parts of Europe settling in great numbers in Greece—either permanently or impermanently. Such a development will be a mixed blessing; the quality of services will improve, no doubt, but the cost will be so high that the average Greek pensioner, whose present pension is below the level of poverty and whose buying ability will progressively diminish due to inflation, will be unable to purchase them.

It is evident that the prospect for the future is rather grim. Unless state and private forces are coordinated immediately, in a way that provides orthological coverage for the dependent elderly as well as support for the family that cares for the frail adult, the coming decades will bring a lot of hardship (because the informal networks will be overburdened and unable to function). Yet during times of hardship people rise to the challenges. The following laconic comment of a dying man in his eighties casts a ray of optimism on the problem: When his wife said to him "where would we be now without our daughter?" he answered: "Life leaves no one without resources." Now is the time to discover, explore, develop, tap, and even harness these resources.

References

Amera, A. (1986). *So we will all age better* (Greek). Athens: Academy of Athens, Publications of the Centre for the Study of Greek Society.

Amera, A. (1990). Family care in Greece. In A. Jamieson & R. Illsley (Eds.), *Contrasting European policies for the care of older people* (pp.72-82). Hants, UK: Avebury; Brookfield, VT: Gower.

Amera, A., & Maratou-Alibrandi, L. (1988). Migration and the family: The socialization of the children in a rural community. *The rural world in the mediterranean area* (in Greek). Athens: National Center for Social Research, Centre for Modern Greek Studies of the National Research Foundation, Franco-Greek Conference with the scientific participation of C.N.R.S.

Archdiocese of Athens. (1988). *Directorate of mutual aid bulletin.* No. 382, Athens: Author.

Avramopoulou, F., & Katsimbraki, A. (1990). *Residential and open-care policies for the elderly.* A research report (in Greek). Athens: Department of Social Work Technological Educational Institutes.

Georgiadis, E., & Amera, A. (1988, October). *Comprehensive care of the elderly in the community: Greece 1988.* Paper presented at the Working Group on the Organization of Comprehensive Care of the Elderly in the Community by WHO, Valletta, Malta.

Heikkinen, E., Waters, W. E., & Brzezinski, Z. J. (1983). *The elderly in eleven countries.* Public Health in Europe No. 21. Copenhagen: WHO.

Ifantopoulos, J. (1988). *Demographic aging and pensions in Greece and the European community* (in Greek). Athens: EDIM.

Kanellopoulos, K. (1984). *The elderly in Greece* (in Greek). Athens: KEPE.

Lambiri-Dimaki, J. (1963, January 31). The employment of women in industry 9 (in Greek). *Economicos tahidromos, 455.*

Ministry of Health, Welfare and Social Security. (1986). *Findings and conclusions of research studies* (in Greek). [Research report]. Athens: Author.

Mossialos, E. (1990). *The consumption of health services in Greece.* Athens: Anixi.

Moussourou, L. (1985). *Family and child in Athens* (in Greek). Athens: ESTIA.

National Committee for the World Congress on Ageing. (1983). *The elderly in Greece: National report.* Athens: Ministry of Health Welfare and Social Security.

Papatheodossiou, T. (1990). *Changing needs in vocational skills.* [Research Report No. 6]. Athens: Ministry of Education, Institute of Technological Education.

Pitsiou, E. (1986). *Life styles of older Athenians* (Vol. 1). Athens: National Center of Social Research.

Psychogios, D. (1987). *Dowries, taxes, raisins and bread* (in Greek). Athens: National Centre of Social Research.

Skoutelis, J. (1990). *Social security: Development and crisis* (in Greek). Athens: Center for Health Social Sciences.

Spinellis, C., & Pitsiou-Darrough, E. (1990). *Violence against the elderly: Abuse and neglect.* [Research Report]. Athens: Ministry of Health Welfare and Social Security.

Stathopoulos, P. (1991). Community development in Greece. In M. Hill (ED.), *Social work and the European community* (pp. 115-128). London: Jessica Kingsley.

Teperoglou, A. (1990). *Evaluation of the contribution of centres of open protection of the aged* (in Greek). Athens: Ministry of Health, Welfare and Social Security, National Centre of Social Research.

Tsaousis, D., & Hatziyanni, A. (1990). *Social and spatial prerequisites for the functioning of the KAPI as linkage institutions between the aged and the community.* Athens: Pantion University of Social and Political Sciences, Ministry of Health, Welfare and Social Security.

13

Family Care of the Elderly in Japan

DAISAKU MAEDA
YOUMEI NAKATANI

Introduction

In Japan, as is frequently pointed out, the traditional family care of the elderly is preserved much more strongly than in other industrialized countries. Even today the Japanese Civil Code still stipulates, in the well-known item 877, that those who are in a lineal relation (as well as siblings) are responsible for supporting and caring for each other. It should be noted, however, that the present policy of the government is very lenient with regard to the enforcement of the legal responsibility of children for supporting and caring for their aging parents.

In the actual administration of the Public Assistance Law, the strictest among various laws with regard to the enforcement of the mutual responsibility for supporting and caring for relatives, the responsibility of children toward their aging parents is regarded to be relative in contrast with the absolute responsibility of parents for rearing their children. The word *relative* means that adult children who became independent from their parents only need to support and/or care for their aging parents when they have enough financial and social capability after securing a decent life for their own families.

Similarly, the current regulations of the Ministry of Health and Welfare on the fees of public community services, that is, day care, respite care, and home help services, only require children who presently live with their aging parents in the same household to bear financial responsibility. In the case of the fee for institutional care in nursing homes and ordinary homes for the aged, only children who have been living with aging parents at the time of admission are required to pay the fee. Thus children who live separately from their parents are not responsible for paying the fee for any public services provided to their aging parents. Not only the financial responsibility but the responsibility for providing care to aging parents is now defined very narrowly in the actual administration of the Law for the Welfare of the Elderly. That is, when aging parents get seriously impaired and need help for their daily living, but a daughter or a son's wife living together is working, they are not required to quit the job to care for them even if the family is well-to-do and her income is not indispensable. They can ask the government to provide care for their aging parents in a nursing home. They are required only to pay a fee according to the regulation mentioned above.

Thus even though the Japanese Civil Code still holds traditional values, the Japanese society has changed to such an extent that the government cannot enforce the traditional value of family responsibility to the people. This chapter discusses the decline of family care in Japan and describes the expanding role of the government in providing social care to the elderly to meet the ever-growing needs of the elderly and their families in this rapidly aging society.

Aging in Japanese Society

Aging Population

The proportion of older persons, aged 65 or over, in Japan was 11.9% in 1990, which is still significantly lower as compared with the Western European countries. The problem is, however, the speed of aging. In 1950 only 4.9% of the entire population was aged 65 or older. The proportion has more than doubled since then, coupled with a fact that the real number of the aging population has almost tripled.

The speed of aging in the future will be still faster. It is estimated that the proportion of the aging population will reach approximately 16.3% in 2000 and 23.6% in 2020, when the proportion is anticipated to reach the first maximum point. In addition, the number of very old persons, aged 80 or older, has significantly increased and will increase as follows: only 371,000 in 1950 and as many as 4.5 million in 2000 (thus, more than a 10-fold increase in half a century), and to more than 17 million in the year 2020 (approximately a four-fold increase in just a couple of decades).

Two factors have caused the rapidly aging population. The primary cause is the decrease of the mortality rate. The life expectancy at birth in Japan has remarkably improved from 50.1 for males and 54.0 for females in 1947 to 75.9 for males and 81.8 for females in 1989. Second, the birth rate has dramatically declined. The total fertility rate in 1950 was 4.54, but the figure in 1989 was 1.57 (one of the lowest in the world).

The Elderly in the Family

The high proportion of elderly persons live together with their adult children. According to the latest National Census of 1990 (GMCA, 1990), approximately 60% of the Japanese elderly, aged 65 or older, live with their children. In addition, the majority of impaired older persons who need assistance in daily life are cared for by, and living together with, their adult children. A nationwide study estimated the proportion of the seriously impaired bedridden elderly (those who have been in such a condition for more than 6 months) in the population aged 65 or older in 1986 at 1.7%. Of all the bedridden elderly, 56% are cared for by their spouse, child, or other relatives in their own home; 23% are in nursing homes; and 21% are hospitalized (MHW, 1985). It can safely be said that traditional patterns of living arrangements are still fairly well-preserved in Japan; however, the proportion of the elderly living with their adult children has been decreasing in the last 30 years (from 81.6% in 1960 to 61.9% in 1988). It seems, moreover, that the rate of the decrease has accelerated in recent years.

**Attitudes of Middle-Aged Persons
on Family Care of the Elderly**

The relatively high proportion of Japanese elderly living together with adult children and receiving care from the relatives can be attributed to attitudes of middle-aged Japanese persons toward family care of the elderly. A survey conducted in 1981 (GMCA, 1981) found that almost 60% of married men and women, aged 30 to 49, thought that one of the children's families should live with aging parents. Furthermore almost 80% of them responded that the children's family should live with them when one of their aging parents gets frail or dies. Similarly, when they were asked about their own plans for the care of their aging parents, more than 80% answered that a child or a child's spouse would provide care, and approximately 10% answered that the parent's spouse should provide care. Less than 3% answered that they were planning to depend upon resources other than family (i.e., a paid housekeeper, public home help services, nursing home, and so forth). Therefore it is clear that the overwhelming majority of middle-aged persons in Japan firmly believed that providing care to the frail elderly is the responsibility of their children.

Declining Family Support and Care of the Elderly

Evidence of Declining Family Care of Aging Parents

Family care is declining slowly but steadily; the percentage of bedridden older persons cared for in their own homes has decreased from 69% in 1978 to 56% in 1984. Almost half of bedridden older persons are hospitalized or institutionalized. Certainly a number of bedridden older persons do not have children, are too impaired to be cared for by family, or have an older caregiver in poor health. Yet many middle-aged persons do not provide care to their aging parents for other reasons such as pursuing a career, or a bedridden older person might prefer to move to a hospital or a nursing home rather than being provided care by a family member who feels physically and psychological burdened, or children might not want to provide care because of difficulty in family relations.

Another evidence of declining family support to the elderly can be observed in the decrease of financial support. Comparing two nationwide studies, conducted in 1974 and 1983 (GMCA, 1974, 1983), the proportion of adult children (married, middle-aged male children) who provide financial support to their aging parents declined as follows:

	1974	1983
children aged 35-39	41%	36%
children aged 40-44	42%	40%
children aged 45-49	48%	42%

When adult children who do not provide financial support to aging parents were asked the reason for not doing so, about half of them answered that their parents were well-to-do enough and did not need such support. During these 9 years between studies Japan's economy had been increasingly developed, and the income of these middle-aged men had substantially improved. Therefore the reduced proportion of financial support to aging parents reflects, in part, the greater financial independence of the elderly brought about by the development of the public pension programs.

**Factors Affecting the Decline of the Family Role
in the Care of Aging Parents**

The following four factors should be considered as causes of the decline
of family care in the context of the Japanese social situation:

1. change in socioeconomic structure as a result of rapid economic development and urbanization,
2. demographic changes,
3. decrease in capability of family to care for their aging parents, and
4. development of formal support and care services.

Rapid Economic Development and Urbanization

Japan has been experiencing rapid economic development and urbanization since 1955. The impact of this change was so profound that it is
sometimes referred to as "the second industrialization." In 1955 the proportion of the population engaged in agriculture was approximately 41%.
This proportion was reduced to 9% in 1985 (GMCA, 1955, 1985). This
reduction of the agricultural population made a profound impact on the
living arrangements of the Japanese elderly.

Industrialization also brought about frequent geographical mobility of
the working population. In industrialized societies people change their
jobs much more frequently than in nonindustrialized societies. Even when
they remain in the same firm, employees are often forced to move to other
industrial areas for various reasons. In such cases aging parents tend to
prefer to remain at the original residence rather than move to an unknown
place. In addition, housing for workers is, generally speaking, not large
enough for two generations to live together in Japanese industrialized areas.

Finally, the awakening of a sense of selfhood among the general public,
aroused by higher education, higher living standards, and the influence
of Western industrialized countries, played a very important role with regard to the change in living arrangements of the elderly; that is, an increasing number of both the older and younger generations prefer to live
separately from each other just for the sake of personal independence and
freedom. All in all, Japanese society is now in a conflicting situation with
regard to the family care of aging parents, where the preservation of traditional culture and the impact of industrialization and modernization
exist side by side.

Demographic Changes

One feature of Japan's recent demographic changes is the increase in the number of unmarried and/or childless old people, along with the increase in the total size of the aged population mentioned earlier. For example, in 1972, 20% of the households had a single person or a married couple and a member aged 65 or older. This proportion increased to roughly one third by 1988 (MHW, 1990).

Due to the aging of the aged population itself, moreover, there are many cases where the age of a caretaking child is also high, and whose health is not good enough to provide needed care to the aging parent(s).

Decreased Capability of Families to Care for Aging Parents

The increased proportion of the elderly living alone or only with their spouse has brought about a significant decrease in the capability of families to care for aging parents. Furthermore, the growing number of middle-aged women who were once the most dependable caregivers of dependent older persons are now working outside the home, limiting the capability of families to care for aging parents, even when aging parents and their adult children live together. The issue of difficulties in family caring will be discussed more fully below.

Development of Formal Support and Care Services

Theoretically, formal support and care services were developed to cope with various problems the elderly and their families face in the industrialized society of present-day Japan. As economists frequently point out, however, supply arouses demand. The development of various forms of formal care services in recent years has made it possible for a family with dependent older persons to rely on these services and seems to somehow influence the decline of family care.

Difficulties of Families Caring for Frail Aging Parents

The impact of demographic and social changes has been so strong that the recent development of formal support and care services could not fully meet the expanding needs of the frail elderly and their families. Thus some families who lack the capability of providing needed care for very frail or seriously impaired elderly still must provide care in their own homes. In such cases the quality of care tends to be poor and, at the same time, the sacrifice of a caregiver is very severe.

A study conducted by the Tokyo metropolitan government in 1990 (Tokyo Metropolitan Government, 1991) found that approximately 80% of family caregivers of the seriously impaired elderly are women. Some 32% of them are spouses, 28% are son's wives, and 22% are daughters. Among the remaining 20% of male caregivers, 15% are the husbands of the impaired elderly, and 5% are their sons. Most of the wives of the impaired elderly are older persons themselves; approximately one out of four are aged 80 or older. It should be stressed that one third of these older caregivers suffer from their own health problems.

In addition, son's wives and married daughters are generally at the prime stage of their life and busy with many duties, such as working and rearing their own children. Unmarried sons and daughters are usually full-time workers. The results of the study show that almost half of the sons and daughters providing care are working, and 12% of the families with impaired elderly members have another person who needs assistance in daily life. In sum, more than 60% of family caregivers have difficulties in caring for their frail or impaired older parents.

From the viewpoint of prioritizing the unmet needs of the frail or impaired elderly and their families, seriously impaired older persons who are cared for by family caregivers and who themselves have serious difficulties in providing care, should acquire special attention. The study estimates that the proportion of such cases in Tokyo, of the total population aged 65 or older, is 5.3 per 1,000.

Many frail elderly still live in the community because of the limited availability of nursing home beds and because of social pressure requiring children to take care of their aging parents. Even today many people are very hesitant to place their frail parents into an institution. Needless to say these seriously impaired elderly (and their family caregivers) need some form of outside support immediately.

Recently a number of studies were conducted on the burdens of family caregivers of the frail or impaired elderly. According to the findings of one such study, a family caregiver feels more burdened when the older person shows problematic behaviors, is bedridden, when the caregiver is engaged in full-time work, and when the income of the household is low (Maeda & Shimizu, 1984). Another study on caregivers of the demented elderly disclosed that, contrary to the findings of the study mentioned above, a caregiver's feelings of burden increases when the individual is not engaged in full-time work, though the influences of other factors seem to be almost similar to those found in the former study (Nakatani & Tojo, 1989).

Development of Public Services for the Frail Elderly

In order to cope with the problems of the impaired elderly and their caretaking families, Japan has been developing various kinds of public services ranging from institutional care to tax-deduction programs. Most of the public programs are administered by local governments with subsidies from the national government. In addition to those programs subsidized by the national government, programs have been established by a number of local governments, although, generally speaking, their effects are limited when compared with those of the nationally-supported programs.

Enactment of the Law for the Welfare of the Elderly

Prior to the 1960s most of the economic resources in the public sector were used for economic development and the construction of very basic social services such as public transportation, running water systems, roads, and so forth. Some of the basic human services (compulsory education, public assistance, etc.) were also given priority. About 1960 Japan succeeded in meeting the basic human needs of the people and began to pay more and more attention to the social and humanistic aspects of their lives. Various public services were developed to meet such needs, including the needs of the elderly for various cultural, health, and social services.

In 1963 the national government enacted the Law for the Welfare of the Elderly (LWE). This law has two characteristics: (a) it is a fundamental law that stipulates several basic principles with which all the other laws, as well as governmental and voluntary actions related to the life of the elderly, should conform and (b) it regulates public social services for the elderly, including institutional services, community services, health-related services, educational services, and recreational services. The LWE has been playing a very important role in the development of public services for the elderly.

Development of Institutional Care

The LWE regulates three types of institutional care for the elderly as follows:

1. Nursing home for the aged (for seriously impaired older persons). Anyone can apply for admission to this home, regardless of their income. When the income of an applicant and family is under a certain level, a fee is waived.
2. Home for the aged (for slightly or moderately impaired older persons with income under a certain amount set by the national government).
3. Home for the aged with moderate fees (for those older persons who are independent in daily life and with a limited income).

In the past 20 years the number of nursing homes has been increasing very rapidly, paralleling the increase of the population aged 65 or older and the decline of family care. The other two types of homes for the aged have not increased very much, mainly due to the government policy that emphasized the expansion of community care services.

Although the increase in the number of nursing home beds was very significant in the past, the proportion of the institutionalized elderly is still remarkably small in Japan. In 1989 only 1.6% of the elderly in Japan were in one of the three types of institutions. The proportion of institutionalized older persons in other industrialized countries is usually 4%-5%. Thus in spite of the recent development of various institutional and community care services, the shortage of nursing home beds is still very serious, especially in large metropolitan areas.

Development of Community Services

No public community services for the elderly had been provided in Japan before 1962, when the national subsidy program for home help services was established. Since then a variety of community services have been started. Currently the national government focuses on three major community services for the frail elderly: (a) home help service, (b) short-term stay service, and (c) day service. In addition, the national government subsidizes several other community services for supporting family care to the elderly.

Home Help Service

The home help service is regarded to be a core of the network of various community services for the elderly and their families in Japan. The number of public home helpers increased from 6,100 in 1970 to 36,000 in 1990. The ratio of the number of home helpers to the population aged 65 or older also increased from one home helper per 1,210 aged persons in 1970 to one per 380 in 1990. The relative number of home helpers in Japan, however, is still considerably smaller when compared to that of the Western European countries.

Short-Term Stay Service

The short-term stay service in Japan is almost equivalent to the respite service in the Western countries. A frail older person can stay at a nursing home for one week for any reason, and this period can be extended when necessary. Started in 1978, the short-term stay service is fairly well-developed, with 7,200 available short-term stay beds in 1990.

Day Service for the Elderly

The national subsidy program for Day Service for the Elderly, started in 1979, is similar to day care for adults in other industrialized countries. One of the differences is that in the Japanese system the services are sometimes given in the homes of the elderly. In 1990 approximately 1,800 day care centers were in operation throughout Japan.

Other Major Community Services

In order to help the community-based elderly living alone or in frail and impaired condition, the national government provides subsidies to local governments so they may provide or lend various types of needed resources, such as a special bed, bath tub, compact water heater, mattress, automatic fire extinguisher, wireless transmitter for emergency alarm, wheelchair, walker, and so forth. The special loan is also available for those family caregivers who plan to build or remodel their houses so as to have a room for their aging parents.

The income tax-deduction program is applied to those taxpayers, regardless of the amount of income, who are supporting a person aged 70 or older. When an older person is seriously impaired, the deductible amount is increased. Almost the same tax-deduction program is available for local taxes.

New and Advanced Approaches of Public Services in the 1980s

The proportion of the elderly aged 65 and older in Japan exceeded 9% in 1980. Since then, the impact of population aging became increasingly apparent not only to those who were directly engaged in work for the elderly but also to the leaders of various areas of Japanese society. In 1985 the national government decided to establish a special subcabinet to deal with policies to be adopted for the coming "Society of Longevity." The following year, in 1986, a Policy Statement on the National Long-Term Program to cope with the "Society of Longevity" was adopted by the Cabinet.

From the viewpoint of social gerontologists, who are well-informed about social policies in advanced countries of Europe and North America, the contents of this Policy Statement are not very new. The goals are described in very abstract terms. Nevertheless, the Policy Statement has been, and is, playing an important role in the development of social policies for the elderly in Japan. Even before the official adoption of the Policy Statement, some national government bodies (and a number of prefectural and municipal governments) established their own policies aimed at undertaking the demands of an aging society. The Policy Statement has actually supported and encouraged these developments. In the following section some of the new approaches of the national government are described.

Enactment of the Law for Health and Medical Services for the Elderly

The Law for Health and Medical Services for the Elderly, enacted in 1982, is based on chapters on health and medical services from the Law for the Welfare of the Elderly. It should be stressed, however, that the previous programs were substantially enlarged in many respects. One of the most significant revisions given to this new law was the lowering of the age limit for health check and preventive services. According to the new law, every local government is required to give health check services regularly to all citizens age 40 and older (as for uterine and breast cancer, those aged 30 or over are covered). The health check services are provided for a moderate fee or free of charge.

The Law for Health and Medical Services for the Elderly introduced a new facility for the impaired elderly—Health Care Facilities for the Aged. Such facilities provide long-term care for older persons who are suffering from chronic diseases but do not need hospitalization. The main purpose of the establishment of this type of institution is to shorten the very long average hospital stay of older persons, thereby controlling the national medical expenditure, which has been rapidly increasing.

The Sheltered Housing Program

In the light of the predicted sharp increase of the elderly living alone and aged couples living by themselves in the community, special housing especially designed to accommodate the frail and/or impaired elderly should be developed. Until recently the national and local governments could not sufficiently fund the public housing program for the elderly due to the serious shortage of public housing for middle-aged wage earners. In 1988 the national government finally decided to start sheltered housing programs for the aged.

Home-Care Support Center

As a variety of community services are provided, information giving and coordination of these services are required. In 1989 the national government started a new subsidy program to local governments for the establishment and operation of Home-Care Support Centers before the end of the twentieth century, hoping to establish 10,000 such centers. These centers operate on a 24-hour basis with at least a nurse and a trained social worker or careworker.

Role of Friends, Neighbors, and Voluntary Organizations

The role played by friends, neighbors, and voluntary organizations in support and care of the elderly living in the community is significantly less important in Japan than in other industrialized countries. The Japanese culture always places very strong emphasis on the mutual help among blood relatives. Generally, asking friends or neighbors to provide substantial help is regarded as a shame in Japan. When a family faces a difficult problem with which family members are unable to cope, the state is expected to provide needed assistance. In fact Japan is one of the oldest countries in starting public relief programs for those who could not depend upon relatives, though the benefit was provided only to aged or disabled persons who were below the subsistence level.

In the actual provision of assistance, sometimes the government utilizes nongovernmental organizations or agencies and provides financial support for them to perform services. Thus voluntary welfare organizations or agencies, which are independent from the government, have not developed. Actually almost all of them are financially dependent upon the government. Thus the weight of contribution from the private sector is very small in Japan.

The number of volunteers working in various social welfare fields, including that of the services for the elderly, has been steadily increasing in recent years in both urban and rural areas. Still their contribution is not as great as in other industrialized countries. Because most volunteers work in existing service delivery systems, they are not regarded as an independent component of the social welfare system.

Future of Family Care

Traditional family care of the elderly in Japan has been declining due to the drastic industrialization and urbanization accompanied by the rapid economic growth. As the aging of the population continues, this trend will be accelerated. Therefore the role of public social services should be expanded, and much more responsibility will be placed on local and national governments in order to supplement and strengthen the family care.

In 1989 the national government promulgated the "Ten-Year Strategy for the Promotion of Health and Welfare Services for the Elderly," known as the "Gold Plan." It presented the following goals to be achieved before the turn of the century: 100,000 home helpers (35,905 in 1990), 50,000 beds for short-term stay service (7,174 in 1990), 10,000 day care centers (1,780 in 1990), 10,000 Home-Care Support Centers (none at the beginning of 1990), 240,000 nursing home beds (152,988 in October 1989), 280,000 beds for the health care facility (18,275 in March 1990), and 100,000 beds in *kea-hausu* (sheltered housing for the elderly with meal services). Other domiciliary and care services are to be provided by community welfare agencies when needed (none at the beginning of 1990) (MHW, 1990). If the plan is completed, the quality of life of frail elderly and their families will be improved significantly, compared to the present level.

It should be noted, however, that the quantitative level of services for the frail elderly, both as institutional and community services, hardly matches that of other industrialized countries. This is due to the extremely rapid increase of the aging population, especially that of the very old elderly. Thus Japan will have to promulgate another long-term plan before the coming of the next century.

References

General Management and Coordination Agency of the National Government (GMCA). (1955, 1985). *Kokusei chosa* (National census). Tokyo: Author.

General Management and Coordination Agency of the National Government (GMCA). (1974, 1983). *Roshin fuyo ni kansuru chosa* (Survey on support and care of aged parents). Tokyo: Author.

General Management and Coordination Agency of the National Government (GMCA). (1981). *Rogo no seikatsu to kaigo ni kansuru chosa* (Survey of opinions on life after retirement and care to be given). Tokyo: Author.

General Management and Coordination Agency of the National Government (GMCA). (1990). *Kokusei chosa* (National Census). Tokyo: Author.

Maeda, D., & Shimizu, Y. (1984). Shogai rojin wo kaigo suru kazoku no shukanteki konnan no yoin bunseki (Factors related to the subjective difficulties of families caring for the impaired elderly). *Shakaironengaku (Social Gerontology), 19,*3-7.

Ministry of Health and Welfare (MHW). (1985). *Kosei gyosei kiso chosa hokoku* (Report of fundamental survey for health and welfare administration). Tokyo: Author.

Ministry of Health and Welfare (MHW). (1985, 1990). *Kosei hakusho.* [White paper on health and welfare administration]. Tokyo: Author.

Ministry of Health and Welfare (MHW). (1990). *Kosei hakusho.* [White paper on health and welfare administration]. Tokyo: Author.

Nakatani, Y., & Tojo, M. (1989). Kazoku kaigosha no ukeru futan: Futankan no sokutei to yoin bunseki (Burden of family caregivers to the demented elderly: Measurement of feelings of burden and factors affecting the burden). *Shakaironengaku (Social Gerontology), 29,* 25-36.

Tokyo Metropolitan Government. (1991). *Koreisha no seikatsu jittai* (Survey on life of the aged). Tokyo: Author.

14

Family Care of the Elderly in the United States

An Issue of Gender Differences?

TIMOTHY H. BRUBAKER
ELLIE BRUBAKER

Family caregiving of the elderly has been a topic of concern for many years within the United States because the number and proportion of older persons has been growing substantially. The declining fertility and mortality rates have encouraged a demographic transition that has resulted in an aging of the United States population (Grigsby, 1991). Currently there are approximately 32 million persons aged 65 years and older within the United States and, by the year 2000, there will be nearly 35 million (U.S. Bureau of Census, 1989). The present number of elderly within the United States represents a dramatic increase during the past 30 years. For example, there were 16.7 million older persons in 1960 and 20.1 million in 1970 (U.S. Bureau of Census, 1984). The increase in the number and proportion of elderly in the United States represents a pattern that is expected to be followed by other countries. For example, it is projected that the older population in Japan (currently 13 million) will double in the next two decades (McContha, McContha & Cinelli, 1991). Grigsby (1991) estimated the growth of an aging population to be based upon countries' rates of mortality and fertility and suggested that other less-developed countries will exhibit similar increases in the number and proportion of elderly within their populations.

The United States, a modern industrial society, has a family structure seldom described as extended (Lee, 1985a). Youth, independence, and autonomy are, and have traditionally been, highly valued within the United States. Achieving independence and autonomy, however, has not resulted in an abandonment of the older generations by younger family members. Indeed, Lee (1985b) commented that the lives of older persons would be "bleak" without the support of family members.

Several analyses of societal values and economic structures concluded that the elderly are most advantaged in agricultural societies in terms of family status and support from younger generations (Balkwell & Balswick, 1981; Ishii-Kuntz & Lee, 1987; Lee, 1984). Within the agricultural societies families are localized and integrated around a centralized authority structure, and the elderly are valued for their participation in activities and as information resources. The status of the older population is generally lower in modern industrialized societies. The elderly have less power and a lower ability to reciprocate the support they receive from younger generations (Lee, 1985b). Within the United States the elderly may not have as high a status as their counterparts within an agricultural society, but they are valued and supported by younger family members.

This chapter focuses on the family caregiving patterns within the United States. The following topics will be examined in terms of traditional and contemporary caregiving patterns: (a) characteristics of family caregiving, (b) expectations regarding caregiving, (c) gender roles in provision of care, and (d) programs that support family caregiving. First, the American family will be characterized with particular attention to the amount of care provided to the elderly by family members. Second, the expectations for the provision of family care will be discussed because the expectations families hold concerning caregiving likely reflect their value orientations toward it. Third, research on gender differences in family caregiving will be examined to describe who provides what type of care, the amount of burden experienced by male and female family caregivers, and trends concerning gender differences in caregiving. Fourth, programs that support family caregiving are discussed. The programs that provide services to elderly individuals often function to support the caregiver, although the intended function may be to support the older recipient of care. Finally, suggestions for changes that may support family caregivers in the future are explicated.

Characteristics of Family Caregiving

Within the United States numerous studies (for reviews, see Brubaker, 1990; Gatz, Bengtson, & Blum, 1990; Mancini & Blieszner, 1989) have indicated that families provide care for older relatives. Historically, family members have provided care to their elderly relatives as well. A recent national survey of caregivers of the elderly reported that the majority of primary and secondary caregivers were family members (Stone, Cafferata, & Sangl, 1987). Others (Brody, 1984; Manton & Liu, 1984) have estimated that 80%-90% of the care received by older persons is provided by family members. Studies of minority families also indicated that elderly black parents rely on extended family for assistance (Chatters, Taylor, & Jackson, 1985; Taylor, 1985, 1986; Taylor & Chatters, 1986). Although American family patterns are heterogeneous, research suggests that family members with diverse backgrounds are providing care for their elderly relatives and, often, the support is provided with substantial sacrifice and, in the least, with an alteration in dealing with one's own priorities (Lewis, 1990).

The elderly population in the United States has increased significantly during this century. The increased older population is due to a variety of factors, including technological advances in medicine, and possibly economic and social conditions (Brody, 1990). As the numbers of elderly increase, it is probable that the number of family members needing as well as providing care will also increase. For example, according to United States Census data (U.S. Bureau of Census, 1989), 12.2% of the United States population was 65 years of age and older in 1987, and it is projected that 13% will be 65 years of age and older by year 2000. The percentage of people in this age group is expected to increase to 21.8% by the year 2030.

Growth in the percentage of people age 85 years and older also is expected. In 1987, 9.6% of the persons 65 years of age and older were aged 85 years and older. It is projected that 13.3% will be 85 years and older in the year 2000, will peak at 15.5% in the year 2010, and will decline to 12.4% by the year 2030. These projections for the older population suggest that there will be more elderly who have the potential of needing care from family members in the future. Thus the number of older people who will need care is likely to increase for many years in the future.

At the same time the number of younger persons to provide care for older persons will likely decrease in the future. The declining fertility rate in the last 30 years within the United States has resulted in smaller families to care for older persons who live longer (U.S. Bureau of Census, 1988). The result, says Brody (1990), is that "contemporary adult children provide more care and more difficult care to more parents and parents-in-law over much longer periods of time than has ever been the case before" (p. 13). Future older generations will have fewer children to provide care for them if they need assistance. Indeed, Cicirelli (1990) recently observed that "social trends towards smaller families, greater employment of women, and increased divorce imply that there will be fewer family caregivers who can assume a primary caregiving role singlehandedly" (p. 228).

Expectations for Family Care

A number of studies (Cicirelli, 1983; Hanson, Sauer, & Seelbach, 1983; Sanders & Seelbach, 1981; Seelbach, 1978, 1984) have indicated that older persons expect their adult children and family members to provide assistance if they need it. Investigations of minority families—black (Taylor, 1985, 1986; Taylor & Chatters, 1986) and Mexican-American (Markides, Boldt, & Ray, 1986; Markides, Hoppe, Martin, & Timbers, 1983)—similarly found that older adults expect assistance from members of the younger generations. Further, this research suggests that many adult children within the United States, similarly, expect to provide assistance to their dependent, older parents, but the expectation of providing assistance is moderated by older parents' desires to not interfere in the lives of their adult children. As Blieszner and Mancini (1987) noted, their sample of older persons wanted their children to routinely interact with them and provide emotional support to them, but they did not want their children to disrupt their own lives to provide care on a long-term basis. In other words, in the United States adult children expect to provide assistance to elderly family members, but older parents do not want to become a burden to their children.

Family members are not only expected to provide support to dependent elderly, but also they are often involved in caregiving activities before the elderly family member becomes dependent (Cicirelli, 1990). This anticipatory form of caregiving suggests that family members are cognizant of the needs of elderly relatives and seek to meet their needs in a variety of ways. Thus as Cicirelli (1990) notes, it is important that the family is recognized as a part of the caregiving network for older persons in the United States.

Given the historical and contemporary normative expectation that family members will provide care to dependent relatives, it is important to identify which family members are providing this assistance. Within the United States family responsibilities are not clearly defined. Consequently, husbands and wives may be working outside the home and both may be involved in household activities. Who, then, are the caregivers within United States families?

Gender Differences in Family Caregiving

U.S. Women as Caregivers

Within gerontological literature it is almost a truism that women are described as the caregivers for dependent older persons within the United States. Numerous research studies have identified women as the primary caregivers for the elderly (AARP, 1988; Brody, 1981, 1985, 1990; Cantor, 1983; Fortinsky & Hathaway, 1990; Horowitz, 1985a, 1985b; Pearlin, Mullan, Semple, & Skaff, 1990; Stone et al., 1987). These studies suggest that between 60%-75% of caregivers are women. For example, the National Long-Term Care Survey (Stone et al., 1987) reported that 72% of the caregivers were female. Not only have women been identified as primary caregivers, but it has been suggested that they spend an average of 16 hours per week performing caregiving tasks (Wood, 1987).

Brody (1981, 1985, 1990) suggests that women are the primary caregivers of the elderly because they are expected to provide care to dependent family members. For many wives, mothers, daughters, and daughters-in-law, caregiving is a career. In a discussion of a study of parent care, Brody (1985) notes that "care of a particular parent at a particular time proved only to be one phase of these women's careers in caregiving, caregiving careers that extend well into late middle age and early old age" (p. 25). Shanas (1979a, 1979b) also commented on the caregiving contributions of wives in the later years. The data suggest that women are the primary caregivers, and it is wives who provide care most often. When wives are not available to provide care, daughters become responsible for care (Abel, 1986, 1989; Brody, 1990). Indeed, in a study of older black adults (Chatters, Taylor, & Jackson, 1986), adult daughters were identified most frequently as a care provider during illness.

Two reviews (Brubaker, 1990; Mancini & Blieszner, 1989) suggest that much of the research related to family caregiving during the 1970s and

1980s focused on women's contributions to caregiving. The gender distribution of most studies clearly indicate that, two thirds to three quarters of the time, women are identified as the primary caregivers—but what about the remaining one third to one quarter? These portions represent an important group of men who are also primary caregivers.

U.S. Men as Caregivers

Evidence from studies of caregivers suggests that even though men may not be the most frequently identified primary caregivers, they are involved in caregiving activities. Their involvement may vary, and the percentages of men providing care varies depending on their relationship to the dependent person. For example, the 1982 National Long-Term Care Survey provided information about the estimated 2.2 million informal caregivers of noninstitutionalized elderly (Stone et al., 1987). According to these data, 28% of the caregivers are men (45% of these are husbands, 30% are sons, and 25% are other relatives or nonrelatives). Another national study of caregivers (AARP, 1988) found approximately one quarter of the caregivers were men. Other studies of primary caregivers reported that men were involved in the caregiving activities. To illustrate, the Montgomery, Gonyea, and Hooyman (1985) study of primary caregivers found that adult children were identified as caregivers most often and slightly more than one quarter of these caregivers were sons. Cantor's (1983) study focused on primary caregivers who received homemaker services in New York City. The overall sample was nearly 30% male, and men were in all categories of relationships to the dependent person (husbands = 51.4%, sons = 25%, other relatives = 14.3%, friends and/or neighbors = 14.3%). Pearlin et al. (1990) reported data from a multiwave study of 555 caregivers in two urban areas. Similar to the Stone et al. (1987) study, more than 40% of the spousal caregivers were husbands and 16% of the child caregivers were sons.

Recent studies of caregivers and employment suggest that male workers identify themselves as caregivers for elderly persons. A survey of employees of a major Southern California employer revealed that 23% (438) were helping an older person and 341 completed the caregiver portion of the survey (Scharlach & Boyd, 1989). One third of the caregivers were male. Another study (Ingersoll-Dayton, Chapman, & Neal, 1990) of employed caregivers revealed that nearly 15% of the participants in a caregiver seminar given on the worksite were male.

Several studies have focused on caregivers of persons with Alzheimer's disease or heart attacks. These analyses also reveal that men are primary caregivers. For example, Fortinsky and Hathaway (1990) focused on the needs of caregivers of relatives with Alzheimer's disease by distributing questionnaires to caregivers involved in support groups and at a conference of caregivers. It was found that approximately one quarter of the current caregivers and nearly 18% of the former caregivers were men. The Kosberg, Cairl, and Keller (1990) study of informal caregivers of persons with Alzheimer's disease had more than one third male caregivers. In another study 20% of the caregivers of persons with confirmed heart attacks were men (Young & Kahana, 1989). Two studies in 1986 that focused on spousal caregivers of dementia patients (Zarit, Todd, and Zarit, 1986; Fitting, Rabins, Lucas, and Eastham, 1986), included husbands who were the primary caregivers. These studies provide additional confirmation that men are caregivers.

The contributions of men to the caregiving of dependent older persons have been the focus of several recent investigations. Kaye and Applegate (1990) examined data from a national sample of 152 caregiver support group leaders and 148 men who were members of a caregiver support group. Stoller (1990) also analyzed the role of men in the provision of care by comparing male and female caregivers in a longitudinal study. Both of these studies suggest that men take an active role in caregiving and, as Kaye and Applegate (1990) concluded, many of these men are caring for women.

Gender Differences in Type of Care Provided

Because the data suggest that both women and men become primary caregivers of the elderly, it is important to determine if they provide similar types of care. Are women and men involved in the same types of activities? Are there gender differences in the levels of participation in caregiving?

Analysis of gender differences in a sample of caregivers of elderly heart attack patients (Young & Kahana, 1989) indicated that during the first 2 weeks after the recipients of their care were discharged from the hospital, women averaged 38 hours per week in caregiving activities while men spent 27 hours. It was also found that the type of activities were gender-specific. Women were more likely to assist in the preparation of meals and laundry, while men tended to provide transportation and complete handiwork. Another study (Stoller, 1990) compared the gender and type of caregiving in a sample of male and female primary caregivers. Generally, gender differences in caregiving activities approximated the traditional divisions of household tasks. Women were more involved in cooking, laundry, and routine household tasks and men participated in shopping, financial management, and heavy chores as often as women. Thus women perform a wider range of activities than men. Also it was found that men were less likely to be responsible for routine household tasks and were more likely to provide limited or intermittent assistance.

Matthews and Rosner's (1988) qualitative study of adult siblings who provided care to an elderly parent revealed differences between the types of care provided by adult sons and daughters. In most cases the daughters provided routine, or day-to-day, care or they were involved in backup care to support a sister who was providing the routine care. When sons were involved in the care of their elderly parents, they were more likely to be involved in a limited type of care (e.g., telephoned once a week but not involved in day-to-day caregiving activities). Interestingly, data from this study suggest that daughters were expected to be involved in caregiving on a regular basis and if they were not, their siblings attempted to "cover" or explain their noninvolvement. For the men, however, their involvement was not expected and if they were uninvolved, little attempt was made to explain the lack of participation. Research suggests that, as Brody (1981, 1990) has argued, women are expected to, and actually do, provide more care on a routine basis than do men.

According to the Kaye and Applegate (1990) investigation of male caregivers (no comparisons with female caregivers were made), men perform a variety of caregiving tasks, and the provision of companionship and emotional support are the most frequently reported activities. The men's feelings of competency with caregiving tasks varied with the type of task. They felt the least competent with tasks associated with personal care because they had little training on how to perform many of these tasks. Overall, however, this study found that the male caregivers had androgynous views of the allocation of caregiving tasks.

Most of these studies suggest that there are gender differences in types of caregiving activities and the level of involvement in caregiving. In the studies in which the types of activities performed by women and men are compared, activities tend to be similar to traditional divisions of household tasks. Further, men's involvement in caregiving tends to be more limited, intermittent, and less routine than women's. On the other hand, as the Kaye and Applegate (1990) study evidences, men can, and do, perform a wide variety of caregiving tasks when they need to do so.

Gender Differences in Feelings of Caregiver Burden

In a recent review of research on caregiving families, Gatz, Bengtson, and Blum (1990) concluded that there is agreement that caregiving is stressful. Because research also indicates that females and males both provide care to elderly persons, one may ask whether women and men experience similar feelings of burden or strain associated with the caregiving tasks?

One study (Fitting et al., 1986) found that husband and wife caregivers reported similar feelings of burden associated with caregiving. The female caregivers, however, were more depressed than the male caregivers. In addition, the husband caregivers reported an improvement, while the wife caregivers noted a deterioration in their marital relationships since they had become caregivers. The Zarit et al. (1986) longitudinal analysis compared husband and wife caregivers during 2 years of caregiving. They reported that wives initially experienced more burden and seemed to have more difficulty than husbands in emotionally distancing themselves from the caregiving tasks. Yet after 2 years of being the primary caregivers, wives and husbands reported similar levels of caregiving burden and women became more able to distance themselves, emotionally, in the provision of care. These studies suggest that while there are some gender differences in feelings of burden associated with caregiving, the differences seem to be minimized over time.

An examination (Young & Kahana, 1990) of caregiving for older heart attack patients suggests that female caregivers experience more strain than male caregivers. This study noted that wives and daughters experienced the most severe strain, while husbands had less strain associated with caregiving. Indeed Barusch and Spaid (1989) found that higher subjective burden was associated with women caregivers, even though the male caregivers were older, had more health problems of their own, and provided care for more disabled persons than the women caregivers. Several studies (Barusch & Spaid, 1989; Fitting et al., 1986; Montgomery, Gonyea, and Hooyman, 1985) suggest that younger caregivers experience more strain than older caregivers. As Barusch and Spaid (1989) noted, men generally become caregivers at a later age than women. Thus, in part, higher levels of caregiver burden may be associated with women because they become caregivers at a younger age.

At a younger age women often are experiencing demands on them from many areas in their lives: employment, family, and social responsibilities. The traditional value that women should be the family caregiver frequently conflicts with the more current value that women should compete successfully with men in the labor market. Brody (1990) suggests that today's women are existing "in a window of time" (p. 55) in which both of these values have strong holds on women and on society in general.

The feelings of burden and the actual demands that women caregivers experience can have long-term effects on their ability to provide care, their relationships with older individuals, emotional status, and on their caregiving aspirations. Brody (1990) noted that women caregivers can experience both depression and family conflict as well as emotional support from family members and the older recipient of care. While the caregiving situation can result in conflict between the caregiver and recipient (Brubaker, Gorman, & Hiestand, 1990), it may not if the previous relationship between the caregiver and recipient has been positive (Horowitz, 1985a). While both women and men tend to experience burden or strain as caregivers, women seem to more frequently be identified as experiencing the most burden as caregivers. The differences are minimized, however, the longer they have provided care.

Programs to Support Family Caregiving

A variety of programs and services funded and administered by diverse private and government agencies exist to support older individuals and family caregivers in the United States. Categories of these resources include those that support older individuals within their own homes and those that provide support outside of older individuals' homes. While family members expect to provide care to their elderly relatives when needed, and the relatives expect that the care will be provided, there exists a need for services to elderly recipients. Most often these services are provided in conjunction with care provided by family members.

Programs That Support Individuals in Their Own Homes

The programs that support individuals in their own homes are varied. Homemaker services exist for older individuals who are unable to carry out certain household responsibilities. The homemaker aide may cook, shop for groceries, and/or clean. The homemaker aide may also be a home health aide, who, in addition to carrying out household tasks, also provides personal care to the elderly recipient. Personal care activities may include monitoring and/or helping the older person with personal hygiene, medications, or meeting other physical needs (Brubaker, 1987). The intended function of homemaker/home health services is to increase the ability of older individuals to remain in their own homes.

Homemaker services, utilized in the early part of this century to provide care to children whose mothers were ill, have changed into programs that primarily serve the elderly. The change, which began in the 1960s, was largely due to demographic changes in society and was possible because of funding from Medicaid and Medicare (Gelfand, 1984).

Home-delivered meals are another in-home service that exist to increase the older recipient's ability to remain at home and assist family caregivers. Home-delivered meals were first provided through Title III of the Older Americans Act; meals are delivered to the homes of older individuals who are unable to cook for themselves. Up to two meals are delivered a day.

Respite care can also be provided in the home of older individuals. Through this service a respite worker comes into the home, allowing the family caregiver to leave for a period of time. The length of time varies depending on the agency providing the service. Some respite workers may stay for 2 hours with the older individual, others for 4 or more hours. As a result of this service, family caregivers are free to utilize their personal time however they desire. The development of respite services signals a recognition that caregivers have responsibilities and needs other than only providing care to the family member, and that these needs must sometimes be met through the use of formal resources. Knight (1986) suggests that respite services are among the most important services needed by family caregivers, but indicates that these services are not always readily available.

Other in-home services include those provided through outreach programs at senior centers. These services are carried out by an outreach worker, often a social worker, who visits the older person's home for a variety of reasons. Visits may include counseling or may involve case management services.

The provision of in-home service may need to be targeted to minority groups to assure the utilization of these services. One study (Harel, 1987) of home-based services to the elderly reported that older black Americans are more economically and socially disadvantaged in receiving these services than older white Americans. Harel (1987) noted that if minority groups are not specifically targeted for services, "it is highly doubtful that minority aged would have access to the home-based and community-based services which they need" (p. 141).

Services Provided Outside of the Home

Services provided outside of the homes of older recipients include adult day care, transportation services, respite care available out of the home, counseling, and support groups. Adult day care services take place in the community of the older individual. Older persons attend the day care program during the day and at night return to their own place of residence or to the residences of their families. Adult day care programs arose from an attempt to minimize the number of elderly persons in nursing homes and other institutional settings. Persons participating in adult day care programs do so for various reasons. These include maintaining a person in the community and/or providing rehabilitation for an impairment. For family members who provide caregiving to an older person within their own homes, the availability of adult day care may serve to increase the functioning of their older family member or may allow family members to be gone in the daytime and still have the older person live with them. Huttman (1985) reports that adult day care programs provide elderly parents and the adult caregiving child independence from each other, resulting in a more positive relationship between the two.

A variety of agencies administer adult day care programs, often with differing goals. The programs may take place in senior centers, nursing homes, hospitals, mental health centers, or churches (Brubaker, 1987). As Dilworth-Anderson (1987) notes, due to the chronic disabilities of some older individuals, as well as the demands on caregiving families, the need for adult day care is clear.

Transportation services operate to allow older individuals the freedom of mobility within their community. Transportation services may take individuals to shop for groceries, doctor's appointments, or other places to which they are unable to transport themselves. These services can be a resource for family caregivers who are unable to transport their older relatives in some situations. Many transportation services began in the 1970s (Gelfand, 1984) in response to the needs of older individuals and their families. Transportation services may be particularly important to minority, rural, and economically-disadvantaged families.

Respite services, described above, may also be provided outside of the home with the older family member staying for a period of time in a facility. Other services to both family caregivers and their elderly recipients include counseling and support groups. Counseling and support groups may be provided in a variety of settings. For example, adult day care centers may provide counseling to its clients (Huttman, 1985), as may community mental health centers, long-term care facilities, and private agencies. Individual and group counseling can be directed toward the older individual, the family caregiver, or both. Knight (1986) states, however, that family therapy is too infrequently utilized with elderly individuals and their families.

Other, less traditional, programs exist for older individuals and can take place in a variety of settings. For example, Aday, Rice, and Evans (1991) report on an intergenerational program in which older individuals were paired with young children. The older participants expressed satisfaction with the experience. A program such as this can result in emotional support for the elderly recipient of family care and, thus, facilitate the family in providing care.

Programs that exist for elderly recipients most often benefit family members as well. For example, a program that provides transportation to the grocery store for an older woman is a resource to that woman's daughter. The elderly mother can now do her own grocery shopping rather than the daughter carrying out that task. Although the intention of the program may be to facilitate the functioning of the elderly individual, the ability of the caretaker to more fully enjoy life is enhanced while providing care.

Certainly services have changed over the years in response to the needs of the older population. The increase of services, due to the various factors discussed earlier within this chapter, has provided options that did not previously exist to both caregivers and elderly recipients of care. Without these services many more caregivers (than currently do) would find themselves in a position of having to choose between work, nuclear, and extended family—in terms of time, physical and emotional energy, and resources. While the value of the family as the provider of care still exists within the United States, that value seems to have merged with the value of receiving support when needed. These combined values do not diminish family care, but, rather, they enhance it. A daughter who does not have to complete household tasks for her mother may be freed to provide emotional support and to deal with her own feelings concerning the caregiving situation. In addition, support can facilitate the well-being of the recipient of care. Finally, it has been reported that formal support to caregivers contributes to a positive use of resources (Huttman, 1985).

Within the United States, in-home and out-of-home services need to be directed toward diverse populations. When compared to majority families, minority and ethnic families have cultural expectations and patterns of behavior that may be unique, and these uniquenesses need to be recognized in the delivery of services (Dilworth-Anderson & McAdoo, 1988). At the same time it should be recognized that minority and ethnic families are heterogeneous (Harel, McKinney, & Williams, 1987). It is clear that the development and provision of services to elderly caregivers and their families within the United States need to be tailored to fit within the cultural environment of the recipients.

Suggested Changes to Support Family Caregivers

The research suggests that there is an inequity in the numbers of women who are identified as primary caregivers of the elderly within the United States. Inequity also appears in the types of caregiving tasks women perform versus those performed by men and in the feelings of burden associated with caregiving. At the same time it should be recognized that some men are intimately involved and committed to caregiving, and they —similar to their female counterparts—feel constraints as caregivers. Changes designed to reduce the gender inequities in caregiving will most likely be beneficial to both U.S. women and men caregivers who are immersed in the responsibilities associated with caregiving.

An agenda for change needs to address the inequity issue on a number of fronts (Abel, 1986, 1989). First, individuals within the United States need to change the way they define responsibilities within families. If an older person needs assistance, family members, regardless of gender, need to decide who is the best equipped and available to provide assistance. To do so, changes in expectations need to occur. Second, U.S. policy needs to be changed to accommodate the needs of caregivers and disabled elderly. These changes are needed at the national level as well as within the workplace. Third, training and education are necessary to equip individuals to perform tasks for which they have not previously been responsible. To develop a feeling of competency in caregiving, basic information is necessary. The fourth area of change includes the tailoring of support groups for male caregivers. Similar to training and education, support groups can help men feel more comfortable with caregiving.

Expectations for Caregiving

One of the reasons for the gender inequity in caregiving within the United States is that both women and men expect women to be the primary caregivers of the elderly (Brody, 1985, 1990; Brody, Johnsen, Fulcomer,

& Lang, 1983; Matthews & Rosner, 1988). Most of the care for older persons occurs within the family, and family members expect women to provide the care. It has been argued (Abel, 1986; Cohler, 1983) that women have internalized this expectation and readily take on the extraordinary responsibilities associated with caregiving. At the same time they continue to attempt to meet their other family obligations and, for many who are employed, continue to fulfill their work demands. Thus it is not surprising that U.S. female caregivers experience more stress than male caregivers.

Within U.S. families, definitions of who is responsible for providing care must change if equity is to occur. Nurturing tasks need to be assumed by family members regardless of gender. The redefinition of the distribution of tasks by women and men will contribute to a more equitable division of activities.

Research on the division of household activities by gender suggest that U.S. men are becoming more involved in domestic tasks but their involvement is limited, infrequent, and nonroutine (Berk, 1985; Pleck, 1985). Thus men's involvement in other household tasks correspond to the patterns of their involvement in caregiving. It is possible that a redefinition of household tasks within families would result in a more equitable distribution of the caregiving responsibilities between female and male family members. Without such redefinition it is unlikely that the inequity will change in the future.

Public Policy

Both female and male caregivers need additional support to decrease the strain they associate with caregiving. It has been argued that a national long-term care insurance program is needed (Brody, 1987). Specifically, such a program would "create a broad array of the kinds of day-to-day sustained services needed by functionally disabled older people and caregiving family members—respite care, day care, in-home services such as personal care and homemaker service and transportation for example" (p. 259). These services would provide support to caregiving women and men whether they are wives, husbands, daughters, daughters-in-law, sons, or sons-in-law. Both women and men would receive assistance to provide care to their disabled loved one within a situation of reduced stress. Thus some of the extrafamilial constraints could be lessened and women and men would be given the opportunity to deal with caregiving in similar circumstances, which, if Thompson and Walker's (1989) observation is correct, should result in more equitable caregiving situations.

United States employers also need to establish parent care policies to enable employees to miss (or leave) work when needed to provide assistance to older, disabled persons. A sizable majority of employed caregivers reported that they utilized a flexible-hours option to provide care (Scharlach & Boyd, 1989). Because some of Kaye and Applegate's (1990) caregivers felt "in the middle" between work and caregiving responsibilities, any workplace policies (e.g., flexible hours, elder care leave programs) would help caregiving men (as well as women) who were employed full-time or part-time.

Parent care programs within the U.S. workplace would be useful to caregiving women and men. Wives and husbands are as likely to quit work because of caregiving responsibilities, but daughters are more likely to quit work than sons as a result of caregiving (Brody, 1985, 1990; Stone et al., 1987). Indeed, a sample of three generations of women noted that they expected their daughters, rather than sons, to quit work or rearrange their work schedules to provide care for disabled family members (Brody et al., 1983). There is need to assure caregivers that they can leave their jobs for a period of time to fulfill caregiving activities and return to their employed positions without the loss of benefits (i.e., pensions, seniority) when their caregiving tasks are completed (Abel, 1986).

If fewer women were expected to quit work to provide care or had employee options to permit them to continue to work on flexible schedules while they provided care, caregiving women's feelings of stress may be decreased. Because both women and men feel the conflicting demands between work and caregiving, parent care programs could assist both women and men caregivers and, thereby, contribute to more equity between the genders.

Training and Education

It is believed that the provision of training and education can equip U.S. women and men to better deal with the caregiving needs of an older person. For example, Couper and Sheehan (1987) described a training program for caregivers that addressed the complexities of caregiving to reduce caregiver stress. This program focused on the multiple sources of strain within the family (see Ingersoll-Dayton et al., 1990). Such training could also include information on how to perform specific caregiving tasks as well as provide information about available services and characteristics associated with old age. Research by Scharlach & Boyd (1989) has found that these types of programs can be very helpful within the work setting. For example, they found that 85% of the caregivers who had participated in the employee-sponsored programs stated that information about senior services was helpful.

Kaye and Applegate's (1990) finding that U.S. men expressed feelings of incompetency with the personal care tasks associated with caregiving suggests that training directed toward male caregivers should include discussions on how to provide personal care. If male caregivers are given information on how to provide personal care, they would have the opportunity to increase their levels of competency in providing care. Thus they may increase their involvement in caregiving.

Support Groups

It is believed that a sensitivity to gender caregiving differences in the establishment of support groups may reduce the feelings of strain associated with caregiving within the United States. From a study by Scharlach and Boyd (1989), it was found that the majority of caregivers noted that employee-sponsored support groups were useful. Support group discussion can emphasize the feelings of overload and multiple demands felt by women caregivers and attention can be directed toward specific ways to deal with personal care for the male caregivers. Giving men the opportunity to discover that other men are having similar difficulties may be worthwhile. In addition, creating a situation in which caregiving men can share their own solutions with other caregiving men may enhance their feelings of competency.

While caregiver support groups with women and men can be useful, gender-differentiated caregiver support groups for caregivers who have recently assumed caregiving responsibilities may encourage more sharing of feelings associated with caregiving. Women may be less reluctant to share their feelings with other women, and men may be more likely to express feelings of incompetency with other men. Thus support group leaders are advised to assess potential (and present) group members regarding their need for same-gender support group sessions.

If U.S. men are included in a support group, recruitment is a concern. Kaye and Applegate (1990) noted that men's lower participation in support groups seems to be a result of lack of recruitment. Once men are recruited and become members of a support group, they are active, feel comfortable, and openly share their feelings about caregiving (Kaye & Applegate, 1990). Thus outreach to male caregivers is crucial if support groups are utilized to assist men in caregiving. Ingersoll-Dayton et al. (1990) suggest that recruitment may need to use differing labels for women and men. For men, informational meetings seem to be more attractive than support groups.

Conclusion

Both historically and currently, older individuals within the United States expect to, and do, receive care from their family members. This is true of minority as well as majority elderly. With the increasing numbers of elderly, and a decreasing younger population, the ability of younger family members to care for older relatives may decrease.

In the U.S. family, caregiving is most often provided by women. Men also provide care to their elderly family members, however. While both genders provide care, the type of care provided is often gender-specific, and the amount of caregiving varies by gender, with women's involvement resulting in more time and continuity. For a variety of reasons women have been found to experience more caregiving stress than men, particularly during initial caregiving.

Numerous resources, in the forms of programs and services, exist to meet the needs of older individuals and their caregivers. These services and programs, ranging from transportation to respite care, require examination to enhance the fit when matching resources to need. For minority, rural, and economically-disadvantaged aged, the match between needs and resources requires particular attention. Demographic changes, expectations of caregivers, gender differences, and resource issues all have implications for the future character of family caregiving in the United States as well as for social services and policy development.

References

Abel, E. (1986). Adult daughters and care for the elderly. *Feminist Studies, 12*, 479-497.

Abel, E. (1989). Family care of the frail elderly: Framing an agenda for change. *Women's Studies Quarterly, 1&2*, 75-86.

Aday, R. H., Rice, C., & Evans, E. (1991). Intergenerational partners project: A model linking elementary students with senior center volunteers. *The Gerontologist, 31*, 263-266.

American Association of Retired Persons (AARP). (1988, October). *National survey of caregivers: Summary of findings.* Washington, DC: Author.

Balkwell, C., & Balswick, J. (1981). Subsistence economy, family structure, and the status of the elderly. *Journal of Marriage and the Family, 43,* 423-429.

Barusch, A. S., & Spaid, W. M. (1989). Gender differences in caregiving: Why do wives report greater burden? *The Gerontologist, 29,* 667-676.

Berk, S. F. (1985). *The gender factory: The apportionment of work in American households.* New York: Plenum.

Blieszner, R., & Mancini, J. A. (1987). Enduring ties: Older adults' parental role and responsibilities. *Family Relations, 36,* 176-180.

Brody, E. M. (1981). Women in the middle and family help to older people. *The Gerontologist, 21,* 471-480.

Brody, E. M. (1984, December). *Informal support systems in the rehabilitation of the handicapped elderly.* Paper presented at Aging and Rehabilitation, a national conference. National Institute of Handicapped Research, National Institute of Mental Health. National Institute of Aging, Washington, DC.

Brody, E. M. (1985). Parent care as a normative family stress. *The Gerontologist, 25,* 19-29.

Brody, E. M. (1990). *Women in the middle: Their parent-care years.* New York: Springer.

Brody, E. M., Johnsen, P. T., Fulcomer, M. C., & Lang, A. M. (1983). Women's changing roles and help to the elderly: Attitudes of the generations of women. *Journal of Gerontology, 38,* 597-607.

Brody, S. J. (1987). Strategic planning: The catastrophic approach. *The Gerontologist, 27,* 131-138.

Brubaker, E. (1987) *Working with the elderly: A social systems approach.* Newbury Park, CA: Sage.

Brubaker, E., Gorman, M. A., & Hiestand, M. (1990). Stress perceived by elderly recipients of family care. In T. H. Brubaker (Ed.), *Family relationships in later life* (2nd ed., pp. 267-281). Newbury Park, CA: Sage.

Brubaker, T. H. (1990). Families in later life: A burgeoning research area. *Journal of Marriage and the Family, 52,* 959-981.

Cantor, M. H. (1983). Strain among caregivers: A study of experience in the United States. *The Gerontologist, 23,* 597-604.

Chatters, L. M., Taylor, R. J., & Jackson, J. S. (1985). Size and composition of the informal helper network of elderly blacks. *Journal of Gerontology, 40,* 605-614.

Chatters, L. M., Taylor, R. J., & Jackson, J. S. (1986). Aged blacks' choices for an informal helper network. *Journal of Gerontology, 41,* 94-100.

Cicirelli, V. G. (1983). Adult children's attachment and helping behavior to elderly parents: A path model. *Journal of Marriage and the Family, 45,* 815-824.

Cicirelli, V. G. (1990). Family support in relation to health problems of the elderly. In T. H. Brubaker (Ed.), *Family Relationships in Later Life* (pp. 212-228) (2nd ed.). Newbury Park, CA: Sage.

Cohler, B. J. (1983). Autonomy and interdependence in the family of adulthood: A psychological perspective. *The Gerontologist, 23,* 33-39.

Couper, D. P., & Sheehan, N. W. (1987). Family dynamics for caregivers: An educational model. *Family Relations, 36,* 181-186.

Dilworth-Anderson, P. (1987). Supporting family caregiving through day-care services. In T. H. Brubaker (Ed.), *Aging, health, and family: Long-term care* (pp. 129-142). Newbury Park, CA: Sage.

Dilworth-Anderson, P., & McAdoo, H. P. (1988). The study of ethnic minority families: Implications for practitioners and policymakers. *Family Relations, 37,* 265-267.

Fitting, M., Rabins, P., Lucas, M. J., & Eastham, J. (1986). Caregivers for dementia patients: A comparison of husbands and wives. *The Gerontologist, 26,* 248-252.

Fortinsky, R. H., & Hathaway, T. J. (1990). Information and service needs among active and former family caregivers of persons with Alzheimer's disease. *The Gerontologist, 30,* 604-609.

Gatz, M., Bengtson, V. L., & Blum, M. J. (1990). Caregiving families. In J. E. Birren and K. W. Schaie (Eds.), *Handbook of the psychology of aging* (3rd ed., pp. 404-426). New York: Academic Press.

Gelfand, D. E. (1984). The aging network: Programs and services. (2nd ed.). New York: Springer.

Grigsby, J. S. (1991). Paths for future population aging. *The Gerontologist, 31,* 195-203.

Hanson, S. L., Sauer, W. J., & Seelbach, W. C. (1983). Racial and cohort variations in filial responsibility norms. *The Gerontologist, 23,* 626-631.

Harel, Z. (1987). Older Americans Act related to homebound aged: What difference does racial background make? In R. Dobrof (Ed.), *Ethnicity and gerontological social work* (pp. 133-143). New York: Haworth.

Harel, Z., McKinney, E., & Williams, M. (1987). Aging, ethnicity, and services: Empirical and theoretical perspectives. In D. E. Gelfand & C. M. Barresi (Eds.), *Ethnic dimensions of aging* (pp. 196-210). New York: Springer.

Horowitz, A. (1985a). Family caregiving to the frail elderly. In M. P. Lawton & G. Maddox (Eds.), *The annual review of gerontology and geriatrics, 5* (pp. 194-246). New York: Springer.

Horowitz, A. (1985b). Sons and daughters as caregivers to older parents: Differences in role performance and consequences. *The Gerontologist, 25,* 612-617.

Huttman, E. D. (1985). *Social services for the elderly.* New York: Free Press.

Ingersoll-Dayton, B., Chapman, N., & Neal, M. (1990). A program for caregivers in the workplace. *The Gerontologist, 30,* 126-130.

Ishii-Kuntz, M., & Lee, G. R. (1987). Status of the elderly: An extension of the theory. *Journal of Marriage and the Family, 49,* 413-420.

Kaye, L. W., & Applegate, J. S. (1990). *Men as caregivers to the elderly: Understanding and aiding unrecognized family support.* Lexington, MA: Lexington Books.

Knight, B. (1986). *Psychotherapy with older adults.* Newbury Park, CA: Sage.

Kosberg, J. I., Cairl, R. E., & Keller, D. M. (1990). Components of burden: Intervention implications. *The Gerontologist, 30,* 236-242.

Lee, G. (1985a). Kinship and social support of the elderly: The case of the United States. *Aging and Society, 5,* 19-38.

Lee, G. R. (1985b). Theoretical perspectives on social networks. In W. J. Sauer & R. T. Coward (Eds.), *Social support networks and the care of the elderly* (pp. 21-37). New York: Springer.

Lee, R. (1984). Status of the elderly: Economic and familial antecedents. *Journal of Marriage and the Family, 46,* 267-275.

Lewis, R. A. (1990). The adult child and older parents. In T. H. Brubaker (Ed.), *Family relationships in later life* (pp. 68-85). (2nd ed.). Newbury Park, CA: Sage.

Mancini, J. A., & Blieszner, R. (1989). Aging parents and adult children: Research themes in intergenerational relationships. *Journal of Marriage and the Family, 51,* 275-290.

Manton, K. G., & Liu, K. (1984). *The future growth of the long-term care population: Projections based on the 1977 national nursing home survey and the 1981 long-term care survey.* Washington, DC: Health Care Financing Administration.

Markides, K. S., Boldt, J. S., & Ray, L. A. (1986). Sources of helping and intergenerational solidarity: A three generations study of Mexican Americans. *Journal of Gerontology, 41,* 506-511.

Markides, K. S., Hoppe, S. K., Martin, H. W., & Timbers, D. M. (1983). Sample representativeness in a three-generation study of Mexican Americans. *Journal of Marriage and the Family, 45,* 911-916.

Matthews, S. H., & Rosner, T. T. (1988). Shared filial responsibility: The family as the primary caregiver. *Journal of Marriage and the Family, 50,* 185-195.

McContha, D., McContha, J. T., & Cinelli, B. (1991). Japan's coming crisis: Problems for the honorable elders. *Journal of Applied Gerontology, 10,* 224-235.

Montgomery, R. J. V., Gonyea, J. G., & Hooyman, N. R. (1985). Caregiving and the experience of subjective and objective burden. *Family Relations, 34,* 19-26.

Pearlin, L. I., Mullan, J. T., Semple, S. J., & Skaff, M. M. (1990). Caregiving and the stress process: An overview of concepts and their measures. *The Gerontologist, 30,* 583-594.

Pleck, J. H. (1985). *Working wives/working husbands.* Beverly Hills, CA: Sage.

Sanders, L. T., & Seelbach, W. C. (1981). Variations in preferred care alternatives for the elderly: Family versus nonfamily sources. *Family Relations, 30,* 447-451.

Scharlach, A. E., & Boyd, S. L. (1989). Caregiving and employment: Results of an employee survey. *The Gerontologist, 29,* 382-387.

Seelbach, W. C. (1978). Correlates of aged parents' filial responsibility, expectations and realizations. *Family Coordinator, 27,* 341-350.

Seelbach, W. C. (1984). Filial responsibility and the care of aging family members. In W. H. Quinn & G. A. Hughston (Eds.), *Independent aging: Family and support system perspectives* (pp. 92-109). Rockville, MD: Aspen.

Shanas, E. (1979a). Older people and their families: The new pioneers. *Journal of Marriage and the Family, 41,* 9-15.

Shanas, E. (1979b). Social myth as hypothesis: The case of the family relations of old people. *The Gerontologist, 19,* 3-9.

Stoller, E. P. (1990). Males as helpers: The role of sons, relatives and friends. *The Gerontologist, 30,* 228-235.

Stone, R., Cafferata, G. L., & Sangl, J. (1987). Caregivers of the frail elderly: A national profile. *The Gerontologist, 2,* 616-626.

Taylor, R. J. (1985). The extended family as a source of support for elderly blacks. *The Gerontologist, 26,* 630-636.

Taylor, R. J. (1986). Receipt of support from family among black Americans: Demographic and familial differences. *Journal of Marriage and the Family, 48,* 67-77.

Taylor, R. J., & Chatters, L. M. (1986). Church-based informal support among elderly blacks. *The Gerontologist, 26,* 637-642.

Thompson, L., & Walker, A. (1989). Gender in families: Women and men in marriage, work, and parenthood. *Journal of Marriage and the Family, 51,* 845-871.

United States Bureau of Census. (1984). *Projections of the population of the United States by age, sex, and race: 1983 to 2080.* Current population reports (Series P-25, No. 952). Washington, DC: Government Printing Office.

United States Bureau of Census. (1988). *Who's helping out?: Support networks among American families.* Current populations reports (Series P-70, No. 13)]. Washington, DC: Government Printing Office.

United States Bureau of Census. (1989). *Projections of the population of the United States, by age, sex, and race: 1987 to 2080.* Current population reports (Series P-25, No. 1018). Washington, DC: Government Printing Office.

Wood, J. (1987). Labors of love. *Modern Maturity, 30,* 28-34.

Young, R. F., & Kahana, E. (1989). Specifying caregiver outcomes: Gender and relationship aspects of caregiving strain. *The Gerontologist, 29,* 660-666.

Zarit, S. H., Todd, P. A., & Zarit, J. M. (1986). Subjective burden of husbands and wives as caregivers: A longitudinal study. *The Gerontologist, 26,* 260-266.

PART V

Aged Countries[1]

Mature countries are defined as those whose populations aged 65 and older represent 15% and over of the total population. Such countries are represented in this book by Austria, Great Britain, and Sweden.

Austria, located in Western Europe, had a population estimated to be 7.6 million persons in mid-1990. An identical population is projected for the year 2020. About 18% of the Austrians were estimated, in 1990, to be under 15 years of age and 15% to be 65 years of age and older. It was determined that 55% of the total population lived in urban areas of Austria. The author of the Austrian chapter is Josef Hörl, Ph.D., University Dozent of Sociology and Social Gerontology in the Department of Social Sciences and Economics, Institute of Sociology, at the University of Vienna.

Great Britain is located in Northern Europe. The following information is on the United Kingdom, while the chapter includes attention to Great Britain (mainly England, Wales, and Scotland). In mid-1990 the population in the United Kingdom was 57.4 million persons, which is projected to grow to 60.8 million persons by the year 2020. In 1990, 19% of the population was determined to be 15 years of age and younger. In that same year 15% of the population was estimated to be 65 years of age and older. Great Britain is the second most urban country represented in this book, with 90% of the population living in urban areas. The author of the chapter on Great Britain is Chris Phillipson, Ph.D., Professor and Head of the Department of Applied Social Studies and Social Work at the University of Keele in Staffordshire.

Sweden, located in Northern Europe, is estimated to have had a population of 8.5 million in mid-1990. The population is projected to increase to 9 million by the year 2020. In 1990 it was found that 18% of the population was 15 years of age and younger. The population 65 years of age and older represented 18% of all Swedes. Thus Sweden has the largest proportion of elderly among countries represented in this book (indeed, in the world). It was determined that 71% of the Swedish population lived in urban areas of the country. The author of the chapter on Sweden is Lars Andersson, Ph.D., Director of the Section on Social Gerontology at the Stockholm Gerontology Research Center in Stockholm.

Note

1. All information used to describe these three countries comes from *1990: World Population Data Sheet of the Population Reference Bureau, Inc.,* Washington, DC, 1990. Mid-1990 estimates are based upon census or official national data or upon U.N., United States Bureau of the Census, or World Bank projections. Year 2020 projections come from the same sources.

15

Family Care of the Elderly in Austria

JOSEF HÖRL

Overview of Sociodemographic Development

The Republic of Austria, one of Europe's smaller countries, has a population of 7.66 million, with a projected slight increase until 2010, after which time there will be a slight decrease. Austria has a considerable number of old people. In 1989, 1.56 million Austrians were above age 60, with half a million of them over age 75 (Findl, 1990-1991).

The percentage of persons above 60 years was 12.2% in 1934, increasing to 15.6% in 1951, 18.4% in 1961, and 20.4% in 1974, followed by an insignificant decline reflecting the birth shortage during and after World War I and the premature deaths of men. In 1989 the proportion of persons 60 and over had soared again to 20.4%. The number and share of older people have increased more or less steadily over the past decades, brought about mainly by the declining birthrate. In 1989 the total fertility rate was 1.45 children per woman (Findl, 1990-1991). At present almost a fifth of the elderly over 60 do not have children. In Vienna this is 30%, and some rural areas are even higher (Mikrozensus, 1989).

Immigration was important during the Austro-Hungarian empire, and following World War II refugees and displaced persons came to Austria. Since the mid-1960s foreign labor has been recruited mainly from Yugoslavia and Turkey, and most recently from Eastern Europe and the Middle East. In 1989 there were about 360,000 legal non-Austrian residents, nearly half aged 15 to 35 and accounting for more than 6% of all newborns.

It may be assumed, due to the fact that markedly smaller birth cohorts will be reaching retirement age, that the proportion of the elderly will remain fairly stable until the end of the century. It will then begin to rise again as a result of the considerable increase in the birthrate around 1940 and during the 1960s, leading to larger birth cohorts reaching retirement age. It is projected that the proportion of persons 60 years and over will reach 24% in 2015 and 31% in 2030; those 75 and over will reach 8% in 2015 and 10% in 2030. This translates to almost 2 million in 2015 and 2.5 million in 2030, up from the current 1.56 million.

Women make up 54% of the total population, but there are only about 60 men per 100 women in the population aged 60 and over, decreasing to 40 men per 100 women aged 80 or greater (as a result of two wars).

Using the concept of the dependency ratio and a delineation of the working age between 15 and 60 years, the following picture can be seen. In 1989 there were 328 elderly and 280 children to every 1,000 persons of an age capable of active work; in 2015 only 239 children but 394 elderly to every 1,000 middle-aged persons are expected; therefore, the total dependency rate is expected to rise from 609 (in 1989) to 816 (in 2030). This trend is not only interesting with regard to the potential economic burden of aged persons on the population of working ages, but also with regard to the decreasing ratio of middle-aged family members who might take over major caregiving responsibilities.

The development of mortality in Austria follows the worldwide phenomenon of decreasing trends since the past century, which are due to economic, social, and medical progress. In the years between 1950 and 1989 life expectancy at birth increased for males from 61.9 years to 72.1 years and for females from 67.0 years to 78.8 years. The decrease has not extended to all age groups to the same extent. Within the last hundred years infant mortality has dropped to less than a thirtieth of its original position. In 1989 only 8 infants per 1,000 live births died before completion of their first year. In consequence of the low level reached, the reduction has slowed down in the last years. Thus the decline of mortality in older age groups gets more attention. For example, men aged 60 in 1989 could expect to have 17.9 more years of life ahead (i.e., 2.8 more years than men in 1950). Women of the same age had, on the average, gained 4.7 further years of life expectancy during this period; women aged 60 can (as of 1989) expect to have 22 more years of life ahead. Since 1984, life expectancy at the age of 60 improved by about 1 year for both sexes.

Societal Values and the Basic Economic
and Social Policy System

Under the Constitution of 1920, Austria is a democratic republic with nine self-governing provinces (or "Länder," each one headed by a governor). Most of the basic rights and freedoms guaranteed by the present constitution were originally listed in the Basic Law on the general rights of citizens of 1867. The Austrian Parliament consists of two houses. According to the doctrine of separation of powers, Austria is traditionally characterized by three powers independent of each other (i.e., the legislative and administrative powers and the administration of justice). Judges are politically independent and cannot be dismissed or transferred.

Austria's perpetual neutrality was promulgated by the Constitutional Law of 1955. While in the 1920s and 1930s the political forces were unable to find a common basis for their nation or to maintain a stable political order, since 1945 there was general agreement, with a remarkably stable distribution of powers between two big political parties, that is, the (moderate leftist) Social Democrats and the (Christian conservative) People's Party. At the present time the overwhelming importance and influence of these two parties is somewhat dwindling away.

Owing to Austria's own efforts and generous foreign relief measures, after 1945 the reconstruction of the Austrian industry progressed much more rapidly than after World War I. In 1950 the level of 1913 (the most prosperous year in the Austro-Hungarian empire) was surpassed for the first time. Since then, the progress of economic growth has continued again on a larger scale. In 1974 the average Western European level of per capita income was exceeded for the first time in Austria's economic history.

Postwar economic stability has been guaranteed by the two most influential power groups, employers and employees. In Austria their cooperation has become institutionalized within a system called "social partnership." The system is designed to keep in check the development of wages and prices by close cooperation between these interest groups. Consequently, strikes are unusual.

Some 45% of the total population was counted as economically active in 1989. As against the situation about 100 years ago (when 56% were active), this signifies a strong decline in the activity rate. This development can be traced back, in the first place, to the reduction of retirement age, the prolongation of education, and the decline in agriculture. The labor force participation of young and middle-aged women increased in the last years. In 1989, however, it was 60% for the 15- to 60-year-old females (Bericht, 1990).

Labor force participation rates in Austria for the elderly are among the lowest in the world. The proportion of gainfully employed men between the ages of 60 and 65 has dropped drastically since the 1960s (1961: 65%; 1989: 15%). Only 2% of men and 1% of women aged 65 and older participate in the labor force (Bericht über die soziale Lage [1989], 1990). Changes in social legislation in the 1960s (e.g., introduction of the early retirement scheme), together with structural changes causing programs formerly employed in agriculture to move to other branches of employment, were responsible for this reduction.

Austrian social policy is characterized by a two-fold system: social insurance and social assistance. The basis for Austrian social policy was established under the monarchy between 1860 and 1890 (the "social issue" forced measures to limit daily working hours, etc.). More or less following the model of social security legislation in Bismarck's Prussia, Austria developed a legal basis for social security. One has to bear in mind, however, that only a very gradual development took place, originally excluding the elderly from social security. General pension insurance schemes for manual workers were not put into force until 1935. After World War II the social security system progressed further. Social insurance, in general, has been compulsory since 1955. As late as 1970, a pension insurance scheme was introduced covering farmers; thus the Austrian social security system developed over a time span of 90 years. Social insurance is by far the most important of all organizational subsectors in Austrian social policy and 99.1% of the Austrian population is covered by social insurance (Weigel & Amann, 1987).

Legislation in social assistance progressed even more slowly. By constitutional law, responsibility for social assistance matters comes within the competence of the nine Austrian provinces. Their laws have created considerable variations between the provinces. Private and charitable services supplied by independent welfare organizations play an important role for the actual implementation of the services, cooperating with provinces and communities.

The following principles are common to all social assistance laws (Amann, 1980):

- Benefits to secure the vital needs are provided only if all other possibilities have been exhausted.
- Benefits are granted on the grounds of individual needs alone.

- Benefits are intended to maintain existing family relationships and to strengthen the ability for self-help.

To summarize, life in Austria is safeguarded by a comprehensive and complex system of social security and public welfare. The financial situation of the elderly has become quite secure, making them independent from family support, even though there are underprivileged groups, especially among widows. If the old age pension is below a legally-prescribed minimum, the difference is paid in the form of supplementary benefits.

Role of the Family in Austrian Society

In principle, Austrians must be characterized as holding rather strong conservative views with regard to family norms and values. Family and children are considered as a life sector more important than work and job, leisure, friends, religion, and so on. Furthermore, "traditional" images of gender relations are frequent even among the younger cohorts; for example, paid work is still seen by only a minority as a desirable status for wives (Wilk & Mair, 1987). Although studies, even in the 1960s, indicated the predominant type of female labor was outside the family, it was seen as an extension of the family function. Husband-wife relations seemed to be influenced by status differences between the sexes, due in part to the large differences in educational levels (Rosenmayr, Amann, Grafinger, & Szinovacz, 1969). This picture is changing only slowly, with the esteem of the wife still largely dependent on her husband's well-being (Scholta, 1989). But old and new attitudes seem to exist side by side, especially among the young and well-educated urbanites. This trend will continue as girls are now enjoying higher education as frequently as boys.

Other sociodemographic figures are indicative of long-term changes in values. The propensity to marriage has diminished since the 1970s, and the median age of first marriages rose from 21.8 years (women) and 24.6 (men) in 1979 to 24.0 (women) and 26.2 years (men) in 1989 (Findl, 1990-1991). Likewise, divorce is increasing (in 1989 about 31% of all marriages ended in divorce), marriages are shorter in duration, and remarriage rates have decreased (Schulz & Norden, 1989). This has resulted in a remarkable increase in single-person households among all age groups, a trend that will continue, especially among those 85 years and older (Hanika, 1989).

Another recent development is the emergence of the multigenerational family (Bengtson, 1986). Some 31% of Austrian women over 75 are great-grandmothers (Mikrozensus, 1989). Whereas four- or five-generation families will last only a few years, three-generation families will exist for about 30 years. This has sparked a debate on the consequences of such long-standing multigenerational constellations, especially regarding intergenerational helping behavior. Until now there has been no cultural pattern developed for appropriate behavior in family situations, where grandparents (in their 40s or 50s) have parents or even grandparents themselves.

The rise in divorce rates, more couples without children, the increase in the number of incomplete families, informal relationships, plus a certain—although rather limited—rise in the number of group cohabitations (even among the elderly), and other minority forms of living arrangements, make it more difficult to define the family as a role system fulfilling prescribed tasks for society. Today "roles" within a family are more and more defined by the members themselves.

This development has been also affecting the elderly. In the 1960s it was found that only a small proportion of Viennese elderly maintained a joint household with their children. The aged wanted to be visited and wanted to participate in certain social activities, yet generally avoided fuller engagement and joint living with the young. These results led to the formula: "intimacy—but at a distance" (Rosenmayr & Köckeis, 1965). It reflected the wish to be "somehow" close—for practical and emotional reasons for support on both sides—and yet, also on both sides, to remain separate for reasons of autonomy and in order to "domesticate" dependencies.

Family cohesion in terms of contact frequencies, helping, and nursing behavior seems to be intact. Family sources, that is, daughters (and to some extent sons, and other relatives) provide about 80% of tangible support with household tasks and personal care.

Microcensus results also show that one third of people aged 60 and older have daily contact with their children or children-in-law and another 30% have weekly contact with their children or children-in-law. The most important aspect of help to the elderly is assistance in their regular provisioning with daily goods, particularly food. Not surprisingly, help depends on age. For example, daily help with shopping is received by only 9% of the 60- to 65-year-olds, but by 27% of the elderly aged over 75. The wish for more help is expressed very rarely. One should not to forget that the elderly also extend help to their kin; babysitting being the most important activity (Mikrozensus, 1989).

Helping activities like shopping, cooking, housekeeping, and so on, can be found most frequently in such living arrangements where both generations live "under one roof" or close together. That means that probably helping and supporting behavior frequently grows out of complicated and sensitive exchange processes working on a long-term basis.

In case of assistance behavior, physical proximity is very important. Such a finding might seem trivial, except that distance from kin may interact with a variety of other factors. One has to bear in mind that proximity has at least two elements to it: it is an expression of social closeness and it enhances opportunities to an extent that it exerts a certain pressure by increasing the visibility of needs. Proximity "enforces" (so-to-speak) mutual aid, although there may be conflicting relations. Social closeness —particularly in the family—does not exclude conflict. If, for instance, nursing needs arise, it is almost impossible to dissolve a common intergenerational household without grave problems.

Considerably more financial assistance is given by the elderly for the benefit of their family than vice versa: 36% of the elderly give, but only 3% receive, financial assistance. This finding comes rather unexpectedly, as the elderly generally have lower incomes than their offspring (Mikrozensus, 1989; Rosenmayr & Majce, 1978). There may be found a string of sociopsychological reasons for this result. One may conclude that parents are highly interested in maintaining harmonious and emotional satisfying relations with their adult children and grandchildren; "good" children seem to be a highly valued symbol for one's own successful and fulfilled life. On the other hand, parents want to avoid unbalanced exchange relations. One has also to bear in mind that today's older generations still may be characterized by a rather low level of "individualistic" aspirations and a certain modesty in their life-style.

Results on nursing expectations (Hörl & Rosenmayr, 1982; Mikrozensus, 1989) by older family members show that the spouse supplies most of the aid in emergency cases, even if a child lives in the same household or same house. For meeting the nursing needs of married women, children play a somewhat greater role than for those of married men. Nevertheless husbands are nominated as primary caregivers by married women as well. Most elderly people would turn to adult children only if there is no marital partner or the partner cannot supply the aid (e.g., because of his or her own health problems), and a substantial minority of elderly would not turn to their children for help for any means.

Although the basic motivation of family caregivers seems to be more or less unbroken, there is a certain danger in overestimating the quality of kin relationships in the lives of the elderly. For instance, empirical research shows that many families develop a severe—if often concealed —crisis when they reach their limitations in providing care needed by the dependent relative. There can be little doubt that the tolerable degrees are frequently exceeded in the intensity and time-consumption of caregiving. Almost all studies report severe restrictions in personal freedom and problems coping with psychological stress, which is even more burdensome than physical tasks (Teilbericht, 1990). The sense of duty and obligation often prevents any serious attempts to alter the situation by the caregivers. When they do attempt to gain more personal independence, caregivers are frequently plagued by guilt-feelings (Rosenmayr, 1985).

There is still much more to be learned about the internal structure of intergenerational relationships, especially about the ambiguities of adult children caring for an older parent. No definitive answer can be given yet to explain what it really is that allows some families to be drawn closer together under circumstances of help and care and for others to fall apart. There is some evidence that compliance, that is, the old person being "grateful" in an appropriate manner, and other forms of reciprocity and mutuality enhance the well-being of family caregivers (Hörl, 1989).

Additional empirical results, especially with regard to long-term care, indicate that the elderly are reluctant to "overstrain" family caring resources. There appears to be a pronounced tendency by the elderly to deny filial obligation toward old parents in the case of long-term care (Hörl, 1989). Maybe this attitude, that they will not burden anyone (even their own children) with their more severe personal difficulties, reflects a fear that a string of other problems might be precipitated.

Social Roles and Importance of the Elderly

The widespread perception that there exists a general negative attitude toward the elderly cannot be supported. On the contrary, surveys show a rather favorable picture. The overwhelming majority of the population does not see serious public conflicts—let alone "war"—between the generations. It is also a common opinion that securing an adequate standard of living for the elderly is one of the government's most important responsibilities. On the other hand, many people perceive a definite lack of understanding on the part of the elderly with regard to problems of youth, and vice versa. Furthermore, the public image of old age is still (wrongly) associated with dependency, sickness, loneliness, depression, and social isolation (Haller, 1987).

As far as the political power of the elderly is concerned, it is weak. At present there is neither an official national statement of rights for the elderly nor a central government bureau for the elderly. Approximately 45% of all Austrians aged 60 and over are members of pensioners' unions (National Report, 1982). Most of these organizations for the elderly have close links with the political parties.

A higher level of education offers professional, economic, and social advantages; a comparison by age groups of the levels of completed formal education reveals, first, a drastically lower educational standard achieved by the elderly, and, second, a considerable sex-specific differentiation. In 1987, 4 out of 10 men and 7 out of 10 women over the age of 65 had no more than compulsory minimum schooling. The figures for the age group 40 to 50 are 2.5 for men and 4.7 for women, respectively (Mikrozensus, 1989). Nevertheless, there has currently been an ongoing relative improvement in educational levels of the elderly compared to the past. This social development is very important, because the higher the level of formal education the stronger the motivation to continue the learning process in old age. Almost invariably, it is the better-educated individuals who seek, and then make use of, information of all kinds.

Social Policy Responses to Social Changes

Social services for the elderly are a major social assistance benefit, covering all domestic health services, assistance in running the household, services for improving social contacts, recreation schemes, and homes for the aged. Both in terms of scope and organization, home help services are the most extensively-developed services in the field of care of the elderly in Austria. They are normally not offered in small municipalities and rural areas, however. Approximately 2% of all Austrians aged 65 and over receive home help or Meals on Wheels. In urban areas, however, these services are much expanded. For example, in Vienna, home help is financed by the municipality and carried out through eight welfare agencies having mostly partisan, but also religious and charitable, backgrounds. Since the early 1970s there has been an eight-fold increase in home help caring hours. Now, almost 5% of all Viennese aged 65 and over are recipients of home help. Of course, this percentage is still far lower compared to Scandinavian countries. The service usually is granted for a maximum of 2 hours per day, 5 days a week. In Vienna (with a population aged 75 and over in 1987 of 144,000), 11,900 clients (aged 80 on the average) were looked after in 1988. There were over 2,700 home helpers employed (including part-time workers), principally fulfilling homemaker tasks, but also providing certain health-related services and companionship. It must be stressed, however, that the elderly are not entitled as a right to these benefits under social assistance legislation. Under recent legislation, qualified home nursing will be covered by social insurance. There are also plans to integrate the problem of nursing care into some kind of special social insurance.

People without kin, who are chronically ill or bedfast, reach a stage where open-care services can no longer effectively meet their needs more often than elderly with kin. For these cases requiring long-term care, provisions are made for institutionalization. It is estimated that 3.5% of all Austrians over 65 are accommodated to some sort of institution, as is true of 7% of those over 75 (Geschäftsstelle, 1990; Hörl & Majce, 1976). The case of nursing homes is most interesting with regard to the outlined dual system of care in Austria. Apart from Germany, Austria—as best as can be determined—is the only European country that differentiates sharply between regular treatment of the sick elderly, on the one hand, and long-term nursing care, on the other. If it is not to be expected that the medical treatment will succeed in rehabilitating the elderly, then medical treatment—as far as the health insurance system is concerned—comes to a stop. This is also true if the elderly person, in need of long-term care, is accommodated as a resident in a nursing home. The costs will have to be taken over by the patient and, in some provinces, also by family members and—if necessary—by social assistance.

Differences in quality between institutions are quite pronounced. Only recently are lawmakers exercising more efforts in introducing at least some legal regulations concerning minimum standards for sanitary equipment, and so on, and the special rights for the residents. It is still the exception to the rule that a home for the elderly has its own doctor; only one third of the total nursing staff has received full training as medical nurses (Hörl & Verschraegen, in press).

There are some efforts made to establish linkages between health and social services. One example is concerned with elderly people admitted to the hospital for treatment of a sudden illness or an accident. After successful medical rehabilitation, although there is no further need for permanent surveillance, it remains doubtful if the patient will be able to live independently in her or his own apartment. So in some hospitals the elderly patient will be informed by a social worker about available social services before discharge. Ideally, upon arrival at one's flat, the discharged older person will find an already well-informed home helper who will immediately start looking after the person. There is evidence that such a program yields a significant increase in the use of social services by ex-patients, not only of home help but also of Meals on Wheels and other programs. There is also evidence that readmittances to hospitals—often primarily due to social reasons—can be reduced through such efforts.

Unfortunately this positive example seems to be an exception and particularly applies to the situation of the home-based elderly requiring both health and social supports. The ability of an older person to continue independent living arrangements relies, in the first place, on effective health care (normally delivered by family doctors and specialists). Doctors, however, usually conceive the treatment of sickness in a rather narrow sense. Often enough they function in complete isolation from the social services.

The standard of housing for the elderly population is considerably worse than that of the population at large. There are special programs to supplement elevators into old apartment buildings. There are also improvement programs with interest-free public loans and easy terms for repayment by elderly apartment renters or owners.

The question of special dwellings for the elderly, or residential homes for the elderly, is largely dependent on the area. According to the 1987 microcensus, 12% of Viennese elderly and their children live in the same house. In rural areas, where homeownership is more common, a substantial proportion of 57% of all older people still live with their children. On the whole, 35% of all Austrians aged 60 or older live "under one roof" (but not necessarily share the same household) with their children (Mikrozensus, 1989). This figure is rather high by Western European standards.

In Vienna (and other larger towns) after 1945, large complexes of public housing were erected, some including special self-contained apartments intended for elderly persons. These flats did not prove as popular as originally expected, however; the local proximity between old and young did not lead to the expected reduction of the social distance between nonkin neighbors of different ages (Rosenmayr & Köcheis, 1965).

Pensioners' homes are meant to house people who, as a rule, are still able to manage their day-to-day activities on their own. These homes for pensioners provide lodging and adequate food, as well as physical care and nursing (in case of emergency). The key feature, however, is that the aged persons lead an independent life in self-contained flats, can move about freely, and can leave the home at any time.

There are considerable variations between the provinces regarding policies for the aged. This is fully justified because, apart from Vienna and a couple of other larger cities, Austria still is a country of small communities. Rural areas demand different kinds of social services. To give one example: in Burgenland, Austria's easternmost province, there is a service called "institutionalized neighborhood help," which is financially subsidized by the provincial government.

In Vorarlberg, Austria's westernmost province, another unique and unconventional form of care can be found: mutual associations, which provide home care for the sick and old on a purely private basis. Through this decentralized system, about one third of the province's population has an immediate right to be supported by a professional nurse in coordination with family lay care (Hauskrankenpflege, 1988).

In Austria, familial engagement for frail relatives is barely compensated, neither in financial allowances nor in other benefits. Only one province, Vorarlberg, has developed such a scheme. Informal caregivers (not necessarily family members) are entitled to receive cash payments of up to $1,200 per month.

Future Predictions and Projections Regarding Family Care of the Elderly

The danger in inadequately defining the family is twofold: we may shut our eyes to the diversity of definitions, understandings, and evaluations of family life; and we may extrapolate an arbitrary selection of existing emotional and social structures into the future. We may do that and overlook the fact that no type of "family" presently viewed to be effective will possibly operate 30 or 50 years from now. There are special reasons that can be identified as limiting the ability of families alone to bear the burden of support and caregiving for their dependent elderly relatives in the future.

Demographic projections leave little doubt that low fertility rates, the increased life span of men and women, and changes in patterns of other social behavior will result in the following:

- The number and proportion of dependent, disabled, and chronically ill people (primarily very old) will continue to increase.

- The family will decrease in size (i.e., the pool of available family caregivers will shrink) and, at the same time, as the older generation increases in age, there is an increased likelihood of more generations within the family.
- Divorce rates and "incomplete family forms" will continue to increase with consequential complication of the generational structure of older persons.

As *family care* is a euphemism for care by female kin, it is not quite unreasonable to expect, sooner or later, a social change in this field of special unequal division of labor. In particular, women will certainly continue to enter the labor market in increasing numbers and try to remain there even during the years of child rearing. Thus it is highly doubtful that tomorrow's daughters will be "ideologically" ready and willing to continue today's pattern of caregiving, and it is even less clear that tomorrow's sons will take their share of caregiving responsibility. To perceive phenomena such as low fertility rates, increased divorce rates, or paid employment of women as origins of social "problems" may be a biased view. Nevertheless these phenomena cause problems for others, particularly for the dependent elderly.

Despite this, the fiscal crisis of the welfare state and a certain conservative backlash in ideology have led some policymakers to recommend a strengthening of family solidarity and even a more or less pronounced "reprivatization" of support tasks. Such statements must go beyond rhetoric if they are to be useful for policy. There is no solution in a policy based on encouraging even more informal support by the kinship system because (a) there is no evidence of a significant pool of potential family caregivers and (b) because irreversible social changes have already occurred.

The rapid expansion of bureaucratic social services is symptomatic of these changes. This development toward increased utilization of formal sources of support does not mean that family and kinship are becoming unimportant, or only "suppliers" of affection. But we should be warned not to overidealize and overburden family support networks with expectations that cannot be fulfilled.

There seems to be evidence that a kind of "superindividualization" is developing, meaning that each family member demands recognition of his or her very own normative concept of the family. "Partial relationships" within the family will lead to the breaking up of the "total role" of mother, father, and so on. In consequence, family interaction will, in the future, probably be determined more by the wider scope and growing weight of self-definition of each individual family as a group (Rosenmayr, 1985; Schulz, 1983).

An individualistic mentality will impact more directly upon behavior patterns. Ideological and life-style pluralism will work in this direction. There is a tendency to demand more and more consideration for the individual case. This will have an impact on the degree and type of integration that these new forms can offer and will be willing to offer to old people who are, in some way, "relatives."

This requires, of course, special agreements to establish who is, at a certain moment and for a certain period, responsible for whom and for what. In addition, there is the need to determine what liberties the person has. The bond of solidarity must constantly be renewed and reestablished. This is already bringing about important problems with regard to the functional and emotional needs of the elderly, and these questions of coordination and assignation will certainly increase. The unlimited aspect of cooperation was part of classical and traditional family solidarity.

Today, for example, the issue of long-term care is much more complex. It seems that losses in the intergenerational and intragenerational social network will have to be compensated by installing even more organized professional social services, unless new interaction and household patterns develop based on nonkin relations. Thus relations between the elderly and their families (in our industrialized societies of today) can only be understood and analyzed when taking into consideration the intervention of the welfare state.

The family and the state (represented in this case by social bureaucracies) cannot live without each other, but their goals and communications may not agree (Sussman, 1977). Knowledge concerning interaction effects between family and social service organizations is salient for social policy planning, because coordination and cooperation between the family and the state is only possible as long as competing, conflicting, or otherwise disturbed relations between both parties are anticipated and comprehended (Hörl & Rosenmayr, 1989/1990).

It must be remembered that there are two target populations in caregiving policy: the elderly and their families. The elderly, due to their vulnerability to chronic disability, have one set of needs. Their families, engaged in the process of helping the older relative, have needs specific to the supportive role they have undertaken. The needs of each population may not always coincide. For example, personal sacrifices in the process of helping may eventually lead to the exhaustion of family support and demand the introduction of social services.

One has to keep in mind that, in Austria, families who require the intervention of a formal social service are still a minority, but they are a rapidly growing minority and the mix and blending between informal (family) and formal systems will, with no doubt, become a central issue of the future.

As far as Austrian empirical research shows, there exists very little coordination or cooperation between the elderly, their family, and social services. Family members are practically not involved in the planning and monitoring of service delivery to their elderly relatives. Occasionally they do comment on social services from kind of an outside position. Panel results have shown that even 9 months after the beginning of social services one third of family caregivers did not make the acquaintance of the home help. There is "coexistence" but no "joint venture" (Hörl, 1992).

Possibly, training programs may develop case management techniques among family members. Until now regarding the linkage functions of the family, the possibilities are not really promoted. Occasionally there are agencies giving advice to caring family members.

If this problem remains further neglected, a spiraling process may slowly move into action: the perfection and ubiquity of services creates demand. If social services seem to be able to offer proved, standardized solutions for problems in life events of every kind, any other alternatives (including self-help or autonomous group work, not only family help) are not even taken into consideration. This will especially be so as social workers and related professions in that field unite in associations and trade unions to promote their very special interests. They are supported by politicians seeking evidence and public approval for their efforts. Such evidence should be underpinned by hard facts; for example, high rates of increase in social services. Finally, as soon as expenditures require a substantial part of budgets, discussions about problems of financing and cutting of funds will arrive in much the same way as they do currently in the sector of pension insurance.

Future social policy will have to find a balance in using highly valued capacities and resources of the family and the professional services. It is crucial to realize that the family does not *fail* when it uses the help of organizations. It cannot be denied that much remains to be done in achieving this balance. Families have not yet developed consciousness regarding the opportunities in getting public assistance for family members with problems. Administrators have not yet given enough attention in analyzing the family backgrounds of clients, with only a few attempts to establish linkages between the bureaucracy and the family. Predominant is a "technocratic" perspective in delivering social services. Increases in the number of "cases" are taken as criteria for success. Thinking in terms of maximum "turnover" may be useful for the politician seeking hard facts to be presented to the public, but it is not self-evident that highly efficient delivery of services is best suited to the needs of recipients. In fact, the more services are performed swiftly and smoothly, the more they may prove disturbing and stressful for the client. The goal cannot be to push personnel and technical equipment to the highest level of efficiency. Rather, the goal must be the development of new measures of success, which include careful assessment of options for the family and for the elderly relative. Only then can there be an assurance of the effectiveness of the system.

References

Amann, A. (1980). Open care for the elderly—Austria. In A. Amann (Ed.), *Open care for the elderly in seven European countries* (pp. 31-59). Oxford: Pergamon Press.

Bengtson, V. L. (1986). Sociological perspectives on aging, families and the future. In M. Bergener, M. Ermini & H. B. Stähelin (Eds.), *Dimensions in aging* (pp. 237-262). London: Academic Press.

Bericht über die soziale Lage 1989. (1990). Vienna: Bundesministerium für Arbeit und Soziales.

Findl, P. (1990/1991). Zur demographischen situation Österreichs im Jahr 1989. Vienna: Akademie der Wissenschaften, Demographische Informationen.

Geschäftsstelle der Österreich. (1990). Altenhilfe in Österreich 1988-2011. Vienna: Rumordnungskonferenz.

Haller, M. (1987). Gesellschäftliche Gleichheit als grundwert des Wohlfahrtsstaates? Die Wahrnehmung und Bewertung unterschiedlicher formen sozialer Ungleicheit. In M. Haller & K. Holm (Eds.), *Werthaltungen und Lebensformen in Österreich* (pp. 141-190). (Ergebnisse des Sozialen Survey 1986). Munich: R. Oldenbourg Verlag.

Hanika, A. (1989). Neudurchrechnung der vorausschätzung der haushalte nach Bundesländern für die Jahre 1988 bis 2015. *Statistische Nachrichten, 44*, 868-875.

Hauskrankenpflege in Österreich. (1988). Vienna: Bundesinstitut für Gesundheitswesen.

Hörl, J. (1989). Looking back to caregiving: Findings from case studies in Vienna, Austria. *Journal of Cross-Cultural Gerontology, 4*, 245-256.

Hörl, J. (1992). *Lebensführung im Alter*. Wiesbaden: Quelle & Meyer.

Hörl, J., & Majce, G. (1976). *Die rekrutierungspopulation wiener Altersheime 1966-1974*. Vienna. Unpublished research paper.

Hörl, J., & Rosenmayr, L. (1982). Assistance to the elderly as a common task to the family and social service organizations. *Archives of Gerontology and Geriatrics, 1*, 75-95.

Hörl, J., & Rosenmayr, L. (1989/1990). Help is not enough. *EURAG Newsletter, 60/61*, 30-54.

Hörl, J., & Verschraegen, B. (in press). Austria. In M. L. Levine (Ed.), *The elderly and the law in a world perspective*. The Hague: Martinus Nijhoff.

Mikrozensus. (1989). *Ergebnisse des Mikrozensus Juni 1987*. Vienna: Statistisches Zentralamt.

National Report of Austria for the United Nations World Assembly on Aging. (1982). Vienna: Ministry for Science and Research.

Rosenmayr, L. (1985). Changing values and positions of aging in western culture. In J. Birren & K. W. Schaie (Eds.), *Handbook of the psychology of aging* (pp. 190-215). New York: Van Nostrand Reinhold.

Rosenmayr, L., Amann, A., Grafinger, S., & Szinovacz, M. (1969). *Die junge Frau und ihre berufliche Zukunft*. Vienna: Sozialwissenschaftliche Gesellschaft.

Rosenmayr, L., & Köckeis, E. (1965). *Umwelt und familie alter Mikrozensus*. Neuwied: Luchterhand.

Rosenmayr, L., & Majce, G. (1978). Die soziale benachteiligung. In L. Rosenmayr & H. Rosenmayr (Eds.), *Der alte mensch in der gesellschaft* (pp. 231-260). Reinbek: Rowohlt.

Scholta, M. (1989). Integration des alten Mikrozensus in das familiale beziehung und stützsystem. In *Lebenswelt familie, familienbericht 1989* (pp. 435-446). Vienna: Bundesministerium für Umwelt, Jugend und Familie.

Schulz, W. (1983). Von der Institution "Familie" zu den teilbeziehungen zwischen Mann, Frau und Kind. *Soziale Welt, 34*, 401-419.

Schulz, W., & Norden, G. (1989). Scheidung, scheidungsfolgen und widerverheiratung. In *Lebenswelt Familie, Familienbericht 1989* (pp. 517-532). Vienna: Bundesministerium für Umwelt, Jugend und Familie.

Sussman, M. B. (1977). Family, bureaucracy, and the elderly individual: An organizational/linkage perspective. In E. Shanas & M. B. Sussman (Eds.), *Family, bureaucracy, and the elderly* (pp. 2-20). Durham, NC: Duke University Press.

Teilbericht der Sachverständigenkommission zur Erstellung des 1. (1990). Altenberichts der Bundesregierung. Heidelberg: Institut für Gerontologie.

Weigel, W., & Amann, A. (1987). Austria. In P. Flora (Ed.), *Growth to limits. The western European welfare states since World War II* (pp. 529-609). Berlin: Walter de Gruyter.

Wilk, L., & Mair, A. (1987). Ehe und familie: Kontinuität und konflikt zwischen konventionellen und neuen Lebensstilen. In M. Haller & K. Holm (Eds.), *Werthaltungen und Lebensformen in Österreich* (pp. 81-109). (Ergebnisse des Sozialen Survey 1986). Munich: R. Oldenbourg Verlag.

16

Family Care of the Elderly in Great Britain

CHRIS PHILLIPSON

Introduction

Understanding the lives of older people is inseparable from the study of the structure and texture of their family relationships. This was highlighted by Peter Townsend (1957) in his classic study entitled *The Family Life of Old People,* conducted in a working-class London borough in the early 1950s. The conclusion of his research was that

> if many of the processes and problems of aging are to be understood, old people must be studied as members of families (which usually means extended families of three generations); and if this is true, those concerned with health and social administration, must at every stage, treat old people as an inseparable part of a family group, which is more than just a residential unit. (p. 227)

Townsend's conclusion reflected, it might be argued, dominant cultural values about the place of older people in society. Even within the framework of a developed welfare state, the care of elderly people was and is still seen as a family affair; this, it is argued by many researchers, reflecting both the preferences of older people as well as traditional patterns of kinship obligations (Shanas & Streib, 1965; Wenger, 1984). The importance of family care in the lives of older people has been confirmed in numerous studies during the past 30 years (Adams, 1967; Hendig, 1986; Levin,

252

Sinclair, & Gorbach, 1989; Qureshi & Walker, 1989; Rosser & Harris, 1965). This research, from a cross section of countries in the developed world, has emphasized the importance of the extended family as a supportive and caring force in the daily lives of older people.

This new picture of the family life of older people raises a number of complex issues. Any assessment of family care has to acknowledge: first, alterations to family structures and relationships in many Western European societies; second, changing attitudes toward both the giving and receiving of care; and third, changes in government social policy toward groups such as older people, with a shift in policy from care in institutions toward care in the community. Against such a background, this chapter has four main objectives: (a) to examine the pattern of family care for older people in Great Britain, (b) to assess some of the changes affecting family care in the 1990s, (c) to examine policy and service initiatives to support carers, and (d) to review the future of family care for older people.

The aging of the population has been a key development in Britain's postwar social history. Table 16.1 shows that the number of people over age 65 has increased from 1.7 million to 8.8 million between 1901 and 1991, or from 4.7% to 15.8% of the population. By the year 2021 the respective figures will be 10 million or 17.2%. Table 16.2 reviews the marital status of men and women based on data from the 1985 General Household Survey.[1] The figures confirm the different experiences and circumstances of older men and women in Britain. Among males aged 65 or older, the majority still live with a partner. Even among males aged 85 and older, some 42% are married. The situation of older women is strikingly different, due to both longer life expectancy and a tendency for women to marry partners older than themselves.

There are important variations in the household circumstances of older people. According to the 1985 General Household Survey (OPCS, 1987), about 61% of women 80-plus live alone as a result of widowhood, with only 11% living with their spouse and two thirds living alone. The decline in the proportion of older British people living with others is a product of the postwar years and reflects a combination of demographic, sociological, and economic factors. The key demographic changes affecting the family life of older people include the general reduction in fertility, the clustering of births in the early years of marriage, the comparative rarity of spinsters and bachelors, and changes in life expectancy (although these are less dramatic than commonly thought). These changes have made it less likely that children will still be at home when parents (or, more likely, one parent) enter late old age (Laslett, 1977). Of added

Table 16.1 Numbers of Elderly People in Great Britain 1901-2021 (000s)

Year	65+	%*	75+	%*	85+	%*
1901	1734	4.7	507	1.4	57	0.15
1931	3316	7.4	920	2.1	108	0.24
1951	5332	10.9	1731	3.5	218	0.45
1971	7140	13.2	2536	4.7	462	0.86
1981	7985	15.0	3052	5.7	552	1.03
1988	8697	15.8	3736	6.8	757	1.4
1991	8795	15.9	3844	6.9	757	1.4
2001	8656	15.3	4082	7.2	1047	1.9
2011	8911	15.7	4053	7.1	1187	2.1
2021	9956	17.2	4401	7.6	1230	2.1

NOTE: *Percentage of total population of Great Britain.
SOURCE: Henwood & Wicks (1984)

significance, however, are sociological and economic factors, including the effects of geographical and social mobility, the increase in employment opportunities for women, and the improvement in the availability of housing for younger families (Bond, 1990).

Household Formation in History

In comparison with the past, some might believe that older people in Great Britain have become socially disadvantaged. Yet the conclusions from historical research suggest a different picture. There has been a decline in the last 4 centuries in the frequency with which both married and nonmarried elderly people reside with their children (Wall, 1984). At the same time, there are also important continuities in residential patterns. For example, the proportion of elderly people living in institutions has remained surprisingly constant from the seventeenth to the late twentieth century (fluctuating between 3% and 6% of all older people). Again, there has always been a significant proportion of older people living alone; studies of English communities in the period 1684 to 1796 show 15% of women aged 65-plus in this position. This contrasts somewhat with the 45% in the 1990s.

Wall (1984) concludes that it is difficult to maintain the notion of a linear progression "from pre-industrial times, when the elderly generally lived with their children or other persons, to modern times, when they live on their own" (p. 491). Indeed, in preindustrial society, 44% of elderly

Table 16.2 Marital Status of Men and Women 65+ and All Men and Women 16+

	Single	Married	Widowed	Divorced/Separated
All men 65+	6	73	17	3
All men 16+	25	67	4	4
All women 65+	10	37	50	3
All women 16+	19	62	14	6

SOURCE: Office of Population Censuses and Surveys (1987)

couples lived alone. Even with the death of a partner, evidence suggests that widows or (more rarely) widowers were, as now, more in favor of an independent household ("intimacy at a distance" to use the phrase of Rosenmayr & Köckeis, 1963).

Additional factors can also be cited to explain the formation of single-person households. At least one in three of those entering old age would have no surviving children with whom they might have lived—figures that are also comparable with the situation in the modern world (Abrams, 1978) that poses particular problems in the context of family care. For those with children still alive, migration (particularly for those in rural areas) would reduce still further the opportunities for coresidence.

As for family care itself, there existed no "binding cultural norm" (Robin, 1984; Hanawalt, 1986) that care would be received. Thus the very existence of elaborate retirement contracts, whereby retirees exchanged their land and buildings in return for specific services and support, suggests the potential tensions between generations; the contract itself leaving little to chance in respect of the provision of food, clothing, and shelter (Hanawalt, 1986).

Care, in short, was no more or less complex as a social relationship in medieval society than it is today. To be sure, it involved different resources, dynamics, and, possibly, sentiments, but its negotiated nature was an important aspect. Older people did not inevitably reside in the houses of their children and where they did, it was through the force of specific events (loss of a partner and/or the loss of a home) rather than through deliberate choice.

If, however, in the modern world, the desire for independence has been retained, older people have also moved both toward a different type of relationship within the family and receive (and expect) different forms of care. It is to the first of these questions—the pattern of care received—to which we now turn.

Family Care in the Industrial World: The Case of Britain

British research on the family life of older people has followed two main traditions. First, up to the 1960s a distinctive body of work examined the position of older people within a network of social relationships including the extended family, friends, and neighbors. Second, and notably in the 1970s and 1980s, extensive research has focused on informal care of older people. This tradition of research confirmed that even if single-person households had emerged as a distinctive feature of late old age, contact with kin was still extensive. The three nations study by Shanas, Townsend, Wedderburn, Friis, Milhoj, and Stenhouwer (1968) found that while two fifths of elderly people in Britain in 1962 shared the same household with an adult child, another two fifths were living within 30 minutes. This tendency for children to live near their elderly parents was strongest among working-class families, with some adult children of middle-class parents tending to live much further away than those of working-class parents. Clare Wenger's (1984, 1989, 1990) influential research showed that among those older people with children, proximity tended to increase with age, with widowhood resulting in a move nearer to children. More than half of the parents in her study saw a child at least once a week, and this rose to three quarters in the case of parents over 80. At the other end of the scale, Wenger found that only 2% of parents never saw their children (though in many cases this was accounted for by the children living abroad as a result of emigration).

Surveys in Britain, based on nationally-representative samples, have confirmed the existence of high levels of contact between older people and relatives and friends (Hunt, 1978; OPCS, 1989). At the same time there is also strong evidence that this is translated into extensive care and support. The 1986 General Household Survey confirmed that for those older people unable to carry out domestic tasks unaided, relatives were the usual source of help. For example, 11% of the 15% of all elderly people unable to do their own shopping received help from relatives and another 2% from friends, while 7% of the 11% who could not clean or sweep floors, and 6% of the 7% who could not could cook a main meal had help from family members (OPCS, 1989). From her review of research in this area, Parker (1990) concludes that "there is no apparent evidence of wholesale abrogation of responsibility by families" (p. 39).

This still leaves open the question of whether different types of family systems/networks are better placed to provide care and support to groups such as older people. Within a broader sociological and social anthropological tradition, there has been a desire to identify distinctive types of family networks together with their implications for family care (Bott, 1957; Wenger, 1991; Willmott, 1986). Willmott (1986) has distinguished three main types of contemporary kinship outside the nuclear family: the "local extended family," in which key relatives, especially women, are in daily contact; the "dispersed extended family," comprising regular and frequent contacts and the provision of support when needed; and the "dispersed kinship network," which rests on the ties between relatives such as parents and children, but where the contact is less frequent than in the other types and maintained by telephone or letter and by stopover visits. Members of this last type of network do not give regular support but might be called upon in times of crisis.

A more sophisticated model of support networks has been developed by Wenger (1989, 1991), who has analyzed five network types ranging from the family dependent to the more community focused. The aim of Wenger's research was to examine the strengths and weaknesses of different support networks and to study the demands that each is likely to make on health and social services. Wenger's conclusion, from her research, was that depending on the type of their support network, older people would have access to different types of support. For example, those with family-dependent support networks may be expected to receive a high level of practical support from kin, but may be isolated from important contact with age peers or extra-familial contacts. By contrast, those with wider community-focused support networks are likely to have good emotional support and high morale. It is likely, however, that long-term support, in the event of a chronic illness, may be less forthcoming.

The value of this sociological/social anthropological tradition has been to relate the family to a broad network of relationships within the community. At the same time it has also showed the extent to which older people are active in reconstructing their lives in old age, and that they provided significant forms of support within and outside of the extended family (Jerrome, 1990). In the 1970s and 1980s, however, research focused on the stresses and the burden associated with the family care of older people. The next section reviews the main findings of British research on this issue.

Patterns of Informal Care

A second area of research and debate, at least during the last 20 years, has been the issue of the pressures facing informal carers of older people

(Parker, 1990). This research reflects more general concerns about the strains affecting the family (and women in particular) within British society. One issue pertains to the position of women in society. Here a number of areas have been raised by research: first, the exploitation of women as unpaid carers; second, the dual responsibilities of women in respect to both paid work outside, and the care of children inside, the home; and third, the changing pattern of kinship obligations, with both older people and their (mainly) female carers indicating alterations in preferences as to who should provide care (Daatland, 1990; Phillipson, 1990).

Underpinning, and reinforcing, these debates has been a growing body of research on the problems faced by informal carers. The main sources in Great Britain have been representative surveys such as the 1985 Office of Population Censuses and Surveys (OPCS) Informal Carers Survey (Green, 1988); studies from academic researchers (Finch & Groves, 1983; Lewis & Meredith, 1988; Qureshi & Walker, 1989; Ungerson 1987); and reports from policymaking bodies such as the Equal Opportunities Commission (EOC, 1982) and the Family Policy Studies Centre (Parker, 1990; Kiernan & Wicks, 1990). These various studies have been unanimous in highlighting both the extent of care provided by the family, in supporting older people, and the resulting pressures on those most closely involved in care provision.

The Nature of Family Care

Much of the statistical data on this topic have been provided by the OPCS survey (Green, 1988), the first nationally-representative government survey of carers of sick, handicapped, and elderly people in the United Kingdom. In terms of numbers the research showed that one adult in seven provides informal care, and one in five households contains a carer. These figures relate to replies to questions that aim to distinguish "caring" from "normal" family care and domestic work and are based on a broad definition of caring arising from subjective responses as to whether people feel they have extra family responsibilities either inside or outside their household. On this basis the survey identifies a slightly higher proportion of women than men as carers: 15% as opposed to 12%.

It should be noted, however, that because the number of women in the population of Britain who are 16 and older is greater than that of men, the number of female carers considerably exceeds that of men—with 2.5 million male carers in comparison with 3.5 million women. Another important point is that the proportion of male to female carers alters considerably if variations in the amount of time devoted to care tasks is taken into account.

Arber and Ginn (1990), in a secondary analysis of the OPCS study, examined age and gender differences according to time thresholds of 5, 20, and 50 hours care work per week. Thus, taking a minimum threshold of 5 hours' "caring" per week reduces the number of carers by over a third, to 7% of men and 10% of women. Because a higher proportion of men than women care for less than 5 hours per week, the gender differential also increases. Using the broadest definition of care, 30% more women than men are carers, but the gender differences increase to 41% using the 5-hour time threshold and to 50% using the 20-hour time threshold.

Age is also an important variable in terms of the provision of care. The OPCS survey found the peak age of caring to be 45 to 64 (20% of carers were in this age group). At the same time 13% of those 65-plus were also identified as carers, with the proportion of carers involved in personal care tasks highest amongst those aged over 65 (see Ungerson, 1987). It is particularly interesting to observe that a similar proportion of the 75-plus age group provide care as the youngest age group, 16 to 29. Of additional significance is the fact that a high proportion (41%) of those over 75, in Britain, are themselves disabled (Evandrou, 1990). Wenger (1990) notes that relatively little attention has been paid to the needs of elderly carers, even though their experience differs in several ways compared with younger carers.

In an earlier report from her study, Wenger (1984) noted that: "informal carers, particularly elderly spouses, apparently provide the bulk of support for the frail elderly at home" (p. 117). Data from the General Household Survey have shown that more than 9 out of 10 older people who need help with domestic and personal tasks receive it from their spouse or partner. The centrality of spouses/partners, in the context of family care, has also been noted in studies of older people with dementia (Levin et al., 1989) and research on users of specialist services for older people (Charlesworth, Wilkin, & Durie, 1984). Research also suggests that equal numbers of men and women can be found caring for their spouse; a finding Wenger (1990) suggests is a challenge to traditional assumptions that most care for elderly people comes from daughters or daughters-in-law.

It is also clear, however, that gender divisions among carers of the elderly who live alone are likely to differ from where the older person lives in the same household as the carer. In the former case, the traditional stereotype of women as the principle carer will almost certainly be confirmed. There is also strong evidence that where elderly people are cared for by relatives of a younger generation (usually offspring), daughters and daughters-in-law are the most heavily involved in the provision of care (Isaacs, Livingstone, & Neville, 1972; Nissell & Bonnerjea, 1982; Townsend, 1957).

These findings need to be interpreted within the context of fairly precise rules in respect of kinship obligations within Great Britain (Finch, 1989). Studies such as those by Isaacs et al. (1972), Qureshi and Walker (1989), and Ungerson (1987) have highlighted the process by which individuals within families are selected to undertake care tasks. These British investigations confirm the existence of a ranking of kin that follows a high degree of predictability with close female kin likely to be called upon first to provide care and support to an elderly person. Following this, daughters take precedence over sons in the provision of care; married sons give access to daughters-in-law; and—where a daughter is the main carer—daughters-in-law can be called upon to provide assistance with care tasks (Ungerson, 1987).

The "Cost" of Informal Care

Research has also highlighted the range of physical, social, and financial costs associated with informal care. The physical stresses of care may include the daily pressures associated with dealing with incontinence, lifting someone in and out of bed, or maneuvering a wheelchair; all of this carried out with limited help and alongside a range of other domestic and nondomestic tasks. Again these activities have to be seen within the context of many carers themselves being in their 60s and 70s, with the likelihood of them also having a chronic illness or disability (OPCS, 1989). The social costs attached to caring will include the isolation and possible loneliness associated with intensive care work, loss of friends, and limited opportunities for holidays and regular breaks.

Levin et al.'s (1989) study of carers of old people with dementia identified a range of social costs arising from this kind of care. For example, only two fifths of the supporters had taken holidays in the previous year and more than half the others had gone without them for at least 5 years. Supporters who did most for their relatives, those who coped with incontinence and other major problems, were no more likely to have had a holiday in the previous year. Similarly many carers experienced difficulties in getting to see friends on a regular basis and felt less free to initiate meetings with friends and relatives.

There is growing evidence that some of the stresses associated with informal care may lead to the abuse and/or neglect of the older person. One British researcher has suggested that approximately 500,000 older people in Britain (around one in 10) are at risk of abuse (Eastman, 1984). A study of caregivers of people with dementia found one fifth reporting that they had, on occasions, resorted to shaking or hitting their elderly relative (Levin et al., 1989).

The social pressures facing carers may be reinforced by financial problems associated with the loss of earnings and promotion. Among sole carers (spouses or parents), Evandrou (1990) notes that a higher proportion is likely to be in poverty (as measured by those with an income on or below 140% of the poverty line) in comparison with other groups of carers. Evandrou (1990) found that nearly one third of sole carers were "in" or "on" the margins of poverty. In the case of carers with the dependent in the same household, 35% had incomes "in" or "on" the margins of poverty.

Services for Carers

For those older people needing help and support it is clear that the informal sector in Great Britain continues to play a dominant role, despite the development of a range of home-care services. This point is brought out by Victor (1991) in her analysis of General Household Survey data, which examined the assistance given to older people in relation to tasks concerned with mobility, personal care, and housecare activities.

In terms of the services that may be available, Victor (1991) found that the most valuable form of family care included home help or home-care services, home meals, home nursing, day care, and respite care. Again it is important to emphasize the relatively low utilization of many of these services. In 1985, 7% of those 65 and older in Britain received home help services and 3% home meals. Even among the very oldest age group (those aged 85-plus) only a minority receive these services: 36% home helps and 11% home meals. In the 1980s there were significant changes to many services concerned with the maintenance of older people in the community. For example, the traditional home help service shifted toward the provision of comprehensive personal and domestic care. "Domiciliary care assistants" and "home carers" are two of the terms used to describe workers engaged in personal care and homemaking tasks to enable older people to stay in their homes.

Another service that became of increasing significance in the 1980s was respite care with the provision of breaks for carers and older people. This service is usually provided by residential homes, nursing homes or hospitals. Such arrangements may be part of a regular program of support with, for example, the older person coming in for residential care every 6 months. Much more common is a looser arrangement where respite care is offered to deal with a situation where the carer is perceived to be in urgent need of help. There is some evidence that carers may feel inhibited about using or suggesting respite care to their dependents (Twigg, 1989). This may arise from difficulties during the process of admission into a residential home.

Innovations in support for carers are likely to emerge with the adoption of case management techniques that are a part of British legislation on community care introduced in 1990. These innovations will almost certainly lead to the deployment of a broader range of services to enable older people to remain in their own homes for as long as possible. The type of services that will need to be developed, on a wider scale than presently exists in Britain, will include: first, intensive domiciliary support to provide 24-hour cover for a disabled person and his or her family; second, organized sitting services to provide relief for carers and to fill the gaps between other services; third, fostering schemes with families "adopting" an older person who has no immediate kin available to provide support; and fourth, counseling facilities to help carers cope both with the stress of care and with the process of grief following the death of a relative or spouse (Bowling, 1984).

Changing Patterns of Family Care

The previous sections set out the main form taken by the family care of older people in British society. The nature of such care is being affected by two kinds of changes operating in the 1990s: first, the debate about social and community care for very elderly people (Phillipson, 1990) and second, attitudes within the family and among older people themselves regarding the giving and receiving of care. This section will review the evidence on these areas, so as to provide a basis for reflecting on the future of family care for older people.

Throughout the 1980s and early 1990s there has been an intense debate in Britain about the structure of the welfare state. Along with an increased demand for community care, the focus in national policy has been to shift care from institutions (hospitals and residential homes) to the community. This development was reflected in two Government White Papers in 1989 (Department of Health, 1989a, 1989b): *Caring for People* (with proposals for reform in the field of community care) and *Working for Patients* (outlining reforms for the National Health Service). These White Papers were implemented in the 1990 National Health Service and Community Care Act. Running through both the White Papers and the legislation was a distinction between care "in" and care "by" the community: the former provided for of a range services for people living in the community; the latter for care by a network of family, friends, and neighbors. A key concern of government has been to maintain the informal care sector as an essential provider of support for groups such as older people. Thus, in the blueprint for community care prepared by Sir Roy Griffiths at the request of the Thatcher government (Griffiths, 1988), the primary role of informal carers in supporting groups (such as older people) was clearly identified.

Underpinning this debate on the importance of informal care has been the emergence of the more general concept of the "mixed economy of welfare" or "welfare pluralism" (Johnson, 1987). This is the idea that welfare provision should properly comprise a mixture of services with a range of providers including the state, the private market, voluntary and charitable organizations, and the informal sector.

The key problem for governments in Britain in the 1990s, however, may be that aspirations to reduce the extent of public services may be frustrated by changes in the nature and extent of family care for the elderly. This point may be illustrated by examining, first, research on care preferences for groups such as the dependent elderly and second, alterations to traditional patterns of kinship obligation among the population in contemporary British society.

Changing Care Preferences

In terms of care preferences, some of the key points can be summarized in the following way: first, we should note the public opinion surveys in a number of countries with established welfare states have shown the extent to which older people are increasingly preferring the support of professionals where they have extensive care needs (Daatland, 1990; Phillipson, 1990). A Gallup survey in Britain carried out in 1988 found that most pensioners believed that responsibility for their care *should shift toward that of the state*. Out of 909 people aged 65-plus who were interviewed, 57% overall expressed this view (*The Guardian*, 1988).

Two surveys by Salvage, Vetter, and Jones (1988, 1989) found that of people aged 75 and older living in the South Glamorgan area of Wales, 98% of the respondents agreed that "retired people should be maintained in their own homes for as long as possible" (p. 273). The achievement of this aim was seen to entail some sacrifice on the part of the family although most respondents, particularly men, felt that this was justified. It was not felt, however, that the sacrifice should be too extreme. For example, the majority of respondents rejected the view that daughters should be prepared to give up work to care for parents.

West, Illsley, and Kelman (1984) explored views about the care of dependency groups and the relationship between the state, professional groups, and informal carers. They presented a community sample in three contrasting areas of Scotland with a series of vignettes of people suffering from various disabling conditions, and asked which of a number of care options they would choose. The least preferred options, for all but one of the vignettes, involved family and informal care alone, on the one hand, or residential care, on the other. The majority of people in this study wanted community-based professional care, along the lines of day care centers, day hospitals, and sheltered housing. According to West, Illsley, and Kelman (1984):

> There is in general much less preference for care *by* the community than care *in* the community; the public are unwilling to place the major burden of care on informal carers which in practice means the family and women in particular. They are especially unwilling to allocate the major responsibility for care to close kin; the children or siblings of dependent persons. (p. 294 [emphasis added])

This is not to say that people will not give the support (as we know they do and invariably at great sacrifice); but it does suggest that care by the community is seen as a less-attractive option than care from professionals, but with the support and involvement of the family.

Changing Kinship Obligations

It might be argued that findings on care preferences reflect important changes in the life-styles and attitudes of older people during the last 20 years (Fennell, Evers, & Phillipson, 1988). These changes have, it is true, received some recognition in proposals for community care, particularly with the emphasis on maintaining people in their own homes and providing greater choice in the provision of services (Department of Health, 1989a. But acknowledgment of changes in attitudes toward the giving and receiving of family care has yet to be followed to its logical conclusion, namely, that older people are moving away from wanting any dependence on children, especially that which implies a long-term commitment arising out of a chronic illness (Lee, 1985) or the need to provide personal care (Ungerson, 1987).

The arguments about changing care preferences are highlighted by research on patterns of kinship obligations. Finch (1989), in a major review of work in this area, has highlighted the complex set of rules determining the provision of family care. She notes that kin relationships do not operate on the basis of a ready-made set of moral rules, clearly laid out for older people and their carers to follow. In particular, the "sense of obligation," which marks the distinctive character of kin relations, does not follow a reliable and consistent path in terms of social practice.

This argument is important because it cuts across a central thrust of government policy on community care; namely, that families act as though there are cultural and moral scripts that they follow in supporting older people in times of crisis or dependency. Moreover, the argument is taken a stage further by some researchers with the assertion that older people themselves follow this path with an almost instinctive tendency to move toward the family rather than bureaucratic agencies.

This argument, however, relies upon a historical perspective that may no longer be acceptable as an accurate portrayal of the kind of care wanted by people. Families are variable in their response to requests for help and, in any event, the care given is always negotiated within a social and biographical context (Finch, 1989). It is this variability that makes the future of family care in Britain somewhat uncertain. People may come to prefer (may, indeed, demand) the provision of a reliable network of public-sector services (supported by other providers such as the private and not-for-profit sectors), these coming to replace the hitherto dominant role of family and informal sector care. According to this line of argument, family care in the 1990s and beyond, although still present—and stronger in some social groups than others—will alter in terms both of the conditions under which care is provided and the range of care tasks that can be performed. Some of the characteristics of family care in the future will be analyzed in the concluding section.

Conclusion

This chapter has reviewed the nature of family care for older people in British society. The support provided by the family is, it has been suggested, undergoing considerable change. Family care is undoubtedly central to the lives of a substantial proportion of older people. Research suggests that this care flows in both directions, from young to old, old to young; from grandparents to grandchildren and vice versa, but the alterations to the structure of family life are also affecting care relations. The family in the late twentieth century is a more diverse institution with higher rates of cohabitation, divorce, and remarriage. These developments will introduce greater complexities to family care in the 1990s, with changing assumptions and attitudes toward the giving and receiving of informal care.

Central to the debate about family care is the position of women. Family care remains unequally distributed with the heaviest responsibility often falling upon female relatives. This has been exacerbated with the growth of community care policies in the 1980s and early 1990s (Arber & Ginn, 1990). Following this, the issue for the 1990s will be how to develop social and community care policies that challenge the traditional division of labor between the sexes. The need for such policies is underlined by sociological and demographic factors. Reductions in family size will reduce the pool of daughters—a crucial group in the provision of family care. At the same time, changing views about the role of women in society have resulted in a reassessment of traditional kinship obligations. These developments raise questions as to the adequacy of, and support for, community care policies that continue to exploit women as both carers and clients. Governments—through the 1990s—will be faced with pressures to increase social expenditure aimed at helping people to remain in their own homes for as long as possible.

It is possible that—in Britain, at least—family care is entering a new phase. On the one hand, the centrality of this type of support (particularly as expressed in the form of care for partners) will be retained. On the other hand, we should also see family carers and older people seeking new alignments in terms of how care relationships are expressed. A key aspect will be the move toward what Qureshi and Walker (1989) describe as "shared care" or "care-partnerships." The principle behind this new approach to informal care is that: "neither families nor female kin should be put under any external obligation to care for elderly relatives and if they choose to do so, the expectation must be that supportive formal services will be available on demand to assist them" (p. 268). The authors go on to suggest an agenda for shared care with the following elements: first, the need to secure effective social and economic policies to ensure that care *for* the community is achieved; second, a loosening in the divisions between the formal and the informal sectors, with the development of care partnerships between professional workers on the one side and family carers on the other; third, an increase in the accountability of professionals and greater participation by older people and carers in the construction of services; fourth, the development of a proactive, instead of a reactive, crisis orientation in the organization of services; and finally, continued attention to the need to share care within the family.

The challenge to gender inequalities will also be reflected in acknowledgment of the type of care families now wish to give and which older people want to receive. In this context, the family of the future may become at least as much an advocate for a vulnerable elder as it is a direct care provider. In short the importance of family care may increasingly lie in how it assists the elder to negotiate the range of formal care agencies characteristic of pluralistic welfare states (Daatland, 1983; Johnson, 1987). What can also be said is that the changing nature of family care will be a crucial area for comparative research. Family care is developing more complex and sophisticated forms; the study of these should be a crucial part of the gerontological agenda over the next decade.

Note

1. The General Household Survey is a national sample survey of the general population resident in private (that is, noninstitutional) households that has been conducted continuously since 1971. It is based on interviews with about 10,000 households (25,000 individuals) per year. Prior to 1982 the achieved sample size was somewhat larger, about 12,000 households. The GHS data are collected from two interview schedules. The Household Schedule covers topics such as housing tenure, consumer durables, and migration and is answered by one adult member of the household, usually the head or his spouse (the definition of head of household used by the GHS means that heads of households are generally men). Each household member aged 16 and older answers an Individual Schedule about his or her employment, job satisfaction, educational attainment, health and use of health services, and income. In addition, topics such as leisure, smoking, drinking, family planning, and the circumstances of elderly people are included in some years.

References

Abrams, M. (1978). *Beyond three score years and ten.* London: Age Concern.
Adams, G. (1967). *Kinship in an urban setting.* Chicago: Markham.

Arber, S., & Ginn, J. (1990). The meaning of informal care: Gender and the contribution of elderly people. *Ageing and Society, 10,* 429-454.

Arber, S., & Ginn, J. (1991). The invisibility of age: Gender and class in later life. *Sociological Review, 90,* 262-291.

Bond, J. (1990). Living arrangements of elderly people. In J. Bond & P. Coleman (Eds.), *Ageing in Society* (pp. 161-180). London: Sage.

Bott, E. (1957). *Family and social network.* London: Tavistock Institute of Social Relations.

Bowling, A. (1984). Caring for the elderly widowed—the burden on their supporters. *British Journal of Social Work, 14,* 435-455.

Charlesworth, A., Wilkin, D., & Durie, A. (1984). *Carers and services: A comparison of men and women caring for elderly dependent people.* Manchester: Equal Opportunities Commission.

Daatland, S. (1983). Care systems. *Ageing and Society, 3,* 1-23.

Daatland, S. (1990). What are families for? On family solidarity and preference for help. *Ageing and Society, 10*(1), 1-17.

Department of Health. (1989a). *Caring for people: Community care in the next decade and beyond.* [Command 849]. London: Her Majesty's Stationery Office (HMSO).

Department of Health. (1989b). *Working for patients.* [Command 555]. London: HMSO.

Eastman, M. (1984). *Old age abuse.* London: Age Concern England.

Equal Opportunities Commission (E OC). (1982). *Caring for the elderly and handicapped: Community care policies and women's lives.* Manchester: Author.

Evandrou, M. (1990). *Challenging the invisibility of carers: Mapping informal care nationally.* [Discussion Paper WSP/49, Welfare State Programme]. London: LSE.

Fennell, G., Evers, H., & Phillipson, C. (1988). *The sociology of old age.* Buckingham: Open University Press.

Finch, J. (1989). *Family obligations and social change.* Oxford: Basil Blackwell.

Finch, J., & Groves, D. (Eds.). (1983). *A labour of love: Women, work and caring.* London: Routledge and Kegan Paul.

Firth, R., Hubert, J., & Forge, A. (1970) *Families and their relatives.* London: Routledge and Kegan Paul.

Green, H. (1988). *Informal carers.* [OPCS Series GHS, No. 15, Supplement A. OPCS]. London: HMSO.

Griffiths, R. (1988). *Care in the community: Agenda for action.* London: HMSO.

Hanawalt, B. (1986). *The ties that bound.* Oxford: Oxford University Press.

Hendig, H. (Ed.) (1986). *Ageing and families.* Australia: Allen and Unwin.

Henwood, M., & Wicks, M. (1984). *The forgotten army: Family care of older people.* London: Family Policy Studies Centre.

Hunt, A. (1978). *The elderly at home: A study of people aged sixty-five and over living in the community in 1976.* London: HMSO.

Isaacs, B., Livingstone, M., & Neville, Y. (1972). *Survival of the unfittest.* London: Routledge and Kegan Paul.

Jerrome, D. (1990). Intimate relationships. In J. Bond & P. Coleman (Eds.), *Ageing in society* (pp. 181-208). London: Sage.

Johnson, N. (1987). *The welfare state in transition.* Sussex: Wheatsheaf Books Ltd.

Kiernan, K., & Wicks, M. (1990). *Family change and future policy.* London: Family Policy Studies Centre.

Laslett, P. (1977). *Family life and illicit love in earlier generations.* Cambridge: Cambridge University Press.

Lee, G. (1985). Kinship and social support: The case of the United States. *Ageing and Society, 5,* 19-38.

Levin, E., Sinclair, I., & Gorbach, P. (1989). *Families, services and confusion in old age.* Aldershot: Averbury.

Lewis, J., & Meredith, B. (1988). *Daughters who care: Daughters caring for mothers at home.* London: Routledge and Kegan Paul.

Nissel, M., & Bonnerjea, L. (1982). *Family care of the handicapped elderly: Who pays?* London: Policy Studies Institute.

Office of Population Censuses and Surveys (OPCS). (1987). *General household survey 1985.* London: HMSO.

Office of Population Censuses and Surveys (OPCS). (1989). *General household survey 1986.* London: HMSO.

Parker, G. (1990). *With due care and attention: A review of research on informal care* (2nd ed.). London: Family Policy Studies Centre.

Phillipson, C. (1990). *Delivering community care services for older people: Problems and prospects for the 1990s.* Stoke-on-Trent: Centre for Social Gerontology, University of Keele.

Qureshi, H., & Walker, A. (1989). *The caring relationship.* London: Macmillan.

Robin, J. (1984). Family care of the elderly in a Devonshire parish. *Ageing and Society, 4,* 505-516.

Rosenmayr, L., & Köckeis, E. (1963). Propositions for a sociological theory of aging and the family. *International Science Journal, XV,* 410-426.

Rosser, C., & Harris, C. (1965). *The family and social change.* London: Routledge and Kegan Paul.

Salvage, A. V., Vetter, N. J., & Jones, D. A. (1988). Attitudes to hospital care among a community sample aged 75 and over. *Ageing and Ageing, 17,* 270-274.

Salvage, A. V., Vetter, N. J., & Jones, D. A. (1989). Opinions concerning residential care. *Age and Ageing, 18,* 380-386.

Shanas, E., & Streib, G. (1965). *Social structure and the family.* Englewood Cliffs, NJ: Prentice-Hall.

Shanas, E., Townsend, P., Wedderburn, P., Friis, H., Milhoj, P., & Stenhouwer, J. (1968). *Old people in three industrial societies.* London: Routledge and Kegan Paul.

Sheldon, J. H. (1948). *The social medicine of old age.* Oxford: Oxford University.

Townsend, P. (1957). *The family life of old people.* London: Routledge and Kegan Paul.

Twigg, J. (1989, July 24). Not taking the strain. *Community Care,* 55-60.

Ungerson, C. (1987). *Policy is personal: Sex, gender and informal care.* London: Tavistock.

Victor, C. (1991). *Health and health care in later life.* Buckingham: Open University Press.

Wall, R. (1984). Residential isolation of the elderly: A comparison over time. *Ageing and Society, 4,* 483-503.

Wenger, C. (1984). *The supportive network.* London: Allen and Unwin.

Wenger, C. (1989). Support networks in old age. In M. Jeffries (Ed.), *Growing old in the twentieth century* (pp. 166-187). London: Routledge and Kegan Paul.

Wenger, C. (1990). Elderly carers: The need for appropriate intervention. *Ageing and Society, 10,* 197-220.

Wenger, C. (1991). A network typology: From theory to practice. *Journal of Aging Studies, 5*(2), 147-162.

West, P., Illsley, R., & Kelman, H. (1984). Public preferences for the care of dependency groups. *Social Science and Medicine, 18,* 417-446.

Willmott, P. (1986). *Friendship networks and social support.* London: Policy Studies Institute.

Young, M., & Willmott, P. (1962). *Family and kinship in East London.* London: Penguin.

17

Family Care of the Elderly in Sweden

LARS ANDERSSON

Introduction

In the same sense as we, to a certain degree, can choose the future, the past, similarly, has been chosen by those who lived before us. These choices have been heavily influenced by the effects of wars, the outcome of power struggles, social or technological inventions, and so on. Thus in referring to the past, we must be careful to specify which past. In one way this is quite obvious, but it is useful to be reminded, from time to time, that the development up to the present-day situation cannot be thought of as totally linear. With a special reference to the elderly, their situation has differed over the centuries, and when we compare the present-day situation with the (good?) old days, we have to specify century or even decade and social class. In this presentation, care of the elderly in Sweden will be mirrored against some historical conditions, which—without doubt— have had an impact on the present-day situation. A few observations on future trends will also be provided.

Sweden Yesterday

Rural Characteristics

Historically there has always been a shortage of farming land in Western Europe. As a consequence, the practice that no family could be formed before a farm was free to be taken over was established. Alternatively, the family had to be prepared to break new ground (Gaunt, 1983). They did not have to wait until the parents were dead, however. In Sweden the parents could be put on *undantag* (i.e., they agreed to move to a cottage separated from the farm house, where they were supported for the rest of their lives by receiving a share of what the farm produced). If the parents accepted this agreement at, say, the age of 60, it meant that the young couple was close to 30 before they could take over the farm. The difficulties in gaining economic independence (i.e., to take over a farm), contributed to another typical pattern in Western Europe: that people got married fairly late. While the brides in Eastern Europe were teenagers, in Western Europe they were close to 25 years of age. The bridegrooms were even older—in Sweden close to 30 years. This pattern did not change when the industrial era started. The salary in industry was not good enough to be able to marry early and to raise a family (Gaunt, 1983).

When did the farmers retire in former days? One could imagine that they waited until it was absolutely necessary. That was quite rare, however. Usually they retired well in advance, which meant that they could live for 10 or 15 or 20 years on *undantag* before they died. Thus it seems realistic to assume that the transfer of the farm had more to do with the wish of the children to take over than it had to do with physical deterioration on the part of the old farmer (Gaunt, 1983).

The second part of the nineteenth century was exceptional in many ways. (It is often the period we think of when we compare today's situation with the "traditional" situation.) Proportionally, farmers became fewer in number, and the ownership of the land became more desirable. Households were more hierarchically organized. Earlier there was less distinction between the farmer's family and the farmhands. They worked, had their meals, and slept together. In the second part of the nineteenth century, however, they were separated. The increase in population during the nineteenth century led to the emergence of a pronounced class-based society in the country. The worsening working conditions for farmhands caused them to turn to the emerging industry, where the pay was somewhat better, or to emigrate.

This can also be regarded as the most patriarchal period. Even though some changes in the law led to improvements for women, it could not outweigh the power accumulated by the male. One major factor behind the power concentration was the change from family production to the situation where the male was the sole breadwinner. Much of what has been regarded as the emancipation of women was actually an attempt to regain the position that at least upper-class women had lost at the beginning of the same century (Gaunt, 1983).

Household Size

Up to the end of the eighteenth century, the term *family* also included farmhands and maids. A study of the household size in a parish in central Sweden in 1643 showed that the mean size was close to 7 persons, ranging from 16 in the manorial, to 1 or 2 persons in several crofts and cabins. There were not many three-generation families (Gaunt, 1983).

If there were too many in the family to feed, some of the children had to leave. It was quite common for a youth to leave the family at a young age to work in another household for some time. When the children in a household were old enough to work, the farmhands had to leave. Thus, among the farmers, laborers were employed on a temporary basis.

The household, defined as the group of people who eat and sleep together, were about the same size in Western and Central Europe from the end of the sixteenth century to the end of the 1880s. The household was made up of four to five persons. In 1890 the average household size in Sweden was 4.56. Currently the size of the average household in Sweden is about 2.2 persons. The household size is larger in the country-side than in the cities. For example, in inner-city Stockholm, two thirds of all households consist of single persons. This increase in the number of one-person households reasonably explains the decrease in household size since the end of last century.

In an affluent society people can choose to live alone instead of having to live as lodgers. Popenoe (1987) poignantly notes that living alone can be regarded as a privilege of affluent people and as an active expression of "individualism."

Care of the Elderly Over the Centuries

The treatment of the elderly differed depending on their position in society (i.e., as to whether the elderly had any property to be inherited or not). According to Gaunt (1983), the situation of the elderly, from a general point of view, was quite wretched during the Middle Ages. They were treated somewhat less miserably, however, from about the middle of the sixteenth century to the middle of the eighteenth century. In the beginning of the eighteenth century, seniority was introduced in the state administration. The situation of the elderly got worse during the latter part of the eighteenth century, and the deterioration continued during the nineteenth century.

As long back as can be traced through the original sources, it was the relatives who were responsible for the welfare of the elderly. More specifically, however, the wording of legislation mentioned heirs as the responsible individuals. It meant that people who had no property to be inherited were not well-protected by the law.

There were different ways to arrange the care of the elderly. How the care was organized, in the main, differed over centuries and between parishes. One type of care, already mentioned, was the *undantag*. Another alternative was that more than one close relative participated in the care of the elderly person, who spent some time with each one of the future inheritors. The time period was proportional to their part of the inheritance. One important part of this system was that the old farmer formally still owned the farm, which meant that he could give notice of the care from someone if it was not good enough. It also happened that some, or all, heirs refused to care for the old couple. If no care was provided, one could receive care from someone else; not because one was respected, but because one could pay. In that case they could let someone else run the farm. After the farmer's death, however, it was the heirs who could take over the farm, not the one who had taken care of the old person (Schultze, 1931). An interpretation of this law is that the elderly, in former days, were not held in particularly high regard.

One alternative for the unpropertied was to move to the poor house, an arrangement that dominated in southern Sweden. Those in the poor house were a mixture of individuals who (for several reasons—economic, physical, mental) were unable to support themselves. To end up in the poor house was regarded as a horror to most members of society. An equally stigmatizing treatment more common to the northern sparsely-populated areas was the so-called *rotegång,* where the old person (*rotehjon*) was sent around the parish, and the farms were obliged to take care of the person for a defined period. The contribution depended on the size of the farm. On the smaller farms, the *rotehjon* just received a meal (Kjellman, 1981).

Another possibility was that the former master agreed to care for the old person. In exchange he received a portion of the annual tithe. The right to receive this share was undermined as time progressed (Odén, 1985, 1988).

A less common form of care, which mainly existed in densely-populated areas, was to become an inmate in an asylum. The main purpose of the asylums was to provide care for the burghers and others who could afford to pay, but as an expression of charity these institutions also accepted a quota of poor elderly in a separate ward. The asylums were established by religious institutions. Gradually, however, they were taken over by other institutions and eventually after the Reformation, which was established at the meeting of Parliament in 1527, the responsibility for the elderly was formally taken away from the church. The asylums were initially intended for lepers. After a few centuries of also accepting elderly inmates, the rules were changed again, giving priority to other groups, above all "lunatics," while the old person had to turn to the parochial poor house for care (Blom, 1991; Odén, 1985, 1988).

During the early part of the Middle Ages another category existed: the slaves. The Norwegian "Gulating" law, from the eleventh century, throws some light on what could happen in old age. If an old, emancipated slave couple owned nothing, they had to dig their own grave in the graveyard and sit there to die. The former master had to care for the survivor. Some researchers see this actually was an improvement of the situation of these elderly because some masters probably took care of their former slaves rather than having to pass by them each time they had to go to church (Gaunt, 1983).

As mentioned, it was customary for an old couple to move out of the main building to live independently in a cottage. If needed, the spouse provided the care. If care was needed in widowhood or if the spouse did not manage, however, then it was customary that the elderly moved back to their children. Support of this notion can be found in a study reported by Gaunt (1983). His study objects were elderly in four parishes in the late seventeenth and eighteenth centuries who had died at age 60 or older. More specifically, he wanted to find out where they had lived at the time of their death. Results showed that just about half of them lived with their married adult children. In addition, some lived with their unmarried children. In total, from two thirds to three fourths lived with their children at the time of their death. In other words, if possible, the elderly were taken care of in the children's households. This only happened during the final stage of frailty, however. Under normal circumstances it was not necessary. That is why we find very few three-generation families in Swedish cross-sectional studies.

During the nineteenth century the population increased substantially, which led to an increased migration. Thus it became more difficult to retain a social network. Gaunt (1983) has studied two parishes, one in central Sweden and one in southern Sweden. Around 1880, less than half of those 60 years and older had been born in the parish. About half had a spouse who was still alive. About 75% had children who were still alive;

however, they had relatively few more distant relatives. And how was the situation for a 50-year-old woman with regard to caring responsibilities? In the studied areas only 37% still had children left in the parish. As many as 83% had no father or mother in the vicinity, and only 5% had both their parents in the parish.

A most efficient way for a widow or widower to be supported was to remarry. Carlsson (1977) has studied the percentage of widows and widowers who never remarried during the first part of the nineteenth century. He found that among farmers, about one fifth were widows, while the percentage among the nobility was 35%. If a widow remarried, however, it could complicate the situation for the children from the former marriage. If the new husband was not too old, they had to wait longer before they could take over the farm.

A delay due to remarriage was an obvious risk because it was quite unusual that widows and widowers married each other. It would be impractical to have two farms at some distance from each other. Instead the widow or widower married an unmarried person close by—usually someone much younger. On occasion younger generations tried to stop the remarriage of their parents. One effect of this was that the position of the woman was strengthened, following from the attempts to make her less interested in remarriage (Gaunt, 1983).

The substantial societal changes during the last part of the nineteenth century dramatically affected the conditions of the elderly. In particular the situation of the unpropertied classes became increasingly precarious. Those who worked as farmhands were less often part of the farmer's household, and those who had become industrial workers were not often covered by the diminishing patriarchal industrial order or by private pension plans (Odén, 1988). In addition, the proportion of elderly rose from the traditional 6% to 8% of the total population. It became increasingly clear to many citizens that the state should take some general responsibility for the support of the elderly. Thus in 1884 the first bill proposing a pension system was laid before Parliament, and in 1913 Parliament passed the first all-inclusive pension scheme (Odén, 1988).

Sweden: From Past to Present

Demography

In January 1990 Sweden had a population of about 8.5 million people. About 17.8% of the population is over 65 years old, and most of these are pensioners. There has been a steady increase in the proportion of elderly during the last century; however, there were also quite a few elderly in the preindustrial society. The high mortality affected chiefly infants and youth. In 1750, 6% of the population was 65 and older, and 3% was 70 and older. The average life span in 1989 was 75.2 years for men and 81.0 years for women.

Not since the nineteenth century have Swedish women given birth to enough children for population replacement. The only exception is the cohort born in the 1930s. The increase in population is due to increased longevity and immigration, although there has only been an increase in population due to migration since the 1930s. Before that, large numbers of Swedes emigrated, especially to the United States. The women who most consequently practiced family planning, to keep down the family size, were those born between 1900 and 1910. When they married in the 1920s and 1930s there was an economic recession, and they gave birth to, on the average, fewer than two children. Recently fertility has shown a steady increase, from 1.6 in 1983 to 2.1 in 1990 (i.e., exactly to the replacement level of 2.1 children per woman).

The percentage of "never married" increased during the eighteenth and nineteenth centuries, and culminated in the early part of the twentieth century. Looking at the situation at the turn of the last century, it is found that the percentage of unmarried women (between the ages 45 and 49) is much higher in the western and central European countries than in the eastern European countries. The figure is often around 15% in Western Europe and around 2% in Eastern Europe (Gaunt, 1983).

The lingering effect of earlier behavior gives the result that, among the elderly today, there is a fairly high percentage who have never married (13%). The number of never married is one factor behind the fact that almost one in four of today's elderly lacks children. In the future there will be a higher percentage who have children. For example, among newly retired, only 15% lack children. The amount of childlessness has implications for support because children today are likely to give as much help as in former times. And for the future, we can expect that from pure demographic reasons, a somewhat larger proportion can have the possibility of receiving help from children.

Modernization

Popenoe (1987) cites Sweden as being the most "modernized" or "advanced" nation in the world. It is also one of the most affluent nations, as well as one of the "oldest" nations in the world with almost 18% of its population aged 65 or older. The measures of modernization include trends toward an egalitarian income distribution, a high level of overall social welfare, secularization, and dominance of the culture by science and rationality.

It is sometimes assumed that the modernization in the Nordic countries, characterized by improved living conditions, is accompanied by a spiritual deterioration resulting in unhappy and frustrated people. From empirical research on the quality of life, however, Nordic countries have consistently been rated among the top nations (Listhaug, 1990). The level of subjective life satisfaction is higher here than in almost any other European country. The data also sustain, with some exceptions, the view that these countries are fairly secularized with an extremely low degree of religion participation.

To the list of indicators of modernization, Popenoe (1987) wants to add the movement beyond the nuclear family. He does not define this family type in detail, but, rather, refers to it as the cultural norm, or ideal, held by most people in Western societies over the last three or four generations. In other words, it is a fairly recent phenomenon. As an ideal type, the "modern" nuclear family was, according to Popenoe (1987), "a monogamous, patriarchal family consisting of a married couple living with their children, the man working outside the home and the woman being a mother and full-time housewife" (p. 174).

Concerning the movement beyond the nuclear family, Popenoe (1987) claims that Sweden has the leading position among Western nations. He notes that other countries may not be able to follow the Swedish trend, as there are characteristics of the Swedish society that are at some variance with the rest of the world. This was noticed a century ago by the French sociologist Le Play who, according to Gaunt (1983), remarked—in the second part of the nineteenth century—that Nordic families were special in some respects. One of his disciples wrote that young people were given freedom to act without interference. This family type promotes great individual initiative. The value of the individual is held in high esteem; while, on the other hand, the contacts with the parents' home are formal and loose. It seems plausible that this individualism could provide an essential requirement for rise of the welfare ideologies where the state, rather than families, is responsible for the social security (Gaunt, 1983).

Another social criticism of modernization concerns the female labor participation. It has been suggested that by causing increased stress, it would have a negative impact on the mental health status. Axelsson (1991) has studied the effects of the development in Sweden from families with a housewife to families with two breadwinners. She finds no support for the thesis that the mental health of the women would have deteriorated during the last decade. During the 1970s the mental health of married women generally improved, with gainfully employed women accounting for most of this improvement. As it turns out, it was the more healthy housewives who joined the labor force, while those with a poorer mental health remained at home. In other studies as well, the change in family composition is not considered problematic (Åberg, 1990; Moqvist, 1990). Findings of poor mental health are claimed to be based on unrepresentative families and are considered a "sociological myth."

Several authors have noted that the nuclear family is a family form that, from the broader viewpoint of history, is unique. It is worth emphasizing that it may just constitute a parenthetic event in history. The period from the nineteenth century to date has certainly been an extreme period in the history of mankind, covering the demographical transition, the Industrial Revolution, and so on. It may well be that it has brought to the fore an extreme family form, one which lacks essential requirements for survival in the future.

Marriage and Cohabitation

The percentage of married women in the age group of 20 to 44 was 59.4% in 1750 and then dropped to 52.1% in 1900, which was a low point. It reached a peak in the mid-1960s, and in 1970 it was 70.4%. Thus marriage was never so popular as it was in the 1950s and early 1960s.

Today Sweden has the lowest marriage rate in the industrial world and, at the same time, one of the highest mean ages of first marriage: 30 for men and 27 for women. The fact that marriage has become less popular does not imply that people are no longer living as couples. What has happened is that marriage is gradually being replaced by nonmarital cohabitation. Popenoe (1987) has estimated that unmarried couples (as a percentage of all couples) in Sweden were 1% in 1960, 7% in 1970, and 21% in 1983 (Popenoe, 1987). During the nineteenth century cohabitation without marriage was quite common in Stockholm. In 1864 close to 40% of the blue-collar workers cohabitated before marriage. The percentage in the middle class was 20% and in the upper class 12% (Matovic, 1980). In 1980 the percentage of unmarried women aged 20 to 24 who lived with someone else, was 68% (79% for men) and in the age group 25 to 29 the percentage was 35% (49% for men). Nonmarital cohabitation is now regarded legally and culturally as an accepted alternative rather than as a prelude to marriage, and virtually all Swedes now cohabit before marriage (Popenoe, 1987). Children born to unmarried mothers numbered 45% in 1984, an increase from 10% in 1956 and 22% in 1971. It should be noted that "born to an unmarried mother" seldom means "born to a single parent."

Already, by the middle of the nineteenth century, the number of children born out of wedlock had been a concern for many scholars. Generally the situation for these children and their mothers was not enviable. There were also positive aspects to this situation, however, and these may have palliated the negative consequences. According to Carlsson (1977), who has studied the period 1800 to 1830 in a parish in central Sweden, 20% of the women bore a child out of wedlock. The positive effects were that the woman might receive economic support from the father; but, more important, the mother could expect support from the child when she got old. In addition, in the lower classes a child could increase the chances of getting married. If the child was at least 10 or 11 years old, it could support itself. And a man who married a 35-year-old woman with a 10-year-old child received extra labor. Finally, the 35-year-old woman could not get so many more children, which was an additional advantage (Gaunt, 1983).

Another aspect concerns the duration of a marriage. Traditionally the marital union is expected to be lifelong. In the eighteenth century marriage for a farmer's wife lasted for about 15 years. Today a marriage could last for 40 to 50 years. The question is whether it is realistic to expect a marriage to last for such a long time, considering the developmental phases that individuals go through. Formerly, marriage got no real test because death almost always came in between. Thus "to love each other until death do you part" seems more feasible if that happens within a narrow period of time.

Family Dissolution—Divorce

Unlike most other countries in Europe, it was possible in the Nordic countries, ever since the sixteenth century, to apply in courts for a complete divorce. Divorces were not particularly common in those days however. Today the number of divorces is about half the number of marriages. In two thirds of those divorces children under 18 are affected. Popenoe (1987) maintains that it is reasonable to posit that Sweden has the highest rate of family breakup in the industrialized world. The proportion of marriages ending in divorce is close to that in the United States. The use of divorce rates can be misleading when making comparisons between nations, however, where the amount of nonmarital cohabitation differ. Thus one has to estimate the dissolution rate of cohabiting couples, and it seems a well-founded conclusion that nonmarital cohabitation does not have the durability of marital cohabitation.

Family Dissolution—Generational Coresidence

The coresidence of elderly with their children has declined from 27% to 9% between 1954 and 1975. The proportion of married elderly living with married children fell at the same time from 1.9% to 0.3%, and today there are hardly any grandchildren present in the households of the elderly (Sundström, 1987).

It is relatively rare for adults to live with their parents. In Sweden about 2% to 3% of those aged 30 and older live in this way. Sundström (1987) challenges the view that adults who live with their parents do so from some kind of altruistic motive and are typically self-sacrificing daughters. He claims, based on his data, that the adults are mostly sons who have never married, many of them with handicaps and little education. For example, in the age group 45 to 59 years, every third bachelor who still has parents alive also lives with them (Sundström et al., 1989). One may also note that coresiding single men tend, at least in advanced ages, more often to have a mother in their household than do single women who live with their parents. Sundström and coworkers conclude that at least the men who "remain" at home constitute an ever more marginal group. For men who are hardly attractive in, or attracted by, the open labor, housing, and marriage markets, the parents may serve as an important refuge. Actually it may often be the child, rather than the parent, who benefits from the arrangement. The older generation shelter those of their offspring who have the least capacity for independence (Sundström, 1987).

Formal Care

The Social Services Act of 1982 emphasizes the right of the individual to assistance. This means that anyone who needs support in everyday life has the right to claim assistance (if needs cannot be met in any other way). Since 1956 children have no legal responsibilities for their aged parents.

In spite of all options for formal care, it is repeatedly shown that informal care is much more widespread than formal care of the elderly. Formal care continues to be mainly a substitute when family care is unavailable or insufficient. It is feared that informal care will decrease in the future, thus putting extra pressure on formal care. One reason for this is demographic factors.

The discussion of demographic factors focuses on the concept of the family. It is known that larger families were more common in the past, and that the children were supposed to care for the elderly parents. Today families have fewer children and, thus, one might assume there to be fewer potential caregivers. What is less observed is that, due to the higher mortality in former days, those elderly parents who reached an advanced age actually had as many, or as few, surviving children as the elderly of today. Today's elderly have almost all their children alive and also have more relatives alive and more contacts with them than ever before. The great majority of grandchildren today have their grandparents alive.

Concerning attitudes to caring, it seems that in most cases, as long as it is a matter of help or temporary care, there are no problems. Both the elderly in need and the potential caregiver find it natural and approve of it. When it comes to continuous care, the picture is quite different. To have a spouse available to give much of the care is the best protection against relying on formal care or having to move to an institution. In Sweden neighbors play an insignificant role in informal care. If the elderly person in need has no spouse, children may take part in the care. In increasing numbers, however, it is the elderly themselves who—when faced with this situation—do not want to be cared for by their children (Andersson, 1986). One reason is that they do not want to strain their relationship with their children. Thus scarcity of informal helpers for continuous care may become apparent due more to attitudinal reasons than from numerical ones.

The municipal governments are responsible for social welfare services, medical services, and care for the elderly. It is the duty of each municipal social welfare committee to keep itself fully informed of local needs of individuals for help and services. Every Swedish municipality provides home help service; a collective concept for many different forms of activity. Home help services provide the elderly, according to need, with help in house cleaning, cooking, and laundry. Other forms of individual and collective services are often used in combination with home help. In most municipal districts these include municipal transport services, technical aids, chiropody, hairdressing, bathing help, food services, telephone services, physical activities, activity and hobby programs, library services, and snow clearing. Some of these activities are now frequently concentrated at special locations called day centers (either constructed as separate units or as part of a service building or residential room). In a number of municipal districts (especially in sparsely-populated areas), home help is supplemented by one or two service buses. Small fees are charged for these forms of public old age service. In Sweden about 20% of the elderly utilize home help, and nearly half of these clients are 80 and older.

During the 1950s and 1960s the number and proportion of those aged 65 and older living in institutions rose from the more usual level of about 4%. The proportion was lower in the nineteenth century, but one can find eighteenth-century parishes where 20% died in the poor house (Kjellman, 1981). Institutional living peaked in the late 1960s and has decreased thereafter. Today about 6.7% of the elderly live in some type of institution (9.3% inclusive of the intermediary "service apartments"), a figure that does not differ much from other Western countries (Ds, 1989).

In the late 1970s and 1980s public policies came to stress the importance of elderly staying in their own homes, as this was the most humane and the most economical approach. The majority of the elderly also want to live at home. Among the oldest-old, or most frail, about half want to move to an old-age home. It is a myth, however, that the elderly in old-age homes have been abandoned by their children; half of them do not have any children, and the majority of the other half have not necessarily been abandoned.

Sweden Tomorrow

There has been much discussion in Sweden about a future limitation of the formal services due to the pressure from an increasing number of elderly people (Andersson, 1991; Thorslund, 1991). The increase will take place among the oldest-old, who are also the major recipients of care. The number of people 80 years and older will increase by 30% between 1988 and 2000. It is claimed that it is impossible to raise the taxes from the already high level, and that the social services will be understaffed because other sectors of the market can offer higher wages. One positive aspect, though, is that the increase will take place in smaller communities where the competition for labor is lower. In Stockholm the number of elderly aged 65 and above is projected to decrease by 14% between the years 1990 and 2020. Even more important, from a caring perspective, is that the number of elderly aged 80 and older is projected to decrease by 30%. In addition, looking at the country as a whole, it is obvious that the greatest yearly increases are in the past. In the next decade the yearly increase of persons aged 80 and above will only be half of what the rate had been in the last decade.

Popenoe (1987) is quite concerned about the "dissolution of the family." The breakup of the first family may result in second or third families, however. This phenomenon might actually have positive consequences for informal care and lead to an interesting development (from the point of view of the elderly). Most models of future generational family structure are still based on the image of the nuclear family (i.e., of a couple that marries in their 20s or 30s, has one or two children, and stays married until either one of them, mostly the male, dies in old age).

What is sometimes called the "dissolution of the family" might actually, for the first time in our part of the world, result in the extended family becoming common (Andersson, 1991). This result, however, is from the perspective of the elderly and is seen by them as "intimacy at a distance." After divorces, grandparents often keep in touch with ex-daughters/sons-in-law and grandchildren, even if the contact is not kept up by the spouse. If, for example, the two children of a woman each have had two families, and the spouses in those families have children from other marriages, the woman (i.e., grandmother) might theoretically have close contact with a total of six sons/daughters and sons/daughters-in-law and at least a dozen "grandchildren" (even if no single family has more than two children). Even if these contacts do not implicate a caring situation, they might lead to an improved well-being in accordance with what has been found in research on social networks and their importance for health and well-being. Nevertheless the chances for being cared for should increase for simple numerical reasons, and, thus, the possibility of a consequential reduction in the need for formal care.

The described family constellation, the "twigs" family (Andersson, 1991), is increasingly more relevant in gerontology in developed countries than the multigenerational family that is incessantly described. Although the four-generation family is not uncommon, the multigenerational family will hardly become prevalent, even with today's average length of life, because it assumes a low age of conception. The children of a five- or six-generation family had to be born to quite young mothers, a phenomenon quite rare in developed countries (Andersson, 1991).

Though there will be a continuous need for care and pressure for resources, it is evident from available data that Sweden has finalized the transition to an aged country. And it is evident that this challenge has also been settled in a reasonably decent way.

References

Åberg, R. (1990). Människan i ett föränderligt industrisamhälle. In Åberg, R. (red.), *Industrisamhälle i omvandling*. Stockholm: Carlssons.

Andersson, L. (1986). Önskemål om informell och formell hjälp och vård. *Socialmedicinsk Tidskrift, 63*, 225-233.

Andersson, L. (1991). The service system at the crossroad of demography and policy making—Implications for the elderly. *Social Science & Medicine, 32*(4), 491-497.

Axelsson, C. (1991). Gifta kvinnors sysselsättningsutveckling—om förutsättningar och konsekvenser. Unpublished doctorial dissertation. Stockholm University, Sweden.

Blom, C. (1991). *Hospitalshjon och fribönder*. Lund: Arbetsrapport nr. 35 i projektet Äldre i samhället—förr, nu och i framtiden.

Carlsson, S. (1977). Fröknar, mamseller, jungfrur och pigor. Uppsala: Ogifta kvinnor i det svenska ståndssamhället.

Ds 1989:27 Ansvaret för äldreomsorgen. (1989). *Rapport från äldredelegationen*. Stockholm: Socialdepartementet, Allmänna förlaget.

Gaunt, D. (1983). *Familjeliv i Norden*. Malmö: Gidlunds.

Kjellman, G. (1981). *De gamlas bostad—fattig-åldringskulturen*. Lund: Arbetsrapport nr. 5 i projektet Äldre i samhället—förr, nu och i framtiden.

Listhaug, O. (1990). Macrovalues: The nordic countries compared. *Acta Sociologica, 33*(3), 219-234.

Matovic, M. (1980). Illegitimacy and marriage in Stockholm in the nineteenth century. In P. Laslett (Ed.), *Bastardy and its comparative history* (pp. 336-345). London: Edward Arnold.

Moqvist, I. (1990). Familjen—beständig och föränderlig. In Åberg, R. (red.), Industrisamhälle i omvandling. Stockholm: Carlssons.

Odén, B. (1985). *De äldre i samhället-förr. Fem föreläsningar*. Lund: Arbetsrapport nr. 22 i projektet Äldre i samhället—förr, nu och i framtiden.

Odén, B. (1988). The role of the family and state in old age support: The Swedish experience up to 1913. *Comprehensive Gerontology, C2*, 42-46.

Popenoe, D. (1987). Beyond the nuclear family: A statistical portrait of the changing family in Sweden. *Journal of Marriage and the Family, 49*, 173-183.

Schultze, A. (1931). Die Rechtslage des Ältern den Bauers nach den altnordischen Rechten. *Zeitschrift der Savigny Stiftung für Rechtsgeschichte G. A., 51*, 258-317.

Sundström, G. (1987). A haven in a heartless world? Living with parents in Sweden and the United States, 1880-1982. *Continuity and Change, 2*(1), 145-187.

Sundström, G., Samuelsson, S., & Sjöberg, I. (1989). Intergenerational transfers: Aging parents living with adult children and vice versa. *Zeitschrift für Gerontologie, 22*, 112-117.

Thorslund, M. (1991). The increasing numbers of very old people will change the Swedish model of the welfare state. *Social Science & Medicine, 32*(4), 455-464.

18

Conclusion

Family Care of the Elderly— Unique and Common Features

JORDAN I. KOSBERG

Introduction

The chapters on family care to the elderly from 16 countries in the world have reflected the occurrence of societal changes that have prodigious ramifications upon the tradition of family caregiving to the elderly. Among the countries represented in this book there is great variation in the dynamics by which the elderly are cared for by family or others. It should also be apparent, however, that between the countries, which vary in the stage of development, form of government, and proportion of elderly, there are also shared commonalities. Unique and common features of countries influence the extent of, desire for, and ability to provide family caregiving to the elderly members of the family.

While the organization of the chapters (countries) in this book is based upon the categorization by the proportion of elderly within the country, it has been acknowledged (in the first chapter) that no assumption is being made regarding the relationships between the proportion of elderly in a country, its stage of development or modernization, status and role of the elderly, and the extent to which the family is the major care system for the elderly. Indeed it can be concluded (from reading about the 16 nations in this book) that there are often greater distinctions in family caregiving dynamics among countries within a category (having similar proportions of elderly) than there are among categories (having different proportions of elderly).

It is the purpose of this final chapter to attempt to come to some general conclusions regarding family care to the elderly in the world (based upon the chapters within this book) and to identify variables that seem to be related to the provision of such care. While descriptively interesting, hopefully each of the chapters in this book will serve as more than a "snapshot" of a country and will provide a better understanding of the dynamics that affect the ability of families to take on caregiving responsibility for their elderly relatives.

Summary of Countries Within Sections

What follows is a brief overview of some of the major characteristics that pertain to the elderly and family caregiving in those countries discussed in this book.

Young Countries: Ghana, Mexico, and Thailand

Ghana is facing poverty, which is resulting in a migration of rural inhabitants to urban areas, thus leaving behind the elderly (and females). The family is being challenged by social and economic forces and the ability of the family to care for elderly relatives needs to be strengthened or public services for the elderly will have to be initiated.

Mexico can be characterized by internal mobility to urban areas (which is seen to challenge traditional values) and by emigration (for economic reasons), which, together, are resulting in the breakdown of the family and its ability to implement traditional roles. There will be a growing need for an increase in the presently limited formal services for the elderly in the country.

Thailand, a Buddhist country that embraces ancestor worship, is being challenged by changes in traditional social relationships such as increases in marital separation, divorce, migration, and fewer children per family. While confirming the necessary role of the family, the government is working with the private sector in the country to provide assistance to the elderly.

Youthful Countries: China, Costa Rica, and Egypt

China, reflecting the teachings of Confucius, is facing an increasing elderly population and a decreasing family size. Although formal services for the elderly are not yet well-developed, there are differences between rural areas of the country and urban areas (where the elderly are more likely to have community resources and pensions).

Family care of the elderly in Costa Rica is being challenged by economic problems (poverty and unemployment) in the country and also by the development of nursing homes and the building of smaller-sized dwellings in the community. Services are needed to assist the family in better caring for their elderly relatives.

The Koran influences the daily life of the Moslem Egyptian; yet the family is undergoing changes (resulting from emigration and poverty) that affect its ability to provide care for the elderly. Family care in rural areas is especially affected by high rates of illiteracy (and, thus, unemployment), underdevelopment, and few resources for the elderly and their families.

Adult Countries: Argentina, Hong Kong, and Israel

The elderly in Argentina are generally not dependent on their families and have reciprocal relationships with them but do need a degree of economic security for such independence. As a result of the economic conditions in the country, the ability for the independence of the elderly is being challenged (as is the family's ability to care for them).

Family care of the elderly in Hong Kong is being affected by a clash between traditional Chinese values (regarding filial piety) and increased Westernization. As a result of this clash and the size of the elderly population without families, there is a growing demand for both community services and institutional care for the elderly in the country.

Generalizing about the elderly in Israel is difficult because the country is composed of a diverse population of Jews of Eastern and Western descent, and Non-Jewish Moslems, Christians, and Druze. Although Israel is an industrialized welfare-state nation, its aged generally live within a family context (which is supplemented by services for the elderly).

Mature Countries: Australia, Greece, Japan, and the United States

Australia is composed of a culturally-diverse population and reflects a governmental commitment for the creation of pluralistic policies to meet the needs of its citizens. The country is undergoing societal changes that adversely affect family care of the elderly and the role and status of the elderly.

Although the family remains the primary social unit in Greece, family care of the elderly is being challenged by the growing aged population, the increased independence of females, and the migration to urban areas. Without necessary community services family members will be unable to find formal respite for the demands from caring for an elderly relative (and this is especially true in rural areas of the country).

The proportion of the elderly is rapidly increasing in Japan in the face of changes that affect filial piety and family care of the elderly. The government has policies for present and future populations of Japanese elderly; yet, given an increase in unmarried or childless elderly and changes in values and attitudes, family care of the elderly cannot be seen as a panacea.

Family care of the elderly in the United States (especially by females; increasingly by males) is quite prevalent, but not without adverse consequences for the family members. There are a variety of services that, potentially, support both caregiving families and independent elderly persons.

Aged Countries:
Austria, Great Britain, and Sweden

Although the Austrian family, as an institution, is undergoing changes in this Democratic Republic, only a relatively small proportion of elderly live with family members. The labor force participation of the elderly is being adversely affected by economic conditions in the country, and they are able to remain independent as a result of old-age pensions and social assistance.

In Great Britain the family is undergoing alterations that affect assumptions and attitudes toward care provision to the elderly. Adversities to the elderly from inappropriate informal support and the inequitable emphasis on females as caregivers are two the major issues being addressed in the country.

Sweden has used formal welfare assistance as a substitute for family caregiving, although the increased number of elderly will limit the extent of future public support. Increases in serial marriages (and relationships) in the country may possibly result in an increase in members of an older person's informal support system (past and present).

Individual and Family Variations

The likelihood of an elderly person needing to rely on one's family is related to characteristics of the country within which the individual is living (that is, its provision of public welfare). Within any country, however, there are also certain idiosyncratic variables that seem to influence the possibility of receiving family care. Of course the ability of the family to provide care is a function, to some extent, of overall national values, prosperity, and demography. Yet several variables will be discussed that were found to be especially related to family caregiving: gender, socioeconomic status, age of caregiver, and urban/rural location.

Gender

Women were found to be the major caregivers in all countries discussed in this book, yet the majority of countries indicated an increased likelihood that women were seeking education or pursuing employment and careers outside the home, thus making them unavailable to provide care to an elderly spouse or relative. Reference had been made to the increased possibility that women, so occupied outside the home, might face dual pressures on the job and from caregiving responsibilities that existed for them at home.

In several of the more rural countries (such as Ghana and Egypt), there was reference made to the emigration of men or their relocation to urban areas (so as to pursue employment opportunities). Thus women were often left behind (in impoverished conditions) to care for their children as well as their elderly parents and/or in-laws. It could also be the case that if a husband had left his wife (for whatever reasons), and her children had relocated to urban ares, the older woman might be alone and dependent upon nonrelatives.

The possible increasing role for men needs to be considered, and the chapters on the United States and Great Britain, in particular, focused upon the need for increased responsibility for men to undertake caregiving roles and tasks. While research has found that women provide care to elderly relatives, and men purchase this care, there is a need to anticipate the consequences from greater gender equity in society and, perhaps, the world.

In every country included in this book, survival rates for elderly women exceeded those for elderly men. And, as was seen, the length of lives is not related to the quality of life. Thus family care of the elderly pertains, in the great majority of cases, to care of elderly women.

Socioeconomic Status

Another variable found to differentiate family caregiving is socioeconomic status. While more impoverished families may have fewer resources to share with their elderly relatives, they seem to uphold more traditional values for family caregiving. The more affluent, who can afford alternative lodging and care for their elderly relatives, may provide only a perfunctory role in the care of their aged. Certainly the more affluent families have options the poorer families do not have in affording to hire individuals to care for the elderly or to place their elderly in institutional (or retirement) settings.

It is said that it is the middle class that is the most inconvenienced of all caregivers of elderly persons, because they cannot either easily afford to purchase care or provide care, nor do they meet eligibility criteria for welfare assistance. Thus they are left with the responsibility of caring for their elderly relatives at the expense of meeting other needs (or they can shirk their responsibilities for their elderly family members because the demands and expenses are unwanted).

Socioeconomic status of an elderly person or family member is related to certain antecedent variables. Education, or level of education, often determines one's occupation, which, in turn, is related to such considerations as health condition, eligibility for pensions, likelihood of savings, and general economic status. Aside from ascribed status (and wealth), as a result of birth, often education is the major determinant for economic stability in adulthood. Accordingly, as was seen in many countries discussed in this book, the likelihood of receiving education seemed to be a function of the general provision of educational opportunities (especially in rural areas of a country) and the freedom for children to attend school (as opposed to their need to supplement family income through employment).

Caregiving Age

Much has been written (within this book and by others) about the "traditional" generation of caregivers: those in their middle-age years. It is such groups of caregivers who face the competing demands from their elderly parents, their younger children, and their own present and future needs and desires. There were suggestions in several of the chapters that the needs of the elderly were being accorded a lower priority (than in the past) when adult children moved to urban areas for work and took on new more self-centered values.

There were also examples of the movement away from an extended family system (where different generations were all a part of the family) to a nuclear family system (of parents and younger children). Although there often remained some contact between elderly parents and their children, it seemed as if the needs of the elderly grandparents were met only after those of their grandchildren and their children (in that order).

Urban/Rural Location

One of the variables that seemed to account for intracountry differences was the urban/rural location of the elderly. On one hand, there was a suggestion that family relationships were maintained in rural areas. Urban life-styles were seen to lead to the breakup of traditional values and standards of behavior. Yet, on the other hand, it was often found that public services and resources were more likely to exist in urban areas.

There are several explanations for this possibility. There is greater efficiency in meeting the needs of a large and concentrated number of elderly (in urban areas) than in serving a dispersed population (in rural areas). Also there may be a greater need for such services (and, perhaps, greater likelihood of family disintegration) in urban areas. Finally, there may be higher government priority given to urban areas of a country rather than rural areas.

Differences Among Countries

As was mentioned, the desire of a family to provide care to elderly relatives and their ability to do so is often a function of the characteristics of the country at any particular time. Based upon the material from the 16 countries included in this book, there are several issues related to the characteristics of countries that seem to differentiate the likelihood of family caregiving for the elderly: the extent of development, proportion of elderly, form of government, religion, mobility, and homogeneity of population. Only the briefest discussion can be given.

Development

Countries represented in this book vary in their stages of development and range from developing to developed nations. Those in early stages of (technological) development may also be relatively impoverished (in relationship to more industrialized nations). Among the consequences for such countries is the scarcity of public resources available for those groups and individuals who are in need. This, of course, includes the elderly.

Countries functioning at a more survival level can ill-afford to provide alternatives to family caregiving. Nor can such countries provide support (in way of public services or economic assistance) to families who wish to care for their elderly relatives.

Proportion of Aged

It does appear that there is some correspondence between the stage of technological development and the proportion of elderly persons in countries represented in this book. Again, as mentioned earlier, there are many explanations for such an apparent relationship. Moreover, less-developed nations do seem to be more impoverished.

The implications are that these more impoverished countries cannot afford to differentiate between different groups in need. This may be due to an inability to afford to provide for competing groups in the country, but also due to the small proportion of elderly in the country. Given erroneous governmental assumptions about the ability of the family to care for its elderly relatives, less-developed nations may be unaware of, or indifferent to, the inability of families to provide care for the needs of elderly. Also there will always be those who do not have family members to care for them.

Form of Government

Countries represented in this book include socialist, communist, and democratic political economies. While this book was not based upon an empirical comparative analysis of countries in the world, the form of government seems to be of some significance in the degree to which family's must take on caregiving responsibilities for their elderly relatives.

For example, two of the three "Aged Countries" (Sweden and Great Britain) are welfare states and provide resources as a matter of course. Democratic nations (such as the United States and Austria) may face "battles" between competing groups for more limited resources.

Religion

On the search for explanations for differences between countries, one could consider the predominance of religion, or degree of religiosity, as an influence on the maintenance of family care for the elderly. In Thailand, China, and Hong Kong, among other countries represented in this book, there existed ancestor worship or other religious philosophies which supported filial piety. The Judeo-Christian mandate for the honoring of one's father and mother exists in the United States, Israel, and Mexico, among other countries.

It is fair to ask whether or not religion can maintain the norm of family responsibility for the elderly in the face of the many forms of changes occurring in countries around the world. In his book, *Ageing in Developing Countries,* Tout (1989) concluded (from his analysis of many of the countries in the world) that even religion could not be relied upon to "stay the processes of disintegration" (p. 15) of marriage of the family. We are given similar evidence within the chapters of this book.

Mobility

The possibility of family care is, of course, dependent upon the existence of family members within some geographical proximity. Family care to the elderly is, thus, related to the extent of geographic mobility of the population. Such mobility includes movement from one location to another within the country, emigration to another country, or the inmigration of persons (either young or old) from elsewhere in the world.

Some countries that have had significant emigration (e.g., Mexico, Egypt, Hong Kong) will need to create other systems and institutions to take over the caregiving responsibilities (such as the community, neighborhood, or formal support). This is true, also, for other countries (e.g., Great Britain, Israel, Greece), where inmigration has resulted in significant numbers of elderly persons who may not have married or whose families have remained in the homeland. Finally there are other—generally larger—countries (e.g., United States, Australia, China) where internal mobility has separated family members from one another. Clearly the consequence of the lack of alternatives for these elderly who do not have family members in close proximity is the increased prevalence of dependent more vulnerable elderly persons.

Homogeneity of Population

One might ask whether the homogeneous composition of the elderly (or any group in need) in a country might influence the provision of alternatives to family care. Sweden, Austria, and Japan have fairly homogeneous populations and do provide, relatively speaking, for the needs of their elderly population. It is true, of course, that these three countries are more industrialized and have a large proportion of elderly persons.

In need of empirical verification is the hypothesis that homogeneous countries are more likely to provide a communal form of assistance than countries with a heterogeneous population (by race and ethnicity)—given a level of economic prosperity. This is to ask whether or not such countries as the United States, Australia, and Great Britain would provide great public assistance to the elderly if such populations were more homogeneous, or that such (racially) homogeneous countries as Ghana and Thailand would provide more in way of assistance to the elderly if the countries were more affluent.

Family Care Cannot Be Considered a Panacea for the Elderly

There are always some elderly, in any country, who are without families. Such elderly may not be married, are widowed, and/or do not have children. The children of other elderly persons might have died or moved away from their elderly parents. In the United States, for example, many elderly move to areas of the country with moderate climates (and with many supportive services and age peers). In other countries, such as Mexico and Egypt, younger members of the family may leave the country in search of job opportunities.

There are some elderly whose family members are too impoverished to provide adequate care. Others have relatives who need to work and cannot afford to either go to part-time employment or leave the job market (so as to care for the elderly relative). In addition, there are also elderly who have lost contact with their family members over the years.

While currently they are not major reasons for the inability of families to care for their elderly relatives in any of the 16 countries represented in this book, widespread famine or disease, internal conflicts, and international war (among other catastrophic events) can decimate a population and alter traditional caregiving systems. Yet certain subcultures (that is, minority groups) within a country might be more susceptible (than the overall population) to certain health and/or economic adversities. This, in turn, is not only related to a decreased likelihood of longevity for the members of such groups, but also a decreased likelihood of family members who will be available and/or able to care for the elderly members of such groups. The AIDS epidemic is one such example.

Another reason why the family cannot be viewed to be a national panacea for the care of older persons pertains to the quality of the relationship between the elderly and their children. Many of the views regarding the obligation that children have for the care of elderly relatives are based upon a belief that good relationships exist between the generations. It should be obvious that such an assumption can be easily challenged by examples of long-standing intergenerational conflict, the abandonment of the family by the husband, and general family disharmony resulting from the clash of personalities, values, and life-styles between generations.

Moreover, traditionally, the elderly expected to be cared for by their children, and adult children had no doubts about their responsibility for their parents. Such expectations and desires have changed. Certainly there is ample evidence of the breakdown of traditional responsibilities as an aftermath of urbanization and modernization.

In addition, there is some suggestion that the elderly, themselves, do not want to be dependent upon their adult children or other family members. This was very clearly described in the Argentine, Swedish, and Austrian experiences. In the United States, too, it has been found that only until such time that an elderly person is facing the possibility of institutionalization will the older relative turn to the family for housing, support, and assistance. Independent of the stage of development, it is suspected that most elderly want to retain their independence, and privacy, as long as possible from family members (and all others).

Several authors alluded to the adversities in their countries that can occur to older persons who are cared for by family members who are ill-suited for, or are overwhelmed by, caregiving responsibilities. Ineffective care may result.

At its worst, there may be the possibility of elderly abuse and maltreatment. For example, in this book references to such potential problems were made by authors from Costa Rica, Great Britain, Greece, and Israel, among others. Thus it is necessary to remember that although some public officials and some private citizens believe that the elderly should be cared for by family members (whether for economic, moral, or ethical reasons), they must not equate family care with effective or humane care. There is too much evidence of the adverse consequences to some elderly persons cared for by inappropriate, overburdened, or impaired family members (see Kosberg & Garcia, 1991, for references to the worldwide evidence of elder abuse and maltreatment). While professionals advocate for screening and assessment of potential or actual family caregivers of impaired and vulnerable elderly persons, governments that provide no alternatives to such care make such screening meaningless.

Communal Responsibility for the Elderly

Quite independent of the desire to provide care to elderly relatives, or having one's family members providing care, there does seem to be a trend for greater publicly-sponsored resources for the elderly by those countries with greater proportions of elderly citizens (again, seen to be related to the stage of development). Further research is needed to better understand this apparent relationship between stage of development, proportion of elderly, and provision of public resources.

Most of the chapters described formal policies, services, and programs for the elderly in the countries discussed. Caution must be maintained, however, before concluding that the examples of formal services for the elderly and their families are necessarily available to all who need such resources. This is to suggest that while the description of resources may be quite impressive, the number (and/or proportion) of elderly who utilize such opportunities might be rather small in number.

Indeed many of the authors acknowledged that elderly beneficiaries might be limited to those living within certain areas of the country (e.g., urban), having certain characteristics (i.e., religion or culture), or meeting certain economic criteria (which can range from level of impoverishment to an ability to pay). Thus it is necessary to ask whether the formal services are equitably available to all elderly regardless of gender, religion, race, country of origin, among other factors. Moreover the existence, availability, and even use of public resources does not necessarily guarantee the effectiveness of such resources.

Another factor that seems to emerge from the pages of this book, as related to the family as caregiver and also to the likelihood of securing formal support for the elderly, seems to be one's place in society by nature of race, ethnicity, and/or religion. All societies have a dominant group (defined either numerically or by held power). This is to indicate that, in any country, those in power to influence the creation of policies may represent a segment of the total population. Thus it might be the case that certain groups of elderly (indeed, from any segment of the nation) may either be favored or disadvantaged by preferential policy decisions.

While this might result from overt discrimination against a minority group (or subculture), so too may these inequities result from the failure of the minority segment to either challenge inequities or to be able to create parallel resources for its own elderly population. Not to blame the victims, but such a failure—where and when it exists—may be a function of a subculture's powerless and economically-disadvantaged position in society. Although social and economic opportunities may be available for all in the society, certain minority groups may refrain from using these resources due to suspicion, lack of understanding, or out of defiance (and not wishing to admit to problems that necessitate receiving help from the dominant society).

Such possibilities may be found in more pluralistic countries. For example, Australia supports the notion of culturally-specific programs and services for the elderly and, collectively, reflects a cultural "patchwork" of resources for the elderly. The United States vacillates between the concepts of "separate but equal" and "the melting pot" in its provision of services to groups in need. The significant variations in some of characteristics between the Arabs and Jews in Israel may, in part, be explained by both the incomparable resources being targeted to both groups and a lack of propensity to seek public assistance and welfare, which is available for all.

Final Thoughts on Family Care

Family care in the world is changing, let there be no doubt. The traditional patterns of the past seem to be crumbling in the face of social, economic, and demographic forces producing and resulting in changes in cultural values toward the elderly, in general, and family care to the elderly, in particular.

Programs and services for the elderly (where and when they exist) vary greatly from country to country. Such resources may be urgently needed by many isolated, dependent, and abandoned elderly, and they might provide much-needed alternatives to family care. Yet many countries reflect an apprehension that the provision of alternatives to family care may be seen to legitimize and encourage the abandonment of family caregiving responsibilities.

Each country must address the question of responsibility for the care of the elderly. Should it continue to be the family? Paraphrasing Kosberg and Garcia (1991), countries need to anticipate and plan for the consequences of changes on the tradition of family care of the elderly through a partnership of the family, government, local community, neighborhood organizations, private sector, and organized religion. A new awareness of the consequences of changes in society must be acknowledged and necessary adjustments take place.

This, then, is the purpose of *Family Care of the Elderly*—to sensitize readers to the changes affecting family care to the elderly in 16 countries in the world. This book was designed to provide an awareness of the existence of problems facing the elderly and their families in countries around the world and an understanding of the dynamics of causes and consequences of these problems. Hopefully this book will also provide ideas and motivations for countries to better meet the needs of the elderly. Such efforts should not only be to support the family's ability to care for its eldest members (through supportive services and benefits), but also to provide effective and equitable alternatives to family care.

As Kosberg and Garcia (1991) have stated:

> To ignore social changes, to persist in out-dated expectations regarding family care, and to resist communal responsibilities for the vulnerable and dependent elderly, is to put both the elderly and their families at great disadvantage and, potentially, at great risk as well. (p. 5)

References

Kosberg, J. I., & Garcia, J. L. (1991). *Social changes affecting family care of the elderly.* **Journal of the International Institute on Aging, 1**(2), 2-5.

Tout, K. (1989). *Ageing in Developing Countries.* Oxford: Oxford University Press.

Index

Abel, E., 214, 224, 225
Accident, fears of, 3
Activities of daily living, 4
    Austria, 240-241
    Great Britain, 256
    Hong Kong, 132-133
    Israel, 148-150
    Sweden, 282-283
Adult countries, 288
    Argentina, 107, 109-121
    defined, 107
    Hong Kong, 107, 123-136
    Israel and, 107-108, 139-154
Adult education, 10, 26
Advice giving by elders, Ghana and, 21-22, 26
Affection, 4
Affifi, E., 96, 103
Africa, elderly population increase in, 2
Age, defining, 9
Aged countries, 289
    Austria, 233, 235-250
    defined, 233
    Sweden, 233-234, 271-284

Age discrimination, 10
Ageism, compassionate, 167
Aging of the world, 1-2
Agriculture, 26, 211
    Argentina and, 110-111
    Austria and, 237
    China and, 69, 72
    Costa Rica and, 85
    Egypt and, 98, 100
    Israel and, 143
    Japan and, 200
    Mexico and, 34-35
    Thailand and, 50, 52, 61
Alzheimer's disease, 216
Amera, Anna, 179-194
Americans for Generational Equity, 8
Andersson, L., 271-284
Applegate, J. S., 216, 217, 225, 226, 227
Arber, S., 259, 266
Argentina, 107, 288
    family structure, 115-120
    social changes, 113-120
    social security and, 113-114
Ashour, A. M., 95-106

Asia, elderly increase in, 2
Attitudes toward elderly, Australia and, 167-169
Australia, 157, 288-289
    community life and, 169-170
    demographics and, 159-160, 162
    economy and, 163
    ethnic women caregivers, 170-172
    family structure and, 166-167
    public policy and, 172-177
    respite care and, 174
    societal changes and, 162
    urbanization and, 165-166
Austria, family care, 233, 235-250, 289
    demographics, 235-236, 239, 246-247
    family structure, 239-242
    future predictions, 246-250
    public policy, 238-239, 242-246
    social roles and, 242-243
    social services, 243-246, 248-250
    societal values and, 237-239
Azaiza, F., 147, 150
Azzer, A., 96, 103

Be'er, S., 140, 144
Beliefs about aging, Ghana, 20-22
Bialik, Raquel, 15, 31-45
Birth rates, 2
    Argentina, 111-112
    Austria, 236
    China, 70
    Costa Rica, 84
    education and, 103
    Ghana, 18-19
    Greece and, 182, 183
    Israel and, 139
    Mexico, 32-33
    Thailand, 51
    U.S., 212-213
Blacks, extended families and, 212
Blieszner, R., 212, 214
Boyd, S. L., 215, 225, 226
Briceno Campos, F., 82-93
Britain, see Great Britain
Brodsky, J., 150, 153
Brody, E., 3, 4, 150, 212, 213, 214, 219, 223, 224, 225

Brown, C. K., 17-30
Brubaker, T. H., 5, 210-227
Brubaker, E., 210-227
Buddhism, 48-49
Burden of care, see Caregiver burden
Burials:
    Ghana and, 28
    Thailand and, 49

Cafferata, G. L., 134, 214, 215, 225
Cantor, M. H., 214, 215
Caregiver burden, 4-5
    Austria, 242
    gender differences and, 218-219
    Great Britain, 260-262
    Israel and, 150-151
    Japan and, 202-203
    public policy and, 224-225
    training and, 225-226
Caregiver support group, 216
Caregiving, family, see Family caregiving
Caregiving age, 291-292
Care-partnerships, 266-267
Carlsson, S., 276, 280
Case management, Great Britain and, 262
Chatters, L. M., 212, 213, 214
Chi, I., 130, 133
Child care, 6, 191
    Australia and, 169
    Austria, 240-241
Chile, 110
China, 67-81, 288
    public policies and, 76-80
    societal changes and, 69-72
    See also Hong Kong
Chow, N. W. S., 123-136
Christianity, 22
Church affiliations, Mexico and, 41. See also Religion
Church organizations, Ghana and, 28
Collective labor, China and, 80
Commodity economy, China and, 71
Community day center, Greece and, 185-186
Community life:
    Australia and, 169-170
    Mexico, 43
Community participation, Ghana and, 25-26

Community services, 12, 297-298
    Australia and, 171-173
    China and, 68-69, 79
    Egypt, 105
    Greece and, 185-189
    Hong Kong and, 127-129, 134-136
    Israel and, 151-152
    Japan and, 204-208
    Thailand, 58, 59
Costa Rica, family care and, 82-93, 288
    demographics, 84-86
    political issues, 82-84
    public policies and, 86, 89-92
    social changes, 86-89
Counseling:
    Israel, 153
    U.S., 221-222
Cowgill, D., 4, 9, 10, 12, 13, 49, 50, 53
Cultural custom, 3
Cultural diversity, Australia and, 165
Cultural values:
    Australia and, 171
    Austria and, 239
    Costa Rica and, 87, 88
    Hong Kong and, 124-125
    Israel and, 143, 145
    Mexico, 40

Daatland, S., 258, 267
Daughter caregivers:
    Argentina, 119-120
    Australia and, 161, 168, 170
    Austria, 240, 247
    Great Britain, 259-260
    Japan and, 202
    U.S., 214, 225
Day care:
    Egypt and, 105
    Great Britain and, 261
    Japan and, 205
Deaths, see Mortality rates
Dementia, Australia and, 172
Demographics, 2
    Argentina, 109-112
    Australia and, 159-160, 162
    Austria and, 235-236, 239, 246-247
    Costa Rica and, 84-86

Egypt and, 96-102
Great Britain and, 253-255
Greece and, 179-183
Hong Kong and, 124
Israel and, 139-143
Japan and, 197, 201
Mexico and, 32-34
Sweden and, 273, 276-277, 282
Thailand and, 48, 51-52
Depression, 55, 218
Developed countries, 8-10
    cost of pensions and, 184
    elderly increase in, 2
Developing countries, 2, 8-10, 17-30, 292-293
Disabled elderly:
    Greece and, 186-187
    Israel and, 149
Division of labor, 6
    gender differences, 217
    Ghana and, 22

Eastern Orthodox Church of Greece, 187-188
Economic changes, developing countries and, 17
Economic prosperity, family care and, 6-8
Economic system:
    Argentina, 111, 113, 114
    Australia and, 163
    Costa Rica and, 83
    Greece and, 181
    Israel and, 143-144
    Japan and, 200
    Mexico and, 34-36
    Thailand and, 50
Education:
    Australia and, 163
    Austria, 237, 239, 243
    birth rate and, 103
    Egypt and, 99-100
    Greece and, 180
    individualism and, 18
    Israel and, 140-142
    Japan and, 200
    Mexico and, 38
    Thailand and, 52-53, 58

See also Adult education
Egypt, family care and, 95-106, 288
   demographic data and, 96-102
   education and, 99-100
   employment and, 100-101
   health care and, 101-102, 105
   social changes and, 102-103
Elder abuse and maltreatment, 5
   Australia and, 170
   China and, 73
   Costa Rica and, 89
   Greece and, 192
   Israel and, 145
Elderly, roles for, 9-10, 22, 242-243
Elderly population growth, 2
   Argentina and, 111-112
   Australia and, 162
   Austria and, 235-236
   Ghana and, 19
   government and, 6
   Great Britain and, 253
   Greece and, 179, 182
   Israel and, 140
   Japan and, 197-198
   Mexico and, 33
   Sweden and, 277
   U.S. and, 210, 212
Elizabethan Poor Law, 6
Emigration:
   Egypt and, 102
   Greece and, 182
   Hong Kong and, 127
   Mexico and, 35, 38
Employment:
   Egypt and, 100-101
   leave policies and, 225
   Mexico and, 36-37
Ethnic aged, Australia and, 160, 172
Ethnic women caregivers, Australia and, 170
Europe, elderly increase in, 2. *See also* specific countries
Evandrou, M., 259, 261
Extended families, 4, 292
   Argentina, 116
   Australia and, 168, 171
   blacks and, 212
   breakdown, 17
   Ghana and, 22, 24

Great Britain, 257
Hong Kong, 127

Factor, H., 140, 144
Family, conflicts in, 5
Family caregiving:
   Argentina and, 109-121
   Austria and, 235
   causes and consequences, 4-5
   China and, 67-81
   Costa Rica and, 82-93
   disincentives to, 7-8
   economic prosperity and, 6-8
   Egypt and, 95-106
   Ghana and, 15, 17-30
   Great Britain and, 252-267
   Greece and, 179-194
   Hong Kong and, 123-136
   international perspective on, 1-16
   Israel and, 139-154
   Japan and, 196-208
   Mexico and, 15, 31-45
   motivations for, 4
   positive consequences, 5
   Sweden and, 271-284
   Thailand and, 15-16, 47-62
   tradition of, 2-4
   United States and, 210-227
Family structure, 292
   Argentina and, 115-120
   Australia and, 166-167, 169
   Austria and, 239-242
   China and, 69-70
   developing countries and, 17
   Ghana and, 23
   Great Britain and, 254-255
   Greece and, 190-191
   Hong Kong and, 126-127, 130-132
   Mexico and, 40
   Thailand and, 47, 50, 53-56
   U.S., 211
Family therapy, 222
Female caregivers:
   China and, 73
   Great Britain, 258-260
   tradition of, 3
Feminine identity, reaffirmation of, 5

Fertility, *see* Birth rates
Filial piety:
    China and, 67-68
    Hong Kong and, 124-126
    Thailand and, 49
Finch, J., 260, 265
Findl, P., 235, 239
Folkways, 21
Friends, Japan and, 207
Functional age, 9

Garcia, J. L., 5, 296, 298, 299
Garrett, W. W., 4, 6
Gaunt, D., 272, 273, 275, 276, 277, 278, 280
Gender differences, caregiving and, 290
    Great Britain, 259
    caregiver burden and, 218-219
    support groups and, 226-227
Gender role socialization, 3, 119
Georgiadis, E., 183, 192
Geriatrics:
    Costa Rica and, 91-92
    Israel and, 145
Gerontology, 12, 44
Ghana, family care and, 15, 17-30, 287
    demographic overview, 18-20
    future projections, 29-30
    social change and, 22-25
    support systems and, 27-29
    traditional beliefs about old age, 20-22
Gibson, M. J., 3, 4, 6, 7, 8
Ginn, J., 259, 266
Golbert, L., 113, 114
Goldsher, E., 147, 150
Gonyea, J. G., 215, 218
Gorbach, P., 253, 259, 260, 261
Great Britain, family care, 7, 233, 252-267, 289
    caregiver burden and, 260-262
    changing patterns, 262-265
    demographics, 253-255
    patterns of informal care, 257-261
    public policy, 262-263
Greece, family care and, 157, 179-194, 289
    church and, 187-188
    demographics and, 179-183
    economy and, 181

future prospects and, 193-194
    social change and, 189-193
    social security and, 184
    social values and, 180-181
Guilt, 4

Habib, Jack, 139-154
Health care:
    Austria and, 244-245
    China and, 77-78
    Costa Rica and, 83-84, 86
    costs, 8
    Egypt and, 101-102, 105
    Greece and, 185, 187
    in home, 219-220
    Israel and, 151
    Japan and, 206
    Mexico and, 34
    Thailand and, 55, 58-59, 61
Heart attack patients, 216, 218
Holmes, L., 9, 10
Home care services, 8, 243-245
    Australia and, 172-173
    Great Britain and, 261
    Japan and, 204-205, 207
    Sweden, 282-283
    U.S., 219-220
Hong Kong, family care and, 107, 123-136, 288
    community services and, 134-136
    demographics and, 124
    family structure and, 126-127, 130-132
    filial piety, 124-126
    public policy and, 125-126
Hooyman, N. R., 215, 218
Hörl, J., 235-250
Horowitz, A., 214, 219
Housing, 7
    Argentina and, 116
    Austria and, 244
    Costa Rica and, 85
    Egypt and, 98-99
    Greece and, 186-187
    Hong Kong and, 127
    Japan and, 207
    Thailand and, 59, 61
Howe, Anna, 159-177

Husband, female caregivers and, 3. *See also*
    Spouse caregivers

Illiteracy:
    Egypt and, 99-100
    Mexico and, 38, 41
    See also Education
Immigration:
    Argentina and, 110, 111
    Australia and, 162, 164-165
    Austria and, 235
    Greece and, 179-180
    Israel and, 139-140, 143, 153
Income distribution:
    Argentina and, 114-115
    Israel and, 142
    Mexico and, 36
    Sweden and, 278
    Thailand and, 61
Independence, desire for, 4
    Argentina and, 119
    Hong Kong and, 127
    Japan and, 200
    U.S. and, 211
Individualism:
    Austria and, 247-248
    education and, 18
    Greece and, 180
    Sweden and, 278
Industrialization, 2, 9-10
    Australia and, 164
    China and, 69
    Greece and, 181
    Japan and, 200
    Mexico and, 35, 39-40
    Sweden and, 272
    Thailand and, 50, 52
Industrial occupations, 17-18
Infant mortality, Mexico, 34
Informal support:
    Australia and, 169
    Israel and, 146
Institutionalization, 8
    Austria and, 244
    fears, 3
    Greece and, 189-193
    Hong Kong and, 136

Israel and, 151, 152
Japan and, 199, 202, 203
Mexico and, 42
Thailand and, 57-58
Instrumental assistance, 7
Interdependence:
    Ghana and, 22-23
    Hong Kong and, 133
Intergenerational program, 222
Intergenerational relations, 3-4, 8
    Argentina and, 119
    Ghana and, 23-24
    Israel and, 145-148
International Institute on Aging, 2
Islam, 22
Israel, family care and, 107-108, 139-154, 288
    demographics and, 139-143
    economic system and, 143-144
    future trends and, 153-154
    intergenerational relations and, 145-148
    public policy and, 150-153

Jackson, J. S., 212, 214
Japan, 158, 289
    declining family care and, 199-203
    demographics and, 197, 201
    economy and, 200
    future of care and, 208
    public policy and, 196-197, 203, 205-206
    social services and, 201, 203-208
    urbanization and, 200
Jews, Israel and, 139-140
Job retraining, 10
Johnson, N., 263, 267
Judeo-Christian religions, family care and, 3

Kahana, E., 216, 218
Kaplan, R., 109-121
Kaye, L. W., 216, 217, 225, 226, 227
Kibbutz, 143, 149-150
King, Y., 147, 150
Knight, B., 220, 222
Köckeis, E., 240, 245, 255
Koran, 103
Kosberg, J. I., 1-16, 216, 286-299
Kwan, A. Y. H., 128, 132

Latin America, urbanization and, 110-111
Latourette, K. S., 125, 126
Lee, J. J., 130, 133
Legal requirements, mandating family care, 6-7
Less developed nations, 2, 8
Levin, E., 253, 259, 260, 261
Lewis, J., 5, 258
Life expectancy:
    Australia and, 162
    Austria and, 236
    Costa Rica and, 84-85
    Egypt and, 101
    Mexico and, 33-34
Life satisfaction, 5, 55
Literacy, 26. *See also* Education; Illiteracy
Living alone:
    Argentina and, 115, 118-119
    Australia and, 162
    Austria and, 240
    China and, 70
    Great Britain and, 255
    Hong Kong and, 127
    Japan and, 207
    Mexico and, 40
Living arrangements:
    Japan and, 198
    Sweden and, 281
Living conditions:
    China and, 71
    Mexico and, 36
    Sweden and, 278
Loneliness, 55
Long-term care:
    Austria and, 248
    Israel and, 144

Maeda, Daisaku, 196-208
Male caregivers:
    Austria, 247
    support groups, 226-227
    training, 226
    U.S., 215-219
Mancini, J. A., 212, 214
Matthews, S. H., 217, 224
Mature countries, 288-289
    Australia, 157, 159-177

defined, 157
    Greece, 157, 179-194
    Japan, 158, 196-208
    United States, 158, 210-227
McCallum, John, 159-177
Meals programs:
    Austria, 243
    Great Britain, 261
    home-delivered, 220
Melting pot, 22
Meredith, B., 5, 258
Mexico, family care and, 15, 31-45, 287
    economic system and, 34-36
    education and, 38
    employment and, 36-37
    industrialization, 39-40
    programs and services, 42-44
Minority groups, in-home service, 220, 222
Mobility, 294
Modernization, 8-10, 17, 53
    China and, 69
    defined, 9
    Sweden and, 277-279
Montgomery, R. J. V., 215, 218
Moral values, Hong Kong and, 124-125
Morales Martínez, F., 82-93
More developed countries, 9
Morginstin, B., 145, 152
Mortality rate:
    Argentina and, 111-112
    Austria, 236
    China and, 71
    decrease in, 2
    Ghana, 19
    Greece and, 182
    Israel and, 139
    Mexico, 32, 33
Moslems, 103
Mossialos, E., 184, 187
Mother/daughter relationship, Israel and, 147-148
Multigenerational family, 240
Multipersonal nonfamily household, Argentina and, 116
Mutual associations, Austria, 246

Nakatani, Youmei, 196-208

Neighborhood relations:
 China and, 68
 Japan and, 207
 Mexico and, 41
Ngan, R. M. H., 130, 131
Noam, Gila, 139-154
North America, elderly population increase
 in, 2
Nuclear family, 4, 292
 Argentina and, 115
 Ghana and, 23, 24, 28
 Hong Kong and, 130
 Sweden and, 278-279
 Thailand and, 53, 61
Nursing homes, Hong Kong and, 132. *See
 also* Institutionalization

Obligation, basis for, 4
Oceania, elderly increase in, 2
Odén, B., 274, 275, 276
Old age, defining, 9
Old-age homes:
 Argentina and, 117
 Australia and, 168
 China and, 78
 Costa Rica and, 87
 Greece and, 188
 Hong Kong and, 128-129
Oriental religions, family care and, 3
Outreach programs, 220

Pantelides, E., 111, 114, 115, 117, 119
Parker, G., 256, 258
Patriarchies:
 China and, 67
 Sweden and, 272-273
Pensions:
 Argentina and, 114
 China and, 75
 Costa Rica and, 85
 Egypt and, 104
 Ghana and, 27
 Thailand and, 56-57
People's Republic of China, *see* China
Phillipson, C., 252-267
Political values, Australia and, 160

Popenoe, D., 273, 277, 278, 279, 280, 284
Population, homogeneity of, 294-295
Population growth:
 China and, 67, 74
 Mexico and, 31, 32-33
 See also Birth rates; Elderly population
 growth
Poverty:
 Argentina, 114, 117
 Costa Rica, 88
 developing countries and, 17
 Great Britain, 261
Progressive aging, China and, 71-72
Public policies:
 Australia and, 172-177
 Austria and, 238-239, 242-246
 China and, 76-80
 Costa Rica and, 86, 89-92
 Ghana and, 27
 Great Britain and, 262-263
 Hong Kong and, 125-126
 Israel and, 150-153
 Japan and, 196-197, 203, 205-206
 mandating family care and, 6
 Mexico and, 42
 Sweden and, 283
 Thailand and, 60
 U.S., 224-225
Public resources, 7

Qureshi, H., 253, 258, 260, 266

Redondo, N., 109-121
Relay model, 69
Religion, 3, 293-294
 Costa Rica and, 83
 Egypt and, 97, 103
 Mexico and, 43-44
 Sweden and, 278
 Thailand and, 48-49
Republic of Austria, *see* Austria
Respect for elders, 68
 China and, 67, 72-73
 Egypt and, 104
 Ghana and, 20
 Israel and, 145

Thailand and, 51
Respite care, 7
    Australia and, 174
    Great Britain and, 262
    Greece and, 193
    Hong Kong and, 128
    Israel and, 152
    Japan and, 205
    U.S. and, 220, 221
Retirement, 10
    Australia and, 167-169
    Austria and, 238
    Ghana and, 27-28
    Mexico and, 40
    Sweden and, 272
    Thailand and, 56
Rights of the elderly, China and, 68
Rosenmayr, L., 239, 240, 241, 242, 245, 248,
    255
Rosner, T. T., 217, 224
Rural areas, 292
    Australia and, 166
    China and, 68-69, 71, 75-79
    Costa Rica and, 84, 88
    Egypt and, 97, 98, 99, 100
    Greece and, 180, 183
    Israel and, 150
    Mexico and, 31
    Sweden and, 271-276
    Thailand and, 52, 61
Rural/urban migration, 17
    Egypt and, 102
    Greece and, 183
    Mexico and, 37, 37-38
    Thailand and, 54-55

Sabório Hernández, F., 82-93
Sandwich generation, 4
Sangl, J., 134, 214, 215, 225
Sarpong, P. K., 20, 21
Scharlach, A. E., 215, 225, 226
Self-satisfaction, 5
Senior centers, 220
Senior citizen clubs, Thailand, 59-60
Sinclair, I., 253, 259, 260, 261
Social activities, Greece and, 185, 187
Social change, 286

China and, 69-72
Argentina and, 113-120
    Australia and, 162
    China and, 69-73
    developing countries and, 17
    Egypt and, 102-103
    Ghana and, 22-25
    Great Britain and, 254-255, 264-265
    Greece and, 189-193
    Sweden and, 276
    Thailand and, 51-56
Socialist country, 8
Social networks, Ghana and, 25-26
Social security:
    Argentina and, 113-114
    Australia and, 160
    Austria and, 238
    China and, 70, 72, 74-78, 80
    developing countries and, 17
    Egypt and, 104
    Ghana and, 27-29
    Greece and, 184
    Hong Kong and, 132
    Israel and, 142
    Japan and, 199
    Mexico and, 40, 43
    Thailand and, 56-57
Social services:
    Austria and, 243-246, 248-250
    Costa Rica and, 89-90
    Egypt and, 105
    Greece and, 181, 182, 184-189
    Hong Kong and, 128
    Japan and, 201, 203-208
    Sweden and, 281-283
    Thailand, 57-59
    U.S., 219-223
Social status:
    China and, 72
    Mexico and, 36, 40
Social values:
    Australia and, 160
    Austria and, 237-239
    Greece and, 180-181
Soviet Union, *see* U.S.S.R.
Spouse caregivers:
    Australia and, 170
    Austria and, 241

Great Britain and, 259
Japan and, 202
U.S., 214-216
Standard of living:
    Greece and, 193
    Japan and, 200
Stathopoulos, Peter, 179-194
Steigman, N., 144, 145
Stone, R., 134, 214, 215, 225
Stress, sources of, 5
Superindividualization, 247
Support groups:
    gender differences and, 226-227
    U.S., 221
Support networks:
    Ghana and, 27-29
    Great Britain and, 256-257
    Hong Kong and, 130-131
    United States and, 131
Sweden, family care, 233-234, 271-284, 289
    asylums, 274-275
    demographics, 276-277, 282
    divorce, 280-281
    marriage and, 279-280
    modernization and, 277-279
    poor houses, 274
    rural characteristics, 271-276
    social changes, 276
    social services, 281-283

Taylor, R. J., 212, 213, 214
Teperoglou, A., 190, 191
Tertiarization, 35, 37
Thailand, family care and, 15-16, 47-62, 287
    demographic change, 51-52
    economic system and, 50
    education and, 52-53
    family role, 50-51
    future and, 61
    public policies and, 60
    social security, 56-57
    societal change and, 51-56
    traditional values, 48-49
Tout, K., 4, 52
Traditions, 21, 72
Training and education, caregiving, 225-226
Transportation services, U.S. and, 221

Ungerson, C., 258, 259, 260, 265
United Nations, 1, 2, 9
United States, family care and, 158, 210-227, 289
    family structure, 211
    gender differences, 214-219
    public policy, 224-225
    respite care and, 220, 221
    social services, 219-223
    support networks and, 131
Urban areas, 292
    Argentina and, 112, 113, 115
    attraction of youth to, 22
    Austria and, 243
    China and, 71, 75, 77
    Costa Rica and, 84
    Egypt and, 97, 98, 99, 100
    Greece and, 180, 181, 183
    Mexico and, 31, 35, 39, 41-42
    Thailand and, 52, 61
Urbanization, 2
    Australia and, 165-166
    China and, 69
    Greece and, 182, 189
    Japan and, 200
    Latin America and, 110-111
    Mexico and, 39
    See also Rural/urban migration
Uruguay, 110
U.S.S.R., elderly increase in, 2

Voluntary activities:
    China and, 79
    Ghana and, 25, 28-29
    Israel and, 144
    Japan and, 207-208

Walker, A., 133, 135, 253, 258, 260, 266
Weihl, H., 147, 150
Welfare programs:
    Hong Kong and, 132
    Thailand and, 57-59
Welfare state, 6
Welfare system, cradle-to-grave, 8
Wenger, C., 252, 256, 257, 259
Werner, P., 145, 152

Westernization, Australia and, 164
Wisdom of elderly, Ghana and, 21, 26
Women, nurturing role, 3
Women caregivers U.S., 214-219, 225. *See also* Daughter caregivers; Spouse caregivers
Women in workforce, China and, 73
Women workers, 18, 290
    Argentina and, 119-120
    Australia and, 164
    Austria and, 237-238, 247
    Egypt and, 100
    Great Britain and, 258
    Greece and, 191
    Hong Kong and, 132
    Israel and, 142-143
    Japan and, 202
    Latin America and, 35, 37, 41
    Mexico and, 33
    Sweden, 278-279
    U.S. and, 218-219, 225

Wongsith, Malinee, 15-16, 47-62
World community, 12

Xiao, Z., 67, 70, 71, 75
Xu, Q., 67-81

Young, R. F., 216, 218
Young countries, 287
    defined, 15
    Mexico, 15, 31-45
    Thailand, 15-16, 47-62
Youthful countries, 288
    China and, 65, 67-81
    Costa Rica, 65, 82
    defined, 65
    Egypt, 66, 95-106

Zhu, C., 67-81

About the Editor

Jordan I. Kosberg, M.S.W., Ph.D., is the Philip Fisher Professor of Gerontology Social Work and Director of the Centre for Applied Family Studies in the School of Social Work at McGill University in Montreal, Canada. From 1981 to 1992 he was a Professor in the Department of Gerontology at the University of South Florida. From 1975 to 1981, he was an Associate Professor in the School of Applied Social Sciences and Associate Director of the Center on Aging and Health at Case Western University. He is the editor of *Working With and For the Aged* and *Abuse and Maltreatment of the Elderly, Causes and Consequences,* and is presently editing an *International Handbook on Services for the Elderly* and *Elder Abuse in World-Wide Perspective.* He has also authored 11 chapters in books and over 50 articles in such journals as *The Gerontologist, Journal of Applied Gerontology, Journal of Gerontological Social Work,* and *Public Health Reports.*

Dr. Kosberg's commitment to international gerontology can be seen by his past activities as a visiting professor in the Department of Social Work and Social Administration at the University of Hong Kong, lecturer for the U.N. International Institute on Aging in Malta, and his election to the U.S. Committee of the International Council on Social Welfare. He has been invited to give lectures and presentations in many countries on social services for the elderly. His current research efforts address family care of the elderly and the unique and common characteristics of informal care of the elderly and formal resources supplementing such care in countries around the world.

About the Contributors

Anna Amera, M.S.W., M.A., is Professor of Social Work, Department of Social Work, School of Health and Welfare Professions, Technological Education Institutes, Greece, and Research Fellow, National Center of Social Research, Greece. She has helped develop community services for the elderly and home-help services for the elderly and the disabled in Greece and has been a member of a team of researchers-consultants at the Department of Aging of the Ministry of Health, Welfare and Social Security. For more than a decade she has been involved, as main researcher or co-researcher, with five projects on the elderly and the chronically disabled that resulted in, among other things, the development of a pilot project of home help services for the elderly and the disabled and the establishment of 220 Community Care Centers for the Elderly (KAPI).

Lars Andersson, Ph.D., is Director of the Section of Social Gerontology at the Stockholm Gerontology Research Center. He is also Associate Professor of Gerontology in the Department of Stress Research at the Karolinska Institute, Stockholm. He has contributed chapters in *Daily Life in Later Life* (Sage, 1988) and *Loneliness* (Sage, 1989), and is presently heading projects on "Loneliness Among the Elderly," "Health Behavior Among the Elderly," "Autonomy in Nursing Homes," and on the situation of the old-old from a Nordic perspective.

Abdel Moneim Ashour, M.D., is Professor of Psychiatry and Director of the Geriatrics Unit, Faculty of Medicine, Ain Shams University. He obtained an M.D. in Psychiatry from Ain Shams University in 1971, and is the founder and the Secretary General of the Egyptian Association for Geriatrics and Gerontology, and the Vice President for the Egyptian Society for the Health of the Elderly. He is also the founder and a board member of the International Psychogeriatric Association as well as the Associate Editor of the *Egyptian Journal of Psychiatry* and *International Psychogeriatrics.*

Raquel Bialik, a social-medical anthropologist, is a researcher and author specializing in sociomedical issues (aging, epilepsy, popular health concepts, etc.) and has written a manual titled *Penetrating the Community* (UNAM, 1989). A field trainer and coordinator of Health Programs for Marginal Populations, she has held several positions in the Mexican Government (Health, Educations and Assistance Ministries). She is a Professor in the Medical School (FM) at the Mexican Autonomous National University (UNAM) and presently heads the Department of Extension and Academic Exchange (FM-UNAM).

Charles K. Brown, Ph.D., is Director of the Center for Development Studies, University of Cape Coast, Ghana. He is a sociologist by training and interested in development issues especially those affecting the most vulnerable and disadvantaged groups in society, including the aging. He is a member of the Collaborating Network of the International Institute on Aging (INIA) in Malta and was a member of the Expert Group that designed the Short-Term Training Course in Social Gerontology for the INIA in May 1989. Currently he is working on a nationwide research project on aging and family care in Ghana.

Ellie Brubaker, Ph.D., is an Associate Professor in the Department of Sociology and Anthropology at Miami University, Oxford, Ohio. Her research has been published in a number of journals, including *Journal of Gerontological Social Work, Gerontology and Geriatrics Education,* and *American Behavioral Scientist.* She is the author of *Working With the Elderly: A Social Systems Approach.* Her research interests are in the areas of social service delivery to older families.

Timothy H. Brubaker, Ph.D., is Director of the Family and Child Studies Center and a Professor in the Department of Family and Consumer

Sciences at Miami University, Oxford, Ohio. His books include *Family Relations: Challenges for the Future* (editor, in press), *Family Relationships in Later Life* (editor, 2nd ed., 1990), *Family Caregivers and Dependent Elderly* (coauthored, 1984), *Later Life Families* (1985), *Aging Health and Family* (editor, 1987), and *Families in Rural America* (co-editor, 1988). His research has been published in numerous scholarly journals, and he has contributed many chapters to scholarly books. Currently, he is editor of *Family Relations.*

Fidelina Briceño Campos, a Social Worker, is Chief of Division, at the Department of Social Development of the Costa Rican Social Security System. She is also a Lecturer in Social Work at the University of Costa Rica.

Nelson W. S. Chow, Ph.D., is currently the Professor and Head of the Department of Social Work and Social Administration at the University of Hong Kong. His research interests include the comparative study of social security systems in East and Southeast Asian countries and the support of the elderly in Asian Chinese communities. He has published a book, *The Administration and Financing of Social Security in China,* as well as articles in *Journal of Social Policy (UK), The Gerontologist (USA), International Social Work (USA), Journal of Aging and Social Policy (USA),* and *The Hong Kong Journal of Social Work.* He is presently Chairman of the Hong Kong Social Welfare Advisory Committee advising the Hong Kong Government on all matters related to social welfare.

Zhu Chuanyi, a Senior Fellow, Institute of American Studies, Chinese Academy of Social Science (CASS), is also Vice-President of the Society of Gerontology Studies (CASS) and an Executive Member of the Society of Chinese Gerontology. His books and articles include: *Rise of Community Social Services, Social Security in the US,* "New Development of Care for the Elderly in Rural China," "A New Vital Social Security Force in Rural China—Mutual Assistance Fund," "U.S. Mandatory Retirement," "The Comparative Study of Elderly Care in China and U.S.," "Orientation of Social Security Development for the Aged in China from an International Perspective," and "The Elderly in the Chinese Society Undergoing Economic and Social Changes."

Jack Habib, Ph.D., is Director, Joint Distribution Committee—Israel, and Professor of the Department of Economics and Baerwald School of Social Work at Hebrew University Jerusalem, Israel.

Flora Saborío Hernández, a Social Worker, is the Head of the Department of Social Development of the Coasta Rican Social Security System. She is also a Senior Lecturer in the School of Social Work at the University of Costa Rica.

Josef Hörl, Ph.D., is Associate Professor of Sociology and Social Gerontology at the University of Vienna, Austria. His principal interest is in analyzing the effects of large-scale phenomena such as bureaucratization on the structure and content of the family and other informal groups. He is currently investigating the determinants of moral values and feelings of obligation among middle-aged families with elderly parents. He is also interested in comparative research on aging and social policies between Eastern and Western European countries.

Anna L. Howe, Ph.D., is the Head of the Office for the Aged in the Australian Commonwealth Department of Health, Housing and Community Services. She is also the Principal Policy Advisor to the Mid-Term Review of the Aged Care Reform Strategy, which is examining progress in the restructuring of the Commonwealth government's aged care programs that has been underway since 1985. She moved into her current position from an academic career combining teaching and research, mainly in the area of health and care services for the aged. Her most recent academic appointment was as Reader in the School of Health Administration at La Trobe University in Melbourne.

Roberto Kaplan, M.D., is currently Chief of the Geriatric Section, Italian Hospital of Buenos Aires. He is a consultant to, and former director of, the Instituto de Geriatria A. Rocca (a 250-bed nursing home that services the Italian community of Buenos Aires). In addition, he is the Director of Postgraduate Course in Geriatric Medicine at the School of Medicine/National University of Buenos Aires, a consultant/advisor (temporary) to the Pan American Health Organization, a Board Member of the Argentine Society of Gerontology and Geriatrics, an Overseas and Honorary Member of gerontological and geriatrics societies (U.K, U.S.A., Uruguay, Peru, and Brazil), and Editorial Board Member of two national journals on the subject.

Daisaku Maeda, M.S.S.A., is President of the Japan Socio-Gerontological Society and Professor of Social Work and Gerontology at the Master's Degree Course of Japan College of Social Work in Tokyo. From 1979 to 1989 he worked for the Tokyo Metropolitan Institute of Gerontology as Director of the Department of Sociology and has been serving various governmental advisory councils at prefectural, national, and international levels, including: Member of the National Advisory Council on Social Welfare for the Minister of Health and Welfare, 1981-1989; Member of the Advisory Council on Statistical Investigation for the Minister of Health and Welfare, 1982-1991; Member of the National Advisory Council on Social Security for the Prime Minister, 1984-1985; and Member of the WHO Advisory Panel on Health of Elderly Persons, 1984-present.

Fernando Morales Martínez, M.D., is National Coordinator of Teaching in Geriatric Medicine and Gerontology, National Center of Strategic Development in Health and Social Security, Costa Rican Social Security System.

John McCallum, Ph.D., is a Senior Research Fellow at the National Centre for Epidemiology and Population Health in Canberra. He is widely published on aging topics both on Australia and Asian countries and is currently involved with a 7-year follow-up study of the aged and a medical and social community study of the elderly. In addition, he advises a number of committees involved with policy for the elderly and, most recently, he reported on the Australian Superannuation System to the OECD in Paris and evaluated, for the United Nations, a Japanese project promoting awareness of aging in Asia.

Youmei Nakatani, M.S.W., is an Assistant Research Scientist in the Department of Social Welfare Research at the Tokyo Metropolitan Institute of Gerontology. He is also an adjunct lecturer of social welfare research in the Department of Social Welfare at the Japan Lutheran College. His research interests are in the area of direct practice to the elderly as well as coordination of long-term care services.

Gila Noam, M.S., is a Senior Researcher at the JDC-Brookdale Institute of Gerontology and Adult Human Development in Jerusalem, Israel, and a doctoral candidate in the Department of Sociology, Hebrew University.

Chris Phillipson, Ph.D., is Professor of Applied Social Studies and Social Gerontology at the University of Keele. His publications include *Capitalism and the Construction of Old Age* (1982), *Ageing and Social Policy* (coeditor, 1986), *A Sociology of Old Age* (coauthor, 1988), and *Changing Work and Retirement* (coauthor, 1991). He has recently completed (with Simon Biggs) a training manual to assist careworkers involved in the field of elder abuse and is currently writing a book on social policies for older people in Britain and America.

Xu Qin, is Assistant Researcher and Head of the Department of Demography, China Research Center on Aging; editor of *Budding of Aging in China;* main author of *Population Aging in China;* and one of the authors of *Data on Sampling Survey on Elderly Population Age 60 and Over 1987;* and *Population Projection for China.*

Nélida Redondo, M.S.S., is currently a grant fellow at the National Scientific & Technical Research Council (CONICET) in the area of sociology of aging and Director of NGO's Centro de Promoción y Estudios de la Vejez (C.E.P.E.V.), Buenos Aires, Argentina. In addition, she is the author of several related publications.

Peter Stathopoulos, Ph.D., is currently teaching at the Technological Institute of Athens (T.E.I.) and is coordinator of an education exchange program involving Social Policy and Social Work departments from seven European countries. He is a member of the academic staff at the National School of Public Administration and has served as faculty preceptor at various colleges and universities in the United States. His consulting efforts have included work that resulted in the development of a National Directory of Social Services. He is currently involved with a project designed to study the attitudes and interests of T.E.I. students.

Malinee Wongsith, is an Associate Professor at the Institute of Population Studies, Chulalongkorn University, Bangkok, Thailand. Her previous publications include "The Impact of Living Arrangements of the Elderly on Government Programs in Thailand" (1991), "Attitudes Toward Family Values in Thai Society," and *Socio-Economic Consequences of the Aging of the Population in Thailand: Survey Finding* (coauthor, 1988).